Indigenous Culture and Change in Guerrero, Mexico, 7000 BCE to 1600 CE

Indigenous Culture and Change in Guerrero, Mexico, 7000 BCE to 1600 CE

Ian Jacobs

University of New Mexico Press

Albuquerque

© 2024 by University of New Mexico Press
All rights reserved. Published 2024
Printed in the United States of America

ISBN 978-0-8263-6893-5 (paper)
ISBN 978-0-8263-6586-6 (cloth)
ISBN 978-0-8263-6587-3 (webPDF)

Library of Congress Cataloging-in-Publication data is on file with the Library of Congress.

Founded in 1889, the University of New Mexico sits on the traditional homelands of the Pueblo of Sandia. The original peoples of New Mexico—Pueblo, Navajo, and Apache—since time immemorial have deep connections to the land and have made significant contributions to the broader community statewide. We honor the land itself and those who remain stewards of this land throughout the generations and also acknowledge our committed relationship to Indigenous peoples. We gratefully recognize our history.

Cover image: Xochipala ceramic sculpture of a seated adult and youth, courtesy of Princeton University Art Museum
Designed by Isaac Morris
Composed in Baltica, Galliard STD, and Paralucent

To Jan, Chris, David, and John, and to my friends in Mexico who helped to make this possible

Contents

List of Illustrations	ix
List of Tables	xi
Acknowledgments	xiii
Introduction	1
Chapter One	16
Guerrero ca. 7000 BCE to 1521 CE: Regions, Peoples, Resources, and Exchange	
Chapter Two	51
Art, Culture, Ideas, Beliefs, Languages, and Population	
Chapter Three	89
Politics and Power	
Chapter Four	109
The Coming of the Spaniards: Invasion, Colonization, and Evangelization	
Chapter Five	138
Power, Adaptation, Resistance, and New Institutions: The Response of the Indigenous Communities of Guerrero, 1521 – ca. 1600	
Chapter Six	182
Encomiendas, Encomenderos, and Guerrero's Indigenous Communities	
Chapter Seven	203
Land, Agriculture, Livestock, and Commerce: Guerrero's Emerging Economy	
Chapter Eight	221
From Gold to Silver: The Mining Economy of Sixteenth-Century Guerrero	
Chapter Nine	236
The Lure of Asia: Acapulco and the Manila Galleon	
Concluding Observations	255

Appendix 1   **265**
Weights, Measures, and Money

Appendix 2   **267**
Rulers of New Spain, 1524 – 1603

Appendix 3   **268**
Some Individuals Engaged in the Peruvian and Manila
Trade with Acapulco, 1583 – 1601

Appendix 4   **272**
Glossary of Place Names

Appendix 5   **275**
Glossary

Notes   **282**

Bibliography   **337**

Index   **376**

Illustrations

Figure 1. Aerial View of the Ballcourt, the Adjacent Plaza, and the Cerro de los Brujos at La Soledad de Maciel 21

Figure 2. El Rey de la Chole, Sculpture from La Soledad de Maciel 22

Figure 3. Plan of La Organera-Xochipala 30

Figure 4. Plan of the Ceremonial Precinct of Teopantecuanitlán, Showing the Metaphorical Ballcourt and the Locations of the Four Monumental Sculptures 32

Figure 5. A Shell Pendant in the Form of a Bird, Probably a Pelican, from El Infiernillo 38

Figure 6. West Mexican Bronze Bell Types 41

Figure 7. A Painted, Lacquered, and Incised Gourd Bowl from Olinalá, Guerrero 42

Figure 8. A Detail of the Chilapa Huipil 44

Figure 9. A Drawing of Mural C-1, Oxtotitlán Cave 52

Figure 10. A Drawing of Mural Group 2, Scene 1, Juxtlahuaca Cave 55

Figure 11. A Drawing of the Interior of the Cave of the Governors, Techan 56

Figure 12. A Mezcala-Style Standing Polished Stone Figurine 59

Figure 13. A Mezcala-Style Polished Stone Architectural Model 60

Figure 14. A Xochipala Ceramic Sculpture of a Seated Adult and Youth 62

Figure 15. A Drawing of the Olmec Stela of San Miguel Amuco 64

Figure 16. A Monolithic Sculpture of a Symbolic Ballplayer in the Ceremonial Center of Teopantecuanitlán 65

Figures 17. A Photograph and Drawing of Stela Monument 3 from Piedra Labrada Depicting the Ruler 10 Nudo 66

Figures 18. A Drawing of the Tepecoacuilco Stela 1 and Stela 2, Depicting the Teotihuacan Storm God 68

Figure 19. A Drawing of Slabs A and B from Placeres de Oro 69

Figure 20. Quesos at Cuetlajuchitlán   71

Figure 21. A Reconstruction Drawing of Structure 11 at
La Organera-Xochipala Showing Talud-Tablero
Walls Decorated with *Clavos*   73

Figure 22. *Lienzo de Chiepetlán II*   76

Figure 23. *Lienzo de Chiepetlán III*   77

Figure 24. *Lienzo de Petlacala* on the Altar during the
Rain Ceremony, 2011   78

Figure 25. *Códice de Azoyú 1*, folio 38   80

Figure 26. *Códice de Azoyú 1*, folio 8   94

Figure 27. *Códice de Azoyú 1*, folio 24   94

Figure 28. Restored Ballcourt at Tehuacalco   97

Figure 29. The Church of Ahuatepec Pueblo, near Chiepetlán   131

Figure 30. The Ruined Church of San Pedro Petlacala   132

Figure 31. *Vista del Puerto y parte de la Ciudad de Acapulco,
sacada desde su Hospital*   239

Maps

Map 1. Guerrero: Precontact Archaeological Sites and Settlements   14

Map 2. Guerrero: Sixteenth-Century Towns and Settlements   110

Tables

Table 1.1. Chronological Chart: Archaic to Postclassic   18

Table 2.1. Approximate Relative Chronology of Some Major Formative Sites and the Occurrence of Mezcala Sculpture, Xochipala Figures, the Corbelled Arch, *Quesos*, and *Clavos*   72

Table 2.2. Population by Language in Guerrero, ca. 1520   85

Table 2.3. Adjusted Population in Guerrero by Language Group, ca. 1520   87

Table 3.1. Annual Cotton Tribute from Tributary Provinces of Guerrero According to the *Codex Mendoza*   104

Table 3.2. Communities in Conflict Under Mexica Rule   107

Table 4.1. Activities of Named Europeans in Guerrero, 1521 – ca. 1600   114

Table 4.2. The Value of Certain Resources in Guerrero and New Spain in the Sixteenth Century   120

Table 4.3. Some Salaries in Guerrero in the Sixteenth and Early Seventeenth Centuries   121

Table 4.4. Individuals Mentioned More Than Once in Legal Documents Concerning Zacatula, 1525, 1527, 1528   122

Table 5.1. Census of the Population of the Costa Grande Aged Seven Years or More in the Diocese of Michoacán in the 1680s   141

Table 5.2. Census of the Population of the Tierra Caliente Aged Ten Years or More in the Diocese of Michoacán in the 1680s   142

Table 5.3. Payments to Municipal Officials of Oapan Every Eighty Days, 1547 – 1554   147

Table 5.4. Payments to Municipal Officials of Oapan, Tecuiciapan, and Tetelzinco Every Eighty Days, ca. 1557   148

Table 5.5. Tribute Paid into the *Caja de Comunidad* in Indigenous Communities of Guerrero, 1558 – 1569   160

Table 5.6. *Cabeceras*, *Sujetos*, and Tributary Population in Guerrero, ca. 1548, According to the *Suma de Visitas*   164

Table 5.7. *Cabeceras* and *Sujetos* in Tlapa Province, ca. 1570	170
Table 6.1. Regional Distribution of *Encomiendas* in Individual Hands in Guerrero in the Sixteenth Century	183
Table 6.2. Regional Distribution of Crown *Encomiendas* in Guerrero, ca. 1548, According to the *Suma de Visitas*	184
Table 6.3. Value of Royal Tribute from Guerrero in January 1560, After Deduction of the *Diezmo*	185
Table 6.4. Tixtla Tribute, 1543	193
Table 6.5. Initial Tribute of Guayameo and Zirándaro	198
Table 6.6. Initial Tribute of Cutzamala	201
Table 7.1. Landowners on the Costa Grande, 1543–1598	204
Table 7.2. Landowners on the Costa Chica in the Sixteenth Century	207
Table 7.3. Landowners in the Montaña in the Sixteenth Century	212
Table 7.4. Landowners in the Center, 1539–1600	213
Table 7.5. Landowners in the North, 1542–1600	215
Table 7.6 Landowners and Renters of Land in the Tierra Caliente, Sixteenth Century	218
Table 8.1. Population of Mining Towns of the Silver Province, 1579–1582	226
Table 9.1. Percentage of Taxes Paid by Large, Medium, and Small Shippers in Acapulco, 1590–1659	245
Table 9.2. Spanish Population of the Philippines	248
Table 9.3. Shippers from Manila, 1591	250

Acknowledgments

The idea for this book began with conversations with David Grove. As we exchanged stories of our travels in Guerrero, David encouraged me to investigate the discoveries published by archaeologists over the last four decades that have brought Guerrero out of the shadows of archaeological obscurity to give the region a more significant place in the broader history of Mesoamerica.

This study owes personal and intellectual debts to numerous other friends and colleagues. At the Universidad Nacional Autónoma de México, Paul Schmidt Schoenberg generously provided encouragement and critical comment, but above all his profound knowledge of Guerrero. I am grateful as well to Michel R. Oudijk, also of the Universidad Nacional Autónoma de México, for his invaluable assistance. Gerardo Gutiérrez, author of numerous essential studies of the Montaña region, was likewise supportive and guided me to important publications. Susan Evans provided many useful observations. David Webster showed a lively interest in my work and made many acute suggestions about its scope.

Alan Knight, a friend since my first visit to Mexico in the summer of 1972, drew on his profound knowledge of Mexico to advise and critique. Susan Deans Smith advised me at several stages of the project and brought to bear her great knowledge of colonial Mexico. Brígida Von Mentz urged me on and provided helpful answers to questions. Anne Warren Johnson showed an early interest in my ideas when she was at the Universidad Autónoma de Guerrero in Tixtla, and later at the Universidad Iberoamericana. Peter Guardino and Alex Aviña, historians who share my interest in Guerrero, helped me shape my ideas at an early stage.

I would like to express a special debt of gratitude to Verónica Oikión Solano of the Colegio de Michoacán. We first met at a conference on regional history in Taxco too long ago for me to remember exactly when. Our friendship resulted in an invitation to spend three months in the Centro de Estudios Históricos, ably led by Claudia Espejel. The welcome extended by Verónica, her husband, Sergio, and numerous colleagues made those months rewarding and pleasurable. Special thanks are due to our neighbors Marco Calderón, Paul Liffman, and Dominique Raby, and to Chantal Cramaussel and Martín González for memorable excursions and conversations. In Morelia, Gerardo Díaz Sánchez, Eduardo Miranda Arrieta, Carlos Paredes, and José Luis Punzo Díaz offered wise advice.

The courtesy and efficiency of the staff of the Colegio de Michoacán's library, especially Isabel Barriga Díaz and Emeterio Martínez Saldívar, made my stay in Zamora especially rewarding. I am also indebted to the librarians of the Anthropology Library at the British Museum, the library of the Institute of Archaeology of University College London, Cambridge University Library, the British Library, and the Wohl Library of the Institute of Historical Research, London. I was also ably assisted in picture research by Pauline Hubner, and Martin Lubikowski expertly executed the line drawings.

Finally, at the University of New Mexico Press, Michael Millman stuck with me through the first and second drafts, the latter much improved by the comments of two generous reviewers, and James Ayers calmly answered my questions about technology and details of presentation of my typescript.

Desgraciadamente mi amigo Paul Schmidt Schoenberg falleció mientras este libro estaba en proceso de publicación. Paul conocía la arqueología de Guerrero como nadie y me apoyó con su amplia sabiduría, dándome aliento y generosos consejos. Espero que el resultado haga honor a su ayuda.

Introduction

The tale told in this study is of a rich material and cultural history fashioned over millennia along the Pacific coast and in the rugged mountains of modern Guerrero, in southwestern Mexico; of cultures rapidly disrupted by the violent intrusion in the sixteenth century of Spanish invaders; of languages extinguished, and the importation of African and Asian peoples; of crops and livestock that transformed the agrarian economy. It is the story of how the Indigenous peoples of Guerrero withstood enormous shocks, including the destruction of their families and communities, and how, although ravaged by epidemics, by social and economic disruption, by forced labor, and obliged to abjure their Mesoamerican view of the cosmos for a new religion, they crafted their place in New Spain. The careers of the European invaders who moved rapidly into the region in the 1520s are case studies in the single-minded pursuit of wealth and power. They rapidly identified the resources, human and material, that held the keys to success, and worked out how to exploit them. Guerrero's natural and human assets helped to create some of the wealthiest, most powerful, and prominent lineages of colonial Mexico. Historians of the later colonial period, and of nineteenth- and twentieth-century Guerrero, will recognize several enduring features that have characterized the region over centuries, features that began to take shape in eight tumultuous decades between 1521 and 1600.

Guerrero as a Unit of Analysis

At first sight, Guerrero as a unit of analysis seems anachronistic. After all, the state did not exist until 1849. Mesoamerican Guerrero was a mosaic of multiple language groups and had affinities and contacts to the east with Oaxaca, to the west with Michoacán, and to the north with Morelos, Puebla, and the Valley of Mexico. In the sixteenth century, the boundaries of civil jurisdictions frequently shifted and ecclesiastical jurisdictions divided Guerrero between the dioceses of (west to east) Michoacán, Mexico, and Tlaxcala. Nevertheless, there are good reasons to adopt Guerrero as the focus of this study. Guerrero is an official archaeological region of the Instituto Nacional de Antropología e Historia (INAH) and studies of its archaeology and colonial history adopt Guerrero as a unit of analysis. There is a geographic logic also. The great Balsas River (in its eastern reaches known as the Atoyac and Mezcala) flows like a defining thread from east to west, until it reaches the borders of Michoacán where it heads south to the Pacific coast. Regional hydrology adds to this geospatial unity—numerous rivers drain from the altiplano or from the Sierra Madre del Sur into the Balsas.[1] Of course, when archaeology and history demand, we can consider connections between Guerrero and other regions. The boundaries of this study are permeable when the evidence requires.

Rationale and Approach

As Guillermo Bonfil Batalla reminds us, Mexico's present is indelibly linked to its Mesoamerican past.[2] Had it been written thirty or forty years ago, this book would have been a very slim volume, for key archaeological findings had yet to be published. There is now a substantial literature about the archaeology of Guerrero, from the first domestication of maize by the Laguna de Tuxpan, near modern Iguala, about 7000 BCE;[3] the shellfish foragers and ceramicists at Puerto Marqués in Acapulco;[4] the remarkably early first-known color wall paintings in Mesoamerica in Oxtotitlán cave in the Center region,[5] together with the architecture and sculpture at Teopantecuanitlán,[6] evidence of a significant flowering of Olmec culture in Guerrero. Notable cultural achievements, such as Mezcala-style sculpture or the ceramic figures of Xochipala style, speak of a region whose people participated actively and creatively in Mesoamerican culture.

There are many studies of particular archaeological sites, zones, or topics in Guerrero, but no synoptic evaluation of prehistoric Guerrero from the earliest evidence to the end of the Late Postclassic in 1521. Consequently, the full history of pre-Hispanic Guerrero remains obscure for archaeologists who specialize in other regions. For historians of colonial New Spain, the scattered archaeological literature is hard to locate, and sometimes rather technical for those not familiar with archaeological methods, theories, and debates. Yet without taking into account this rich archaeological record, the deep history of pre-Hispanic Guerrero will remain a closed book to colonial historians. The first goal of this study is, therefore, to tell and interpret the story of the people who inhabited this region for thousands of years before the arrival of the Spaniards.

In recent decades trailblazing archaeological accounts of Postclassic Guerrero have included in their studies of the region's material culture the rich evidence of colonial Guerrero's pictographic codices and *lienzos*. Similarly, historians of the early colonial period have drawn on archaeological evidence to complement documentary sources. These studies have revealed much about the history of specific locales and regions and about particular aspects of that history. However, there is no unified narrative that connects these studies and relates the entire regional history. My second goal is, therefore, to tell the history of the early colonization of Guerrero, and to examine the immediate impact of European imperialism on its centuries-old cultures and the fashioning of a new society.

Much excellent research has begun to document the Spanish colonial project in the sixteenth century. However, the regional coverage of these studies is uneven and the questions they address vary. The Montaña region of eastern Guerrero has received much attention from ethnohistorians studying a rich crop of Indigenous documents. In the mining and agricultural region of the North, historians have paid substantial attention to Spanish colonial policies and their impact since silver mining was an important driver of the colonial economy and society. More recent studies have brought into this picture the Indigenous peoples of the region and how they navigated rapid and profound changes. Other regions of Guerrero—the Tierra Caliente, Center, Costa Grande, and Costa Chica—have received less attention from historians.

A regionwide account over a very long period is valuable for a number of reasons. For example, detailed studies of particular regions are invaluable, but by pulling together studies of these regions we gain new insights into Guerrero's history. For instance, as early as the second millennium BCE, coastal settlements participated in networks of exchange along the Pacific coast to Tehuantepec, Michoacán, and Colima, the uplands of Michoacán, Oaxaca, and Morelos, and to the valleys of Toluca and Mexico. The placer gold of Guerrero's coast and the route to Asia attracted the attention of the Spaniards, and before the sixteenth century ended, the economy and population of the coast had been drawn into a global maritime market.

Second, a history of both Mesoamerican and early colonial Guerrero identifies the region's key resources, how they were differently valued in pre-Hispanic and colonial Guerrero, and how this changed economy and society. For example, Guerrero's greenstone, Pacific shells, metals (especially copper and bronze), cacao, and cotton were highly prized in other regions of Mesoamerica, and in the Late Postclassic were sought by the Mexica and Tarascan empires. Greenstone and shells were worthless to the Spaniards, but silver funded the invasion and colonization of Mexico, while cacao and cotton could be converted into capital to invest in mining or livestock.

A discussion of resources does not imply neglect of culture broadly conceived, including cosmology, beliefs, rituals, or concepts of rulership and lifeways in general. Indeed, many of pre-Hispanic Guerrero's resources were important precisely because of their intrinsic cultural significance. Metallurgists fashioned ritual objects, and shells were made into artifacts of social and ceremonial significance. In the sixteenth century, while evangelization changed the ritual life of Indigenous communities, elements of Indigenous religion permeated church rites. Spanish legislation changed the ways in which communities were governed, but significant aspects of pre-Hispanic community practices persisted.

Third, a comparative regionwide approach provides new insights into Guerrero's history. For example, the Postclassic Montaña was a populous region, rich in placer gold and greenstone and skilled weavers of high-status garments. Its position astride key routes of exchange between the coast and central Mexico profited the elites who, in the fourteenth and fifteenth centuries, fashioned the largest and most stratified polity of precontact Guerrero. Under Spanish rule, a group of powerful absentee Spanish families exploited Indigenous administrative skills to extract the region's surplus without direct investment. In the North, by contrast, the polities were much smaller, and mining required direct investment of substantial capital, exploitation of human and natural resources, and a large Spanish presence.

As the literature has grown, the need for synthetic studies that pull together our accumulated knowledge of Guerrero's history up to ca. 1600 has become much greater. The value of the present synthesis is twofold. First, a comparison of the historical trajectory of Guerrero's regions yields new insights into their histories, histories both shared and disparate. Second, this study provides a platform for other scholars to identify topics and areas for new research. I considered whether archival research offered a realistic prospect of filling those gaps. However, it soon became clear that useful archival research in addition to the task of analyzing the voluminous secondary literature covering eight and a half millennia was beyond an individual researcher. Further, published documents concerning sixteenth-century New Spain could be mined to extract data not yet exploited in the literature.

For example, Manzanilla López's study of the Costa Grande surveys the key sites, settlement patterns, and social organization from the Archaic to the Postclassic, and includes some brief material on the early decades of the colonial period.[7] Labarthe's broad survey of the province of Zacatula from the Late Postclassic to the end of the eighteenth century is particularly valuable for lists of *encomiendas* and land grants, Spanish military expeditions to the region, and its evangelization.[8] The current study adds to these two studies in various ways. For example, recent studies suggest that Formative Guerrero's Pacific coast was a corridor for exchange of obsidian, and they demonstrate that coastal communities used boats for fishing and possibly coastal navigation.[9] Moreover, Guerrero's Formative coastal communities can now be understood in the broader context of social developments along the Pacific coast; for instance, at La Consentida[10] in Oaxaca and Cerro de las Conchas[11] in Chiapas. For the period 1521–1600, the present study further adds to Manzanilla López and Labarthe's accounts by comparing the information concerning encomienda tribute in *El libro de tasaciones*[12] with data concerning mining and commercial activities in the Zacatula region in the *Índice y extractos de los Protocolos del Archivo de Notarías de México*.[13]

The Postclassic archaeology of the Montaña region has been documented by Gutiérrez, who compares the archaeological record to the ethnohistory of the region as narrated in the *Códices de Azoyú 1* and *2*.[14] Danièle Dehouve's ethnohistorical work, drawing on an important body of pictorial documents from the region, ethnographic fieldwork, and archival research, is fundamental for understanding the historical trajectory of the Indigenous peoples of the Montaña after the Spanish invasion.[15] The present study builds on the work of Gutiérrez, Dehouve, and others to paint a longer-term picture of the history of the Montaña, examining, for example, the role of exchange and resources from and to the coast from the Formative to the early colonial period. Further, I demonstrate that in the sixteenth century, fewer Spaniards were present in the Montaña than in other regions of Guerrero.[16] So rich is the ethnohistorical material that the activities of these Spaniards in the region have been less discussed and understood. The present study draws on documentary[17] and secondary sources to document a broad array of Spanish enterprises. For example, in the Montaña there were very few encomiendas, but they were large, yielded rich tribute, and were held by exceptionally powerful individuals who used their tribute to fund commercial ventures.[18]

Important discoveries about the Olmec culture have been published by David Grove, who studied the cave paintings at Oxotitlán[19] in the Center, and Martínez Donjuán[20] and Niederberger[21] documented the Olmec site of Teopantecuanitlán in Guerrero's North. Teopantecuanitlán was an important center of manufacture and distribution of prestige and ceremonial goods created from materials of the Pacific coast, which is part of a bigger story of resources and exchange along an exchange route from the coast, a theme that the present study examines in both the precontact era and the early colonial period.[22]

The fate of the North in the sixteenth century was dominated by silver mining, the subject of Von Mentz's foundational study,[23] which has the great merit of examining the North in the round, including an analysis of the Indigenous polities of the region in the Late Postclassic and how Spanish colonization affected them, as well as of the mineowners and the mining economy. Amith's study of the North[24] focuses on landowning and mercantile interests, the redefinition of space and its impact on Indigenous communities from the sixteenth to the end of the eighteenth centuries. My study sets Von Mentz's and Amith's findings in a regionwide context, tracing the careers of mineowners in Zacatula on the coast and Zumpango in the Center, who later made fortunes in Taxco.[25] Moreover, an analysis of the activities of Spaniards in Guerrero from 1521 to ca. 1600 shows, unsurprisingly, that more were involved in mining in the North than in any other region of Guerrero. However, there was also a preponderance of Crown officials and clergy, the civil and spiritual instruments of social control.[26]

I have engaged with theories, debates, and interpretations that help to organize our understanding of the history of Guerrero. For example, archaeologists have debated whether the Gulf Coast Olmec constituted a mother culture (a diffusionist explanation in archaeological terms) from which concepts diffused to other regions, or whether regions like Guerrero contributed to the development of sister cultures that shared such concepts (a multivariate approach).[27] Some have interpreted the role of the Indigenous elites as that of self-serving collaborators who worked with the Spaniards to further their own interests in the sixteenth century. Other scholars such as Yanna Yannakakis[28] have argued for a more nuanced view of the elites as intermediaries who served their own and community interests at the same time.

I owe a debt to processual archaeology's[29] emphasis on the interconnectedness of different aspects of society and the environment and how these factors stimulated change. Thus the rise of Teopantecuanitlán can be attributed, inter alia, to control of a route of exchange of highly prized resources; a ruling elite that had functions of secular rulership and sacred roles as intermediaries with the supernatural; the elite's shared concepts with other centers such as Chalcatzingo; the elite's mobilization of labor for construction of ceremonial-administrative zones, irrigation works, and so on; and craft specialization in designated manufacturing-residential zones. In the sixteenth century, Taxco's rise as a significant economic pole of the regional economy can be ascribed, for instance, to the discovery of easily mined silver; small, stratified Indigenous polities in the vicinity ruled by elites capable of delivering labor and resources; the availability of agricultural land in the Iguala Valley and of livestock grazing and salt in the Tierra Caliente; and a concentration of clergy in the region to exercise social control of Indigenous communities.

Outline Structure

The first three chapters analyze our current knowledge of precontact Guerrero from the Late Archaic to the end of the Postclassic (3500 BCE–1521 CE). Chapter 1 surveys the geography, topography, and hydrology of Guerrero, settlement patterns, and societal development. The chapter also examines resources and exchange. These factors all combined to stimulate the development of settlements and, eventually, polities ruled by elites whose power and prosperity was built on the control of exchange, of routes and transport, combined with the manufacture of prestige items of ceremonial and social significance.

Chapter 2 assesses our knowledge of the material cultures, religious beliefs, ideologies, and cultures of the Indigenous peoples of Guerrero. A major topic is the Olmec culture in Guerrero and its implications for the origins of the first great culture of Mesoamerica. Guerrero's various art forms, notably the famous Mezcala stone sculptures and Xochipala ceramic figurines, are discussed, as is the region's wealth of Indigenous pictographic manuscripts. The chapter ends with a discussion of the many languages spoken in precontact Guerrero and the Indigenous population about 1521. Chapter 3 concludes the survey of precontact Guerrero with an exploration of what is known about the local polities, beginning with the Archaic, up to the emergence of Postclassic entities such as the Yopes on the coast, and especially the important Kingdom of Tlapa-Tlachinollan in the Montaña. The chapter ends with the late Postclassic empires of the Tarascans and the Mexicas.

Chapter 4 examines the military invasion of Guerrero following the defeat of the Mexicas, and then discusses how the Spaniards established control of Guerrero through civil and ecclesiastical arms of government. A novel feature of this chapter is an analysis of the activities of the Spaniards in Guerrero's regions, highlighting significant regional differences. A discussion of the evangelization of Guerrero addresses the regional differences in the character of the church's work, the responses of the Indigenous peoples, and how they participated in and shaped the development of the new faith.

Changes in the Indigenous communities are the theme of chapter 5, beginning with the enormous damage wrought by epidemics, the consequent changes in the demographic composition of Guerrero, and how Indigenous elites resisted but also sought accommodations with, and benefits from, the new colonial system. New institutions of Indigenous government both changed and preserved aspects of the precontact systems, and novel institutions, the *caja de comunidad* (a community fund) and the *cofradía* (a religious sodality), were integrated into the structures of village power and government. The imposition of civil and ecclesiastical jurisdictions and enforced resettlement programs, combined with fissiparous tendencies within Indigenous society, restructured territory and Indigenous jurisdictions.

The focus of chapter 6 is the encomienda, a foundational institution of sixteenth-century New Spain. The chapter analyzes the significant differences that characterized the encomienda and the *encomenderos* in the various regions of Guerrero. The encomenderos relied on Indigenous elites to administer tribute, which they used to finance their commercial activities, but Indigenous elites also negotiated benefits for themselves and/or defended their communities against excessive demands. Around midcentury, as chapter 7 demonstrates, Spaniards began to turn their attention to direct acquisition of land as the encomienda became less significant, but again the regional variations were significant. The chapter further examines the development of agriculture, livestock, and commerce, and the importation of African and Asian slave labor to replace the decimated Indigenous workforce. Once again, the analysis demonstrates very different regional variation in these factors.

Chapter 8 discusses the critically important mining industry, beginning with a very early gold rush on the coast, followed by a short-term boom in silver in the Center. In these early booms Spaniards would develop the commercial practices that would characterize the much richer silver strikes of Taxco and other mining centers of the Silver Province in the North. The chapter also examines the social and environmental problems caused by mining in Taxco. The other major economic event of the sixteenth century was the opening of the Asian trade with Acapulco in 1565, the subject of chapter 9. Acapulco was drawn into a new global economy fueled by American silver. Those who became immensely wealthy from this trade, which contraband and corruption ensured never conformed to the model prescribed in royal ordinances, were the merchants of Mexico City and Lima and Chinese traders in Manila. Very little benefit accrued to Acapulco, although the economic and cultural influence of the trade could be detected throughout Guerrero. Chapter 10 draws together the principal themes of Guerrero's history from as long ago as 7000 BCE to 1600 CE.

Sources

In our multidisciplinary age, it is imperative to incorporate insights from many disciplines. Danièle Dehouve, the ethnohistorian of Guerrero, lamented in 1994 our "great ignorance of Guerrero's distant past," observing that archaeology and linguistics are the only disciplines that shed any light on Guerrero's past before the twelfth or thirteenth centuries.[30] Fortunately, today we need not be quite so pessimistic, since several disciplines can contribute to an insightful history of pre-Hispanic and colonial Guerrero. This study draws on the now substantial body of work of archaeologists, linguistic historians, historians, ethnohistorians, ethnographers, and art historians.

Histories written in the decades after the fall of Tenochtitlan in 1521 shed some light on the history of Guerrero since the fourteenth century CE. However, both accounts written by Indigenous elites of central Mexico and by conquistadors—Augustinian, Franciscan, and Dominican friars—display a marked Mexican bias.[31] As Silverstein has demonstrated, accounts written by central Mexican Indigenous individuals and Spanish chroniclers of the defeat of Oztuma and other Chontal kingdoms in the Tierra Caliente of Guerrero that rebelled against the Mexica *tlatoani* (sources differ as to which ruler, and, therefore, the chronology) are contradicted by local colonial-era documentary sources and archaeological evidence.[32] Two categories of document created by Indigenous peoples of Guerrero offer testimonies in their voices. The first is pictographic documents, often with glosses in Nahuatl, dating from the first half of the sixteenth century to the eighteenth. The majority originated in eastern and northern Guerrero. Documents from the Tierra Caliente are few, for the Costa Grande we have only two, the Costa Chica five, and four from the Center. These documents are valuable for the precontact and early colonial periods, but must be treated with caution, since they were created to address colonial problems faced by the pueblos.[33] There are also documents written in alphabetical Nahuatl, whatever the native language of the group that had them made, for bureaucratic or legal dealings with the Spanish administration, many of which refer to precontact local history.[34]

Documents related to the history of Guerrero impose a significant chronological limit. For example, the *Códices de Azoyú 1* and *2*, made in the sixteenth century, tell the history of the ruling lineage of Tlapa-Tlachinollan and their territorial acquisitions, beginning in the fourteenth century, the polity's incorporation into the Mexica Empire in the mid-fifteenth century, and its sixteenth-century history. The successors of the rulers of Tlapa-Tlachinollan had the codices created to claim their hereditary rights before the Spanish authorities.[35] Several other documents produced in the region relate aspects of the same history.[36] No equivalent documents record the history of the Tarascan Empire in Guerrero. Scholars once argued that the Tarascans had no system of writing. However, studies of early colonial pictographic documents suggest the contrary. Moreover, archaeological evidence for the western Tierra Caliente of Guerrero challenges the view that the Tarascans ruled with an iron military grip as document-based historical studies had argued.[37]

The *Relaciones Geográficas*[38] and other Spanish sixteenth-century documentary sources describe the societies and the subsistence crops and resources of the Indigenous peoples and the routes they traveled to source them. However, since the emphasis was on the resources the Spaniards valued, some that had previously been of great economic and cultural value and that had stimulated interregional exchange for centuries were ignored.[39] Archaeology, not documents, tells us that the regional and extraregional demand for these products had stimulated exchange for centuries.

In short, the documentary evidence must be carefully interpreted, nor is it comprehensive and thoroughly trustworthy. Moreover, the chronological reach of the documents is limited. Archaeology cannot fill all the gaps and may not prove or disprove accounts in documents, but it can question its veracity, increase the chronological scope of our knowledge, and expand our understanding of Indigenous societies. Archaeologists would advise caution. Guerrero's archaeology suffers from large-scale looting and a consequent lack of archaeological context. Thus, despite the advances of recent decades, the shortage of securely dated remains precludes a completely chronological account.[40] A combination of chronological and thematic analysis provides a richer and more informed history of pre-Hispanic Guerrero.

Archaeology and History

Archaeology and history work to different chronological scales. Historians can often date an event to a year, month, or day. Archaeology works to much longer scales of centuries.[41] Similarly, archaeology can rarely discover the ethnic identity of populations,[42] and, as Michael Smith has pointed out, for example, it is difficult to identify in the archaeological record preimperial and postimperial artifacts of the Mexica, whose empire was formed after 1428 during the Postclassic.[43] Thus, the themes of the history of ancient Guerrero are drawn in broad chronological terms, but they are nevertheless significant. For example, human activity in the valley of the river Balsas dates at least to 7050 BCE. Then, between 7040–6660 BCE, something momentous for the future of Mesoamerica happened: On the shore of a small lake, the cultivation of maize occurred for the first time.[44]

Until recently, pre-Hispanic Guerrero was considered a very marginal region of Mesoamerica. Three distinguished archaeologists dismissed as "unlikely" Miguel Covarrubias's suggestion that the Olmecs originated in Guerrero, a region "of desert valleys and rugged, desiccated mountains," but discoveries such as Teopantecuanitlán challenge that assessment.[45] Formative Guerrero (1500 BCE–300 CE) was far from marginal, but rather it was an important participant in the cultural, social, and economic life of Mesoamerica. Thus, in 1521–1522, when Spaniards first trod the soil of Guerrero, they found societies that had formed, over many centuries, lifeways adapted to regional conditions. In the following chapters, we will examine the themes that shaped pre-Hispanic societies and, in turn, the colonial period in Guerrero.

Terminology

I have preferred the term *Mexica* instead of *Aztec*. However, although modern scholars tend to prefer *Purhépecha* to the traditional *Tarascan*, I have used the latter since the term is still used in scholarly publications and is familiar to nonspecialist readers.[46] Concerning Nahuatl terms, a reviewer of this text pointed out that Classical Nahuatl did not distinguish between singular and plural nouns, a distinction that emerged in the colonial period. Thus, *altepetl* is both singular and plural, as are *tecpan*, *calpolli*, *calpixqui*, and *tlatoani*. In general, I have avoided applying Nahuatl terms to non-Nahuatl polities and persons. Thus, a Chontal ruler or lord is not a tlatoani, and the polity is not referred to as an altepetl, but as a community, polity, and so on, although altepetl is sometimes the most convenient way to refer in general to Indigenous polities. For Indigenous persons referred to in the *Códices de Azoyú 1* and *2*, I have used the Spanish language names (thus, Señor Lluvia, not Lord Rain) cited in the literature, since their names are not cited in an Indigenous language. The Spanish term *estancia* had two meanings in colonial Mexico: a cattle ranch, or a community dependent on a *cabecera* (head town), also termed a *sujeto*.[47] Here *estancia* refers to a cattle ranch and *sujeto* to a dependent community, unless text containing the term *estancia* is quoted. The term *minero* is used in sources to mean both a mineowner and a worker in a mine (generally referring to a Spanish supervisor). Here *minero* is reserved for mineowner, and mineworker is used for its other sense. Finally, I have preferred to use the term *Spanish invasion* instead of *Spanish conquest*, since much of the fighting was done by Indigenous allies without whom the Spaniards could not have succeeded.

The naming of historic settlements requires some clarification. Toponyms are often spelled in more than one fashion in the sources, and on occasion alternative names differ considerably (e.g., modern Culác may be Cualac or Cuaulasyotepetl). Since a modern town usually sits on the archaeological remains of the precontact settlement or is very close by, I have used the modern names unless there is a good reason not to. For a list of names used in the text, alternative spellings used in sources and the literature, and modern place names, see appendix 4.

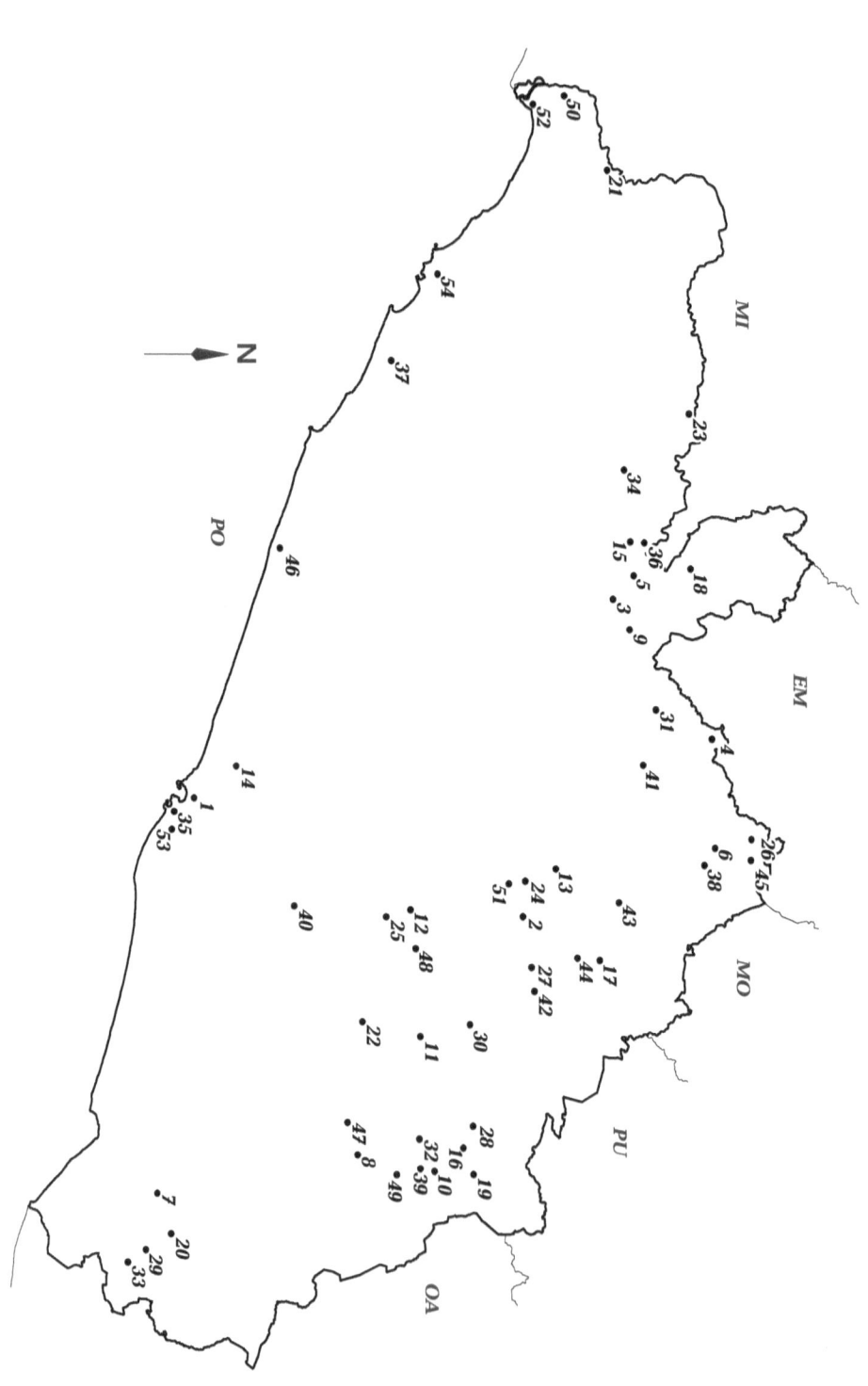

Map 1. Guerrero: Precontact Archaeological Sites and Settlements

Locations

1. Acapulco
2. Ahuináhuac
3. Ajuchitlán
4. Alahuizlán
5. Amuco Abelino
6. Azala
7. Azoyú
8. Cauadzidziqui
9. Cerro de los Monos
10. Chiepetlán
11. Chilapa
12. Chilpancingo
13. Coacoyula
14. Coyuca [on Costa Grande]
15. Coyuca [in Tierra Caliente]
16. Cualác
17. Cuetlajuchitlán
18. Cutzamala
19. Huamuxtitlán
20. Igualapa
21. El Infiernillo
22. Juxtlahuaca
23. Mexiquito
24. Mezcala
25. Mochitlán
26. Noxtepec
27. Oapan
28. Olinalá
29. Ometepec
30. Oxtotitlán
31. Oztuma
32. Peltacala
33. Piedra Labrada
34. Placeres de Oro
35. Puerto Marqués
36. Pungarabato
37. La Soledad de Maciel
38. Taxco el Viejo
39. Techan
40. Tehuacalco
41. Teloloapan
42. Teopantecuanitlán
43. Tepecoacuilco
44. Tequicuilco
45. Tetipac
46. Tetitlán
47. Texmelincan
48. Tixtla
49. Tlapa
50. La Villita
51. Xochipala
52. Zacatula
53. La Zanja
54. Zihuatanejo

Keys for surrounding areas

MI. Michoacán
EM. Estado de México
MO. Morelos
PU. Puebla
OA. Oaxaca
PO. Pacific Ocean

CHAPTER ONE

Guerrero ca. 7000 BCE to 1521 CE

Regions, Peoples, Resources, and Exchange

Geography and Settlement Patterns

Guerrero is a rugged region of great topographical and climate variety, shaped by two great geographical features. The Sierra Madre del Sur gives Guerrero a mountainous spine pierced by rivers and streams that flow down either to the narrow coastal plains and lagoons or in the opposite direction, draining into that other determinant of Guerrero's geography, the Balsas River (also known upstream as the Mezcala, and further upstream still as the Atoyac). The Balsas flows from the modern states of Mexico, Morelos, and Puebla across northern Guerrero before it descends along the frontier with Michoacán to the Pacific. Guerrero combines hot and humid tropical coasts, temperate mountain valleys watered by seasonal rains, cooler higher land, and the hot lands of the Balsas Valley. This varied terrain can be divided into six regions. The Costa Grande stretches to the northwest of Acapulco to the estuary of the Balsas, while the Costa Chica takes the traveler south and east to Oaxaca. The highlands of eastern Guerrero are known as the Montaña, to the west of which is the Center. To the north of the Balsas is the North. To the west along the river basin is the aptly named Tierra Caliente. This complex mix of topography, climate, and hydrography created a diversity of ecological and resource niches that the peoples who made their lives in Guerrero over many centuries exploited to develop networks of exchange along which traveled not just goods but also ideas—ideas about power, society, culture, art, and cosmology.

The plains of the Costa Grande and the Costa Chica were a tropical region of high seasonal rainfall. The rivers that flow from the sierras water the region, forming lagoons on the coast. The coastal plain was narrow, hot, and, according to an Italian traveler in 1697, plagued by mosquitos.[1] In places the terrain rose abruptly toward the Sierra Madre del Sur.[2] Tropical crops, such as cotton and cacao, prospered, alongside foods such as tomatoes. At higher elevations, such as upland sections of the Costa Chica and Costa Grande and parts of the aptly named Montaña, a more temperate climate permitted the cultivation of most of the nontropical crops essential to the Mexican diet. Higher still, a colder climate and rugged terrain limited cultivation to modest yields of maize and similar crops. The proximity of these three distinct zones promoted the exchange of resources within Guerrero and beyond.[3]

The Center was a region of mountains, drained to the south by the Papagayo River and to the north by the Mezcala (or Balsas) and their tributaries. The high Sierra Madre ran across the Center.[4] The well-named Tierra Caliente followed east to west the course of the Balsas, fed by tributaries that drained the high plain of central Mexico and the high sierra. Relatively scarce alluvial flatlands in the Balsas basin were suitable for crops that included cotton and cacao.[5] The North was a zone of high temperatures but not the searing heat of the Tierra Caliente. The mountains here were less rugged than in the Center, and some rivers and streams flowed all year to supplement the seasonal rains.[6]

This, then, was a rugged territory with a great variety of terrain, climate, and ecology. In his study of Aztec markets, Ken Hirth states that a resident of Mesoamerica who wished to reach an ecological region with a different climate and resources had only to travel a maximum of 90 kilometers. Furthermore, many settlements were located only 30 kilometers from a zone that offered products not available locally.[7] Gerardo Gutiérrez notes that this generalization applied perfectly to the Costa Chica and the Montaña of Guerrero.[8] Ecological variety was a fundamental context within which the lifeways of Guerrero's inhabitants and the pattern of their settlements, and the exchange of resources and ideas, occurred throughout the precontact history of the region. It is to the regional contexts of settlement patterns that we turn first.

1.1. The Costa Chica and the Costa Grande

Shell mounds, which occur from El Salvador to San Blas, are the earliest known sites along the Pacific coast of Mesoamerica. From the Middle Archaic (5500–3500 BCE), communities such as Cerro de las Conchas in modern Chiapas lived from a combination of marine and terrestrial

TABLE 1.1. CHRONOLOGICAL CHART: ARCHAIC TO POSTCLASSIC		
ARCHAIC		8000–1500 BCE
	Early Archaic	8000–5500 BCE
	Middle Archaic	5500–3500 BCE
	Late Archaic	3500–1500 BCE
FORMATIVE		1500 BCE–300 CE
	Early Formative	1500–1200 BCE
	Middle Formative	1200–400 BCE
	Late Formative	400 BCE–1 CE
	Terminal Formative	1–300 CE
CLASSIC		250/300–900/1000 CE
	Early Classic	250/300–600 CE
	Late Classic	600–900 CE
	Epiclassic	650/700–900/1000 CE
POSTCLASSIC		900/1000–1521 CE
	Early Postclassic	900/1000–1200 CE
	Middle Postclassic	1200–1430 CE
	Late Postclassic	1430–1521 CE

resources, founded small settlements, and eventually cultivated crops. We know from evidence of forest disturbance that the inhabitants employed slash-and-burn methods to modify their environment for farming. By the Late Archaic this was a full-fledged agricultural community.[9] Studies of La Consentida in modern Oaxaca, which flourished during the Late Archaic and the Early Formative, show us something of the lifeways of its inhabitants beyond the harvesting of marine resources and the emergence of early farming. La Consentida's residents subsisted on a mixture of seafood, preferring large fish caught in an ocean environment, and by the Early Formative horticulture and some maize cultivation were developed. The eighty or so inhabitants lived in architectural structures on earthen mounds. Finds of musical instruments and decorated ceramics suggest intermittent feasting, music, and perhaps dancing. The architecture of La Consentida implies the organization of communal labor and the emergence of a degree of social hierarchy. However, there is little evidence of the hereditary hierarchies that would characterize later periods of Mesoamerican history.[10]

Several similar early coastal sites have been found along the Pacific coast of Guerrero, although inundation due to sea-level rise and the formation of lagoons at the estuaries of rivers have doubtless obliterated traces of other sites that once existed. The best studied case is what is now known as Puerto Marqués in Acapulco. From the Late Archaic to the Formative (3500 BCE–300 CE), the inhabitants collected shellfish from the beaches and lagoons. They also fished, and analysis of fish bones reveals that, like the people of La Consentida, they were fond of some species that could only be caught with nets (there is no evidence of hooks or lines) in the deepest waters of the bay, and perhaps at sea. Thus, they had some kind of sea-going vessels. In the Late Archaic and the Formative, the population of Puerto Marqués was larger than that of La Consentida, but still modest at between one hundred and five hundred people. Nevertheless, the exploitation of marine resources had ecological effects to which the community adapted. The diet initially included locally gathered estuarine shellfish, but around 900–500 BCE, as the population increased, a greater variety of mollusks from farther afield was sourced directly, possibly using boats or by trade. Modifications to subsistence also included the cultivation of maize.[11]

Maritime navigation and fishing were not the only technological achievements of the people of Puerto Marqués. In the Late Archaic they made tools using local stone and obsidian. There are no sources of obsidian in Guerrero, so its presence is evidence of extraregional exchange at an early date.[12] Analysis of obsidian artifacts demonstrated that in the Early and Middle Formative, the inhabitants of Puerto Marqués obtained finished obsidian blades from the central Mexican highlands and the Valley of Oaxaca, and possibly also from the Gulf Coast and the Isthmus of Tehuantepec. Thus, Puerto Marqués and the Guerrero coast were part of a Pacific coast network of exchange.[13] Another achievement that indicated significant social and economic changes was the manufacture of Pox ceramics dated by Charles Brush to 2300–2400 BCE. If this date is correct, Pox could be the oldest ceramic of Mesoamerica.[14] The date has been keenly debated, some scholars arguing for a later date, while others suggested that Pox might be still older.[15] The general consensus of recent research is that Pox dates to around 1400 BCE, contemporary with other early ceramics such as those found at Barra de Chiapas or Purrón in the Tehuacán Valley.[16] Nevertheless, the presence of early ceramics combined with other evidence tells us that the people of Puerto Marqués were resourceful and were in contact with distant regions. Ten Early Formative sites around Acapulco

Bay and in the hills behind indicate a general increase in population that lasted at least until the Classic (250/300–900/1000 CE).

By 1400 BCE, one of these settlements, a site now called La Zanja, was established on the shore of the Laguna de Tres Palos, approximately 5 kilometers from Puerto Marqués. Here the residents lived from shellfish collection, fishing, and cultivating maize, beans, and squash. Like their neighbors in Puerto Marqués, they used some kind of boat to source seafood farther afield. By this time the exchange of ceramics, obsidian, and other resources had intensified through networks from the Isthmus of Tehuantepec along the Pacific coast.[17] Portable X-ray fluorescence analysis has confirmed that in the Early and Middle Formative (1500–400 BCE), La Zanja participated in long-distance exchange of obsidian from Ucareo-Zinapécuaro in Michoacán (360 kilometers in a straight line), and, from the Middle Formative, from Otumba (337 kilometers) and Pachuca (380 kilometers).[18]

To the northwest of Acapulco Bay, on the Laguna de Coyuca, eleven shell mounds at Tetitlán have yielded data concerning the subsistence strategies and diet of Formative coastal inhabitants, from 1390 BCE to 320 BCE. From 1220 BCE to 870 BCE, they harvested an estimated 1.2 tons of seafood meat annually. Between 870 BCE and 620 BCE, the average increased to 5.8 tons, a substantial amount that indicates a similarly sustained growth of the population. The presence of pollen is evidence of agriculture from quite an early date, but in some periods, hunting (deer, crocodile, duck, and crab) compensated for a reduction in cultivation. The inhabitants of Tetitlán responded to several ecological challenges—changes in rainfall and temperature and the flooding of the lagoon by seawater—by adjusting the mix of marine resources, hunting, and agriculture.[19]

According to Manzanilla's studies, Formative societies of the Costa Grande consisted of pretribal hunter-gatherers and lacked class distinctions and any notion of property, although research at La Consentida suggests at least incipient hierarchy and social distinctions in coastal communities. The inhabitants lived in independent settlements but exchanged goods and ideas. Evidence indicates exchange beyond the region: from Zihuatanejo and La Villita along the coast to Michoacán and Colima to the northwest, as far as Tehuantepec and Guatemala to the southeast, and from Atoyac, Coyuca, and San Jerónimo across the sierra to the basin of Mexico. People of the Formative lived either on the coastal plain, on low hills where they had access to rivers or springs of fresh water, or in settlements scattered

Figure 1. An aerial view of the ballcourt at La Soledad de Maciel, Guerrero, with the adjoining plaza to its west (left) side, and the Cerro de los Brujos to the rear of the plaza. Reproduction authorized by the Instituto Nacional de Antropología e Historia (INAH), Mexico City.

over the hill slopes. They cultivated crops on the river estuaries. They used grinding tools, axes, chisels, and hoes. Ceramic tablets with concave areas, perhaps for mixing pigments, suggest an interest in colors, perhaps for ritual purposes. This interpretation is supported in later periods by the palettes for mixing colors found in El Infiernillo in the Tierra Caliente.[20]

The Classic Period (250/300 CE–900/1000 CE) witnessed the emergence of more hierarchical societies and of sites with ceremonial centers and substantial structures on the Costa Grande. The settlement pattern remained dispersed, but some noticeable changes were introduced because of increases in population. Complexes of three or four houses arranged round a rectangular or square patio were located on the flat lands or, for the first time, on terraces to provide both more living space and more cultivable land. This pattern also allowed fallow periods or rotation of crops on the coastal plain.[21]

Figure 2. The statue of El Rey de la Chole, originally from La Soledad de Maciel. The face of the figure is divided in two by a skull with no skin. There is a year marker in the headdress. Museo de Sitio de Soledad Maciel, Xihuacan, Guerrero. Reproduction authorized by the Instituto Nacional de Antropología e Historia (INAH), Mexico City.

The most impressive of these is the site known in most of the published literature as La Soledad de Maciel (recently renamed Xihuacán), near present-day Petatlán, dated from the Middle Formative to the Late Postclassic (1100 BCE–1521 CE). A plaza was enclosed with massive structures, ballcourts, altars, and terraced habitational areas. The settlement had four stepped temple structures. The orientation of the ceremonial structures and the iconography of the decoration of Building B and of Epiclassic ceramics at the site refer to the solstice and the equinox, which were important for agricultural planning and reckoning the rainy season. La Soledad de Maciel is one of only two sites at which carved monumental stelae have been found on the Costa Grande. Known as El Rey de la Chole, the figure carved on this stela has been interpreted as a fat priest. The figure wears a mask with a human face divided in the middle by a skull with no skin (possibly a reference to Xipe Tótec, the flayed god). A year sign is visible on the figure's headdress. Numerous finds of figurines include some distinctive new forms, suggesting an interest in asserting locally generated ideas rather than simply absorbing influences from more powerful polities.[22]

During the Postclassic, in the Balsas delta near Zacatula a dispersed settlement was located on five contiguous hills—constructed in two phases, 800–1200 CE and 1200–1521 CE. Las Tamacuas was a ceremonial center of limited access, with residential units probably occupied by people of high social status. Barranco de Marmolejo was a ceremonial, administrative, and political center, with mounds, large open spaces, and a cemetery for funeral rituals. El Cuartel was a residential zone. Monte Don Venus was a ceremonial site and served as a watch site to observe movements along the river and the coast. There are also other sites in the locality, some dated as early as 200 CE.[23]

The Classic ceremonial centers and other aspects of the material culture of sites such as La Soledad de Maciel reflect influences of the two great cities of the period, Monte Albán in Oaxaca and, above all, the metropolis of Teotihuacan in the Valley of Mexico. By adopting the visual language of such important polities, local elites bolstered their power, emulating on a reduced scale the dominant states of the day. At Zihuatanejo, ceramic evidence speaks of interactions with Teotihuacan and the Costa Chica of Oaxaca from 200 CE to 900 CE. From the Early Postclassic (900 CE to 1200 CE), figurines and ceramics reflect Toltec influence. There is also evidence of violent conflict with settlements such as Pantla, Ixtapa, and Petatlán.[24]

On the Costa Chica, a site survey carried out by Gerardo Gutiérrez identified nine sites. The most significant is Piedra Labrada, dated to the Classic and Postclassic. This is a large site of 90 hectares, which makes it the largest site of the western Zapotec region and probably the largest on the Costa Chica. There are indications of Zapotec, Teotihuacan, and Mixtec influences. It was occupied from the Late Formative to the end of the Late Postclassic. The site has twenty-five structures, including pyramid mounds up to 20 meters tall, and at least five ballcourts. Piedra Labrada is most notable for its twenty-one carved granite and sandstone sculptures (one is of a red stone).[25] A much smaller settlement, Terreno de Cohimbre, consists only of small mounds, but it is notable for a carved stela that bears similarities with monuments at Piedra Labrada and at the important Montaña site of Texmelincan.[26]

In short, by 1521 communities on the coast had lived for more than 4,000 years from marine resources, hunting, and the cultivation of maize, beans, squash, and other crops typical of the Mesoamerican diet. From early times there were contacts with Michoacán, central Mexico, and Oaxaca. In addition to subsistence crops, the coast was also a source of some valuable tropical resources, which enabled coastal communities to trade within and beyond Guerrero. The climate was ideal for cultivating cotton and cacao, much in demand in the cooler highland regions. Clay spindles found in quantity in Postclassic contexts in Guerrero (wooden spindles may have been used but have been not preserved) confirm cotton's importance to the pre-Hispanic economy.[27] Coastal cacao was similarly prized in regions where the climate prevented its cultivation.[28] The coast was also a source of placer gold,[29] salt,[30] and much prized marine shells.[31] Toward the end of the Formative, the hunter-gatherers of the Costa Grande lived in chiefdoms, with storage systems, organized in larger settlements to protect their territory and resources, with some degree of specialization of activities and ideologies that validated the new social system. By the sixteenth century, rulers governed sociopolitical units of a modest scale and controlled the labor force.[32] In the Classic and Postclassic there was contact with more distant regions,[33] and evidence suggests contact, direct or indirect, by land or sea, with the Andean region.[34] This was certainly not an isolated or backward region.

1.2. The Montaña

Above the Costa Chica lies the Montaña, an apt name for this region of sierra, small valleys, and rivers that do not always flow in the dry season. As one ascends the valleys one reaches the great basin of the Balsas.[35] Within a relatively short distance the traveler passes through very distinct ecological regions: the Balsas region is relatively dry with high temperatures; the highest parts of the sierra are cold with meagre rainfall; at lower elevations toward the coast temperatures rise and rainfall increases, but it is still inadequate at times.[36] The well-watered alluvial soils of the valleys form productive mini-zones of varied ecologies, as the noted writer Ignacio Altamirano observed of Tixtla in the nineteenth century, no doubt exaggerating the attractions of his native region: "An agreeable and fertile valley sheltered by an amphitheatre of handsome sierras covered in luxuriant vegetation . . . Cold in the highlands, temperate on the plain and hot in the low-lying land . . . The Indians keep handsome and sizeable gardens where they cultivate the vegetables of Mexico."[37]

However, since the fertile land was never abundant, the Indigenous peoples of the Montaña built channels to increase the irrigated area and a system of walls of twigs, shrubs, stones, and pine branches, known as *trompezones*, behind which they captured the fertile alluvial soils when the rivers washed them downstream.[38]

One might assume that the shortage of cultivable land would inhibit the development of prosperous settlements. To the contrary, rather dynamic societies developed here. Mastodons and mammoths were probably hunted here in the Paleoindian period (12,000–8000 BCE), since their remains have been found in the adjacent Mixteca of Oaxaca.[39] Temporary encampments from the Archaic in the valley of Huamuxtitlán signal the presence between 5000 and 2000 BCE of hunter-gatherers, who used tools made of flint.[40] Thus, some 2,000 years after the domestication of maize in the Iguala valley,[41] and around the time when the people of Puerto Marqués lived off shellfish and fish, hunter-gatherers still roamed the Montaña. Unlike the residents of the coast these people seem to have had no access to obsidian or ceramics. These different lifeways reflected distinct resources, social organization, patterns of exchange, and chronologies of change.

According to linguistic historians, from 2500 BCE, people who spoke a predecessor of the Tlapanec language inhabited eastern Guerrero. The region had links to the Mixteca, and around 500 BCE, Mixtec speakers settled there. After the eleventh or twelfth century CE, Amuzgos, also from Oaxaca, were living in parts of the Montaña, and around the eleventh century, Nahuatl speakers arrived to the north, founding the polities of Huamuxtitlán and Olinalá.[42] Clearly, the Montaña had sufficient attractions to bring migrant groups here over several centuries. A survey carried out by Gutiérrez recorded forty-eight sites in the Tlapa Valley, ninety in the valley of Huamuxtitlán, seven in the small Igualita Valley, and fifty-four elsewhere, some in the Montaña Alta. These figures include very small sites, no doubt scattered dependencies of larger centers, and most have not been dated. Nevertheless, evidence of settlements since the Formative, and later the presence of platforms, mounds, ballcourts, *tecpan* (elite residences), and *talud-tablero* architecture, suggest a long history of human activity and participation in Mesoamerican culture.[43] By the Postclassic some of these settlements would be capable of dominating others and forming the largest polity in Guerrero.

The inhabitants of twin towns a mere 1.8 kilometers apart in the Tlapa Valley, Contlalco and Cerro Quemado-La Coquera, organized their urban area to make the most of the terrain. These were Formative settlements, dating to 900 BCE–300 CE; Contlalco occupied a little more than 85 hectares, Cerro Quemado-La Coquera some 35 hectares. Their combined extent made them probably the largest settlement in the Montaña, but was less than half that of Teopantecuanitlán, a Formative site to the north of the Tlapa Valley. Their subsequent occupation is obscure, but it seems they were abandoned during the Classic and occupied again in the Postclassic. Contlalco is the most complex site of the Montaña. Its inhabitants converted a hill that was 80 meters high on one side and 100 meters on the other, with stepped terraces to form an exceptionally tall pyramid. In sector 1 was a 2.7-hectare terrace, with a 1.5-hectare plaza on which stood several mounds, a ballcourt, and a tecpan located in an area divided by four patios. In the upper part of sector 2, which consisted of several rectangular terraces, was a platform 60 meters by 40 meters, with two mounds and a ballcourt. The rulers of Contlalco developed their settlement progressively to make it more imposing: one patio was stuccoed up to twenty-three times, and the creation of the main terrace was the result of frequent additions, retained by talud walls filled with material excavated for the works. Cerro Quemado-La Coquera had a plaza 150 meters by 43 meters, on which stood two mounds. There was a ballcourt and a drainage system to capture rainwater. The terracing was identical to that of Contlalco. The initial embankment on the hill slope was leveled and supported by talud walls. Subsequently, more terraces were added repeatedly to raise the level.[44]

In terms of extent, Contlalco and Cerro Quemado-La Coquera are minor settlements indeed compared to the great urban centers of central Mexico, such as Teotihuacan and Tenochtitlan, or of Monte Albán in Oaxaca. Yet they display certain features—such as monumental ceremonial structures, palatial residences, and drainage systems—they share with those great cities. The general settlement pattern of the Montaña, and indeed of precontact Guerrero as a whole, was of dispersed small-scale communities. Yet, if we concentrate on the scale of settlements to the exclusion of other aspects of sites, we fail to understand the essence of social organization in Guerrero. As Gutiérrez argues, the Mesoamerican altepetl should not be considered a single built point in space. Furthermore, the Mesoamerican model of the altepetl did not distinguish between the urban and the rural. Rather, it consisted of dispersed subunits of varying scale that could agglomerate into larger units ruled over by a dynastic lineage residing in a nucleated site with a temple, a tecpan, a market, and other urban features. In the case of the Montaña, the twin centers of Contlalco and Cerro Quemado-La Coquera probably reflect the dual dynastic structure, known as the *yuhuitayu*, of the Mixtec urban state, or *ñuu*. The yuhuitayu was formed by the marital alliance of a male ruler of one ñuu to the female ruler of another. They ruled in two urban centers. Thus, Contlalco and Cerro Quemado-La Coquera were likely ñuu ruled by a yuhuitayu, which probably governed other ñuu, each with its own subject dynasty.[45]

There were a further forty-six sites in the Tlapa Valley, which measure 12.5 kilometers long and, at its maximum, 1 kilometer wide. These sites ranged from settlements of 1 hectare with a few terraces and perhaps a mound to 21 hectares. Since the sites have not been dated, it is not clear which were contemporary with Contlalco and Cerro Quemado-La Coquera, but it seems likely that the Formative inhabitants of the valley undertook a general transformation of their territory.[46]

Many sites in the Huamuxtitlán Valley were small, but one of the largest is Alpoyeca-Las Minas, occupying almost 27 hectares. The area, which included the principal structures, is 3.5 hectares in extent, formed by three levels of terraces, on which two ballcourts and several platforms were constructed. A possible tecpan measuring 48 meters by 40 meters lies to the west of this area. Alpoyeca-Las Minas was strategically located to control two roads to the Mixteca of Oaxaca. There was also ample agricultural land, a substantial portion of it irrigated.[47] Beyond the valleys, in the high Montaña, were at least fifty-four sites. Few had any form of monumental architecture, one of the exceptions to this rule being Cochoapa-Yuu Kivi. Here the principal structures were ranged round a sunken plaza measuring 27 meters by 25 meters. To the north of the plaza was a large ballcourt (43 meters long by 9 meters wide), in which two ring-shaped markers carved with anthropomorphic designs were found, as well as a serpent head. This site's prominence may be due to its location on a possible route connecting the Costa Chica with central Mexico.[48]

How did significant settlements in regional terms develop in a mountainous area with limited agricultural land? The Montaña was a significant source of gold and also of beeswax and honey, which were exchangeable in other regions.[49] Maize and beans could be grown, but not cotton nor cacao. Cotton was sourced from the coast and woven by local craftspeople to make everyday garments, as well as elite wear.[50] The importance of the Montaña was not principally in its products but rather in its strategic position on routes of exchange, despite its mountainous terrain, which the Spaniards would consider an impediment to trade in the colonial period.[51] Nevertheless, narrow routes of trampled earth and stone provided access to the resources of Guerrero. The Montaña was equidistant between Monte Albán and Teotihuacan and surely benefited from the transport of products between Oaxaca and the central altiplano, both before and after the rise of those two great cities. The first indication of such routes consists of Olmec or "Olmecoid" (Olmec-influenced) objects, evidence of contact between Guerrero and the Gulf Coast. Archaeologists had long theorized that Olmec demand for greenstone, called *chalchihuitl* by the Mexica, was the driver of exchange. Recent discoveries confirm that greenstone, marine shells, and other materials were exchanged along routes through the Montaña to Morelos from the Formative onward.[52] Colonial trade would later follow similar routes.[53]

1.3. The Center

To the west of the Montaña lay the Center, an equally mountainous region of small valleys, crossed by the Sierra Madre del Sur. The elevations here range from 350 meters to 3,000 meters, but generally are 500 to 1,500 meters. The climate is hot and dry, although in the highest part of the sierra rainfall was sufficient for pine and evergreen oak forests. A relatively low pass between tributaries of the Balsas and the Papagayo has for centuries been the route between central Mexico and the coast.[54] The agricultural potential of the region from the Balsas to Zumpango, one of the driest in Guerrero, was limited.[55]

The area in the Center with the largest number of recorded sites, some of them excavated, is the valley of Chilpancingo. The region to the west is relatively unexplored, although survey work has found sites whose level of development is unclear.[56] A 2004 survey found fifty-seven sites dated from 800 BCE onward in the valley of Chilpancingo. Between 650 and 900 CE the population of the valley increased, and large settlements appeared at higher and lower elevations.[57] A site called Pezuapan, whose population reached its maximum between 800 and 1100 CE, demonstrated the importance of being located on an exchange route. Analysis of shells excavated here shows that 70 percent were from the Pacific, 26 percent from coastal lagoons (probably of the Pacific), and 4 percent from fresh water. The people of Pezuapan constructed an elite residence, consisting of platforms, possible storage facilities, and areas for manufacturing shell objects.[58] This region experienced periods of prosperity when regional and interregional exchange stimulated the economy.[59]

To the north is the large plain of Xochipala, an area today of 2,200 hectares of good cultivable land, which is the granary of the sierra. Flat, fertile land was a precious resource. Therefore, the inhabitants of Xochipala constructed settlements and ceremonial centers on higher land, reserving the plain for cultivation. Consequently, there was no large urban center. Rosa María Reyna Robles argues that the site of La Organera occupies only 9 hectares and cannot compare with the large cities of the Valley of Mexico, but nevertheless it exhibited features (temples, palaces, other monumental architecture) characteristic of urban centers. Together with contemporary sites around the Xochipala plain, she argues, La Organera constituted a different type of urban organization, a discontinuous city. She has estimated its total settled area at 200 hectares, a modest size compared to contemporary sites in central Mexico, and smaller than Olmec Teopantecuanitlán, which flourished several centuries earlier in the North of Guerrero.[60] Paul Schmidt's first systematic investigation of Xochipala identified ninety-three sites varying from 1 to 100 hectares. Based on the ceramic sequence and two radiocarbon dates, Schmidt identified eight phases and dated occupation between 585 BCE and 965 CE, and probably later.[61]

La Organera was occupied during the Middle and Late Formative, followed by an urban settlement from 700 CE to 1000 CE. It was subsequently inhabited as a small domestic site from about 1000/1050 to 1100/1200 CE, then abandoned until around 1400 CE, when it was settled as a domestic site. The period of urban settlement included stone palaces with porticos, temples, two large structures with sunken patios separated by a probable tomb with a corbelled arch, plazas, patios, and a ballcourt. The site underwent considerable public works. First, substantial areas were leveled, creating by means of cuttings and terraces, and fill, six flat areas. The difference in height between the ballcourt on the highest, northern level to the southern area is more than 15.5 meters. Hydraulic works were constructed: water tanks, channels, and drainage. The plan included passageways, stone paving, and stairways to connect and separate the structures and spaces, some of which were large and open, others small and enclosed. La Organera's small, densely constructed space had many of the features of larger urban centers.[62]

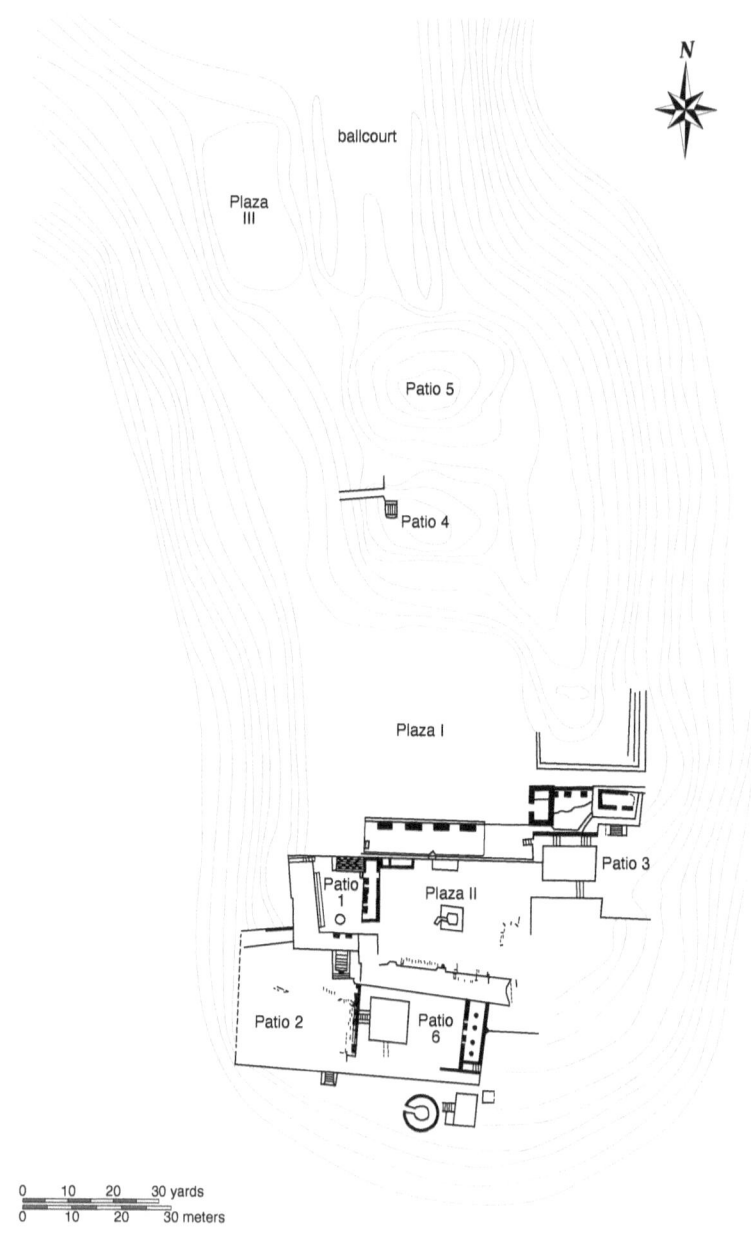

Figure 3. Plan of La Organera-Xochipala, 700 CE to 1000 CE. The ballcourt is on the highest, northern, elevation. Land was leveled to create plazas and patios. Patios 2 and 6 are more than 15.5 m lower than Plaza III. Drawing by Martin Lubikowski, adapted from Reyna Robles, *La Organera-Xochipala*.

1.4. The North

Although this region has areas of high sierra, in general elevations are lower than in the Center, the Montaña, and the elevated zones of the Tierra Caliente. The climate in some parts is hot, while in others temperatures are more moderate. Rainfall is seasonal. Tributaries of the Balsas flow year-round and in places form small lakes.[63] A number of valleys are propitious for agriculture, notably the Iguala Valley, where research has suggested that by the Laguna de Tuxpan, a short distance from modern Iguala, maize domestication began, and about 7000 BCE, humans sheltered and prepared a meal in the Xihuatoxtla rock shelter.[64] In the colonial period, the valley would supply maize to the Taxco and Zacualpa mines, and in times of scarcity to Mexico City and Guanajuato.[65]

Since the Formative, settlements with ceremonial and administrative centers were large enough to support a governing elite. The best documented such site is Teopantecuanitlán, a Formative settlement first occupied from 1400 BCE that eventually covered at least 280 hectares,[66] a very sizeable area in Guerrero, even in later centuries. In comparison, Formative San José Mogote in Oaxaca, with a population of some 1,000, covered 60–65 hectares, and Cuicuilco in the Valley of Mexico, 400–500 hectares.[67] If Teopantecuanitlán was as densely settled as San José Mogote, its population would have been 4,300–4,600, or 860–920 families. Teopantecuanitlán had three habitational zones, systems of drainage, and irrigation. An impressive ceremonial center speaks of a ruling group with sufficient resources and the ability to mobilize labor to undertake four phases of construction.[68] Niederberger describes Teopantecuanitlán as a key element in exchange networks, perhaps a regional capital by the beginning of the first millennium BCE.[69]

Teopantecuanitlán is the earliest example of urbanism in Guerrero. Before 1200 BCE, when construction of a sunken patio began, an elite that participated in the Olmec culture ruled there. This first phase of construction was of adobe. Between 1200–100 BCE successive modifications were made to the patio precinct. In the third phase access to the patio was restricted by narrow passageways. On two sides platforms further narrowed the passageways, and two stairways interrupted them. Together with two sculptures with Olmec iconography, this represented a new language of elite power. Between 1000–800 BCE the adobe walls were dressed with stone blocks weighing from 50 kilograms to 5 tons. Four new stone sculptures were installed. Two were placed so that at the spring

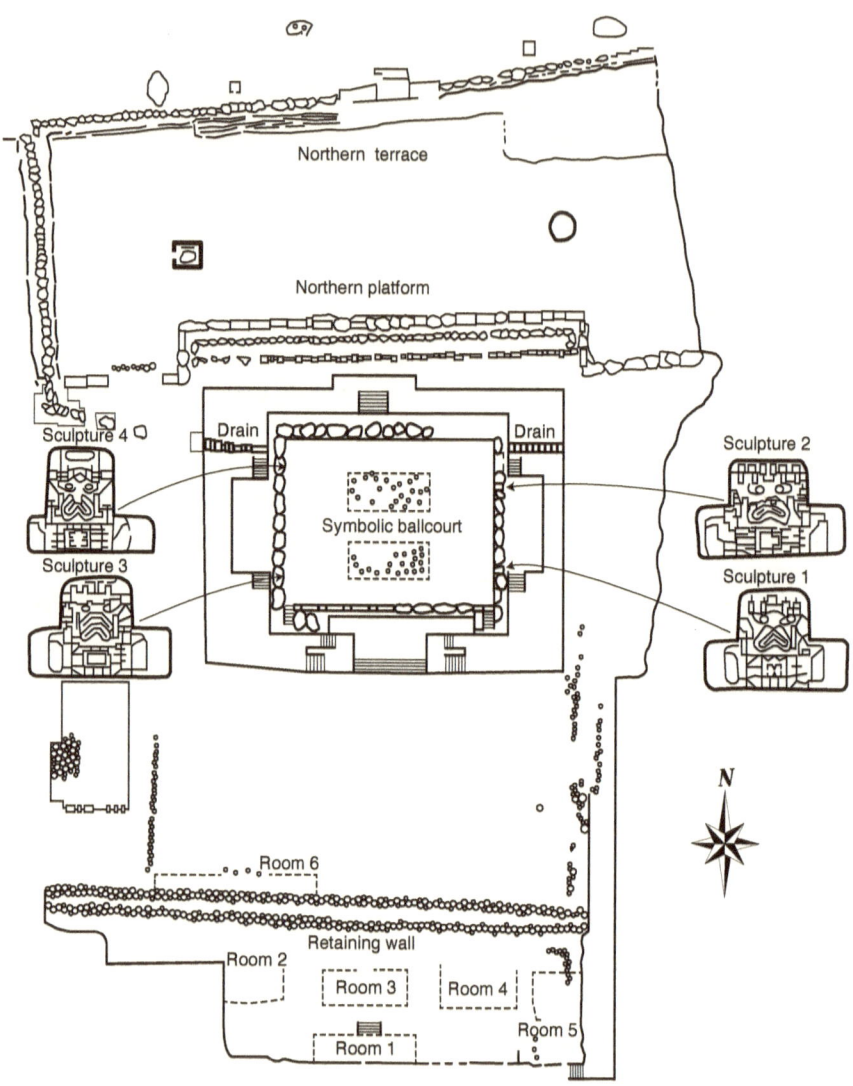

Figure 4. Plan of the ceremonial precinct of Teopantecuanitlán, 1000 BCE to 700 BCE, showing the location of the symbolic ballcourt and the four monolithic sculptures thought to be of ballplayers. Drawing by Martin Lubikowski, adapted from Martínez Donjuán and Solís Ciriaco, "Producción especializada."

equinox their shadows crossed in the center of the patio, indicating that the precinct had ceremonial functions and cosmological connotations. The patio has been interpreted as a symbolic ballcourt and its sculptures as players. Between 800–600 BCE the patio was filled with material that included burnt matter suggestive of conflict and covered by an esplanade. Teopantecuanitlán also had residential zones, some for elite use, others for artisans. A ballcourt with a temple and sweat bath was constructed, as were tombs with corbelled arched roofs, and irrigation works including a dam and channels at least 100 meters long.[70] In short, the urbanism of Teopantecuanitlán developed over 1,800 years. This required control of labor and planning capabilities from quite early dates of the Formative.

Not far from Teopantecuanitlán, Cuetlajuchitlán, strategically situated as a lookout at a pass that controlled an exchange route, was occupied from about 800 BCE in the Middle Formative until around 300 CE in the Classic and reached its maximum significance between 200 BCE and 300 CE. There were residential zones, some for the elite, a ceremonial center, and a system of drainage and irrigation. There are five other sites nearby. Despite its strategic position, life at Cuetlajuchitlán could be precarious, for it was abandoned from 300 CE, perhaps, as botanical evidence of increased temperatures and reduced rainfall suggests, because of a decline in subsistence agriculture. The site remained abandoned until the fifteenth century.[71]

Where the waters of the Tepecoacuilco River meet the Balsas, between 800 and 400 BCE, Ahuináhuac developed. The first structures were residences of adobe and straw, but by 500 BCE stone construction began. Ahuináhuac had a public area that included a ballcourt and residential zones of variable materials and finish, including an area of relatively luxurious residences, indicative of high-status groups and differentials of power. Columns of circular stones supported the flat roofs of residential buildings. These buildings had four contiguous rooms, patios, and altars very similar to those of Teotihuacan dated to 300 CE, but which in Ahuináhuac dated much earlier to 500–200 BCE.[72] Paradis reports four similar sites contemporary with Ahuináhuac in the southern reaches of the Tepecoacuilco river valley. Although each covered a small area, the organization of space at these sites suggests urban settlements. The pattern was of dispersed communities organized in different formal and functional sectors. A further forty-five such sites, with different characteristics and functions, have been dated from the Middle or Late Formative to the Classic (500 BCE–750 CE), when the population increased. These were densely populated settlements, some with a civic-religious zone, smaller residential quarters, and areas of workshops. In Ahuináhuac itself, during the first centuries CE, several structures were abandoned and covered with fill, but new structures were also built, and some existing ones were modified.[73]

This pattern of dispersed settlements persisted in sites in the Cocula River Valley. The earliest settlements date from the middle Formative, but they are few and the population was probably small. During the Classic and the Postclassic, residential settlements with civic-ceremonial structures emerged. Classic sites had residential structures identified as tecpan, broad stairways, and covered drainage systems. At some sites the ceremonial area consisted simply of pyramid bases around plazas and patios, but the larger sites had ballcourts and small altars in the center of the plaza. Talud walls, supporting vertical tablero walls, were stuccoed and painted red, as were the floors. Postclassic sites had residential structures on terraces and plazas of several levels. Wells or water sources were encased in stone. There were paved causeways and access ramps, and a ballcourt, sometimes two. Formative sites were located on low hill slopes and Classic settlements generally sat on low-lying land or hill slopes, while Postclassic communities occupied strategic sites with restricted access.[74] The changes in site location during the Formative, Classic, and Postclassic may reflect an increased population seeking land, but Postclassic sites may have selected defensive locations in a time of increased conflict.

In summary, from early Formative times settlements in the North were relatively prosperous. They exhibited economic and social organization and hierarchy, and were in contact by routes of exchange with peoples outside the region. By the Postclassic, the area was one of hierarchically organized polities, ruled by lineages that lived off lands worked by laborers. The rulers established their residences in sacred and, therefore, strategic locations. Many, for example, Tetipac and Noxtepec, were Chontal ministates linked by matrimonial alliances, but they were rivals in war.[75]

1.5. The Tierra Caliente

One of the most impressive hydrological systems in Mexico—the basin of the River Balsas—dominated this region. The Balsas is 800 kilometers long and its basin covers 107,000 kilometers^2 of rugged land pierced by numerous tributaries, all in turn fed by affluents. The great river flows through Guerrero from east to west and then descends to the Pacific near Zacatula where it forms a delta.[76] Where it turns toward the coast, the Balsas links to the Tepalcatepec, which flows in from Michoacán[77]. The Balsas has been a determinate factor for the settlement pattern and history of pre-Hispanic Guerrero. The river carries precious water to the regions of low rainfall through which it runs, linking settlements to one another, and facilitating communication and contact.[78] In the Amuco region, the Balsas opens out into an extensive valley floor, but in many places steep slopes enclose the narrow valley.[79]

Archaeological evidence tells us that the Balsas region was well populated from at least the Middle Formative. In 1939 and 1941, Robert Lister documented numerous settlements, ranging from villages of simple huts to settlements with terraces, platforms, mounds, truncated pyramids, and ballcourts. In 1944, Pedro Armillas surveyed the Balsas from Tetela del Río to Zacatula on the coast, reporting a considerable number of sites in some stretches, but in others few archaeological remains. Most of these sites have not been dated, although some had fifteenth- or sixteenth-century Tarascan features.[80]

Paradis's study of Amuco Abelino confirms that this region was settled by at least the Early Formative. She dates Amuco Abelino and associated sites from 1530 BCE ± 230 years to 100/125–575 CE, but settlement continued in some form to the end of the Postclassic. There were sixty-nine pre-Hispanic sites around Amuco, of which forty-one consisted solely of residential units, twenty-two had a single mound, and only six featured more than one mound. The Balsas Valley is at its widest here, making it an attractive location for farmers. Consequently, forty-three of the settlements (including thirty-five residential units) were situated on the banks of the river or on the valley bottom.[81] Not far from Amuco, in the area bounded by the Cutzamala and Alahuiztlán rivers, 126 sites have been recorded. Research in this area has focused on the fifteenth and sixteenth centuries, but the area was doubtless settled much earlier.[82]

To the east of Amuco in the Postclassic, the merchants of Oztuma controlled exchange between the coast, Michoacán, and central Mexico. Oztuma's control of exchange routes and the region's resources (metals, salt, cotton, and cacao) made the town an important polity before the resources and strategic location of Oztuma prompted the incursions of the Mexicas.[83] Silverstein's survey around Oztuma recorded 125 settlements, only 38 of which were Postclassic. Of these 125 settlements, 92 were classified as key sites because they had substantial mounds or had been looted. Evidence of bronze working and of lithics manufacture at large ceremonial sites, dated from the Late Classic to the Late Postclassic, indicates the emergence of several regional states from the Late Classic. In the Late Postclassic, five Mexica fortresses stretched along a 70 kilometers tract of the frontier with the Tarascans.[84]

Downstream, from where the Tepalcatepec joins the Balsas, is the El Infiernillo archaeological zone, where a survey documented 104 sites, located on both sides of the Mexica-Tarascan frontier. Sites varied from ceremonial complexes to others with only a single mound, and still simpler, smaller sites, principally located where rivers and streams join the Balsas, providing good conditions for subsistence. This area was occupied at least from 600 BCE to the end of the Postclassic. The existence of a powerful ruling group is documented by elite burials with sumptuary objects of ritual importance. Metal artifacts were found in exceptional quantities. There were also artifacts of shell, some from the Gulf Coast, turtle shells, fragments of textiles, and various other types of offering. Half of the 290 burials were at the Classic La Luz site, radiocarbon dated between 325 BCE and 630 CE, and the Postclassic San Antonio. They seem to have been principal settlements to which others were subject. El Infiernillo is notable for finds of large quantities of color palettes and pigments, dated from 100 or 200 CE in the Classic to the Postclassic. These palettes suggest shared traditions with west Mexico and perhaps the distant Hohokam of Arizona.[85]

Thus, the Tierra Caliente bears comparison with the Costa Grande (desirable and prestigious products) and the Montaña (some desirable products, but above all a strategic position on routes of exchange). The Tierra Caliente combines both factors: it had important resources (copper, gold, cotton, cacao, salt) and was also a gateway for exchange with other regions.[86] The Balsas Valley enabled two-way exchange with the Costa Grande and provided access to the valley of Toluca and Morelos. The confluence with the Tepalcatepec was the gateway to Michoacán and Jalisco. The presence of shells from the Gulf Coast in El Infiernillo confirms long-distance exchange.[87] As late as 1941, Mazahua merchants followed ancient exchange routes from the valley of Toluca to the Balsas and Acapulco, carrying goods from Toluca to exchange for local products such as salt and dried fish.[88]

1.6. Regional Contexts and Settlement Patterns: Conclusions

The apparently forbidding terrain and climate of Guerrero provided opportunities from the Formative to the Postclassic. Guerrero may not have been a Mesoamerican land of milk and honey, but its potential went well beyond hunter-gathering and subsistence agriculture. Human interaction with ecological niches formed specific contexts for the ways in which the peoples of the region organized their communities. The resources of each region and their abundance or scarcity in neighboring areas stimulated exchange between the regions of Guerrero and farther afield. A full account of the history and social changes of precontact Guerrero, therefore, requires an understanding of the key resources of the region's ecological niches and how exchange operated. Certain communities benefited from being the origin of resources such as salt, shells, cotton, and cacao on the coast, of greenstone in the Montaña, or of salt, cotton, cacao, and metals in the Tierra Caliente. Others thrived because they occupied strategic locations on routes of exchange. Furthermore, such regional differences, some of which the Spaniards recorded in the sixteenth-century *Relaciones Geográficas*, would also shape each region's experience of Spanish colonialism.

1.7. Resources and Exchange

The exchange of Guerrero's resources stimulated local and long-distance contacts that were not solely economic but also cultural and ideological. Many of the region's resources were highly valued. Frances Berdan suggests that various factors conferred value on resources in Mesoamerica. One was durability. Resources that had scarcity value tended to be prized. Products were also valued for their social significance, their material properties, the skills and technologies required to process them, their aesthetic qualities, and the labor involved in their manufacture. Finally, restricting access to a resource to the elite was an important aspect of value.[89]

Concerning cultural value, the South occupied a very special place in Mexica cosmology. The South was associated with water and fertility. Huitzilopochtli, one of the principal Mexica deities, to whom one side of the Templo Mayor in Tenochtitlan was dedicated, was god

Figure 5. A shell pendant in the form of a bird, probably a pelican with its wings extended, and two perforations in its neck, height 7.8 cm, width 5.7 cm, depth 0.2 cm, 600 CE to 900 CE, from El Infiernillo, Bejucos, Guerrero. Museo Nacional de Antropología, Mexico. Photograph © Archivo Digital MNA. Reproduction authorized by the Instituto Nacional de Antropología e Historia (INAH), Mexico City.

of the South. Numerous offerings in the Templo Mayor are objects typical of Guerrero: shells, artifacts made of shell, and polished greenstone, including Mezcala-style sculptures. Most of the offerings that probably originated from Guerrero were deposited when Moctezuma Ilhuicamina (1004–1459 CE) and Axayácatl (1469–1481) were the tlatoani of Tenochtitlan, at precisely the time that the Mexica Empire expanded into Guerrero.[90]

1.8. Shells

Marine and, to a lesser extent, freshwater shells were exchanged from a very early date. Obsidian had been exchanged from the Archaic onward, but since Guerrero had no obsidian deposits, it was imported from considerable distances.[91] While there is no direct evidence to confirm the exchange of shells for obsidian, the ubiquity of unprocessed, semiprocessed, and finished shellwork in inland sites dating to various periods suggests a long-term demand. It seems likely that such a prized product would be involved in obsidian exchange.

Shells were abundant on the coast, but transport to distant centers of consumption involved long-distance porterage along mountainous paths. Moreover, intermediate sites exercised control over the transport and processing of shells. The elite of Teopantecuanitlán owed some of its social and economic power to the control of shells, their acquisition, and processing.[92] Cuetlajuchitlán operated on the same principles.[93] In the Center at Pezuapan, at least 146 unprocessed shells were found. Formative Chalcatzingo, Morelos, was a redistribution center for marine shells and greenstone from Guerrero's mountains.[94]

Thus, Pacific shells met some of Berdan's conditions for value. There was a reliable source of supply, but control of distribution and manufacture restricted access. Shells were also aesthetically pleasing and durable,[95] and they occur in socially and ceremonially important contexts (the Templo Mayor in Tenochtitlan, offerings in tombs).[96] Experiments using Mesoamerican manufacturing methods confirm the enormous cost of shell objects in terms of labor and highly skilled processing. A study based on objects from the Templo Mayor, including Pacific shells, estimates that the manufacture of eleven *epcololli* ear ornaments took some 1,007 hours, and thirty-five *anahuatl* (pectorals) required 1,382 hours.[97]

1.9. Metals and Metallurgy

Barely had the Mexicas been defeated before Hernán Cortés turned his attention to Guerrero, where, he was told, there was fabulous wealth in gold.[98] Because of their value and transportability, gold and silver provided the essential financing of the Spanish invasion and the bulk of colonial economic activity.[99] Mesoamericans were also anxious to access metals—the Tarascans and the Mexicas went to war, in part, over them—but metal meant very different things in Mesoamerica than in New Spain. Metallurgy arrived quite late in Mesoamerica. Dorothy Hosler has dated this to around 650 CE,[100] but recent research suggests that a later date is more likely.[101] The technology was imported from the much older metallurgical tradition of Ecuador. A widely supported theory is that metallurgy arrived by a Pacific maritime route, perhaps brought by merchants seeking spondylus shells, which were of great ceremonial importance in South America. Guerrero's coast may have been a link in the chain of transmission. The earliest metal objects came from a well-defined metallurgical zone, or "copper belt," that included the middle Balsas region of Guerrero and Michoacán, as well as some parts of Jalisco and Nayarit. Hosler has defined two technological traditions. The lost wax method was used to make small bells and adornments. Jewelry or small tools were made by cold working of a smelted blank.[102] Some pre-Hispanic foundry sites have been found in the Balsas area and on the Costa Grande.[103] At Texmelincan, where small leaves, beads, and other gold objects were excavated, there were shallow tunnels, tools to mine gold (large hatchets and stone rings, components of hammers), and grinding tools to process the ore. At Huitzapula, grinding tools were decorated with human faces, perhaps related to a mining cult.[104] Guerrero was also a source of placer gold, in Tlapa-Tlachinollan, for example, where the Mexicas exacted considerable quantities of gold tribute.[105] Cihuatlán and other regions of Guerrero paid tribute in gold or copper.[106]

Although Mesoamerican metallurgy was of South American origin, the purposes of Guerrero's metalworkers were specifically Mesoamerican. Precontact metalworkers made some utilitarian objects, such as fishing hooks, needles, and burins. However, the archaeological record suggests that the most important uses were ceremonial, ritual, cultural, and as markers of social hierarchy. These included small bells, musical instruments, rings, pincers, ornamental shields, and axe monies, the latter possibly functioning as currency. The sounds of bells were

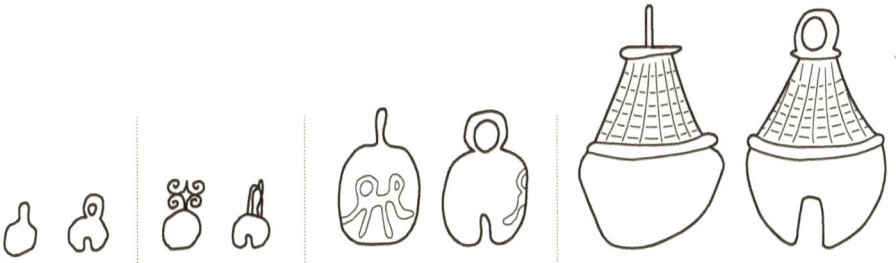

Figure 6. West Mexican bronze bell types. Drawing by Martin Lubikowski, adapted from Hosler, "Ancient West Mexican Metallurgy."

associated with the deities Tláloc, Xipe Tótec, and Quetzalcoatl, and metallic colors with the sun and moon.[107] At El Infiernillo in the Balsas, metal objects were found at 55 percent of sites excavated, and twenty-eight of sixty-seven burials contained metal ear plugs, nose ornaments, rings, lip ornaments, and pincers. In many burials metal and shell objects were found together, underlining the importance of Guerrero's two plentiful resources.[108] In short, metals were abundant in Guerrero, and in the Postclassic were prized resources that the Tarascan and Mexica empires sought in Guerrero and were a key factor in exchange networks along the Balsas and, in Michoacán, the River Lerma. The labor and skills involved in mining, smelting, and working the metal gave metal objects rarity value and doubtless occupied an artisan class of miners and metalworkers.[109]

1.10. Cacao and Painted Gourds

Like metals, cacao had important social functions. Cacao cultivation was well suited to two regions of Guerrero: the coast and the Tierra Caliente, although we do not know when cacao was first exploited there. However, since the domestication of cacao in Mesoamerica probably began with the Olmecs in the Formative, it is possible that cultivation in Guerrero dates to that period. The Mayan elite drank chocolate from elegant ceramic cups. For the Mexicas, chocolate was of ceremonial and ritual importance, and signaled the elevated social rank of those who could savor it. They drank chocolate from *jícaras pintadas*, gourds decorated with paint or lacquer.[110] Painted gourds did not preserve well in an archaeological

Figure 7. A painted, lacquered, and incised gourd bowl from Olinalá, Guerrero, 1980–1981, National Museum of the American Indian. Gourd, paint, lacquer, height 17.8 cm, width 8.6 cm. National Museum of the American Indian, Smithsonian Institution (Cat. No. 26/8759). Photograph by NMAI Photo Services.

context, but fragments have been found in burials in El Infiernillo and northern Guerrero. We know that jícaras were tribute items in various regions in Guerrero and that exceptionally exquisite jícaras were sold in the market of Texcoco.[111] Lacquerwork continues to be an important product of some regions of Guerrero, notably Olinalá in the Montaña.[112]

According to Litvak King, the coastal province of Cihuatlán in Guerrero supplied 3,689 kilograms of cacao annually as tribute, a quantity that could be harvested from about 25 hectares, which suggests a modest level of tribute. The Mexica empire acquired its cacao from various regions of Mesoamerica. The main center of production was distant Xoconochco (modern Soconusco). Cihuatlán was much closer to Tenochtitlan, but nevertheless it took twenty-two days to deliver cacao tribute.¹¹³ Thus, transport to central Mexico was costly and supplies were limited, which contributed to cacao's prestige and scarcity value.

Cacao had an additional function in Postclassic Mesoamerica. There were four types of cacao, only one of which was used to make drinks. The remaining three functioned as a combination of commodity and currency. Cacao was sufficiently important as a currency that its use would survive into the early colonial period as a substitute for metal coinage.¹¹⁴ Cacao, then, joined shells, polished stone, and metals as valuable prestige products of Mesoamerican Guerrero. The main consumers were the elite groups of Mesoamerica. The consumption of chocolate from elegant vessels testified to its social and ceremonial significance.

1.11. Cotton and Other Textiles

Cotton is rarely preserved in archaeological contexts. However, the use of cotton in Guerrero can be confirmed indirectly. Textiles are depicted on figurines, and textile fragments found in El Infiernillo have been preserved by contact with copper. A single radiocarbon date associated with these fragments suggests a date about 1220 CE. Finds of spindles at sites throughout Guerrero confirm that weaving was widely practiced.¹¹⁵ The few surviving pieces attest that the textile artisans of Guerrero were highly skilled in a wide variety of techniques. The range of weaves, from simple methods to complex techniques, is impressive, as is the overall quality of some items. There were at least two traditions. Some pieces were made of tough fibers used to make articles of variable quality and appearance. The second tradition is of highly accomplished attire, of which the Chilapa huipil (blouse) is an exceptional example. The huipil has been radiocarbon dated to about 1290 CE. This women's garment combines several colors: rose red, white, blue, pink, olive green, and light brown. The rose red was woven after the other colors, which were dyed before weaving. The maker of the huipil decorated it with a fringe of shells from the Gulf of Mexico, suggesting that no expense was spared in its manufacture. A notable feature of the garment is the use of rabbit or hare fur. Documentary sources report the sale of rabbit and hare fur, but the Chilapa huipil is the sole surviving example of the fur in use. This garment was clearly made for a woman of high social status.¹¹⁶

Textiles were made not only for utilitarian purposes. The textiles found in the Cuevas de Atzcala also include miniature *cactli* (sandals),

Figure 8. A detail of the Chilapa huipil, ca. 1290 CE, showing diamond, *xicalcoliuhqui* (step fret designs), and zigzag motifs. Museo Nacional de Antropología, Mexico. Reproduction authorized by the Instituto Nacional de Antropología e Historia (INAH), Mexico City.

made of palm leaf fibers, their size suggesting that they were a votive offering. There is also a miniature *xicolli*, a ceremonial jacket with short sleeves worn by men. Xicolli are recorded in Mixtec codices and Spanish documentary sources, but the Atzcala miniature is one of only two surviving examples. Its owner may have been of low status since it is not made of cotton. The Atzcala textiles include several items made with fibers such as palm or bark. Tools used to pound bark have been found in sites in this region of the Balsas basin.[117]

Although fibers of various types and different grades of prestige or luxury were used in pre-Hispanic Guerrero, cotton was the textile of choice in Mesoamerica.[118] Cotton was grown on the coast, in Tierra Caliente,[119] and in small quantities in other areas where conditions were suitable. However, cotton was spun and woven throughout Guerrero for centuries before the Spanish invasion. The control of cotton production, transport, and exchange was an important objective of local, regional, and extraregional rulers. For example, the rulers of Postclassic Tlapa-Tlachinollan controlled the exchange route between the coast and the Montaña and on to Oaxaca, Puebla, and central Mexico, along which traveled sought-after products such as cotton, cacao, and salt.[120]

Cotton was also an important item of tribute in the Mexica and Tarascan Empires. Litvak King calculated that Cihuatlán paid in tribute annually 18,403 kilograms of cotton thread and 184,000 kilograms of cloth, and that Tepecoacuilco contributed 16,500 kilograms of cloth (these quantities, if correct, represented a substantial tribute burden).[121] Tlapa's tribute also included warriors' suits.[122] In the Tierra Caliente, both the Tarascan and Mexica Empires demanded cotton clothing. Here, too,

Mexica tribute included warriors' suits.[123] Indeed, cotton was the most significant Mexica tribute item in terms of quantity and was demanded from all the tributary provinces of Guerrero, even if they did not cultivate cotton.[124] Like cacao, cotton cloth (*quachtli*) also functioned as a currency to facilitate Postclassic exchange.[125]

1.12. Other Significant Resources

Guerrero's varied ecological zones were the source of several other culturally or economically significant resources. Copal, an incense produced from the resin of the Protium copal tree, was used on ceremonial and religious occasions. Copal was associated with the deities Huitzilopochtli and Tezcatlipoca. In Tenochtitlan it was used during sacrifices, and rulers and priests wore small bags of copal.[126] Incense burners found in numerous sites confirm that copal was used throughout Guerrero. An example found near Tlapa has been dated to 600 CE ± 150 years.[127] Indeed, Guerrero provided 50 percent of the copal delivered to Tenochtitlan.[128] Another product of Guerrero was rubber, used in Mesoamerica for ceremonial and social as well as utilitarian purposes. Social and ceremonial uses included rubber balls for ballgames and figurines; utilitarian uses included the soles of sandals and rubber bands.[129] Tlapa Province sent substantial quantities of rubber and rubber figurines as tribute to Tenochtitlan.[130] Rubber balls must also have been used in Guerrero, since some stunning clay figurines of the Xochipala tradition depict ballplayers,[131] and ballcourts have been found in all regions of Guerrero.[132]

Guerrero produced several other products for which there was regional and extraregional demand. Salt was produced on the coast and inland, for example, in Oztuma and Alahuiztlán in Tierra Caliente.[133] The Chontals of the Tierra Caliente, especially Oztuma and Alahuiztlán, specialized in salt, honey, and copal. Salt was an important factor in exchange and was culturally significant since it was associated with Chalmeca Cihuatl, the white god.[134] Honey and beeswax were sought after by the Tarascans and the Mexicas.[135] Guerrero was a source of several other products, such as *chía* (a variety of sage), *huauhtli* (amaranth), fruits, pumpkin seeds, and basic staples such as maize and beans. In summary, Guerrero was a source of several products of substantial ceremonial, social, and economic value, as well as others of less significance, which were exchanged within and beyond the region. This leads to the question of how these products were transported and exchanged.

1.13. Exchange and Transport

Extraregional exchange had already occurred in Guerrero before the Formative (i.e., before 1500 BCE). It is not always easy to detect exchange in the archaeological record, still less easy to document exchange networks, but a discussion of regional and extraregional exchange is essential for understanding the societies that existed before Spaniards set foot in the mountains of Guerrero. Exchange cannot be understood solely in material and economic terms, consisting only of commodities and artifacts, but also in terms of social contacts and the interchange of ideas and information.[136] Indeed, several of Guerrero's resources were of not just economic significance but also of social and ideological importance.

At first sight, Guerrero's topography might be assumed to have impeded transport and exchange. Moreover, there were no beasts of burden in Mesoamerica. There was no wheeled transport, which in any case would have been useless over Guerrero's narrow mountainous tracks. Difficult terrain separated many centers of consumption from other regions that supplied resources, so Guerrero was at no great competitive disadvantage compared to other sources of supply. The centers of consumption either had to send their own *tamemes* (porters) to collect resources, wait for them to be transported by bearers from their source, or deal with an intermediary who controlled or facilitated exchange. Diversity of resources encouraged exchange, creating multiple spheres of distribution.[137] Now, Guerrero consisted of numerous ecological niches, each region the source of particular valued products. The example of Formative Teopantecuanitlán's participation in the exchange and manufacture of shell and polished stone suggests that Hirth's analysis of the factors that stimulated exchange need not be limited to the Late Postclassic but can be applied to much earlier periods.

Nevertheless, Guerrero's terrain necessarily imposed costs on the supply of any goods. Several archaeologists have modeled the costs of transport by tamemes. For example, Robert Drennan's calculations assumed a load of 30 kilograms transported 36 kilometers per day, and that the bearer must have carried enough maize to generate the calories needed to complete the journey. During a return journey of thirty-one days, or 1,116 kilometers, the carrier would consume the equivalent of the entire load and, thus, would reap no profit in caloric terms. Drennan argued that, in the Formative at least, only prestige goods could be transported over long distances and in quantities too small to be of economic significance. This does not mean that materials of great prestige or cultural value were not significant, but that their exchange could not provide sufficient economic stimulus to account for the origins of complex societies in the Formative, as some models suggest.[138]

However, the question can be addressed from a more nuanced point of view. Consider, for example, artifacts of shell, greenstone, or bronze. Certainly, the quantities transported were probably small. Nevertheless, the examples of Teopantecuanitlán, Cuetlajuchitlán, and Tlapa-Tlachinollan suggest that the transport, control, and manufacture of such items could confer power and prestige on a ruler, who could deploy increased influence to dominate neighboring altepetl, accumulate land, and control labor, and thus become a powerful local or regional figure. In short, it is possible that in those settlements social relations and power structures changed precisely in response to the exchange of luxury and prestige materials. A calculation of caloric losses or profits related to transport of materials of low value is useful, but it does not explain everything.

Litvak King calculated the burden of transporting the tribute exacted by the Mexicas to Tenochtitlan from the tributary provinces of Tepecoacuilco and Cihuatlán. Based on a study of maize production and consumption in the Mayan zone, assumptions about the load a tameme could carry, and the distance traveled in a day, Litvak estimated that the delivery of cotton (18,403 kilograms) and cacao (3,689 kilograms) tribute from Cihuatlán required the equivalent of fifty-eight bearers employed all year. The maize required to feed them was equivalent to the maize surplus of fourteen families, which did not seem to be a burdensome cost. However, cotton and cacao were relatively high-value products. Tepecoacuilco's tribute, on the other hand, included lower value and bulky staples: maize, beans, chía, and amaranth. In this case, the number of bearer loads was substantial, the equivalent of 1,578 men working all year. Moreover, because the tamemes would consume more foodstuffs than they delivered, the surplus production of 982 families was needed to feed them. Thus, the cost of this tribute was very substantial indeed. However, two alternatives suggest themselves. It is possible that Litvak King's assumptions and calculations are not an accurate reflection of the transport costs of tribute. Equally, it is possible that while the tribute was expressed in terms of food staples, the Mexicas' demands were met by an equivalent payment in other higher value and less bulky goods.[139]

Hirth offers an alternative explanation. He suggests that a load factor of 23 kilograms (a figure mentioned by Bernal Díaz del Castillo) is insufficient. Ethnohistoric and ethnographic studies suggest a minimum of 40–70 kilograms and a maximum of 85–90 kilograms. Further, Hirth assumes that a tameme could walk 30 kilometers daily. These calculations suggest that the cost of bearers was substantially lower than Drennan's and Litvak's estimates. Hirth adds another factor: the role of markets, at least in the Postclassic. Each altepetl had a market, whose size and frequency varied according to local needs, where a family could source something it needed and could exchange its domestic surplus or products it had manufactured for the desired goods. The merchant who transported products from another region could attend several markets, thus reducing the distance between the consumer and the source of the goods, avoiding traveling substantial distances to acquire what was needed. Hirth argues that markets reduced the marginal cost of buying and selling in areas of high transportation costs and that the more centralized commercial activities became the greater the cost reductions. Moreover, "the level of commercial activity found [in Mesoamerica] . . . suggests that some of our assumptions about transportation efficiency limiting exchange are either incorrect, or do not capture the way that prehispanic households operated with regard to resource provisioning." Archaeological evidence suggests that the *tianguis*, or formal market, emerged at least by 500–350 BCE. Before that, it may well be true that regional and extraregional exchange operated on a small scale.[140]

One of the most reliable indicators of exchange in Mesoamerica is obsidian, the highest quality material available to make essential tools to cut, scrape, perforate, and so on. When it is possible to identify the source of obsidian, we can confirm contact between Guerrero and a specific region. The earliest examples of obsidian are from the coast as early as 2940 BCE, but the ubiquity of obsidian during various periods confirms that local products were exchanged for obsidian throughout Guerrero.[141] Several other indicators confirm vigorous exchange networks from early dates. For example, shells from the Pacific Coast and the Gulf of Mexico have been found at Teopantecuanitlán.[142] However, Teopantecuanitlán was not just engaged in the exchange of raw materials: it was also a manufacturing center, with specialized workshop zones for shell, serpentine, mica, mirrors made from iron ore, onyx, and pigments. Thus, Teopantecuanitlán was a storage, specialized manufacturing, exchange, and redistribution center, which controlled exchange between the northern region of Guerrero and Morelos and the Pacific coast.[143]

Formative intermediary sites, such as Teopantecuanitlán, reduced the cost of access to the goods by aggregating a range of them in a single location, similar to the way described by Hirth in the Postclassic. Such strategies continued into the colonial period. In colonial Guerrero many of the pre-Hispanic exchange routes were used by human bearers and by mule drivers. It not surprising, therefore, that some of the precontact mercantile practices survived in New Spain. In colonial Guerrero small-scale merchants operated a "stepping-stone" strategy that linked local markets. Merchants sold their wares gradually along the route, selling some of the goods from a more distant region, while topping up their stock with local merchandise to be sold further down the line.[144] This stepping-stone strategy, which enabled exchange in difficult terrain, is remarkably similar to Hirth's model.

Other examples from later periods confirm that a range of materials and products were exchanged. The metal objects and pigment palettes of El Infiernillo are examples.[145] Another is Blanco Granular, the only type of ceramic found in Guerrero from the Early Formative to the Postclassic. It occurs in sites in the Montaña Baja and the Center from the Early Formative, and somewhat later in the North. Blanco Granular has also been found in Morelos, the valley of Toluca, Puebla, and in small quantities in Teotihuacan. It is possible that Guerrero's honey tribute to Tenochtitlan was transported in Blanco Granular containers. Blanco Granular continued to be made in Guerrero during the colonial period and is made in local workshops to this day.[146]

In the Classic period in the Middle Balsas an exchange network distributed utilitarian ceramics among the large settlements of the region, perhaps using river transport.[147] Artifacts found at the El Monte Don Venus site in the Balsas delta suggest contacts around 200 CE with the central altiplano and Oaxaca.[148] Similarly, Oztuma and its environs, farther up the Balsas, occupied a strategic position as the exchange gateway to Michoacán, the valley of Toluca, and Morelos for salt, cotton, cacao, copper, and gold.[149] Commerce accompanied Mexica military campaigns in the Late Postclassic, and tribute paid to the Mexicas was sometimes adjusted by a process of negotiation and exchange. This stimulated exchange in general and increased economic activity in the tribute-paying altepetl.[150]

Ethnographic studies of the twentieth century suggest that rural families in Guerrero employed a range of similar economic strategies, some of which provided a modest return on investment but which, nevertheless, were a valuable part of a family's economy. For example, until the 1950s, petty merchants of the Balsas Valley who traveled for seven days to the Costa Chica to acquire salt loaded two burros and themselves with a load for the eight-day return journey to extract the maximum profit from the trip.[151] A study of transport strategies of pueblos near the market in Chilapa in 1990–1991 showed that, although vehicular and mule transport were available, 10 percent of maize and 38 percent of garlic was carried to Chilapa on a human's back. These data tend to confirm Hirth's hypothesis that markets performed an integrating function and facilitated economic activity, even when the means of transport was not very efficient.[152]

1.14. Resources and Exchange: Conclusions

In summary, from early on, despite Guerrero's mountainous terrain and consequently high transport costs, the region was in contact socially and economically with other regions to exchange local resources for goods available only there. Natural resources, craft products, and regional and extraregional exchange all combined to stimulate the development of settlements and, eventually, polities ruled by elites whose power and prosperity were built on the control of exchange, of routes and transport, combined with the manufacture of prestige items of ceremonial and social significance. Exchange implied the sharing not just of material goods but also of beliefs, ideologies, and cultures in which Guerrero was an active, and in some respects innovative, participant from the Formative onward. This is the subject of the next chapter.

CHAPTER TWO

Art, Culture, Ideas, Beliefs, Languages, and Population

The paths along which resources were exchanged were also routes for communication of political ideologies, social concepts, and ceremonial, religious, cultural, technological, and aesthetic thinking, for the migration of people and the diffusion of languages. Evidence suggests that the exchange of such ideas was particularly fruitful in the Formative, but traces of contact with Teotihuacan, Monte Albán, Tula, and other regions confirm that the flow of ideas never dried up. The mix of peoples, ideas, and material resources gave each region of Guerrero distinctive characteristics that formed the societies that would encounter the Spaniards in 1521.

2.1. The Olmec Question

The most debated topic in Guerrero's archaeology is the Olmec question, which in turn links to debates about the formation of the essential characteristics of Mesoamerican culture. David Grove has observed that the term *Olmec* is problematic since it has been applied not only to a style with certain iconographic features but also to an archaeological culture of the Gulf Coast. This dual usage is a problem because artifacts with Olmec features occurred in several regions of Mesoamerica, as distant as Honduras, although these objects often differed in some ways from those found in the Olmec Gulf Coast heartland.[1]

The debate centers on the question of whether the Olmec heartland is the sole origin (the mother culture) of the Olmec phenomenon, or whether a hypothesis of multiple origins (sister cultures) best accounts for the Olmec. The debate is not entirely settled. For example, an analysis of Olmec ceramics at San Lorenzo (a Gulf Coast Olmec site) and of Early Formative pottery at sites in the Valley of Mexico, Oaxaca, Chiapas, and the isthmus of Tehuantepec concluded that wares at the sites outside the heartland were either imports from San Lorenzo or local emulations of Olmec heartland wares, but that none of the local wares had been exported to San Lorenzo. The study argues that this proved that social developments in other parts of Mesoamerica were originated by the Gulf Coast Olmec.[2] Other scholars contend that there is evidence of exchange between the regional Olmec centers, that most specialists reject the mother-culture model, and that it has lost its analytical utility.[3]

In this study of Guerrero, Olmec refers to iconographical features identical or similar to artifacts found in the Gulf and other regions, and it examines evidence of Olmec developments that were specific or unique to Guerrero. Finds with Olmec characteristics have been discovered in substantial quantities throughout Guerrero,[4] including rock art, carved stone stelae, figurines, ceramics, and objects of polished stone and shell.[5] Their quality and ubiquity prove beyond doubt that from the beginning of the Formative Guerrero participated actively in the ideas, beliefs, symbols, and means of expression that characterized the Olmec. This raises the question whether the region simply adopted these ideas or, instead, modified or initiated some of them.

2.2. Rock Art

Grove notes that monumental stone sculpture first appeared in Gulf Coast sites in the Early Formative, before it emerged elsewhere in the Middle Formative, and that the techniques and fundamental canons are those found in the Gulf.[6] Colossal heads, a fundamentally Olmec form of monumental sculpture, are found only in the Gulf (there is a quasi-exception at Teopantecuanitlán).[7] However, rock art with Olmec features first appeared in Guerrero and is not known in the Olmec heartland, nor indeed anywhere else in Mesoamerica at this early date.

In 1970 Grove published an analysis of paintings in Oxtotitlán Cave in the Center of Guerrero. He described a mural, 3.8 meters wide and 2.5 meters tall, that depicts a human figure seated on the head of a jaguar monster. The figure wears an elaborate headdress, an owl mask, and adornments similar to Olmec examples found at San Lorenzo and Chalcatzingo, such as jade ornaments and a pectoral. The figure wears a cloak with a "step" motif and a skirt with a scroll element, both known in various forms in Olmec art. The head of the jaguar monster is like those

Figure 9. A drawing of Mural C-1, Oxtotitlán cave, Guerrero, Formative Period, depicting a human figure seated on the head of a jaguar-monster and wearing an owl mask. Drawing by Martin Lubikowski, adapted from Miller, *The Art of Mesoamerica*.

of the Olmec carved stone altars of the Gulf, none of which are known in Guerrero. A second mural, in poor condition, measures 4 meters wide and 3 meters tall. There is an owl, fragments of an apparently reptilian face, the outline of two hands, and a circular band with a feather motif, known at the Gulf Coast Olmec site of Tres Zapotes, but also in central Mexico during the Postclassic. A human figure whose face has certain Olmec features stands behind a jaguar whose tail connects with the figure's pubic area, an apparent sexual reference unknown in Olmec art elsewhere. Grove noted a baby face, which is typically Olmec, and another figure wearing a helmet (note that the colossal heads wear helmets). Three circular elements may be the glyph of the number six, which may be the oldest glyph in Mesoamerica. Finally, a creature with reptilian, mammalian, and avian features, similar to a vessel at Teotihuacan identified with Quetzalcóatl, suggests that this part of the mural may be an early reference to elements of Classic beliefs. The two main paintings are polychrome. Several small paintings in the north chamber are in black, and those in the southern chamber principally are red.[8] The cave is visible from an adjacent site known as Cerro Quiotepec, which was occupied from the Middle Formative to the Late Postclassic. This suggests that the cave was used as a sacred space for a very long time.[9]

The Oxtotitlán cave art includes paintings with clearly Olmec features, some unique to Guerrero, some difficult to interpret, and others that seem to date long after the Olmec period. Radiocarbon dating of parts of the paintings underlines the importance of Oxtotitlán. The seated figure in the first mural was painted before 1520–1410 BCE, and may predate 1500, the beginning of the Formative. The latest dateable paintings were done in 600 CE. The earliest portions of the paintings antedate the intensive construction of ceremonial complexes in Guerrero and the Gulf Coast. Furthermore, although rock art is found throughout Mesoamerica from the Archaic onward, Oxtotitlán is the first example of polychrome painting anywhere in Mesoamerica. Moreover, Oxtotitlán's artists painted complex figurative scenes long before complex scenes painted in polychrome on stucco emerged. Therefore, Oxtotitlán represents an exceedingly important moment in Formative culture. Indeed, it is possible that the mural tradition of Mesoamerica originated in this cave in the mountains of Guerrero.[10]

It is difficult to exaggerate the importance of the Oxtotitlán paintings. They prove that at the beginning of the Formative (perhaps even before), and therefore at the very birth of the Olmec (or even earlier), ritual and social ideas at the very heart of Mesoamerica's cosmovision were current in Guerrero. Moreover, the Oxtotitlán artists did not borrow their aesthetic and media from elsewhere. Rather, they were the originators. The ideas they expressed in Oxtotitlán were shared with other regions—for example, in the Olmec altars (or thrones) of the Gulf coast—[11]but the Oxtotitlán artists chose to articulate in paint ideas expressed on the Gulf Coast in stone, seating a human figure (probably a ruler and/or shaman) on the head of a jaguar monster.[12] In short, Oxtotitlán speaks of a society that was developing new ideas and forms of expression, a society that was not a mere importer of concepts and techniques from elsewhere.

Moreover, Oxtotitlán is not the only example of Olmec rock painting in Guerrero. Another polychrome painted cave is 30 kilometers to the south at Juxtlahuaca. One of the paintings depicts two human

Figure 10. A drawing of Mural Group 2, Scene 1, Juxtlahuaca cave, Guerrero, Formative Period, depicting a large human figure wearing a feathered headdress and a probable jaguar-skin cloak, holding an apparent rope connected with a smaller, seated masked figure. Drawing courtesy of Martha Cabrera.

Figure 11. A drawing of the interior of the Cave of the Governors, Techan, Guerrero, Formative Period. Drawing by Martin Lubikowski, adapted from Gutiérrez and Pye, "Gobernadores de Techan."

figures. One, standing, wears a feathered headdress and a probable cloak of jaguar skin. His left hand holds an apparent rope that connects with a smaller seated figure, its face covered with a black mask. A second painting apparently depicts a serpent, perhaps the plumed serpent, with a red body and black head. In a third painting, an animal, possibly a jaguar, faces the serpent. The paintings have not been dated but appear to be of a similar date to those at Oxtotitlán.[13] A recent study notes that the Juxtlahuaca artists employed drawing, engraving, the color of the rock, light and shade, as well as paint, in various combinations. This study argues that Juxtlahuaca and Oxtotitlán were located on exchange routes, including one that led to Zazacatla and Chalcatzingo in Morelos.[14]

A third set of cave paintings has been found at Cauadzidziqui Cave in the Montaña. Here paintings with Olmec iconography are superimposed on earlier paintings in red that probably date to the Late Archaic. These earlier paintings consist of simple anthropomorphic, geometric, and vegetal motifs and may belong to a tradition shared with Morelos and southern Puebla. The paintings with Olmec iconography are polychrome. One depicts the torso and head of a human who wears a helmet similar to those of Olmec colossal heads. A second, full-length figure extends his arm toward the other. Gutiérrez suggests that the superimposition of Olmec iconography on a local style indicates an intrusion of Olmec ideas, adopted by local elites from Teopantecuanitlán or Chalcatzingo along an important route of exchange.[15] However, there are no polychrome paintings at Teopantecuanitlán or Chalcatzingo. Perhaps the painters of Cauadzidziqui were heirs to, and innovators of, an older regional tradition. Wherever the ideas may have come from, the visual expression of them is clearly an innovation of Guerrero's artists.

A further argument in favor of an Olmec rock-art tradition born in the caves of Guerrero is the discovery of the Cueva de los Gobernadores (Cave of the Governors) of Techan in the Montaña. As in Oxtotitlán, Juxtlahuaca, and Cauadzidziqui, artists converted the Techan cave into a ceremonial space; indeed, a performance space. However, here the medium was sculpture, including the modification of the cave itself. Four human-feline figures, provisionally dated between 900 and 500 BCE, were sculpted in high relief. Sculptors carved the entrance to the cave into a triangular shape and modified the entire interior. Clearly, this was the work of skilled artists who had a profound understanding of Middle Formative beliefs. Here, in a confined space, were performed ceremonies connected to the rain and wind to receive supernatural messages that were communicated to the populace.[16] The caves in which painted and sculpted images are found are difficult to access and their interior space is limited. They were reserved for ruler-shamans, as demonstrated by the famous bas relief called *El Rey* in Chalcatzingo, which depicts a powerful person or shaman performing a ceremony related to the rain deity.[17]

In summary, the rulers and artists of Guerrero discovered a distinctive visual language that combined pan-Mesoamerican concepts with a regional aesthetic and techniques. In Formative Guerrero, painters and sculptors communicated ideas that justified the authority of the rulers of settlements. The paintings of Oxtotitlán, Juxtlahuaca, and Cauadzidziqui, like the sculptures of Techan, are outstanding examples of an abundant rock-art tradition in precontact Guerrero. By 2013, 310 rock-art sites, in caves, rock shelters, and on large boulders, had been recorded in the region.[18]

2.3. Mezcala Sculpture

Guerrero was home to an outstanding sculptural tradition admired in ceremonial contexts in antiquity by the Mexicas and today in museum collections.[19] These were the famous Mezcala-style sculptures, so named because many originated in the region of the Mezcala River. A large proportion of Mezcala sculptures are anthropomorphic pieces measuring from 2 to 54 centimeters tall. Nearly all lack indication of their sex. Only 4 or 5 percent are clearly female. The upper part of about half of the pieces was left uncarved or carved in such a way as to appear uncarved. There are also heads, faces, and masks. Zoomorphic figures such as birds, monkeys, iguanas, frog, toads, tadpoles, dogs, fish, and bats are less common. There are some musical instruments.[20] Figures found in their primary context suggest a ceremonial or ritual use.[21] The sculptures share a marked preference for abstraction and a sensitivity to the qualities of the stone.

Architectural models, probably made as funerary offerings, are an additional category. Some depict small buildings with two columns and a single door, some larger structures with as many as eight columns, two buildings with two columns on a single base, and others three or four structures on a circular base. There are also towers of two or three stories. In some a schematic human figure stands in the doorway, or stands, sits, or lies down on the roof. In others the figure is an animal. They are made of stones of various colors, some veined or with patches of colors. Recent excavations have confirmed that the models depict building types that existed in Guerrero, perhaps temples or palaces, of precisely the kinds in the models.[22]

The chronology of Mezcala sculpture has been shrouded in mystery because, of approximately 22,000 known pieces, only some 300 have been reported in context,[23] the majority in their secondary context in the Templo Mayor, far in time and place from their origins. In 1990 Louise Paradis found seven anthropomorphic masks and figures at Ahuináhuac, in a context radiocarbon dated to 700–230 BCE. Schávelzon has dated the architectural models to 700 BCE–300 CE.[24] It seems that Mezcala sculpture was made from the Formative at least to the Early Classic for some 1,000 years, perhaps more if the dates for the Ahuináhuac sculptures are ante quem and post quem.

The puzzle of Mezcala sculpture is deepened further by the enigma of where and why they were made. The term *Mezcala*, itself, can cause confusion. The known oeuvre includes pieces in various styles. Some display apparent Olmec or Teotihuacan influences. Others have been

Figure 12. A Mezcala-style, standing polished stone figurine, height 35.6 cm, width 12.4 cm, first to eighth centuries CE, Metropolitan Museum of Art, New York. Bequest of Jane Costello Goldberg, from the Collection of Arnold I. Goldberg, 1986 (Acc. 1987.394.718).

Figure 13. A Mezcala-style polished stone architectural model, height 14.3 cm, width 10.8 cm, depth 2.5 cm, first to eighth centuries CE, Metropolitan Museum of Art, New York. Bequest of Arthur M. Bullowa, 1993 (Acc. 1994.35.630).

classified as of Chontal style, originating in the region of Teloloapan, or of Sultepec in the state of Mexico.[25] The territory from which the sculptures are thought to originate extends north to south from the southern slopes of the Nevado de Toluca, in the state of Mexico, to Xochipala, Zumpango del Río, Tixtla, and Mochitlán in Guerrero. To the west it includes the middle Balsas and to the east Olinalá and parts of Puebla.[26] The variety of styles and content and the longevity of the tradition testify to its importance. The sculptors who made them must have been specialists with valued skills. They worked with specialized techniques, with stone that varied in color and hardness. The difficulty of carving the harder stones contributed to their prestige value.[27] The sculptors doubtless enjoyed privileges. In Teopantecuanitlán those who worked with serpentine and shell had a superior diet of freshwater species, deer, rabbits, hares, and dogs.[28] In Ahuináhuac the sculptors lived in hierarchical settlements with specialized functions, including polished stone workshops. An elite with the resources and power to patronize the Mezcala sculptors lived in zones with elite residences, civic-religious areas, and a ballcourt.[29] Schmidt and Reyna Robles suggest that the Mezcala sculpture tradition represents a broader culture consisting of other elements.[30] A consideration of the Xochipala figures suggests that these might have been one such element.

2.4. Xochipala Ceramic Figures

In the Xochipala region in the Center of Guerrero a sculptural tradition quite different from the Mezcala figures developed. The Xochipala figures are very naturalistic and expressive and made of ceramics, while the Mezcala figures are abstracted and carved in stone. The majority of the Xochipala pieces depict vividly Mesoamerican people: some suck their thumbs, others touch their head with their hands. The finest examples display remarkable aesthetic sensibility and superb modeling of the human form. The smaller figures are solid; the larger, which measure up to 66 centimeters tall, are hollow. There are a few sculptures of animals (e.g., a dog, a frog, a tortoise), and some vessels that Gay attributed to the same tradition.[31] One notable category of figures portrays ballplayers, some kneeling, others wearing protection on their heads, hands, or waist. A figure in the Princeton University Art Museum may have worn perishable padding. He holds a ball at breast height and is poised to play.[32] The figures were made by ceramicists capable of superb visual expression. The quantity

Figure 14. A Xochipala ceramic sculpture of a seated adult and youth, Late Formative Period, Xochipala, red-brown micaceous ceramic, height of left figure 13.5 cm, height of right figure 11.0 cm, Princeton University Art Museum. Gift of Gillett G. Griffin in honor of David W. Steadman, Graduate School Class of 1969 (Acc. y1972-38, 39).

and quality of the pieces indicate their social significance, no doubt for ceremonial or votive purposes.

There are an estimated 20,000 Xochipala figures,[33] but their interpretation and dating suffer from the same problem as the Mezcala-style sculptures: nearly all are looted. The Xochipala figures seem to have originated in the Mezcala region where the site of Xochipala is located. Paul Schmidt has dated the Xochipala ceramic sequence from 585 BCE to 965 CE, probably beyond the latter date.[34] A recent thermoluminescence analysis of figures in the Princeton University Art Museum suggests that, at a minimum, the Xochipala tradition dates from 880 BCE to 392 BCE.[35] Thus, the Xochipala and Mezcala traditions were contemporaneous and flourished in the same region of central and northern Guerrero (as were architectural features such as the corbelled arch and decorative *clavos* and *quesos*, discussed in 2.6). This suggests that Schmidt's and Reyna Robles's speculations that the two traditions were part of a broader culture may be correct.

2.5. Monumental Stone Sculpture

A third sculptural tradition of monumental stelae, carved and uncarved, endured from the Formative to the Postclassic. The earliest known example is a bas relief stela, whose Formative iconography is clearly Olmec, found at San Miguel Amuco in the Middle Balsas. It measures 85 centimeters tall and 42 centimeters wide and depicts a human wearing a cloak and a bird-serpent mask carrying a symbol of ceremonial import or denoting high status. Monolithic sculptures as early as this are rare outside the Gulf. Before this discovery, the corpus of Olmec sculpture in Guerrero was limited to portable objects that could have been acquired by exchange rather than made locally. The San Miguel Amuco stela is so large that it was surely carved in situ. The style and composition are similar to rock carvings of Chiapas, Honduras, and perhaps Veracruz, which again suggests that Formative Guerrero was in contact with various regions along exchange networks. Radiocarbon dates strongly suggest it was carved between 1530 BCE ± 230 and 1260 BCE ± 110. If this is correct, the Amuco Abelino stela is one of the earliest Olmec-style sculptures in Guerrero and, indeed, in Mesoamerica.[36]

In Formative Teopantecuanitlán the first sculptures in the ceremonial precinct were of clay modeled on stone columns. They included Olmec iconography and what seem to be jaguars. They have been dated by their similarity to stone sculptures at Ojo de Agua, Chiapas, to between 1200 BCE and 1000 BCE. The sculptures were arranged on the walls and steps of a sunken patio, probably a representation of the underworld and a model of the cosmos. Just as the Cueva de los Gobernadores bears similarities to Monument 1 (*El Rey*) at Chalcatzingo, the ceremonial precinct at Teopantecuanitlán resembles Monument 9 at Chalcatzingo, which depicts a sunken patio. However, integration of sculpture with architecture at such an early date is currently known only at Teopantecuanitlán.[37] The iconography, possibly also shared with nearby Zazacatla, suggests that these communities shared a cultural worldview. Between 1000 BCE and 700 BCE the walls of the precinct were dressed with stone and four sculptures in the form of an inverted *T* were installed. They depict the torso, arms, and face of a deity with almond-shaped eyes and a "were-jaguar" mouth, measuring 1.4–2.2 meters wide, 1.15–1.5 meters tall, and 0.7–0.9 meters deep. They weigh 2.5–3.0 tons. The sunken patio is thought to represent a metaphorical ballcourt and the sculptures ballplayer-deities, which had astronomical and calendrical

Figure 15. A drawing of the Olmec stela of San Miguel Amuco, Formative Period, depicting a human wearing a bird mask and a cloak and carrying an object with a ceremonial meaning or that denotes high status. Drawing by Martin Lubikowski, adapted from Grove and Paradis, "Olmec Stela from San Miguel Amuco."

functions, and represented an axis mundi. These cosmological concepts were later commonplace in Mesoamerica. When the precinct was buried beneath new structures, the four sculptures were knocked down, and two other anthropomorphic sculptures were mutilated.[38]

At Piedra Labrada, on the Costa Chica, carved and uncarved stelae and sculptures in the round date probably to the Early Classic (250/300–600 CE) and reflect the influence of the powerful cities of Monte Albán and Teotihuacan. A stela 2.5 meters tall and 0.8 meter wide (now identified as Monument 3), bearing what Piña Chan interpreted as a Zapotec-style glyph for number one, depicts an individual disguised as a "tiger" (or jaguar), wearing a large feather headdress. An

Figure 16. A monolithic sculpture of a symbolic ballplayer in the ceremonial precinct of Teopantecuanitlán, 1000 BCE to 700 BCE. The shapes of the eyes and the downturned "were-jaguar" mouth are characteristically Olmec. Photograph by Gillett G. Griffin, slide archive, GGG3237. Courtesy of the Princeton University Art Museum.

unfinished stela 3.5 meters tall by 0.65 meter wide depicts Tláloc or the goddess Chalchiutlicue and bears stylistic similarities with Teotihuacan, but also with urns depicting Cocijo, the Zapotec god of lightning and rain, at Monte Albán. A third stela 4.33 meters tall and 0.9 meter wide depicts a human figure with a headdress similar to Teotihuacan portrayals of Tláloc. It bears a number one glyph and another that means either tiger or Cocijo. Sculptures in the round represent a jaguar and a tortoise.[39] When Gutiérrez visited the site in recent decades he found twelve sculptures with glyphs, carved from an extremely hard granite.[40] Urcid's study of Zapotec glyphs identified stelae dating to 600–900 CE in the Late Classic. If this is correct, stelae with Teotihuacan characteristics were made when Teotihuacan's center had already been destroyed in the sixth century. Thus, the great city's influence continued long after its decline, while Monte Albán remained powerful until 800 CE. Some consider that the stelae depict deities, while Urcid argues that Monument 3 honors a deceased local ruler in the form of a man-jaguar.[41] Gutiérrez

Figure 17. A photograph and drawing of Stela Monument 3 from Piedra Labrada, Classic Period, depicting the ruler 10 Nudo (Knot) as a jaguar-headed figure. Photograph and drawing courtesy of Javier Urcid.

rejects relationships with Monte Albán, arguing that the epigraphy is like that of Xochicalco, Teotenango, and Cacaxtla in the Central Highlands. He reads the glyph in the center of the ruler's chest as 10 Nudo (10 Knot).[42] In any case, a vigorous tradition of monumental sculpture for ceremonial-political purposes existed during the Classic, perhaps until the Postclassic, and the choice of stone difficult to carve speaks to the value attributed to monumental sculpture.

A Classic tradition of carved stelae in the North reflected in stone the influence of Teotihuacan, although stelae were rare in Teotihuacan where murals were preferred. One interpretation of two sculptures attributed to the Tepecoacuilco region is that they depict the rain god Tláloc, the Teotihuacan equivalent of Tláloc or Chalchiuhtlicue. Another study suggests they represent Teotihuacan warriors with iconography affiliated with the martial Storm God aspect of Tláloc. Stela 1 holds a dart dripping with blood and has goggle eyes. Stela 2 holds jade beads and wears a medallion marked with symbols of the Storm God.[43] Three slabs from Tequicuilco, not far from Tepecoacuilco, depict a human face surrounded by rays of the sun, the sun together with a bird and a jaguar or serpent's mouth, and a jaguar or serpent mask. The iconography relates to the sun, creation, and the end of the solar cycle. Associated ceramics suggest dates between 650–700 CE, but three numerical glyphs, of Zapotec and Xochicalco style, suggest dates between 700–900 CE.[44]

Two carved slabs, also dating to the Classic, found at Placeres de Oro, seem to represent a style of anthropomorphic monumental sculpture local to the Mezcala region.[45] Slab A combines five faces. A "grotesque" face occupies the upper register, its eyes circled by two serpents. Below, two highly abstracted faces in profile, their eyes diamond-shaped and their lower jaw missing, face upward. In the lower register, two profile heads face outward, the eyes again diamond-shaped, the noses curled up, and the jaws lined with triangular teeth. Slab B has a similar face to Stela A in the upper register, but the lower register has an empty rectangle in the center, flanked by geometric designs. Above and below the rectangle are abstracted faces in profile facing one another, their eyes almond-shaped and noses upturned. The slabs were found in a funerary context, with offerings that suggest the burial of a prestigious person.[46] A slab found to the northeast of Arcelia is of a very similar design, and two more similar stelae have been reported at Cerro de Los Monos.[47] However, three columns at Cerro de Los Monos, possibly sections of a ballcourt marker, carved with geometric elements and motifs such as half-stars and circular disks, have been interpreted as being of a clearly Teotihuacan style,[48] and

Figure 18. A drawing of the Tepecoacuilco Stela 1 (left), Classic Period, height 1.14 m, and Stela 2 (right), height 1.24 m, possibly depicting the Teotihuacan Storm God. Drawings courtesy of Nicolas Latsanopoulos.

there was also a large stela at Mexiquito, carved in Teotihuacan style with half stars.[49] Thus, the Mezcala-region style did not exclude styles and iconography from Teotihuacan.

The end of the power of Teotihuacan and Monte Albán disrupted power relationships in Guerrero. The stela of Cohimbre on the Costa Chica suggests that local elites consequently lost power. The stela's generic depiction of a god of death contrasts with earlier stelae at Piedra Labrada, which represented a specific ruler as an intermediary with the gods. Perhaps the Cohimbre stela reveals a new relationship of humans with gods, characteristic of the transition from the Classic to the Postclassic. If correct, this implies a reduction in the intermediary role of rulers in favor of more direct community communication with deities.[50]

In the Montaña, between 1932 and 1937, archaeologists saved

Figure 19. A drawing of Slabs A (left), height 71 cm, width 46 cm, depth 5 cm, and B (right), height 84 cm, width 38 cm, depth 3 cm, Classic Period. Drawings by Martin Lubikowski, adapted from Placeres de Oro. After Reyna Robles, "Esculturas, estelas y lápidas."

from looters at Texmelincan an impressive collection of jade, gold, obsidian, copper, ceramics, alabaster, fragments of carved bone, turquoise, and other stones, all with similarities to artifacts at Monte Albán. Excavation revealed four low relief stelae depicting high status figures and warriors.[51] According to Jiménez García, stela one is similar to reliefs at Xochicalco, stela two is of Toltec style, and stela three exhibits traits of both Xochicalco and Tula, possible evidence of Toltec rulers at Texmelincan and Cualác about 900 to 1200 CE. Whether or not Toltecs were present, the stylistic features reflect changes in cultural and political contacts between the Montaña and Central Mexico after the decline of Teotihuacan and Monte Albán.[52]

In short, throughout Guerrero there was a deeply rooted tradition of expressing in monumental stone sculpture cosmological, ceremonial, political, and social ideas. These ideas were the basis of Mesoamerican thought, which Guerrero's rulers and sculptors expressed with distinctly regional accents. They also reflect the influence, whether military or political-cultural, of powerful cities in central Mexico and Oaxaca. The quantity and quality of the surviving examples underlines the importance of stone sculpture in Guerrero.

2.6. Architecture

Our earlier discussion of regional settlement patterns demonstrated that the general trend was one of dispersed settlements that were small relative to other areas such as the Valley of Mexico or Monte Albán in Oaxaca. Sites with ceremonial zones and elite residential areas emerged in Guerrero in the Formative, a development that continued into the Classic and Postclassic. While the large urban centers such as Teotihuacan, Monte Albán, Tzintzuntan, or Tenochtitlan were orders of magnitude, more complex societies than the smaller settlements of Guerrero, communities of modest scale emerged that nevertheless exhibited certain features of urbanism. The architecture included building types common to other areas of Mesoamerica, such as platforms, mounds, plazas, ballcourts, and tecpan, and construction methods such as talud-tablero walls. Nevertheless, some aspects of architecture were specific to Guerrero and are discussed here.

Indeed, an important architectural innovation may have been first introduced in Guerrero. The corbelled arch, a development usually attributed to Mayan society, was possibly in use in Guerrero before it appeared at Mayan sites, although generally for tombs and not for large structures as was the case of Mayan cities. Corbelled arches have long been reported in Guerrero: as early as 1896 at Coacoyula in the North; at La Organera-Xochipala and in a tomb at Pueblo Viejo III in the Center; four chambers, one of them measuring 4.6 meters by 3.7 meters, roofed with corbelled arches were reported at Oxtotitlán; and at Teopantecuanitlán. In 1986 a tomb with corbelled arches, measuring 2.2 meters by 1.15 meters at the Coovisur site in Chilpancingo, was dated by reference to eleven Olmec ceramic vessels. The tomb was in use from 1000 to 400 BCE. These dates suggest that the Coovisur corbelled arch may be the oldest in Mesoamerica, perhaps antedating Mayan examples by more than a millennium. By 2002 more than twenty-eight corbelled arches had been recorded in Guerrero and the areas of Morelos and the

Figure 20. Quesos at Cuetlajuchitlán in a masonry workshop area. Reproduction authorized by the Instituto Nacional de Antropología e Historia (INAH), Mexico City.

state of Mexico that are within the region in which the Mezcala sculptural tradition flourished.[53] The rough chronological and spatial coincidence of the corbelled arch with Xochipala and Mezcala sculpture, all within the geographical locus of the Mezcala tradition, is intriguing, to say the least.

Two other features of Guerrero's architecture, quesos and clavos, are emblematic of the Center and North, once again within the region where Mezcala and Xochipala sculpture flourished. Quesos (literally, cheeses) are round stones used to make columns that support flat roofs. They were a favored method of construction at La Organera-Xochipala and at sites in the North.[54] Clavos were conical stones with round heads, often carved with human faces, some perhaps representing deities. The earliest reported clavos were at Teopantecuanitlán,[55] but the majority are found in Classic contexts, often embedded in horizontal rows in tablero walls. They were found in abundance at La Organera-Xochipala, where some tableros were concave rather than flat.[56] Clavos, like quesos, have been interpreted as a feature of Mezcala culture.[57]

TABLE 2.1 APPROXIMATE RELATIVE CHRONOLOGY OF SOME MAJOR FORMATIVE SITES AND THE OCCURRENCE OF MEZCALA SCULPTURE, XOCHIPALA FIGURES, THE CORBELLED ARCH, *QUESOS*, AND *CLAVOS*

	Early Formative 1,500–1,200 BCE	Middle Formative 1,200–400 BCE	Late Formative 400 BCE–1 CE	Terminal Formative 1–300 CE
Oxotitlán	▬			
Teopantecuanitlán	│	│		
Cuetlajuchitlán		│	│	
Ahuináhuac			│	
Xochipala		│		
Mezcala figures		│	│	
Mezcala architectural models		│	│	
Xochipala figures		│	│	│
Corbelled arch		│	│	│
Quesos			│	│
Clavos			│	│

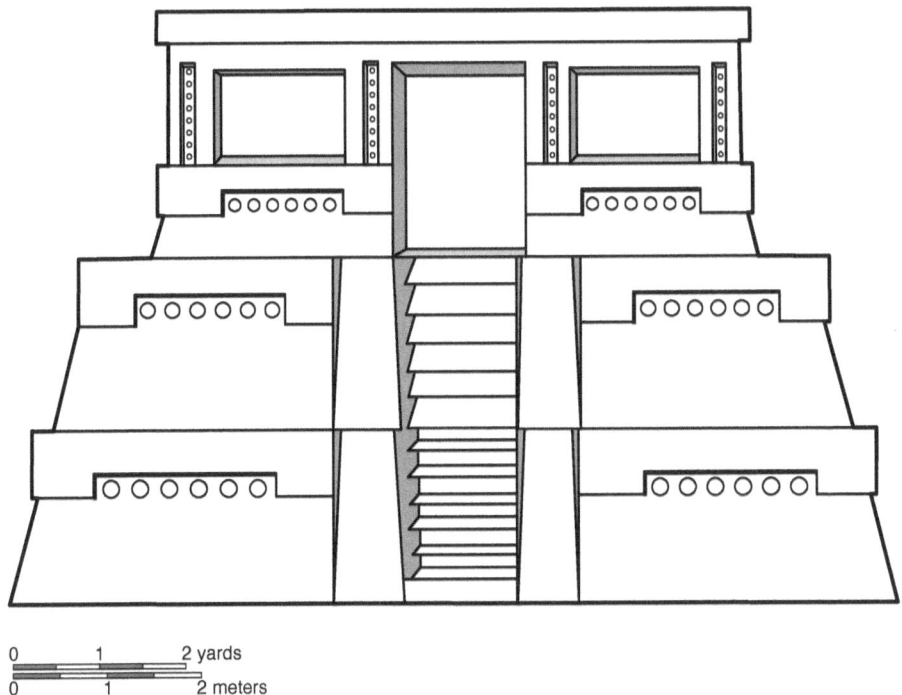

Figure 21. A reconstruction drawing of Structure 11 at La Organera-Xochipala showing talud-tablero walls decorated with horizontal and vertical rows of clavos. Drawing by Martin Lubikowski, adapted from Reyna Robles, "La cultura arqueológica Mezcala."

2.7. Other Forms and Media of Expression

We have already encountered several other forms of expression in Guerrero, such as metal artifacts, Pox and Blanco Granular ceramics, shellwork, painted gourds, and the color palettes of El Infiernillo. That there was a preoccupation with color from the Formative onward is evident in Olmec-style rock art. The serpentine and jadeite of Guerrero were admired not only for their polished finish but also for their colors. The area around Formative Teopantecuanitlán was rich in pigments, which were an important element of the exchange economy. For example, there were deposits nearby at Huitzuco of cinnabar, which was prized for its bright red color and was found in abundance under buildings and in ceramic vessels at Teopantecuanitlán, where colored materials, such as golden mica, were recorded, as were a variety of pigments: white, orange, ochre, yellow, blue, and red. At a Formative cemetery in Chilpancingo, associated with a settlement occupied since the second millennium BCE, burials were laid on a layer of red pigment. In the Postclassic the Montaña's tribute to the Mexicas included yellow and blue pigments for dyeing textiles.[58]

Clay and stone anthropomorphic and zoomorphic figurines were abundant and have been found throughout Guerrero. At Formative Ahuináhuac a variety of stone figurines in Mezcala style and ceramic ones in a variety of styles have been recorded. At Teopantecuanitlán hollow Olmec-style baby face and solid OSP-type (*ojos sin pupila*) figurines have been reported. Olmec baby-face figurines have been found at Chilpancingo in the Center, in the Montaña at Tlapa, as well as Olmec-style figurines at Olinalá. In the Oztuma region of the Tierra Caliente figurines similar to central Mexican examples of the Middle and Late Formative to the Postclassic have been found. Figurines at La Organera-Xochipala similar to those from Monte Albán and Veracruz date to the Classic and Early Postclassic. The figurines of Zacatula, on the Costa Grande, reflect contacts along Guerrero's coast, with Oaxaca and the Central Highlands. These figurines depict local dress and adornment: a kind of skirt, a *quezquémetl* (a form of stole) on the shoulders, necklaces, earplugs, simple hair styles, teeth filed to a triangular shape, facial scarification, or painted faces. Figurines at Texmelincan in the Montaña have been related stylistically to examples at Monte Albán.[59] Classic figurines with traits indicative of contact with Teotihuacan and Monte Albán were widespread.[60] In sum, Guerrero had a long-lasting and ubiquitous tradition of figurines that document contact with other regions as well as local forms.

2.8. Codices and Lienzos

Marion Oettinger remarked that, alone in the Americas, "Mesoamerica was the land of written books." The people of Mesoamerica recorded time, historic or mythical events, and narratives of migration. Their books kept accounts of tribute obligations, wars, ruling lineages, and propaganda, all told in pictographic texts.[61] The earliest Mesoamerican paper beater, found on the coast of Guatemala, dates to about 1000 BCE. Beaters at Teotihuacan have been dated to the sixth century CE.[62]

Paper beaters found in archaeological contexts tell us that paper was made in Guerrero,[63] although they have not been dated. The evidence for a tradition of pictographic documents in Guerrero is a substantial number of documents with clear pre-Hispanic roots, known as codices, *mapas*, and lienzos,[64] made soon after the Spanish invasion and in the seventeenth and eighteenth centuries, and preserved or later copied in villages of Guerrero. Some of them date from the sixteenth century: the *Códices de Azoyú 1* and *2* to 1565, the *Codices de Ohuapan, Tecuiciapan and Tetelzinco* to 1557, the *Pintura de Muchitlan* to 1582. It is possible that the so-called *Palimsesto de Veinte Mazorcas* (Palimpsest of Twenty Corn Cobs) and the *Lienzo de Chiepetlán I* date from pre-Hispanic times with colonial retouching.[65] It is probable that the scribes of Guerrero had been painting documents at least several centuries before the arrival of the Spaniards.

The fact that these documents were made under colonial rule, signaled inter alia by the integration of Spanish figures in them, cautions care in their interpretation. Churches replaced temples, but Indigenous iconography persisted: footprints record processions round the boundaries of a community's land and rulers carry fans, a bag of copal, and sit on an *icpalli*, symbols all of rank. We meet founding *principales*, but King Charles V of Spain may join them as mythical founders. Many of these documents were created to defend the interests of a village in dealings with the colonial administration, civil or ecclesiastical, or to record tribute obligations. Very soon after the Spanish invasion the Indigenous scribes of Guerrero adopted the European pen alongside the paintbrush. They combined pictographic modes of representation with glosses in Nahuatl to clarify their glyphs and images. These were hybrid, evolving documents. They incorporated traditional elements but were not merely texts from "time immemorial." They were dynamic responses to a new reality. From the 1530s Indigenous peoples were active in civil and ecclesiastical proceedings.[66]

Several documents refer to precontact or early colonial migrations of Nahua groups. The motives for migration included environmental catastrophes, lack of land, poor infrastructure, excessive tribute, wars, and conflicts.[67] For example, two eighteenth-century documents created between 1691 and ca. 1711, copies of sixteenth-century originals, record the foundation of Ocotequila and Xalatzala in the Montaña.[68] The *Lienzo de Chiepetlán II* tells of the foundation of Chiepetlán in 1490. Three groups set out from central Mexico: the settlers of Xalatzala from Toluca,

Figure 22. The *Lienzo de Chiepetlán II*, ca. 1691 – 1711, paint on cloth, 1.01 m x 1.67 m. The glyph for Tenochtitlan is top right. To its left, the gloss in Latin characters reads "Moyotlalia." Feet depict migration journeys. Courtesy of the Chiepetlàn community, Guerrero.

the Ocotequila group from Xochimilco, and the future residents of Chiepetlán from Moyotlalia. The migrations lasted a long time: eighteen, twelve, and thirteen years respectively. The migrants halted along the way to rest and grow food. Their routes and stopping places were almost identical. When they arrived at their final destinations, they requested land from the local ruler and offered him gifts. The groups were not large: the Chiepetlán group totaled forty-five.[69]

The *Lienzo de Chiepetlán II* is one of six lienzos held by the pueblo and constitutes an interesting case study of the fashioning, refashioning, and transmitting of community history and memory. The originals of all but *Lienzo I* were destroyed in a fire in 1691 and replaced by the surviving versions. *Lienzo I* was made in the early sixteenth century, possibly before the Spanish invasion, and like all the Chiepetlán lienzos, its multilayered narrative serves several functions. At one level it is a map that positions Chiepetlán, a Mexica tribute collection center, as economically dominant and also religiously supreme, since Chiepetlán was the site of the temple of Xipe Tótec, the preeminent deity of the region. Furthermore,

Figure 23. The *Lienzo de Chiepetlán III*, also known as the *Códice de Chiepetlán*, 1691 – ca. 1711, red, green, blue, maroon, and black paint on cotton, 96 cm x 83 cm. In the central panel, seven Indigenous figures sit on *tolicpalli* (high-backed seats), identifying them as nobles. A further Indigenous figure is identified by his head only. Two Spanish officials are also present. Beginning at the bottom right, landmarks arranged counterclockwise in a spiral leading to the center record the route of the review on foot of the boundaries of Chiepetlán's land. Reproduction authorized by the Instituto Nacional de Antropología e Historia (INAH), Mexico City.

Figure 24. The *Lienzo de Petlacala*, 78 cm x 99 cm, on the altar during the rain ceremony, with offerings of food, drinks, flowers, and candles, 2011. 1953, beige, brown, blue, gray, pink, and white paint on cotton, 77 cm x 99 cm. Photograph by Gregorio Serafino, 2011. From Gregorio Serafino, "La comida ritual de los nahuas de San Pedro Petlacala por la petición de Lluvia," Nuevo Mundo Mundos Nuevos (http://journals.openedition.org/nuevomundo/67391). 1953 copy of an earlier original.

Chiepetlán is politically superior because it is the seat of government and a military headquarters. The prestige and power proudly documented in the lienzo is represented by the arrival of the "civilizing ambassadors" of the Mexicas and their defeat of the Tlapanecs.[70] The remaining four lienzos were probably created in the late seventeenth century. *Lienzo III* records a confirmation of the boundaries of Chiepetlán's land. *Lienzos IV, V,* and *VI* mark an important date in 1696 when an official document concerning the village's lands arrived.[71]

The *Lienzo de Petlacala* records a migration to the Montaña that may have taken place in the Postclassic, either 1428–1440 or 1450–1455, or perhaps in the early colonial period, 1520–1535. Like other migrations to the same region, Petlacala's lasted several years, with pauses to cultivate land. The fact that several migrations from the Valley of Mexico ended in the Montaña suggests that this was the intended terminus, that the migrant groups knew where they were going, and that the region was an attractive destination. In addition to recording with pride Petlacala's origins in a long migration, the lienzo emphasizes the importance of mythical or historical founders. The document portrays three Indigenous principales, all of whom were depicted wearing eighteenth-century clothing, and an Indigenous woman, María Nicolasa Jacinta, who is depicted in the style of pre-Hispanic stone sculptures that were placed on altars. These were the original founders, but they are joined by King Charles V of Spain, to accord the foundation of Petlacala the authority of the Crown. In sum, the lienzo is a colonial-era document that records an Indigenous identity based on the foundation of the settlement but refashioned to incorporate Spanish authority figures.[72] The *Lienzo de Petlacala* records possession of the village lands. The presence of leaders of Petlacala, of neighboring villages, and of Spanish officials, and indeed of Charles V, sanctioned possession of the land. The lienzo is still an indispensable part of contemporary rituals of clear pre-Hispanic origin, but with Spanish components. In modern times it is kept in the house of the village shaman, emphasizing its ceremonial and community significance. This precious manuscript is still brought out for special occasions, including ceremonies associated with land and rain.[73]

Gruzinski states that an important function of Mesoamerican documents was "to keep safe the memory of the lineage or the community."[74] The most notable documents produced in Guerrero as a record of lineage are the *Códices de Azoyú 1* and *2*,[75] the first made in Tlapa ca. 1565, with possible seventeenth-century additions; the second made, also in Tlapa, in the late 1560s with later sixteenth-century additions. These documents record the history of Tlapa-Tlachinollan and its ruling lineage 1300–1565 CE to justify and preserve under colonial rule the power and prestige of the lineage.[76] The *Humboldt Fragment 1*, the *Palimsesto de Veinte Mazorcas*, the *Lienzo de Tlapa*, the *Lienzo de Aztatépec y Citlaltépec*, and the *Lienzo de Chiepetlán I* are related documents whose data serve to confirm and interpret the *Azoyú* codices.[77] The codices record the rulers of Tlapa-Tlachinollan, who ruled in pairs (a Mixtec arrangement known as a *yuhuitayu*), their eventual dominance of other communities in the Montaña to create the most significant polity of Guerrero, and their subjugation by the Mexicas. The codices tell of the first conquest of Tototepec between 1349 and 1355, a victory commemorated with human sacrifices. Under Señor Lluvia (1454–1477) the Mexica conquest of Tlapa-Tlachinollan began. In about 1461 Lluvia met the Mexica ambassador Señor Abeja, who appointed Lluvia as tribute collector.

Figure 25. The *Códice de Azoyú 1*, folio 38, ca. 1565, paint on amate paper, 20.5 cm x 23 cm, depicting a judge holding his staff of office standing in front of the empty tolicpalli of the governor of Tlachinollan in 1559. A lord named Señor Flecha, in precontact dress and seated in a tolicpalli, sits opposite a Spaniard in a Spanish-style seat above the glyph for Acocozpan. Top right, Señor Conejo and another lord lie dead in coffins rather than traditional mortuary bundles. Biblioteca Nacional de Antropología, Mexico. Reproduction authorized by the Instituto Nacional de Antropología e Historia (INAH), Mexico City.

According to Oudijk, the last colonial Indigenous rulers recorded in the *Códices de Azoyú* were Señor Flecha (1551–1564) in *Azoyú 1*, folios 37–38, and Señor Conejo (1557–1564) in *Azoyú 2*, folio 17, although there had been difficulties and disputes in earlier years, since Conejo's long rule from 1541 or 1542 was apparently interrupted for a time by Señor Agua.[78]

Technical analysis of the *Códices de Azoyú 1* and *2* reveals that they were painted on fig bark paper with pre-Hispanic pigments. They were not created at one time. There are additions to the original, which do not overpaint any original images. There are also patches stuck over the original, but they are not much later than the rest of the documents. On the obverse of folio 17 are five Spanish personages, two of them depicted with hatched shading, a European technique.[79] The two scribes who painted the codices worked in the Mexica style, incorporating Mexica iconography in their depictions of banners, temples, elements of costume, and the like, following the practice of other Late Postclassic artists in Guerrero, who incorporated Aztec iconography into sculpture, for example.[80] The codices, lienzos, and other colonial documents of Indigenous origins provide glimpses of the nature of rulership in the Montaña. A ruler enjoyed privileges and tribute but also had obligations: to safeguard the community and its land; to defend the community in negotiation or in battle; to preside over ceremonies and rituals (ceremonies depicted in rock art are early examples). Sometimes a leader's decisions were a matter of life or death. *Códices de Azoyú 1* and *2* tell of rulers who resisted Tlapa-Tlachinollan and paid the high cost of military defiance.[81] Other rulers preferred to negotiate (often under duress) or to form a marital alliance, and thus avoid the destruction of their temple and human sacrifices.[82]

The colonial Indigenous documents of Guerrero testify to the intermediary role of the local elite, defending the community from natural disasters and war, while protecting their own interests and privileges. Life in Mesoamerica could be precarious. The ruler was the intermediary of deities such as Tláloc, god of rain and fertility, still the protector of crops in contemporary villages.[83] Traveling far from one's village was a dangerous affair.[84] In return for tribute and services, a ruler offered his community protection from such dangers. The documents also exhibit an intense attachment to and pride in the community, its history, and foundation.

2.9. Languages

Studies of Guerrero in the second half of the sixteenth century describe the region as a mosaic of languages. Dehouve mentions the principal languages: Chontal, Cohuixca, Cuitlatec, Mixtec, Nahuatl, Purhépecha, Tlapanec, and Yope. Drawing on the *Relaciones Geográficas*, Vélez Castro lists twenty-nine tongues, including Cinteca, spoken only in Cintla, and Cuauhteca, limited to Cuahuitlán. Marino Flores relies on the work of Orozco y Berra, listing twenty-one languages, of which nine were spoken only in one, two, or three settlements.[85] In other words, many languages were spoken in Guerrero, although exactly how many we cannot say. By 1930 the state officially recorded the following: Amuzgo, Matlatzinca, or Pirinda (two speakers), Nahuatl, Mixe, Mixtec, Popoloca, and Tlapanec.[86]

Guerrero's linguistic diversity reflects a long history of migration into Guerrero. According to Vélez Calvo, around 2500 BCE only two languages were spoken, Prototlapanec and Protocuitlatec, the latter the result of migration from Michoacán. By the early Formative, about 1500 BCE, Protomixtec, Protozapotec, and Protoamuzgo had added to Guerrero's linguistic diversity. By 600 BCE there were additional languages: Nahuatl, Protomazahua, Protomatlatzinca, Protonahua, Chichimeca, Protochontal, and Prototepuzteca, joined by Purhépecha around 400 CE and by 700 CE Mixtec.[87] Glottochronological studies of the Tierra Caliente of Michoacán suggest that migrants entered the region about 2500 BCE. The most significant linguistic migrations occurred between 1500 BCE and around 400 CE, when Yutoazteca groups from the north moved along the coast toward the Balsas, displacing the Tarascans who expanded into Cuitlatec territory in Guerrero. The Cuitlatec are thought to have immigrated from Michoacán to the Costa Grande and Tierra Caliente of Guerrero by 1500 BCE. The population of the Tierra Caliente was Cuitlatec and Chontal until the Tarascans and Mexicas imported settlers in the Late Postclassic.[88]

It is difficult to confirm this chronology. The archaeological record does not link archaeological finds and cultures with languages. Moreover, many languages have left not a single word for historical linguists to study, and for others very little is documented. Von Mentz argues, based on cultural, historical, and anthropological data, that the Chontals were the oldest inhabitants of the North of Guerrero. Evidence from the *Relaciones Geográficas* and documents concerning the *congregaciones* of the late sixteenth century confirm that the Chontal-speaking population was sizeable. Nevertheless, Nahuatl replaced Chontal in the colonial period, and no data survived to make dating of Chontal's presence in Guerrero possible.[89] Concerning Yope, some researchers argue that it was an independent language, while others state that it was identical to Tlapanec.[90] In short, the linguistic history of Guerrero remains shrouded in a good degree of mystery. However, linguistic diversification certainly occurred in parallel with social and cultural developments that manifested themselves, for example, in the presence of the Olmec style and the creation of sites such as Teopantecuanitlán, Cuetlajuchitlán, and Ahuelicán.

Linguistic diversity had consequences for social, political, and economic interactions. Most Indigenous communities had neighbors who spoke another tongue. For example, in the Montaña, in Tlapa and its subject villages, Mixtec, Náhuatl, and Tlapanec were spoken. The residents of Azoyú probably spoke only Tlapanec, while neighboring settlements spoke Amuzgo. Friendly dealings with other language groups would have facilitated the transportation and exchange of resources. However, communities were regularly in conflict, as the depiction of burning temples and the sacrifice of defeated opponents in the *Códices de Azoyú* demonstrate.[91] Nor did speaking the same language guarantee solidarity or harmony. In the middle Balsas region, Chontal Alahuiztlán, Oztuma, and Teloloapan mustered enough unity to revolt against Mexica domination, but the Chontals of Tetipac and Noxtepec, in the North, did not come to the assistance of their ally Oztuma when the Mexica attacked. The Cuitlatecs of Tetela were frequently at war with those of Ajuchitlán, as well as with the Tarascans and Tepuztecos of Tlacotepec.[92]

In the linguistic mosaic of Guerrero bilingualism, indeed trilingualism, was surely commonplace. Even in single language groups there were distinctions of dialect and geographic origins. For example, the Nahuas in the North had a strong affinity with the dialects of Michoacán, Durango, and Jalisco, those of the Center with Tenochtitlan and, in some cases, with the Huasteca.[93] Moreover, communication between different groups was facilitated not only by language but also by cultural and ritual norms. The accounts of migrations to the Montaña demonstrate how the principales who led the migrations negotiated access to land with local rulers. The migrants' leaders observed rhetorical norms. The supplicants offered gifts that they deplored, while the local ruler flattered them as venerable elders and invited them to rest (till the land).[94] Migrants would have brought with them new ideas, beliefs, customs, and social practices, and perhaps also conflict. New ideas stimulated social dynamism and the acceptance of change.

Studies of Guerrero's languages generally conflate language and ethnicity. However, it is not clear that this assumption has any explanatory power. Renfrew and Bahn have observed that often language and ethnicity correlate. However, "human societies can exist quite well without tribal or ethnic affiliations: there is no real need to divide the world up into named and discrete groups of people."[95] Language was significant but was not in itself a basis of identity. Family ties, allegiances, social status, or gender may have been more consequential.[96] A study of the Tierra Caliente of Guerrero, Michoacán, and the state of Mexico concludes that linguistic groups cannot be considered as distinct ethnicities, since they shared a cosmovision and a material culture independent of their language.[97] James Lockhart observed that the commoners of the Nahua communities of colonial central Mexico were much more attached to their autonomous municipal unit than to their Nahua neighbors.[98]

2.10. Population

Raúl Vélez Calvo makes the only estimate of the total population of Guerrero ca. 1520, based on reports of the number of speakers of the diverse languages of Guerrero in the *Relaciones Geográficas*, the *Suma de Visitas*, the *Relaciones del Obispado de Antequera*, and other sources from the second half of the sixteenth century. Since these reported only the tributary population, he multiplied the numbers by four to estimate the total population, and then multiplied this by the rate of population decline between 1520 and the end of the sixteenth century calculated by Peter Gerhard.[99] Since he used Gerhard's ratio of population decline, Vélez Calvo's estimate can be tested against Gerhard's calculations. Gerhard estimated that the density of the Indigenous population of Guerrero ca. 1620 was less than one inhabitant per square kilometer. Further, Gerhard accepts the population estimates of the "Berkeley School" which calculated that the ratio of the precontact Indigenous population ca. 1519 to the population by 1581 was 12.2:1. Assuming a density of one per square kilometer, and since the surface area of Guerrero is 64,458 square kilometers, the precontact population might have been 786,000, a density of 12.2 per square kilometer.[100] Vélez Calvo's estimates imply an unlikely density of 26 per square kilometer.

TABLE 2.2. POPULATION BY LANGUAGE IN GUERRERO, CA. 1520. BASED ON THE ESTIMATES OF VÉLEZ CALVO

Language group	Population
Acatecas	3,000
Amuzgos	60,000–68,800
Apanecas, Ocuiltecas, and Tecos	No estimate
Ayacachtecas	3,600
Chontals	160,000
Chumbias, Coyotomatecas, Olimecas, and Pantecas	No estimate
Cintecas	70,000?
Cuauhtecas	20,000
Cuitlatecs	300,000
Huehuetecas	10,000
Ixcucas, Matlames, Texomes, and Tlahuicas	No estimate
Mazatecas	No estimate
Mixtecs	34,244
Nahuas	701,440
Purhépechas	105,700
Tepuztecas or Tepehuas	68,000
Tlapanecs	115,000
Tuztecas	189
Yopes	5,728
Zapotecs	10,000
TOTAL	1,666,901–1,675,701
Inhabitants/km2 (total area 64,458 km2)	25.86–26.00

Sources: Vélez Calvo, "Etnohistoria (¿–1521)," 164–340; Gerhard, *A Guide to the Historical Geography of New Spain*, 22–28.

Gutiérrez's work on the archaeology, territorial extent, and estimated precontact population of the polity of Tlapa-Tlachinollan in the Montaña provides a second test of Vélez Calvo's figures. Gutiérrez estimates that the territorial extent of Tlapa-Tlachinollan was 6,000 kilometers^2, and its population a minimum of 50,000, perhaps as high as 150,000.[101] Thus, the precontact density was between 8.3 and 25 per square kilometer. Now, it is clear from archaeological data and sixteenth-century documentary sources that Tlapa-Tlachinollan was more densely populated than several other regions of Guerrero. Thus, a density of 26 per square kilometer implied by Vélez Calvo's estimate for Guerrero as a whole is improbable. Another comparison can be made with the Mexica tributary province of Tepecoacuilco, a region of 12,000 kilometers². Archaeological and documentary sources suggest that the population of the province, like the Montaña, was relatively high, evidence supported by Litvak King's calculation that the area was capable of feeding a population as large as 184,615 families or 1,080,767 individuals.[102] If one assumes that the density was similar to that of Tlapa-Tlachinollan, then the actual population of Tepecoacuilco Province might have been 100,000–300,000. That the rest of Guerrero, which included areas with a much lower carrying capacity than Tlapa-Tlachinollan and Tepecoacuilco Province, should average 26 per square kilometer, as Vélez Calvo suggests, is untenable. It is worth noting that in modern times the population density of the Montaña, which includes ancient Tlapa-Tlachinollan, is above the average for the state.[103]

An estimate of 786,000 seems more reasonable. Now, if one applies Vélez Calvo's data for the relative populations of the various language groups of Guerrero to a figure of 786,000, the results are as shown in table 2.3. Broadly speaking, historical linguistics and other data confirm that the Cuitlatecs, Chontals, and Tlapanecs were relatively numerous, and that the Amuzgos and Mixtecs were smaller but significant groups. The numbers for Cintecas and Tepuztecas (or Tepehuas) are much more speculative because they are extinct and reliable data are scarce. Now, the adjusted Tlapanec, Amuzgo, and Mixtec population (most of whom lived in the Montaña) totaled 98,000–102,000. Since a portion of Guerrero's Nahua population also inhabited the region, these data broadly suggest that Gutiérrez's higher estimate of 150,000 may be credible.

A comparison with Borah and Cook's calculations of the population of the communities recorded in the *Suma de Visitas* ca. 1548–1550 lends some credence to a figure of 786,000.[104] They estimated the total population of New Spain ca. 1548–1550 to have been 6.4–7.3 million. In another work, they estimated the total population of New Spain ca. 1520 to have been 22 million.[105] The ratio of the ca. 1548–1550 population to the population ca. 1520 was, therefore, 6.4–7.3:22. Borah and Cook's estimate for the total population of Guerrero, except for the province of Zacatula ca. 1548–1550, was 188,044. If one applies the ratio of 6.4–7.3:22 to this figure, the result is 602,000–684,000. If an estimate of 786,000 for the total population of Guerrero is correct, the population

TABLE 2.3. ADJUSTED POPULATION IN GUERRERO BY LANGUAGE GROUP, CA. 1520

Language Group	Population	%
Nahuas	330,000	42%
Cuitlatecs	141,000	18%
Chontals	75,000	10%
Tlapanecs	54,000	7%
Purhépechas	50,000	6%
Cintecas	33,000?	4%
Tepuztecas or Tepehuas	32,000	4%
Amuzgos	28,000–32,000	4%
Mixtecs	16,000	2%
Subtotal	759,000–763,000	
Other languages (19 in total)	23,000–27,000	3%
Total	786,000	100%

Source: Vélez Calvo, "Etnohistoria (¿–1521)," 164–340.

of Zacatula would, therefore, have been 102,000–184,000. The second figure seems to be excessive, since it is larger than the estimated population of the Montaña, which archaeological and documentary evidence does not support. Thus, Borah and Cook's analysis suggests that the total population of Guerrero ca. 1520 may have been around 700,000, and perhaps at a maximum 780,000.

Finally, it is useful to bear in mind a few observations concerning the regional distribution of the major language groups at the end of the Late Postclassic as we examine the Late Postclassic polities of Guerrero and their early colonial trajectory. The Montaña in the east was occupied by Tlapanecs, Mixtecs, Amuzgos, and Nahuas. This had been the polity of Tlapa-Tlachinollan, then the Mexica tributary province of Tlapa, and much of it would form the largest encomienda of sixteenth-century Guerrero. The Indigenous identity of this region would endure into modern times. In the North and the Tierra Caliente, the predominant languages were Nahuatl, Chontal, and Cuitlatec, the latter reaching down to the Costa Grande, and in the far west Tarascan. Chontal would endure into the sixteenth century but would soon become extinct. Cuitltatec would last longer but was eventually destined for extinction.[106]

2.11. Art, Culture, Ideas, Beliefs, Languages, and Population: Conclusions

Guerrero participated actively in Mesoamerican culture. Cosmological-religious ideas, social organization, and ideologies of rulership had much in common with the rest of Mesoamerica. In certain periods Guerrero participated and contributed more actively than in others, notably in the Formative. But the currents of Mesoamerican culture flowed through Guerrero throughout the pre-Hispanic period. Moreover, Guerrero made important contributions: polychrome rock art, Mezcala-style sculpture, Xochipala ceramic figures, monumental stone sculpture, shells and shell artifacts, polished stone objects, metallurgy, pigment palettes, painted jícaras, and textiles. These artifacts expressed ideas about cosmology, society, and power.

Guerrero's cultural artifacts speak of ideas, ways of conceiving society and the world, the nature of rulership, and social and economic contacts with other parts of Mesoamerica. It is not always easy to see clearly the human beings behind the artifacts, and there are limits to our ability to read in them the lives of communities. Nevertheless, from the caves of Oxotitlán, Juxtlahuaca, Cauadzidziqui, and Techan, and in the sunken patio of Teopantecuanitlán, we learn that the people of ancient Guerrero did not distinguish, as we do today, between sacred and secular power. For the rulers of precontact communities ruled in the sacred and the secular spheres, they protected their privileges but also the territory and livelihoods of those they ruled over. The codices, lienzos, and mapas of colonial Guerrero speak of pride in a community's origins, both historical and mythical, in its deities, and of a powerful attachment to its land above other ties of ethnicity or language. Community ties persisted tenaciously through times of change and perils, such as the decline of Teotihuacan, or the incursions of the Mexicas and Tarascans. In the next chapter we will see how these and other factors affected power and politics in Guerrero.

CHAPTER THREE

Politics and Power

3.1. The Archaic and Formative

Ceramics, lithics, and evidence of boats and nets used for sea fishing tell us that by the end of the Late Archaic and in the Early Formative coastal settlements such as Puerto Marqués were forming settled communities that exchanged with peoples from distant localities. Nothing in the archaeological record suggests that these were hierarchical societies. Nevertheless, there may have been some degree of specialization in toolmaking or fishing. These were certainly more elaborate societies than their hunter-gatherer predecessors. From the Early to Late Formative their inhabitants had diversified their subsistence strategy to include some cultivation of maize and other crops, allowing settlements such as La Zanja to expand. According to Manzanilla, by the Middle Formative, the area between Acapulco and San Jerónimo was integrated into networks of exchange along the coast of Oaxaca to Chiapas and Guatemala, inland to the upper Balsas and the Basin of Mexico, and further afield to Veracruz and Tabasco. By the later Formative, figurines suggest social distinctions. Ceremonial centers, indicative of rituals performed by specialist elites, and more organized agricultural activities evidence a degree of increased social hierarchy, and of centralized control, probably by groups whose prestige and authority rested on their roles in rituals. In short, the society and economy were diversifying, suggesting greater social differentiation and the presence of ruling groups. Nevertheless, these were small polities consisting of dispersed settlements.[1]

Further north, the rock art of Oxtotitlán and Juxtlahuaca are evidence of Early Formative ideologies and the social practices of a ruling elite. This process was accentuated in Teopantecuanitlán, which was probably a significant regional center, in contact and sharing ideas with other exchange centers. Teopantecuanitlán's ceremonial precinct evidences the presence of a ruling group that participated in the iconography, cosmology, and ideology associated with Olmec style to reinforce its social status. This is evidence of the beginnings of social complexity, of a high-status elite and relations with a social-ruling culture shared beyond the region. Excavations at Cuetlajuchitlán and Ahuelicán suggest that the processes at work in Teopantecuanitlán were evident on a smaller scale in other settlements involved in the exchange of prestigious resources.[2]

3.2. The Classic

Formative Guerrero had been an active participant in the currents of ideas and iconography associated with the Olmec. During the Classic, the influences were external, from the powerful city-states of Teotihuacan and Monte Albán. For example, coastal rulers adopted provincial imitations of the symbols of power and prestige espoused by the more powerful rulers of the Valley of Mexico and Oaxaca. Thus, the plumed serpent appeared on ceramics, and iconography associated with Tláloc was adopted, as were symbols from Oaxaca such as Zapotec glyphs. Expanded settlements and more elaborate ceremonial centers with enlarged platforms, sunken plazas, ballcourts, talud-tablero architecture characteristic of Teotihuacan, and carved and uncarved stelae evidence more powerful elites and a more entrenched social hierarchy.[3] Similar developments, with regional variations, occurred elsewhere. For example, in the El Infiernillo region of Tierra Caliente, burial offerings and architecture suggest that the elite lived in ceremonial centers, while their subjects resided in smaller sites with modest structures.[4]

    Markers of the influence of Teotihuacan were particularly widespread and in places abundant. For example, in the Montaña several instances of Teotihuacan influence have been found: a mask, censers, and sites with talud-tablero construction. Reciprocally, artifacts from Guerrero have been found in Teotihuacan. It is significant that Teotihuacan iconography continued to be used from 600 to 800 CE long after the great city had declined.[5] The enduring presence of Teotihuacan-style finds raises the question of the nature of interaction between Guerrero and Teotihuacan. Classic sculpture in Guerrero has been interpreted as evidence that Teotihuacan may have exercised direct control in some places in Guerrero,[6] but it is equally possible that Guerrero's rulers imitated their powerful peers as a means to consolidate and validate their authority. Gutiérrez notes evidence of strong interaction between the Montaña and Teotihuacan from 450 to 650 CE. Some scholars suggest that the Montaña may have been a tributary province of the great city. Others attribute interaction with Teotihuacan to the presence of colonists, perhaps in the Tlapa region. Well-documented migrations from the valley to the Montaña in the Postclassic indicate that is a feasible hypothesis.[7]

Reyna Robles sees evidence of migration from Guerrero to Teotihuacan in the Classic. Teotihuacan finds are more prevalent in the North and on the Costa Grande, less so in the Mezcala region. Perhaps the North exported labor, and the coast exported exotic and prestigious resources rather than labor. In return Guerrero imported Teotihuacan's ideology. Reyna Robles further proposes that Puerto de Allende in western Guerrero was the gateway from Teotihuacan to the coast. If this were the case, travelers from Teotihuacan would have passed through the region where pigments and pigment palettes were made and perhaps used to create the murals of Teotihuacan.[8] Perhaps Guerrero, the pioneer of polychrome rock art, also played a role in the development of mural painting in Teotihuacan.

Traces of interaction with the Toltecs have also been detected in Guerrero. Finds include ceramic vessels of Toltec style at Zacatula on the Costa Grande and traces of Toltec contact on the Costa Chica, in the Montaña, and in Oaxaca. Toltec contact has also been suggested in El Infiernillo. In Pezuapan, in the valley of Chilpancingo, Toltec characteristics have been detected in a tecpan. Particularly significant traces of the Toltec, perhaps suggesting the presence of Toltec warriors, have been reported in Texmelincan and Cualác in the Montaña.[9] The data are fragmentary, but since long-distance exchange was important for the Toltec economy,[10] it is not surprising that evidence of the Toltecs has been found in Guerrero, possibly accompanied by the adoption of Toltec ideas of rulership.

3.3. The Postclassic: Introduction

In Postclassic Guerrero, some long-term themes continued: the region's resources continued to be in demand; the population continued to increase; migration persisted. However, there were new developments. In the Montaña, Tlapa-Tlachinollan gradually pieced together the largest polity seen in Guerrero by the late fourteenth and early fifteenth centuries. More or less in the center of the coast, another polity took shape: Yopecingo. On the Costa Grande, population increased and there are indications of conflict. In the North, several small Chontal polities flourished. And toward the end Guerrero suffered the intrusion of the two great empires of Postclassic Mesoamerica, first the Tarascans, then the Mexicas, to climax in the still greater shock of Spanish colonization.

Gerardo Gutiérrez estimates that in eastern Guerrero in the fourteenth to sixteenth centuries there were some 35 polities in a territory of approximately 15,000 kilometers^2.[11] On average, a polity occupied 429 kilometers^2, and if that were true of the rest of Guerrero, there would be a total of 150 polities. If the population of Guerrero were, as calculated in chapter 2, 700,000–786,000, the average polity would be home to 4,670–5,240 souls, perhaps 930–1,000 families. The polities of eastern Guerrero were more hierarchical and larger than those in many other parts of Guerrero. Therefore, in the entire region there probably would have been more, smaller polities. In Postclassic Guerrero it was often in the interests of rulers of small polities to form alliances with, or alternatively to attack or resist, neighbors or extraregional powers such as Tenochtitlan or Tzinzuntzan. The skill set of successful rulers included negotiations and the calculation of costs and benefits of submitting to or resisting another lord. These skills would be at a premium when the Spaniards set foot in Guerrero in the 1520s.

3.4. Tlapa-Tlachinollan

Several factors combined to create the conditions in which the kingdom of Tlapa-Tlachinollan developed. The region was an important source of gold and greenstone. Its major settlements occupied strategic positions on key routes of exchange and became intermediaries in the exchange of products. Demand resulting from the rapid growth of the population of the central altiplano incentivized greater control of territory to profit from exchange and tribute, and to increase the power and prestige of Tlapa-Tlachinollan's elite. The territory covered 6,000 square kilometers, occupied by between ten and twelve polities whose territories averaged between 500 and 600 square kilometers.[12] In the Postclassic this mountainous region of small fertile valleys was home to a relatively dense population. The average distance between Tlapa and the polities it would dominate was only 23 kilometers, a day's walk, and the maximum was 50 kilometers.¹³ The mobilization of resources required to control another community was modest in Mesoamerican terms. Hassig considers that a small Mexica army might consist of 8,000 warriors and 333 tamemes.¹⁴ Since the average population of eastern Guerrero's polities was 13,636–16,666,¹⁵ the army of a Montaña ruler would have been much smaller.

The *Códices de Azoyú 1* and *2* record the history of Tlapa-Tlachinollan's expansion and eventual domination by the Mexicas. The governmental system here reflected Mixtec methods of rule. In Mixtec terms, each settlement in the polity was a *ñuu* (rather than the Nahuatl term *altepetl*). Two rulers governed from twin capitals (Tlapa-Tlachinollan and Caltitlan), a Mixtec structure of government known as *yuhuitayu*.¹⁶ Tlapa-Tlachinollan's territory was occupied by speakers of Tlapanec, Mixtec, Amuzgo, and Nahuatl. The conquests began with Tototepec between 1349 and 1355 and continued until 1447. Eight polities succumbed to force, but not all those absorbed into the kingdom were conquered in battle. Some submitted to the threat of force; others formed marital alliances or negotiated their incorporation. The rulers of the subject communities acknowledged the authority of the rulers of Tlapa-Tlachinollan and paid tribute. Expansion did not always proceed smoothly. For example, between 1433 and 1439, Tlazallan rebelled and had to be reconquered.¹⁷ Alliances provided protection against Tlapa-Tlachinollan's enemies, and as the kingdom expanded toward the coast, the range of tribute increased to include cacao, cotton, shells, fish, and other coastal products.¹⁸

By the 1440s Tlapa-Tlachinollan was threatened by Nahua migrants who had settled to the north. Around 1440 the forces of the Mexica tlatoani Moctezuma Ilhuicamina first entered Guerrero.¹⁹ The *Códice de Azoyú 2* depicts the temple of Tlapa-Tlachinollan in flames by 1447, probably the result of an attack by Nahua migrants rather than the forces of Tenochtitlan. Señor Calandria Flecha responded by attacking Petlacala and Axoxuca-Oztocingo, both Nahua settlements. In about 1461 Moctezuma sent Señor Abeja to negotiate with Señor Lluvia, Calandria Flecha's son and successor. In return for paying homage and tribute to Tenochtitlan, Lluvia remained the preeminent figure in the region and received Mexica support for future conquests. This change in the power structure disrupted the alliances between the lineages of the region. A conflict broke out between predominantly Nahua and Tlapanec polities and those ruled by Tlapanecs and Mixtecs. Since there were Tlapanecs on

Figure 26. (*opposite, top*) The *Códice de Azoyú 1*, folio 8, ca. 1565, paint on amate paper, 20.5 cm x 23 cm, recording Tlachinollan's conquest of Tototepec between 1349 and 1355. In the lower register, a warrior sacrifices a captive. The upper register depicts two lords holding their staffs and bags of office. On the right, Señor Pájaro-Lagarto, and on the left, Señor Venado, who is listening to an individual on the far left. Biblioteca Nacional de Antropología, Mexico. Reproduction authorized by the Instituto Nacional de Antropología e Historia (INAH), Mexico City.

Figure 27. (*opposite, bottom*) The *Códice de Azoyú 1*, folio 24, ca.1565, paint on amate paper, 20.5 cm x 23 cm, depicting the meeting between Señor Lluvia of Tlapa-Tlachinollan (right), seated on a high-backed tolicpalli, and Señor Abeja, the Mexica ambassador (left), 1461. The gloss above the glyph in the center reads "tenochtitlan" and the gloss above Lluvia reads "montecsuma," a reference to Lluvia's status as a ruler subordinate to Moctezuma Ilhuicamina. Biblioteca Nacional de Antropología, Mexico. Reproduction authorized by the Instituto Nacional de Antropología e Historia (INAH), Mexico City.

both sides, this conflict was not drawn along ethnic-linguistic lines but was rather a fight between lineages. Lineage was the key factor in the next conflict when Lluvia died in 1477. His sons Mono and Xihuacoatl (or Couaxiuitl, in Spanish Serpiente de Turquesa) disputed the succession. Since this threatened Mexica control, Tenochtitlan resorted to military force between 1468 and 1474, capturing Tlapa-Tlachinollan and killing eighteen individuals of high rank. Xihuacoatl survived but was now a subordinate to the Mexica tlatoani. The lords of Tlapa-Tlachinollan supported the Mexica in further military campaigns, ending in 1510–1516 with the conquest of Alcozauca and Tenanco.[20]

The creation of the kingdom of Tlapa-Tlachinollan is documented in the *Códices de Azoyú*, other Indigenous documents, and in the archaeological record. The *Códices de Azoyú* were created by the colonial successors of the ruling lineages to lay claim to their territory, power, and privileges. Testimony to the colonial authorities confirms not just the existence of the kingdom but also the alliances and loyalties that held it together, and the seeds of interpolity conflict that threatened it. In these documents we witness how the pre-Hispanic rulers calculated their interests and sustained their position through lineages and alliances.[21] In a little more than a century, the dual governing lineages of Tlapa-Tlachinollan created the largest polity in Guerrero until that time. Archaeological data document the existence of earlier regional centers such as Teopantecuanitlán. Perhaps the lords of Tlapa-Tlachinollan were heirs of Formative and Classic rulers in the sense that their predecessors developed ideologies of ceremonial, social, and political power developed over centuries and adapted to the contexts of different periods of Guerrero's history. Tlapa-Tlachinollan deployed the ruling tools of its day (force, negotiations, marital alliances) to create something new: a regional mini-empire.

3.5. Yopecingo

To the south of Tlapa-Tlachinollan lay the kingdom of the Yope people, Yopecingo. No sources from Guerrero for this polity exist, and certainly there are none that originated from the Yopes. Sahagún, in the Florentine codex paints a none too flattering picture of the Yopes:

> The Yopime, whose name [is] also Tlappaneca; these are inhabitants of Yopitzinco. The [term] Yopime is taken from their home [land], which is a place called Yopitzinco. And they are Tlappaneca because they paint themselves with red ochre, and because the name of their god was Totec, the red Tezcatlipoca. His array [was of] red ochre. Likewise were his priests and all the commoners; all painted themselves with red ochre. These were rich. . . . The common name of these was Tenime, because they spoke a barbarous tongue. These were completely untrained; they were just like the Otomí; yet they were really worse. They also suffered affliction. They dwelt in a land of misery; but nevertheless, [they were] knowers of green stones; [they were] people of wisdom.[22]

Davies, drawing on Sahagún, concluded that the Yopes exhibited some characteristics of civilization before the Mexicas rose to power, but that those characteristics disappeared.[23]

There are several reasons to doubt this negative depiction of the Yopes. It is curious that the only group in Guerrero said to have regressed culturally was a fierce enemy of the Mexicas, whom they defeated, and of the Spaniards, who subjugated them with great difficulty. The Yopes had historical links to the Toltecs and to important archaeological sites such as Texmelincan. Sahagún's assertion that the Yopes inhabited a very poor region is curious, since archaeology attests that for centuries inhabitants of the coastal region had lived from fishing, shellfish, hunting, and maize

Figure 28. The restored ballcourt at Tehuacalco. Photograph © Enrique Hudson/Dreamstime.com.

cultivation, and if "barbarous" is interpreted to mean warlike, this was a typical characteristic of Postclassic peoples. Moreover, Sahagún reported that the Yopes were excellent goldsmiths and craftspeople in precious stones, and their lords were honored guests at important ceremonies of the Mexicas, who admired their culture and military skills. Some scholars claim that the cult of Xipe Tótec, much venerated by the Mexicas, originated among the Yopes, although others dispute this. The *Códice Tudela* describes them as agriculturists and hunters who learned to hunt with bow and arrow from seven years of age. Sources also record that Yope rulers administered a well-organized, if harsh, system of justice. A husband had the right to rid himself of a lazy wife and adultery was severely punished. Moreover, some evidence suggests that the Yopes participated in exchange networks of metals and tropical goods. Mexica sources frequently peddled propaganda against the enemies of Tenochtitlan, and it is likely that sources combine elements of truth mixed with propaganda to justify the Mexicas' failure to defeat the Yopes. The Yopes occupied a territory of some 3,000 square kilometers, from Coyuca in the west to the river Nexpa, and inland to the Papagayo and Omitlán Rivers, which they assuredly shared with other linguistic groups.[24] According to Gerhard there were four Postclassic Yope states.[25] Consistent and fierce Yope resistance to intruders suggests that these states were closely allied. Since the Yopes were firmly established in their territory it is likely that their polities were of some antiquity. Recent excavations at Tehuacalco, a site in the northern reaches of Yopecingo, have cast further doubt on the Yopes' purported lack of civilization. The site had a ceremonial center with substantial architecture. Preliminary estimates suggest occupation from the Epiclassic to the end of the Postclassic in 1521.[26]

3.6. Mexcaltépec, Oztuma, Cototolapan, Oapan, and Chontal Kingdoms of the North and Tierra Caliente

Some information has survived about several other polities. For example, Gerhard states that the Cuitlatec polity of Mexcaltépec, which became part of the Mexica tribute province of Cihuatlán, exercised some degree of control over nine semi-independent states on the Costa Grande. In addition, there were numerous autonomous states on the Costa Grande. On the Costa Chica, the kingdom of Ayacastla, consisting of the sizeable communities of Tlacolula, Ometepec, and Igualapa, may, like Yopecingo, have been independent of the Mexicas.[27]

A small polity in the Montaña, the kingdom of Cototolapan, is documented in the *Códice de Cualác*, apparently made in the late sixteenth century. Cototolapan (close to the modern Cualác) was probably founded around 1428–1440 by migrants from the central altiplano or Morelos. The codex identifies the ruler of Cototolapan as Tequespalteuhtli, who governed thirty-two subject communities. Tequespalteuhtli was married to Calxotin, but the opportunity arose to marry a new wife, Susianicapi, who brought with her twenty-three additional communities. Among the now fifty-five subject settlements were Olinalá and Cuaulasyotepetl (modern Cualác). Also listed as a subject of Cototolapan was Tlapa. This may have been a sixteenth-century ploy to claim that Cualác had been the cabecera of Tlapa or, alternatively, perhaps the Nahua descendants of Cototolapan were emphasizing that Tlapa had been subject to Mexica rule. The codex depicts two residences of rulers, perhaps indicating that Cototolapan was a yuhuitayu as practiced elsewhere in the Montaña. There are also two armed groups wearing different clothing, suggesting conflict. The codex depicts important Mesoamerican deities: Cihuacóatl, Tezcatlipoca, and the Scorpion of the Underworld. A mythical bird represents a cave in front of which seven rulers sit, perhaps a reference to Nahua migration. Evidence suggests that the kingdom was divided in two when Moctezuma Ilhuicamina (1440–1469) conquered the region. It may be that the codex was created to recover jurisdiction over all the subject communities once controlled by Cototolapan.[28] The *Códice de Cualác* confirms characteristics of politics and power in the Montaña: dual rulership, the formation of larger polities by conquest or marital alliances, the role of migration, the link between ceremonial caves, and rulership.

Documents in two cases, concerning who was entitled to the tribute of nine sujetos of Chilpancingo, brought before the Audiencia of Mexico by two encomenderos and their Indigenous allies from 1531 to 1561, shed light on politics and power in the Center and North of Guerrero in the last decades of the Postclassic. The encomenderos and their Indigenous allies referred to precontact political structures and social alliances to justify their arguments. This enables us to reconstruct aspects of pre-Hispanic governing alliances in this region, which was part of the Mexica tribute province of Tepecoacuilco (or Cohuixcatlacapan). Oapan, one of nine altepetl in this province, was structured thus: The tlatoani of Oapan exercised direct authority over Tixtla, Chilapa, Mochitlán, Chilpancingo, and their constituent calpolli. Another altepetl, Zumpango, provided services and tribute to Tixtla, and thus indirectly to Oapan. The rulers of these altepetl in turn ruled subject calpolli, each governed by two *teuctli* (lords). Chilpancingo, for example, had eleven calpolli. At this local level, government was dual, as it was in the Montaña. Until 1522 the tlatoani of Oapan was Coapotlal. However, his authority was not beyond challenge, since in 1515 Chilpancingo had rebelled and attacked Zumpango.

Spanish court documents identify other individuals who had held positions of authority in the region before 1521. Under the Mexicas, a tlatoani such as Coapotlal shared authority with Mexica calpixqui (tribute collectors). The court documents refer to one Juan de Aguilera (his Nahuatl name is not recorded), who from ca. 1510 had been the calpixqui in Tepecoacuilco, to the north of Oapan. Juan's position entitled him to wear the attire of a tlatoani and to eat and play games of chance with the elite of Tepecoacuilco. Another calpixqui in Zumpango collected and assessed the value of tribute due from the mines. The documentation of the case also suggests that elite marriage alliances were important in the precontact era and continued to be so after the Spanish invasion. In 1535 a group of elite men and women from Oapan walked 57 kilometers to Mayanalán, near Tepecoacuilco, to arrange the marriage of Ana Conxochil, daughter of the local *cacique*, to the cacique of Oapan. Once arrangements had been made, more principales joined them to walk to the monastery in Chilapa where the couple were married.[29]

Several small Chontal kingdoms were a feature of the political structure of the North and the Tierra Caliente in the Late Postclassic. The Chontal rulers derived their power and wealth from the excess produced on their farmlands by tenant farmers, who might be Chontals, Cohuixcas, or Matlatzincas. Since the control of land and people defined power, wars with other Chontal or Otomí polities were frequent. Territory changed hands, was not contiguous, and was often intermingled with the territory of another ruler, since a victorious elite would appropriate fields in a defeated rival's territory. Victory in war also provided access to increased tribute or control of key resources. Chontal rulers formed alliances with the Mexicas and appealed to them to resolve territorial disputes. Nahuatl became the language of power, used by Chontal rulers to conduct their relationships with the Mexicas. The elite resided in the principal settlements located on hills or on strategic plains. However, the rest of the population lived in small, dispersed settlements occupied by some five families, or twenty to thirty individuals. Sacred functions were an important source of elite power. Nobles adopted sacred names from the altiplano (and after 1521, Christian names). Sumptuary goods, such as cacao, gold, textiles, greenstone, small copper bells, and shells, were significant symbols and sources of power. Salt had both economic and ritual importance and was associated with a white goddess. Family and lineage were the foundation of government. The ruler's family occupied important posts and formed marital alliances with other ruling families. Chontal lineages could be traced back many decades and some continued in power into the seventeenth century.[30]

3.7. The Mexica and Tarascan Empires

In the mid-fifteenth century, the rulers of Guerrero faced two new threats: incursions, first of the Tarascans and then of their rivals the Mexicas. The first Mexica incursions in the North of Guerrero occurred under Itzcóatl

(1428–1440), but the two expanding empires first clashed later in the valley of Toluca between 1455 and 1462. In response, in 1475–1477 the Mexicas sent armies to the Oztuma area of western Guerrero to contain the Tarascans who already occupied territory in Guerrero, though during 1479–1480 Mexica forces from the Valley of Mexico suffered a disastrous defeat when they attacked Michoacán. From then on, the two empires faced off along a frontier in Guerrero formed by the Balsas River.[31]

Guerrero was a tempting prize for the Tarascans because of its resources, above all copper, since they were expert metalworkers. According to Helen Pollard, exchange was important for the Tarascan state not only to acquire sumptuary resources, such as feathers and greenstone, nor solely as a sign of submission to the *cazonci*, since by 1520 the nucleus of the state was no longer a viable economic unit. Thus, exchange and the provision of services were indispensable for the Tarascan economy.[32] Tarascan expansion in the Balsas Valley was logical, since the peoples of the middle Balsas had exchanged resources, ideas, and technology with people to their west centuries before the Tarascan state emerged. Between 400–900 CE the Santiago-Lerma and Balsas-Tepalcatepec rivers were major routes of exchange. Around the Middle to the Late Postclassic, contact between these areas and central Mexico declined, while exchanges with regional cultures increased, sharing cultural traits and beliefs that would become characteristic of the Tarascans. Both the Tarascans and the Mexicas were attracted to the Balsas by its copper, gold, iron pyrites, lead, greenstone, cacao, pigments, and salt.[33] But Mexica expansion affected larger areas of Guerrero than the Tarascan incursions. Moctezuma Ilhuicamina (1440–1469) attacked the polities of the North and Center of Guerrero. Axayácatl (1469–1481) concentrated his efforts on the region that bordered Tarascan territory. Ahuítzotl (1486–1502) suppressed the Chontal rebellion of Oztuma, Alahuiztlán, and Teloloapan, and brought the Costa Grande under Mexica control with the objective of outflanking the Tarascans. Finally, Moctezuma Xocoyotzin (1502–1520) consolidated some of Guerrero's polities into the Mexica domain.[34]

The Tarascans and Mexicas operated very different models of political expansion. The Mexica Empire did not permanently occupy the territory of subject altepetl, did not exercise intrusive control, and local rulers who paid tribute to Tenochtitlan retained substantial freedom. The Mexica Empire was founded on the projection of military power. However, the Mexicas relied not only on military conquest but also on threats, intimidation, alliance formation, and negotiations. Hassig contrasts this model with that of the Tarascans, who sought direct and total control by stationing warriors or colonists in conquered territory.[35] Still, Yopecingo remained entirely independent of the Mexica Empire, while other regions of Guerrero may have retained degrees of autonomy. Indeed, Berdan and Smith have hypothesized that the Mexica dominion was by no means total, comparing it to a holey Swiss cheese. There were two types of imperial province: tributary and strategic. The principal obligation of tributary provinces, especially the more distant, was to pay tribute. Strategic provinces had military functions in frontier zones, in the case of Guerrero the Balsas region and the frontier of Yopecingo.[36] Moreover, Mexica domination had limits. The lists of Mexica conquests mention some altepetl more than once, perhaps because they had to be reconquered. For example, Moctezuma Ilhuicamina had to retake Tepecoacuilco and Tlalcozautitlán, and under Ahuítzotl a considerable number of Chontal kingdoms rebelled.[37] Since the population of Guerrero was not evenly distributed across its mountainous terrain, some areas must simply not have been worth the costs of conquest. Indeed, the Mexicas preferred not to resort to risky and costly military force. Many "conquests" were the result of the projection of superior power, threats, and negotiations. In the case of the Chontal kingdoms of the North and the Tierra Caliente, the Chontal elites governed with, not under, the Mexicas, a negotiated arrangement beneficial for both.[38]

In the Mexica Empire the ruler of a "conquered" community who was not rebellious and paid tribute remained in power and local laws and customs were unchanged. Both the local lord and the Mexicas made a calculation. Resistance and conquest were risky. It might be better to limit or avoid them.[39] If, in order to meet tribute obligations to the Mexicas, the local ruler did not have to reduce his own tribute and services, and if submitting to the Mexicas did not disrupt the local hierarchy, at the elite level little changed. However, if the elite miscalculated, the consequences could be serious. For example, in 1487 the Chontal rulers of Teloloapan, Oztuma, and Alahuiztlán repudiated their allegiance to Tenochtitlan. The elite of Teloloapan, defeated by a Mexica army, avoided punishment by shifting blame for the rebellion on to the rulers of Oztuma and Alahuiztlán, who paid with their lives.[40]

Nevertheless, some things did change when a ruler promised loyalty to Tenochtitlan. The Mexica Empire was sustained by a shared system of elite values, symbols, ideas, privileges, and obligations. *Codices of*

Azoyú 1 and *2* suggest how local elites absorbed Mexica values. Although the *tlacuilo* (scribe) of *Codex 1* had a better grasp of Mexica canons than the scribe of *Codex 2*, both painted in the Mexica manner. The banners, temples, and elements of the costume and bearing of the elite are characteristically Mexica.[41] Nevertheless, the adoption of Mexica ideas and styles did not imply total acceptance of everything Mexica. While locally made sculptures are clearly Mexica in style, there are few similar stylistic affinities in Guerrero's ceramics or architecture.[42] However, in the case of Oztuma, Alahuiztlán, Teloloapan, and some of their subject communities such as Acapetlahuaya, Mexica influence was more direct since the Mexicas settled 2,000–9,000 colonists from the Valley of Mexico, in addition to Otomís and Oaxacan Mixtecs. Furthermore, Mexica *tlacatecuhtli* (governors) and calpixqui were installed in Oztuma. Nevertheless, the archive of Ixtepec demonstrates that this did not eliminate the local elite, since a proud descendant of Oztuma's precontact Chontal ruling lineage continued to govern Oztuma in the late sixteenth century.[43]

Negotiations between the elite and the Mexicas to minimize or to avoid a violent conquest and to maintain local customs may have proved beneficial to the commoners since they limited disruption to their lives. The principal negative impact was the amount of tribute demanded by the Mexicas. Berdan observes that the transport of sumptuary tribute seems to have been on a quite small scale,[44] and Barlow's lists of tribute paid by altepetl in Guerrero confirm this. The transport of eight hundred red shells from Cihuatlán, five strings of *chalchihuites* from Tepecoacuilco, or twenty vessels of *tecoçahuitl* pigment from Tlalcozautitlán cannot have been very onerous.[45] However, Litvak King calculates that Cihuatlán's cost of cultivating and transporting its cacao and cotton tribute was equivalent to the annual subsistence production of 39 families and the annual labor of 58 tamemes. Cihuatlán's tribute included a variety of other items, such as chile, mats, gold, and slaves, but it is difficult to assess how much they added to the burden.[46] In the case of Tepecoacuilco, Litvak King's calculations suggest that the burden of supplying bulky produce such as maize, beans, amaranth, and chía amounted to the equivalent of the maize surplus of 982 families and the annual equivalent of 1,578 tamemes.[47] These numbers are sufficiently large to be treated with skepticism, but they do suggest that the provision of bulky produce was a substantial burden. Tepecoacuilco's tribute included several other items that were doubtless much less costly to acquire and transport.[48] Thus, the nature and burden of tribute varied substantially by region.

TABLE 3.1. ANNUAL COTTON TRIBUTE FROM TRIBUTARY PROVINCES OF GUERRERO ACCORDING TO THE *CODEX MENDOZA*

Çihuatlan	Tlapan	Tepecoacuilco	Tlalocoçauhtitlan	Quiauhteopan	Tlachco
3,200 orange-striped mantas four brazas in length	800 women's tunics and skirts	800 quilted mantas	800 large white mantas	800 large white mantas	800 loads of rich cotton mantillas
4,800 white mantas	800 red-striped mantas	800 black-striped mantas	One warrior costume and shield	One warrior costume and shield	800 loads of skirts and women's tunics
800 loads of brown cotton	1,600 large mantas	800 rich diagonally divided mantas			Two warrior costumes and shields
	Two warrior costumes and shields	800 women's tunics and skirts			
		800 white mantas			
		3,200 large white mantas			
		22 warrior costumes and shields			

Source: Berdan and Anawalt, *The Essential Codex Mendoza*, 2:76–89.

It is likely that the tribute dispatched to the Mexica capital was additional to the existing obligations of the commoners to pay tribute to the local elite. Mexica conquests and alliances, therefore, implied an additional burden for commoners. Before they expanded beyond the Valley of Mexico, the Mexicas acquired cotton goods by exchange from cotton-producing regions, but tribute cotton was cost free. All the tributary provinces of Guerrero sent cotton to Tenochtitlan, as table 3.1 demonstrates. The quantity and composition of tribute demanded from each province varied considerably. Cihuatlán provided both woven and raw cotton, while other provinces supplied only woven items. Tepecoacuilco provided the largest volume and variety, which included substantial quantities of elaborate warrior costumes.[49] Thus, provinces that paid cotton tribute bore not only the cost of cultivation and transport, but they also lost income previously derived from cotton.

Mexica tribute demands had some additional consequences. For example, Tlapa's tribute included gold, cotton textiles, warriors' costumes, shields, tecomates, blocks of rubber, and rubber figurines. Evidence suggests that some of these items were produced elsewhere and were acquired by exchange, the volume of which therefore increased under Mexica domination. Moreover, high quality sumptuary items, such as cotton textiles, warriors' suits, shields, and tecomates were made by specialist artisans. Thus, tribute obligations implied an increase in specialist work and in subsistence goods to maintain the artisans.[50] The beneficiaries of increased economic activity were the elite, intermediaries, and specialist artisans.

A special feature of Guerrero's experience of the Mexica Empire was that a substantial number of altepetl were located close to two active frontiers, with Yopecingo to the south and with the Tarascans to the west. These were the strategic provinces, whose principal obligations were to contribute to the defense of the Mexicas' domains rather than paying tribute. Frontier populations supplied fighting men, equipment, and foodstuffs to Mexica garrisons.[51] The burden of being a frontier community was substantial, but conflict was a fact of life even away from the frontiers, as table 3.2 suggests. War was a fact of life in Guerrero before the Mexica incursions, but under their rule military activity on the frontiers was especially intense. Skirmishes and sieges of fortifications were frequent.[52] Continuous warfare created a no-man's land near Oztuma and Alahuiztlán, which included two fertile valleys. The inhabitants built a defensive wall to protect their agricultural land, without success, and eventually had to abandon their fields.[53]

In summary, the Mexica Empire did not achieve total domination of Guerrero, did not affect all communities equally, and its duration was relatively short (e.g., much less so than the kingdom of Tlapa-Tlachinollan). The ruler who resisted or rebelled risked death. Local elites were inclined to negotiate arrangements that protected their privileges and power, in return paying tribute and homage to Tenochtitlan, remaining loyal and tolerating the presence of Mexica officials, and, in some zones, of colonists. Commoners, on the other hand, suffered an increased tribute burden, variable according to their province, and reduced standards of living.

The Tarascan Empire was of a different character from its Mexica rival. "In return for tribute and state control of lands, forests and minerals, the elite exported 'elite culture', a state religion, and the organization necessary to maintain and defend the borders of the kingdom." Resources required to maintain the Tarascan state flowed from the periphery into the Pátzcuaro basin at the heart of the empire.[54] This was a polity that exercised a high degree of control in its subject territories. The Tarascans built forts, defended by troops sent from other parts of the empire, along the frontier in Tlalpoxahua, Tlaximaloyan, Zitacuaro, Tozantlan, Cutzamala, and Ajuchitlán. This costly strategy limited the potential for expansion of the empire, since the Tarascans lacked the population, the network of alliances, and the logistics that the Mexica had at their disposal.[55] In 1522 the Tarascan empire occupied some 75,000 square kilometers, including land in western Guerrero along the border with Michoacán, as far south as Zacatula, whose skillful ruler managed to maintain his small kingdom's independence by playing the Mexica and the Tarascans off against one another.[56] Other regions were thoroughly assimilated into the empire. For example, in southeast Michoacán, on the frontiers with Guerrero, the Tarascan language was still spoken as late as 1750 because Tarascan workers had been sent there to work in mines and foundries.[57]

The Tarascan cazonci controlled his territory by means of a network of administrative centers, responsible directly to him. In Guerrero the administrative centers were Coyuca, Pungarabato, Ajuchitlán, and Cutzamala.[58] Coyuca administered seven or twelve subject towns, Pungarabato seven to thirteen, Ajuchitlán twenty to thirty, and Cutzamala, the most important of the administrative centers, thirteen to twenty-one. A Tarascan governor represented the empire in the region. The languages spoken in the region were Tarascan and Cuitlatec, the latter the result of the immigration of Cuitlatecs under Tarascan auspices about 1454.[59] Despite the constant military activity, merchants were able to trade across the frontier. Obsidian from Zinapécuaro and Ucareo was available in markets in Morelos, and Tarascan bronze objects have been found in Morelos.[60] Although the two empires imposed an increased tribute burden on the commoners of subject communities, resentment of the imperial power was not necessarily the result. For example, a sixteenth-century encomendero complained that the people of Cutzamala continued to deliver their tribute to Tzintzuntzan, 45 leagues (207 kilometers) distant.[61] According to the author of one *Relación Geográfica*, the residents of Zirándaro and Guayameo "continued to respects the sons of the nobles of Mechoacan, stating that their fathers were their slaves and captives, and, for that reason, they love and esteem them, without [paying] any other tribute."[62] Similarly, when the descendants of the nobility of Tlapa-Tlachinollan requested from the Spanish authorities the restoration of their pre-Hispanic rights and privileges, in the *Códices de Azoyú 1* and *2* they expressed their pride in being allies of the Mexica.

TABLE 3.2. COMMUNITIES IN CONFLICT UNDER MEXICA RULE		
Altepetl	In frontier zone with	Conflict with
Alahuiztlán	Tarascans	Ixcapuzalco
		Tlatlayan
		Tarascos
Chilacachapa		Iguala
		Cocula
		Cuetzala
		Teloloapan
Chilapa	Yopes	Yopes
Cocula		Chilacachapa
		Cuetzala
Cuetzala		Apaxtla
		Chilacachapa
		Coatepec
		Cocula
		Tenantzinco
		Tenepantla
Ixcateopan		Ixcapuzalco
		Noxtepec
		Taxco el Viejo
Malinaltepec		Yolos*
		Chinantecos*
Noxtepec		Ixcateopan
Oztuma	Tarascans	Tarascans
Teloloapan	Tarascans	Tarascans
		Chilacachapa
Taxco el Viejo		Cuauhnahuac
		Ixcateopan
Ixcapuzalco		Alahuiztlán
		Ixcateopan
Iguala		Chilacachapa

*A linguistic group rather than an altepetl. Source: Berdan, Blanton, Boone, Hodge, Smith, and Umberger, *Aztec Imperial Strategies*, 118.

3.8 Politics and Power: Conclusions

At the end of the Postclassic, a variety of polities had taken shape, some small, some a larger hierarchy of units under a degree of control of a dominant power, some owing allegiance to varying degrees to the Mexica Empire, a smaller number under the firmer rule of the Tarascans. However, the rule of the two external empires lasted only some eight decades. In that time many things did not change. Crops, prestige resources, and routes of exchange remained the same. In most cases, the ruling elite, ceremonial life, and rituals changed little. Tribute demands increased the economic burden borne by commoners, the level of conflict increased, and settlers changed the balance of population along the frontier, but migration had long been a familiar feature of life in Guerrero, so the arrival of incomers was not unfamiliar. Some polities resisted inclusion in the empires, whether by determined resistance or by clever political and diplomatic maneuvers. For more than 3,000 years, the peoples of Guerrero had exchanged with other Mesoamerican regions ideas, technologies, and resources. Some of the practices of the Postclassic would have been quite familiar to a commoner or a noble of Formative or Classic Guerrero, in particular the sacred aspect of rulership and the obligations of ruler and ruled alike. This does not mean, of course, that Guerrero's societies had been immutable, since powerful polities waxed and waned, different external powers with different models of influence or of exercising power had come and gone. The population had increased and with it the frequency and intensity of exchange.

The polities of Guerrero functioned in a multilingual environment and were accustomed to absorbing migrants and other external influences. A key skill required of the elite was negotiation and dealing with newcomers. When representatives of a new empire appeared in 1521, Guerrero's rulers had to make the same calculations they faced in dealing with the Mexica and the Tarascans: Negotiate or resist? Whether they chose the former or the latter, those who governed Guerrero's communities and their subjects were not merely passive objects of a change imposed by strangers but active participants in the creation of a new society. Their labor, skills, and resources, their attachment to their local community, notions of how their communities should be organized, and their cultural resources all interacted during the first decades of European colonization with the structures, laws, religious doctrines, and ambitions of the Spanish Crown, conquistadors, and *pobladores* to fashion New Spain.

CHAPTER FOUR

The Coming of the Spaniards

Invasion, Colonization, and Evangelization

4.1. Invasion

When news of the defeat of the Mexicas reached Guerrero, Indigenous rulers of the Cohuixcas (a Nahua people) of the Center, Chontals of the North, and Matlatzincas of the Toluca region, who had ties formed through trade and war, joined together to resist the foreign invaders. After a battle near Ocuila, in the modern state of Mexico, with forces led by Andrés de Tapia, the Cohuixcas, Chontals, and Matlatzincas withdrew, but at Talasco an army of 18 Spanish horsemen, 100 Spaniards on foot, and perhaps as many as 60,000 Indigenous allies, commanded by Gonzalo de Sandoval, defeated them. Thereupon lords from Taxco el Viejo, Iguala, Oapan, Huitziltepec, Mochitlán, and Tixtla journeyed to Tenochtitlan to offer their allegiance to Hernán Cortés.[1]

The Chontal alliance may not have been entirely unanimous, since the rulers of Noxtepec, for example, later recalled that they had opted for negotiations rather than battle and had presented themselves to Cortés. Many years later, the people of Noxtepec recorded their account of the events of 1521 in a document produced for a *composición de tierras*, a legal confirmation of the village's titles to its land. Three "elders" of the community and two of their dependents met the great tlatoani Cortés, who introduced them to their new tlatoani, the encomendero Juan de Cabra. The Spaniards gave the nobles of Noxtepec Castilian food, but they could not eat it and took it home to the men of their community, who could not eat it either. Cabra instructed them to build a church and, after considering the instruction, they asked for twelve years to complete it, whereupon Cabra came to Noxtepec and marked out the boundaries of the pueblo's land in the traditional manner of the Mexica.[2]

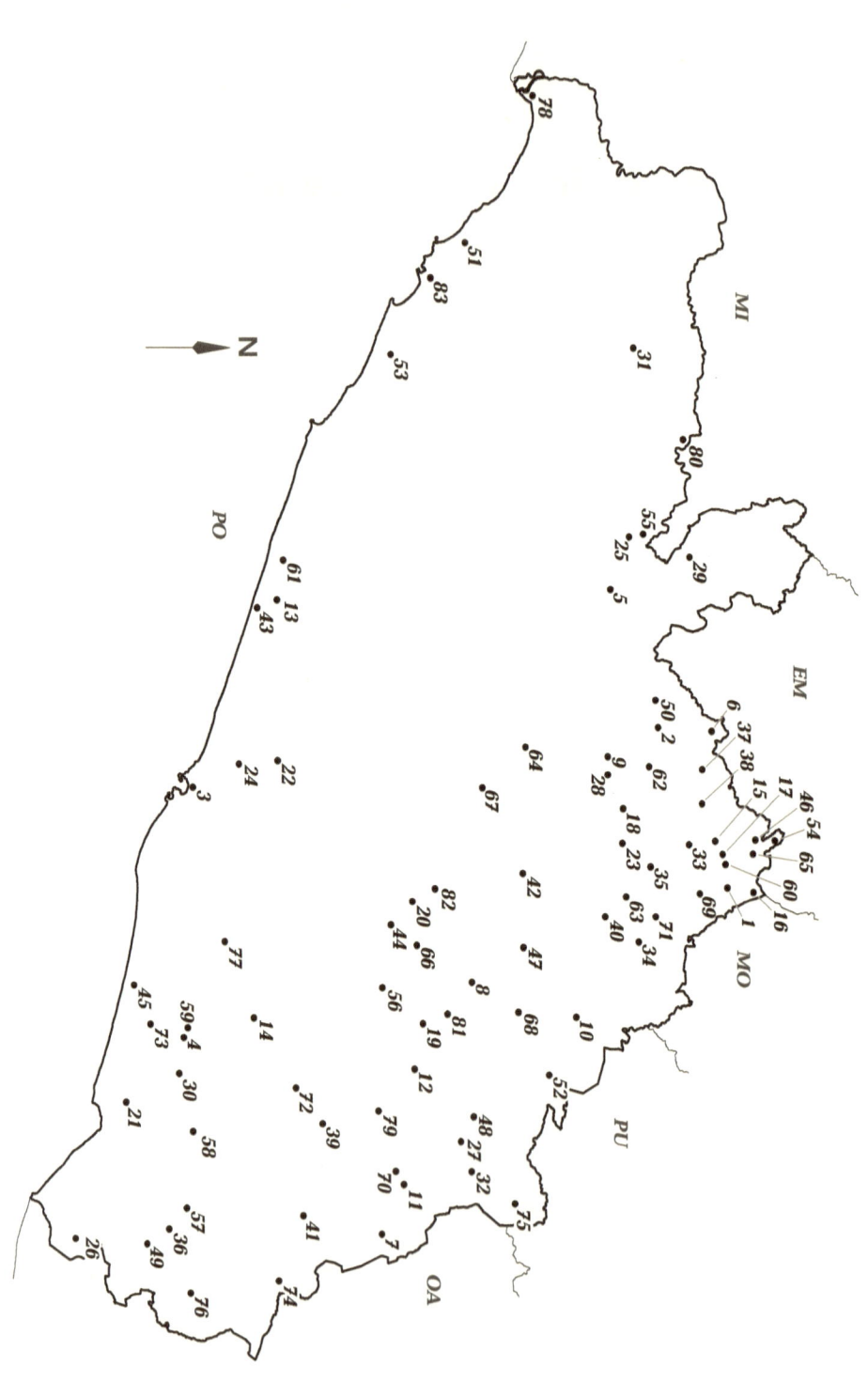

Map 2. Guerrero: Sixteenth-Century Towns and Settlements

Locations

1. Acamixtlahuaca
2. Acapetlahuaya
3. Acapulco
4. Acatlán
5. Ajuchitlán
6. Alahuiztlán
7. Alcozauca
8. Apango
9. Apaxtla
10. Atenango
11. Atlamajac
12. Atlixtac
13. Atoyac
14. Ayutla
15. Azala
16. Cacahuamilpa
17. Cacalotenango
18. Chilacachapa
19. Chilapa
20. Chilpancingo
21. Cintla
22. Citlaltomahua
23. Cocula
24. Coyuca [on Costa Grande]
25. Coyuca [in Tierra Caliente]
26. Cuajinicuilapa
27. Cualác
28. Cuetzala
29. Cutzamala
30. Cuyhutla
31. Guayameo
32. Huamuxtitlán
33. Hueyistac
34. Huitzuco
35. Iguala
36. Igualapa
37. Ixcapuzalco
38. Ixcateopan
39. Malinallepec
40. Mayanalán
41. Metlatónoc
42. Mezcala
43. Mitla
44. Mochitlán
45. Nexpa
46. Noxtepec
47. Oapan
48. Olinalá
49. Ometepec
50. Oztuma
51. Pantla
52. Papalutla
53. Petatlán
54. Pilcaya
55. Pungarabato
56. Quechultenango
57. Quetzalapa
58. San Luis Acatlán
59. Sochitonala
60. Taxco
61. Tecpan
62. Teloloapan
63. Tepecoacuilco
64. Tetela del Río
65. Tetipac
66. Tixtla
67. Tlacotepec
68. Tlalcozautitlán
69. Tlamacazapa
70. Tlapa
71. Tlaxmalac
72. Totomixtlahuaca
73. Xalapa
74. Xicayán
75. Xochihuehuetlán
76. Xochisitlahuaca
77. Xoculla
78. Zacatula
79. Zapotitlán de Tablas
80. Zirándaro
81. Zitlala
82. Zumpango
83. Zihuatanejo

Keys for surrounding areas

MI. Michoacán
EM. Estado de México
MO. Morelos
PU. Puebla
OA. Oaxaca
PO. Pacific Ocean

The Europeans who participated in the civil war against the Mexica did not constitute a formal army of the Spanish state. Rather, they were freelancers who, once victory was achieved, sought a payoff. Cortés was told that there was fabulous wealth in gold on the coast of Guerrero. Because of their value and transportability, gold and, soon, silver provided the essential financing of the Spanish invasion and the bulk of colonial economic activity.[3] Therefore, the coast was the Spaniards' first objective. In 1521 Cortés sent Gonzalo de Umbría to Zacatula. He returned with 300 pesos of gold dust. This prompted further expeditions, one in 1521, led by Francisco Chico and Juan Rodríguez de Villafuerte. Villafuerte, who would be an important encomendero on the coast in the early years of the colonial period, moved though the Costa Grande and Michoacán demanding gold. However, the Indians remained hostile, necessitating two further campaigns commanded by Cristóbal de Olid and Gonzalo de Sandoval in 1523. In that year Villafuerte founded the Villa de la Concepción de Zacatula with a population of 120 or so Spaniards.[4]

Meanwhile, in 1522 Cortés sent Pedro Alvarado with 200 Spaniards and 15,000 Mexica and Zapotec allies to conquer Tututepec, capital of the coast of Oaxaca, and the Costa Chica of Guerrero.[5] In 1524 Diego de Pardo founded San Luis Acatlán on the Costa Chica, on the frontier of Yopecingo. Nevertheless, the coast was not yet pacified. There were uprisings in 1523–1524 near Zacatula. Around 1529 the Yopes attacked Pardo as Indigenous slaves working for him were looking for gold. The Yopes mounted the most determined opposition. In 1531 Pardo, hardly an impartial source, denounced them as "disorderly, rowdy and cruel." Their rebellion continued well into the 1530s. Indigenous uprisings continued until around 1570.[6]

To the north, Juan de Cabra and Juan de Salcedo were ordered to Taxco to seek gold and copper. By 1524, tin, copper, and iron were being mined and, soon after, gold was worked in placers of the region. The first silver strike occurred in 1534.[7] According to the "Relación de Sirandaro y Guayameo," the Tierra Caliente was subdued by Captain Antonio de Carvajal, three other Spaniards, and a Black man, Juan Garrido, omitting to mention that they would have been accompanied by quantities of Indigenous allies who did most of any fighting. This band was en route to Zacatula, where Garrido tried his luck at mining and then moved on to Zumpango by 1539.[8]

Thus, in the first decade since the defeat of Tenochtitlan, the Spaniards had founded a few small Spanish towns and had initiated mining operations, even as they addressed lingering resistance. In fact, not all were Spaniards, for alongside them were tens of thousands of Indigenous allies, a few Blacks and Mulattos, and assorted Europeans, Portuguese, Flemings, and other nationalities. Some of the adventurers who entered Guerrero were active there only briefly, but others left their mark on the colonial society that emerged over the next three centuries. These Spaniards and assorted Europeans now started that long process with urgency and determination.

4.2. Colonization

The Europeans inserted themselves rapidly and decisively in the economy and societies of Guerrero. Contracts and other legal and official documents of the late 1520s and 1530s identify merchants, day laborers, cowboys, swineherds, mineowners, blacksmiths, ship's carpenters, tailors, priests, royal officials, and numerous other professions.[9] Data from sources consulted for this study provide a bird's-eye view of the Europeans active in Guerrero until ca. 1600 (table 4.1), which, however, should not be considered a complete census of the region during the period under study. Demographic and biographical information is more abundant for some regions of Guerrero than others. Moreover, the time periods covered by different series of documents vary. For example, many Spaniards who submitted *probanzas de méritos*, petitions to the Viceregal government for favors, mentioned their participation in expeditions to Zacatula, Yopecingo, or the Southern Sea.[10] The documents (contracts, powers of attorney, agreements to form a company, deeds of sale, creditor and debtor agreements, testaments, and the like) indexed by Millares Carlo and Mantecón[11] cover the periods 1525–1528, 1536–1538, and 1551–1553. During the first period the main area of activity was Zacatula's ephemeral gold-mining boom, and during the second the spectacular silver strikes in Taxco and other mines of the *Provincia de la Plata* (Silver Province).[12] Concerning the religious, the abundant data compiled by Schwaller from accounting documents of the *Real Hacienda* (Royal Treasury) begin in 1555, becoming more abundant from 1565. They record the secular clergy but not the friars of the regular orders.[13] Many documents refer in general to the presence of Spaniards in the mines of the Tierra Caliente or selling goods on the coast, but they do not identify individuals.

TABLE 4.1. ACTIVITIES OF NAMED EUROPEANS IN GUERRERO, 1521–CA. 1600							
Activity	Costa Grande	Costa Chica	Montaña	Centre	North	Tierra Caliente	Total
Attorney/granter of power of attorney	57	0	0	5	10	1	73
Conquistador/ participant in military campaigns	117	2	0	0	2	2	123
Encomendero	23	20	6	9	12	22	92
Inheritor of encomienda	18	20	12	9	20	22	101
Owner/vendor of slaves	66	2	0	5	23	4	100
Landowner and/or livestock owner	67	12	2	8	27	17	133
Mineowner	28	7	1	33	125	13	207
Official	48	21	9	20	73	33	204
Lender/debtor	61	7	0	0	20	3	91
Clergy	44	39	10	29	74	71	267
Seller of animals	7	0	0	0	0	1	8
Other activities	59	5	1	10	71	8	154
Resident of the province of Zacatula	92	-	-	-	-	-	92
TOTAL	687	135	41	128	457	197	1,645
Sources: Data from various sources consulted for this study.							

Nevertheless, important themes of the history of sixteenth-century Guerrero are apparent. Some 117 Spaniards/Europeans were involved in expeditions to Zacatula, the Costa Grande, and Yopecingo, the main objectives in the first years of colonization. Many of them were also active in Michoacán and Colima. The number of residents of Zacatula indicate that it was the base of operations for that extensive region in the 1520s and early 1530s, undoubtedly because it was an early center of mining operations (gold placers). Contracts, documents of sale, and the like identify twenty-eight mineowners and sixty-seven owners or sellers of slaves who were laboring predominantly in mines. Sixty-one individuals extended credit or were debtors. Many were both since many transactions were financed by transferring debt from the seller to the buyer. Power of attorney (fifty-seven individuals) was critical for commercial activities in a frontier settlement distant from the nascent cities in central Mexico.

However, the boom of Zacatula was fleeting.[14] By the second half of the century, the Spaniards of the coast concentrated on acquiring land for livestock and agricultural enterprises, partly to supply demand generated by Acapulco, partly for lack of other opportunities. In contrast, apart from the encomenderos, their heirs, officials, and clergy, very few Spaniards were residents on the Costa Chica. Nor do records indicate the levels of debt and powers of attorney seen in Zacatula. There were fewer mineowners.

The contrast between the coast and the Montaña is starker still. On both coasts the encomiendas were generally small scale, but nevertheless an important factor, and on the Costa Chica it was the preponderant activity. In the Montaña there were few encomenderos, but they were powerful individuals and the yields of their encomiendas were substantial. Since these Spaniards used the existing Indigenous infrastructure to manage their commercial activities, there were fewer Spanish mineowners and slavery was generally absent. Indigenous tribute supplied the gold, not Spanish-owned mines. Landownership for livestock enterprises was largely absent. Instead, livestock owners in Puebla rented or commandeered Indigenous land for grazing on a seasonal basis. Absent these kinds of activities, the lack of credit and powers of attorney is notable.[15]

The Center exhibited some similarities with the Montaña. Encomiendas were few but their yield was ample. The encomenderos were exceedingly powerful and influential, most of them members of a group of families tightly connected with one another and with the highest levels of the royal administration.[16] The Center, however, was a mining zone of some significance in the first years of colonization. The mines were mostly in Zumpango, but they were soon eclipsed by the spectacular silver strikes in Taxco. Nevertheless, some mineowners, who would later be important figures in Taxco and elsewhere in the Silver Province, began their careers in Zumpango.[17]

In the North, silver mining in Taxco and neighboring areas dominated everything. Sixty percent of the mineowners identified in Guerrero operated there. Here the encomendero was almost always a mineowner, their encomiendas supplying labor and critical resources. The figure for buyers and sellers of slaves to work in the Taxco mines (twenty-three) must be an underestimate, since resident and absentee mineowners relied on plentiful Indigenous labor and at least a few African slaves to work, for example, as overseers.[18] Indigenous labor was indispensable, most supplied by two colonial institutions, the encomienda or the *repartimiento de indios*. The former was a grant of Indians to an individual who received tribute in kind, money, or labor, in return for an obligation, frequently ignored, to ensure that the Indians were well treated and religiously observant.[19] The repartimiento was an allocation of rotational obligatory labor to an individual or a community undertaking.[20] Twenty creditors and debtors have been identified, but there were surely many more since investments in mines, refining mills, salt and mercury to process ore, mules, and other supplies required substantial capital outlays. Ownership of land was almost entirely connected to mining for constructing refining mills, housing for workers, or for grazing livestock.[21] Mineowners in the Tierra Caliente were fewer in number. Consequently, there were fewer owners and sellers of slaves, creditors, and debtors, and a smaller group of people making use of power of attorney. Here the encomienda was significant, because it supplied labor, foodstuffs, cotton clothing, salt, and other indispensable supplies for Taxco, Zacualpa, Temascaltepec, and other mines of the Silver Province. Landowners here were mostly cattlemen, their business built on the mines' insatiable demand for meat, leather, and tallow.[22]

The clergy and royal officials were two numerous groups in Guerrero as a whole. More than half the clergy officiated in the North and the Tierra Caliente for reasons that were partly demographic. The population of the Tierra Caliente was quite numerous compared, for example, to the coast. In the North the population was swelled by Indigenous laborers imported to work in the mines, as well as a large resident European population. These two regions may also have attracted priests for economic reasons. A substantial population was a source of income from fees for masses, weddings, funerals, and other services. In addition, some priests sold goods in the mines. A little less than a third of priests worked on the Costa Chica and the Costa Grande. Although the population here was relatively small, it was also dispersed, which perhaps required a reasonable number of clergy to officiate and to maintain social control. Very few secular priests are recorded in the Montaña since this was a region where the regular orders predominated.[23] Some priests stayed in a single parish for a long time. Bartolomé López officiated in Olinalá from 1576 to 1597. Juan Baez was the incumbent of Tlalcozautitlán from 1586 to 1587 and then 1590 to 1599, as was Benito Muñoz de Amarilla 1587 to 1588 and 1590 to 1599. Martín Rodríguez officiated in Taxco and Tenango for more than twenty years. Others were notably mobile. From 1569 to 1578 Francisco Hernández Negrete was the priest of Acapulco, on the Costa Grande, Huitzuco and Atenango in the North, and Zumpango in the Center.[24]

The face of royal government at the local level was the *corregidor*, whose jurisdiction was a *corregimiento*, or *alcalde mayor*, who presided over an *alcaldía mayor* (the terms were interchangeable). These officials were responsible for local justice, implementing royal edicts and the instructions of the viceroy, and collecting tribute. Their staff consisted of a *teniente*, an assistant, an *escribano*, scribe or notary, and perhaps an *alguacil*, constable. This small group of officials relied on Indigenous municipal officials to carry out most of their instructions, although Indigenous officials might also act without reference to Spanish officialdom.[25]

The distribution of officials reflected the economic interests of the Crown. Two regions, the North, a mining area, and the Costa Grande (where there was early mining in Zacatula, and from 1565 the Asian trade of Acapulco) encompassed 59 percent. Another 16 percent were in the Tierra Caliente, an important source of inputs for the mines of the Silver Province. The Costa Chica and Center each had 10 percent of officials. The populous Montaña had only 4 percent, probably because the Indigenous structure of administration required fewer Spanish officials. Officials were of varied social and economic positions. Johan Coronel, corregidor of Chilapa in the Center, 1535–1546, earned 300 pesos, while Alvar Gómez, teniente de corregidor of Tlapa, 1538–1539, was paid only 150 pesos. Other officials had interests in Guerrero other than their government roles. Antonio Castrejón, alcalde mayor of Zacatula in 1585, was a landowner on the Costa Grande. Alonso Martín de Jerez, encomendero, livestock owner, and moneylender on the Costa Grande, was corregidor of Sochiguautla in 1537 and of Zacatula in 1545. Álvaro de Castrillo, *escribano de registro* (registrar of cargo) in Acapulco in the second half of the 1590s was also an agent of Lima merchants active in the Manila trade, a clear conflict of interest. Pedro de Medinilla, administrator of the mines of Martín Cortés in Taxco, was teniente de alcalde mayor there in 1593. Several important mineowners were also officials. Gonzalo Cerezo, a mineowner in Zumpango and Taxco and encomendero of Cocula, was appointed as judge in Zumpango in 1542. Francisco Vázquez de Coronado, famous as the governor of Nueva Galicia who, in 1540, led the unsuccessful *entrada* across New Mexico to seek the fabled Seven Cities of Cíbola, was corregidor of Tlapa ca. 1544, owned a mine in Taxco, and was encomendero of Cutzamala and Tlapa. Luis de Castilla, richest of all Taxco mineowners, and one of the most influential men in New Spain, was alcalde mayor of

Taxco and Tenango, 1542–1543. An interesting case was Alonso Espinoza, who combined a portfolio of official posts with other activities. This slaveowner and mineowner in Zumpango and Taxco, proprietor of land in the Tierra Caliente, Almoloya, and Zacualpan, and of an inn in Tehuacán, was corregidor of Texupa on the Costa Grande in the 1540s, teniente de corregidor in Xalapa, Cintla, and Acatlán on the Costa Chica in 1537, and again 1539–1540, and also was corregidor of Ixcateopan 1538–1539.[26]

On the Costa Grande ninety-two resident Spaniards have been identified. The equivalent number for Taxco is thirty-one. This is surely a considerable underestimate, although Spaniards were a minority even in the mining towns. Sources identify sixteen people engaged in Taxco as merchants. For example, Antón de Carmona, a Mexico City merchant, purchased maize, beans, and *ají* (a kind of chile pepper) from the Bishop of Mexico City's tithes for sale in Taxco.[27] Tomás de Fonseca was a Portuguese Jewish merchant resident in Taxco who traded in silver and salt. Commerce depended on mule trains to transport merchandise. Fonseca owned a string of mules managed from him by the *arriero* Marco Antonio.[28] Sources identify seven named individuals who were mule drivers, mule owners, or sellers of mules. Labor shortages were a persistent problem for Taxco mineowners. Most mineworkers were Indians or African slaves. Nevertheless, the wealth of the Taxco mines attracted European laborers, such as Alonso de Almodóvar and Francisco Méndez, noted as *jornaleros sin indios ni esclavos* (day laborers without Indians or slaves) in the baptismal records of Taxco in 1590 and 1595 respectively.[29] There were also specialist laborers such as Luis Damián, head of the carpenter's guild of Taxco, and Ventura Díaz, head of the stonemason's guild.[30]

Guerrero offered many temptations to the Spaniards, other Europeans, and the occasional African who came to the region seeking recompense for their role in delivering New Spain to the Crown. In parallel with subjugating the Indigenous population, the Spaniards sought commercial opportunities. The first step was to identify resources that promised a good return. Gold was most desirable or, alternatively, silver. Cotton and cacao were also attractive. For a time, they functioned as currency, as they had in Postclassic Mesoamerica, and funded early enterprises. For example, Cortés was paid 24,000 cacaos for 900 tamemes to deliver flour to the Taxco mines.[31] Salt was important in the diet, but also to process silver ore.[32] On the other hand, resources such as shells, greenstone, and warriors' suits that had been highly valued previously now lost their value overnight. An additional attraction of Guerrero was its population, structured in polities with elites that were experienced collectors of tribute. Many rulers of the region now had several decades' experience of collecting tribute for the Mexicas and Tarascans. Their existing administrative systems could be repurposed to meet Spanish demands. Thus, it was relatively simple for the Spaniards to extract in the form of tribute the resources and labor they required.

As they sought existing resources, the Spaniards also introduced European crops and livestock at speed. By the late 1570s Indigenous communities were growing a variety of Castilian crops.[33] This intensive search for opportunities placed a high value on certain resources and overturned Mesoamerican notions of value, as table 4.2 suggests. A horse or mule was valued much more highly than an Indigenous slave. The latter was worth the equivalent of 4.7–7.6 *fanegas* of maize. Named female Indigenous slaves (probably household slaves) were worth much more than a male Indigenous slave. The sources do not explain this price differential, but both cases cited the slaves were young women, nineteen or twenty years old. Perhaps their value was related to their age and appearance.[34] African slaves were much more valuable than Indigenous slaves, probably because African slaves were less plentiful than Indigenous slaves, perhaps also because some Africans were considered suitable for supervisory tasks in mines or on cattle ranches. According to Von Mentz an African slave could cost as much as 250–350 pesos in the sixteenth and seventeenth centuries.[35]

These prices can be set in the context of the purchasing power of some officials, priests, and workers in sixteenth-century and early seventeenth-century Guerrero. These wages suggest that for most salaried Spaniards the purchase of a horse or mule was impossible. The maximum annual salary of an Indigenous worker was the equivalent of 4,600 kilograms of maize in Zacatula and 3,680 kilograms in Taxco. Since the annual consumption of maize of a family of five in pre-Hispanic Guerrero was 2,560 kilograms, a worker needed twenty-eight weeks of work in Zacatula and thirty-five weeks in Taxco to feed a family. The maize equivalent of a skilled worker's wage was 10,304–13,800 kilograms, and of a priest's salary 4,600–18,400 kilograms. However, many priests were fed by their parishioners, and some charged extra fees or engaged in commercial activities to increase their income.[36] Similarly, the salary of a corregidor was not the only source of income from the office. The friar Antonio Vázquez de Espinosa recorded the salaries of some corregidores in Guerrero in 1612, which had not changed since 1546. He observed that Tlapa and Igualapa were nevertheless "good" corregimientos,[37] suggesting that they provided other sources of income.

TABLE 4.2. THE VALUE OF CERTAIN RESOURCES IN GUERRERO AND NEW SPAIN IN THE SIXTEENTH CENTURY

Resource	Value	Place	Year
Horse	310 pesos de oro	Zacatula	1525
Pregnant mare	184 pesos de oro	Zacatula	1527
Lame horse	55 pesos de oro	Zacatula	1528
Mule	150 pesos	Mexico City	1536
Indigenous slave with tools	4 pesos de oro and 6 tomines	Zacatula	1527
Indigenous slave, branded	3 pesos	Zacatula	1527
Indigenous female slave, Leonorilla, aged 18 or 19	30 pesos de oro	Zacatula	1527
Indigenous female slave, Juana, with mining tools and clothing	100 pesos de oro	Zacatula	1528
Indigenous slave	25 pesos	Mexico City?	1537
African slave	100 pesos de oro	Mexico City	1536
Female African slave, Leonor	160 pesos de oro	Mexico City	1536
African slave	42 pesos de oro	Taxco	1536
African slave	58 pesos de oro and 3 tomines	Mexico City	1537
African slave in the mines, minimum price	210 pesos		1574
Rental of an Indigenous laborer from an encomienda	13.75 pesos	Taxco	1536
Rental of an Indigenous laborer from an encomienda	14 pesos de oro and 2 tomines	Minas de Taxco	1537
Rental of an Indigenous laborer for a year	26 pesos de oro and 6 tomines	Minas de Taxco	1537
Fanega of maize	4 reales	Zacatula	1527
Fanega of maize, beans, or chile	5 reales	Taxco	1527
Fanega of maize, beans, or chile	5 reales	Sultepec	1536

Sources: Millares Carlo and Mantecón, *Índice y extractos de los Protocolos del Archivo de Notarías*; *Cartas de Indias*, 302.

TABLE 4.3. SOME SALARIES IN GUERRERO IN THE SIXTEENTH AND EARLY SEVENTEENTH CENTURIES

Profession	Annual salary
Repartidor de indios (allocator of Indigenous labor) in the Taxco mines	2,000 pesos
Administrator, specialist, or overseer in the mines	300–700 pesos
Corregidor of Ajuchitlán 1535–1546	250–300 pesos
Corregidor of Taxco 1535–1546	200–300 pesos
Corregidor of Tlapa 1535–1546	200–300 pesos
Castellan and alcalde mayor of Acapulco 1612	200 pesos
Corregidor of Xicayán 1535–1546	200 pesos
Corregidor of Xalapa, Cintla and Acatlán 1535–1546	140–200 pesos
Corregidor of Ixcateopan 1535–1546	120–200 pesos
Teniente de corregidor of Tlapa 1535–1546	150 pesos
Teniente de corregidor of Ajuchitlán 1535–1546	120 pesos
Teniente de corregidor of Taxco 1535–1546	100–120 pesos
Teniente de corregidor of Xalapa, Cintla, and Acatlán 1535–1546	100–120 pesos
Teniente de corregidor of Ixcateopan 1535–1546	100–120 pesos
Priest, Acapulco 1577–1592	200 pesos
Priest, Ajuchitlán 1543–1599	150 pesos
Priest, Taxco 1545–1599	116–180 pesos
Priest, Xicayán 1552–1597	100–150 pesos
Priest, Zirándaro 1575–1599	150 pesos
Priest, Ixcateopan 1550–1599	69–118 pesos
Priest, Atenango and Ixcateopan 1559–1599	50–100 pesos
Chaplaincy	75–125 pesos
Skilled worker (e.g., carpenter, blacksmith) in the mines	112–150 pesos
Indigenous repartimiento worker in the mines working 50 weeks	50 pesos

Sources: Schwaller, *Partidos y párrocos*; Von Mentz, *Señoríos indígenas*, 321–23; Ruiz Medrano, *Reshaping New Spain*, 265–97; Vázquez de Espinosa, *Compendio y descripción de las Indias Occidentales*, 266–70.

Thus, over the first eight decades of the colonial period, a very small number of Europeans relative to the Indigenous population participated in the creation of a new colonial society. The numbers of the newcomers and activities they engaged in varied by region. Exactly how these variations played out is one of the major themes of this study. Since Zacatula and the Costa Grande were the first destinations of substantial numbers of outsiders, a brief account of how some of these newcomers operated on the coast demonstrates the modus operandi of the earliest pobladores (settlers).

TABLE 4.4. INDIVIDUALS MENTIONED MORE THAN ONCE IN LEGAL DOCUMENTS CONCERNING ZACATULA, 1525, 1527, 1528

Individuals	Mentions	Activities	Notes
Jerez, Alonso Martín de	10	Creditor, attorney, granter of power of attorney, purchaser, employer	Encomendero, landowner, and official, vecino of Zacatula
Llerena, Gonzalo de	8	Creditor, debtor, purchaser, dowry	Tailor, vecino of Zacatula
Martínez, Francisco	6	Creditor, attorney	Priest and vecino in Zacatula
García Moreno, Pedro	5	Creditor, attorney	Merchant, slaveowner, vecino of Mexico City
Sánchez, Antón	5	Attorney, granter of power of attorney, purchaser, debtor	Carpenter, encomendero, mineowner, official
Aguilar [y Córdoba], Alonso de	4	Granter of power of attorney, debtor	Encomendero in the Montaña, mineowner, landowner, vecino of Zacatula
Cartagena, Juan de	4	Attorney, granter of power of attorney, creditor, debtor	Slaveowner, vecino of Zacatula
Gallego, Hernando	4	Granter of power of attorney, creditor, purchaser	Slaveowner, mineowner, vendor, vecino of Zacatula
García, Alonso	4	Attorney, granter of power of attorney, creditor, debtor	Vecino of Zacatula
Oliveros, Francisco de	4	Attorney, debtor	Vecino of Mexico City
Rodríguez de Zacatula, Francisco	4	Granter of power of attorney, purchaser, vendor	Encomendero, slaveowner, vecino of Zacatula
Dávila, Alonso	4	Granter of power of attorney, attorney	Slaveowner, landowner, encomendero in Michoacán, vecino of Mexico City
López, Gonzalo	4	Attorney, debtor, purchaser	Slaveowner, vecino of Mexico City
Gómez, Juan	3	Debtor, vendor	Slaveowner, sale of animals, vecino of Zacatula
Pedro López	3	Muleteer, attorney, creditor, granter of power of attorney	
Muela, Diego de la	3	Attorney, purchaser	Slaveowner, mineowner
Pérez, Juan	3	Granter of power of attorney, creditor, purchaser	Slaveowner, vecino of Mexico City
Rodríguez de Villafuerte, Juan	3	Granter of power of attorney, attorney, debtor	Conquistador, owner of animals, slaveowner, encomendero on the Costa Grande, mineowner in Centre of Guerrero vecino of Zacatula
Barahona, Martín de	2	Debtor, vendor	Slaveowner
García, Miguel	2	Attorney	Vecino of Zacatula
García, Ruy	2	Attorney, vendor	Merchant, vendor of slaves
Hernández, Cristóbal	2	Attorney, creditor	Miner, landowner, vecino of Zacatula
Jiménez, García	2	Debtor	Owner of animals
Jiménez, Martín	2	Slaveowner	Mineowner
López, Martín	2	Granter of power of attorney, vendor	Vecino of Mexico City
López Galbito, Pedro	2	Creditor	Agent of Zacatula mineowners Andrés de Monjarrás and Blasco Hernández
Medel, Hernando	2	Attorney, creditor	
Morón, Alonso	2	Granter of power of attorney, debtor	Slaveowner, mineowner, vecino of Zacatula
Juan Pérez	2	Granter of power of attorney, creditor, purchaser	Slaveowner, vecino of Mexico City
Rodas, Juan de	2	Attorney, debtor	Vecino of Zacatula
Torres, Hernando de	2	Formed company, employer	Slaveowner, mineowner
Vargas, Juan de	2	Attorney, vendor	Slaveowner, merchant

Source: Millares and Mantecón, eds., *Índice y extractos de los Protocolos del Archivo de Notarías*, vol. 1.

4.3. Commerce and Colonization in Practice: A Case Study of Zacatula

The commercial arm of colonization was not far behind the military, as a sample of eighty-two legal documents relating to commercial transactions in Zacatula demonstrates. Six were signed in 1525, thirty-one in 1527, and forty-five in 1528. Thus, Spanish commercial activities on the coast began only four years after the fall of Tenochtitlan and intensified in 1527 and 1528. Forty-three of the documents concern debts (many creditors were also debtors); forty-one granted powers of attorney; twenty-seven referred to a sale; fifteen mentioned individuals who owned slaves; thirteen concerned mining enterprises, of which eight involved the formation of companies. The documents name 116 individuals. Thirty-two individuals are named in several documents. Table 4.4 summarizes their activities.

Many transactions involved debts. In 1525 Juan Núñez, a *vecino* of Tenustitán, as Mexico City was referred to at that time, appointed Alonso Martín de Jerez to collect from Alonso Morón, a vecino of Zacatula, 66 gold pesos and six *tomines*. Jerez next appears in eight documents registered in four months in 1528. The Tenustitán merchant Cristóbal Ruiz commissioned Jerez to collect from Alonso de Aguilar y Córdoba, a mineowner in Ayoteco (modern Puebla), Chilapa, and Yopecingo, and encomendero of Olinalá and Papalutla in the Montaña, 100 gold pesos and four tomines. Jerez also loaned money: 180 gold pesos to Pedro Hernández, a Zacatula carpenter; to García Jiménez 55 pesos, for a lame horse; the substantial sum of 216 pesos to Bartolomé Quemado; and to Diego Martín 80 pesos. Jerez appointed Juan Rodríguez de Villafranca and Juan Méndez, a *hortelano* (gardener), attorneys to collect Quemado and Martín's debts. Jerez also owed money; for example, 125 pesos to Rodríguez de Villafranca, which he would settle by collecting Quemado's debt. Jerez similarly cleared a debt of 55 pesos owed to Hernán Pérez de Bocanegra by appointing him attorney to collect García Jiménez's debt.[38]

Debts were frequently discharged by appointing a creditor to collect a debt owed to the debtor. This method of financing commercial activities depended on trusted networks of friendships and commercial relations, especially when a debtor was in Zacatula, 90 leagues (414 kilometers) distant from Mexico City. Such relationships also facilitated noncommercial arrangements. In 1528 Jerez paid Juan de Burgos, encomendero of Cutzamala in Tierra Caliente and of Teutenango in the valley of

Toluca, and a trader in slaves and horses, to free Alonso de Torres, who was imprisoned for an unpaid debt.[39] Jerez's other commercial interests were his encomienda, buying and selling horses, and raising pigs, cows, and sheep, which required Spanish labor. He hired three Spaniards in 1528. García de la Peña was employed to care for pigs purchased a month earlier from Bartolomé de Morales. De la Peña was paid in kind with 120 sows and 3 boars. Gonzalo de San Martín guarded Jerez's cows and sheep in return for lodging and a share of the animals, while Francisco Sánchez worked on Jerez's encomienda.[40] Jerez clearly prospered quickly in Zacatula, his enterprise built on his encomienda, credit, and livestock.

Zacatula's priest, Francisco Martínez, also had commercial interests. No information about his salary survives, but later in the century the incumbent of Zacatula earned 100–200 pesos. Martínez was trusted by Spaniards with interests in Zacatula. In 1525 Juan Núñez, a vecino of Tenustitán, appointed him attorney to collect from Alonso Morón a debt of 66 gold pesos and 6 tomines, probably the debt Núñez had owed to Jerez. Two years later Martínez became Morón's attorney to settle all his disputes. Shortly afterward, Alonso de Aguilar y Córdoba appointed the cleric as his general representative to look after his interests. A month later Catalina Martín entrusted Martínez and the Michoacán encomendero Alonso Dávila to recover the property of her deceased son Francisco de Robledo. Martínez was quite wealthy in his own right. In October 1527 he loaned the sizeable sum of 685 gold pesos to Francisco de Oliveros, a resident of Tenustitán, and 150 pesos to the Zacatula tailor Gonzalo de Llerena.[41] Thus, in a single year Martínez loaned sums equivalent to several years' salary. His debtor Llerena relied heavily on debt. In 1527 he also owed 52 pesos to Diego Hernández, 50 pesos to *maestre* (ship's master) Martín of Tenustitán, and, in 1528, 15 pesos and 6 tomines to Pedro de Calvo of Tenustitán. Llerena's debts were more than double the annual salary of a priest.[42]

Zacatula attracted tradespeople such as carpenters and blacksmiths, whose skills were required in the shipyard and the mines. In 1525 Antón Sánchez, encomendero and ship carpenter, borrowed 30 gold pesos from Miguel Rodríguez de Guadalupe. Sánchez was also a lender, since in 1527 he and his partner, Hernando Gallego, appointed the mineowner Diego de la Muela to collect their debts. In 1528 Sánchez and blacksmith Pedro Hernández (a debtor of Alonso Martín de Jerez) borrowed an unspecified sum from Francisco de Almansa of Tenustitán, who transferred the debt to Alonso García. Hernández was the general representative of Diego de Correas, encomendero of Mitla, near Zacatula. Another blacksmith, Hernán Martín, was Hernández's attorney in Tenustitán.[43] Again, crisscrossing relations of creditor-debtor-attorney lubricated the wheels of commerce.

A certain Pedro López is an early example of a character who would be a fundamental participant in Mexican society and commerce for centuries to come: the arriero (muleteer). In 1528 López was employed by Ruy García and Juan de Vargas to transport from Tenustitán to Zacatula merchandise to the value of 353 pesos. López transported forty-six male and two female Indian slaves branded on their faces with his name and a cross. He also carried thirty-two *arrobas* of wine in *botijos* (ceramic vessels used to transport liquids), five of vinegar, three of olive oil, and one of raisins. Other goods were a sword, a dagger, seven hundred iron nails, two chains with padlocks to shackle the slaves, some breeches, a doublet, four cheeses, four strings of garlic, and three packs of playing cards.[44] Thus, before the end of the decade, market demand in Zacatula called for slaves, items of the Spanish diet and clothing, and metalwork that was useful for shipbuilding or for mining operations.

The two principal drivers of these activities were gold placer mining in the coastal rivers and livestock, which will be addressed later in this study. However, a few of the features of the activities outlined in this small sample would become characteristic of commercial activities throughout Guerrero and, more widely, in New Spain: Indigenous labor, enslaved and free, the rapid introduction of European livestock, networks of personal contacts, the importance of credit, and the use of devices such as power of attorney to transact as securely as possible. If this commercial arm of colonization quickly made itself felt in Guerrero, the spiritual arm of the Catholic church was not far behind, as the following discussion demonstrates.

4.4. Evangelization

Since the priest Francisco Martínez is documented as commercially active in Zacatula as early as 1525, the Catholic church had some presence on the coast only a few years after the defeat of the Mexicas.[45] A secular priest, *bachiller* Cristóbal Carrasco, officiated in San Luis during the 1520s until rebellious Yopes drove the Spanish population out of town in 1532.[46] Moreover, the Indians of Noxtepec started building their church perhaps as early as 1521, finishing it in 1533.⁴⁷ However, the first major campaigns of evangelization, conducted by the regular orders, did not begin until the 1530s. Juan de Grijalva's history of the Augustinian order in New Spain tells how Tlapa and Chilapa, considered to be rugged and remote provinces still in the depth of their errors, were assigned to the Augustinians by the Audiencia. Fray Jerónimo de S. Esteban and Fray Jorge de Ávila, chosen to undertake the spiritual conquest,⁴⁸ arrived in San Luis (de los Yopes, or perhaps San Luis Acatlán, both Spanish foundations) in 1531, Chilapa and Olinalá in 1533, Huamuxtitlán in 1534, and Tlapa in 1535. They founded monasteries in existing cabeceras (e.g., in Tlapa, Atlixtac, Totomixtlahuaca, and Chilapa), apart from Alcozauca, a mere estancia. In 1537 an earthquake destroyed the monastery in Chilapa, because, according to prophecy, Father Coruña had organized (perhaps forced) gangs of Indigenous labor to connect the monastery to the royal road by a causeway.⁴⁹ For a time the Augustinians also ministered in Igualapa on the Costa Chica.⁵⁰ Thus, the Augustinians had a substantial influence in the Montaña in competition with the secular clergy. Consequently, the numbers of secular priests in the Montaña were lower than in other areas of Guerrero.⁵¹

In the 1530s and 1540s the Dominicans evangelized Tututepec on the coast of Oaxaca and Ometepec on the Costa Chica of Guerrero.⁵² In the late 1530s the Franciscan Fray Pedro de Garrovillas was the first member of the religious orders to minister on the Costa Grande and the highlands behind it. The order established a monastery in Acapulco, under the jurisdiction of Michoacán.⁵³ In 1526 Franciscans based in Cuernavaca visited Taxco, Pilcaya, Noxtepec, Ixcateopan, and Iguala. In 1533 the Augustinians evangelized in the Tierra Caliente. In Tetela del Río, the sixteenth-century church of Santa María de la Asunción, whose facade design is characteristic of Augustinian churches, was decorated with two medallions of Franciscan design. Thus, the faithful of Tetela acknowledged the role of the two orders in their region.⁵⁴

While the regular orders predominated in the first phase of evangelization, from the 1540s to 1600 the accounts of *partidos* (parishes) funded by the royal treasury, rather than by encomenderos, recorded twenty-one parishes in which secular priests officiated, seven in the Tierra Caliente, five in the North, five on the Costa Grande, two on the Costa Chica, and only one in the Montaña and one in the Center,⁵⁵ both areas where the Augustinians were dominant. Two reports about priests and parishes in the Tierra Caliente and the North by archbishops of Mexico,

Don Fray Alonso Montúfar in 1570[56] and Don Pedro de Moya y Contreras in 1575,[57] provide information about the caliber of individual clerics, the logistics of ministering to a large parish, and the abuses committed by some priests whose behavior ranged from poor to appalling.

An example of a particularly large parish was Teloloapan in Tierra Caliente, a *cabecera de doctrina* (head town of a parish) consisting of five other cabeceras, each with their *barrios*, and a total of thirty-two sujetos. In the five decades following the Spanish invasion, the Indians of the parish had undertaken a substantial church building program, resulting in the construction of forty churches, although Priest Diego García de Almaráz complained that only the church in Teloloapan had any of the customary ornaments. Teloloapan had also built a hospital, which the priest described as "very poor," that owned an estancia (ranch) with thirty sheep. Despite the priest's bad opinion of his parish churches, his Indigenous faithful must have expended a considerable amount of labor to build new places of worship, in addition to their tribute obligations and providing labor for the mines. The tributary population was 2,199. The majority spoke Chontal, others Nahuatl, Izcuca, and Mazateca. Almaráz could hear confession only in Nahuatl. However, many speakers of other languages had a basic command of Nahuatl, which enabled 1,688 to take confession. Indigenous assistants taught the parishioners Christian doctrine, assembled them for confession, and interpreted Almaráz's sermons. There were only a few non-Indigenous residents: a mineowner, his Spanish servant, and some Blacks (presumably slaves).[58]

The large parish of Tepecoacuilco in the North, an important encomienda and commercial center, had an adult population of 5,377. Father Joan Martínez reported that there were thirty-six estancias, each of which had a church. Since there would also have been a church in Tepecoacuilco, the flock ministered to by Martínez had also been busy building churches. Seven of the sujetos were a league (4.6 kilometers) or less from Tepecoacuilco, twelve were more than 10 leagues (46 kilometers) away. The closest sujeto was half a league (2.3 kilometers) distant, the furthest 15 leagues (69 kilometers). In each sujeto an alguacil and a *tequitato* ensured that parishioners attended church on Sundays and holidays. Five languages were spoken: Nahuatl, Chontal, Matlame, Tuzteca, and Texome. Those who could not speak Nahuatl could not take confession. Martínez's parish included the mines of Techichiquilco, where three Spaniards and eleven Blacks lived, the only non-Indigenous residents. The priest's salary was 210 pesos.[59]

The incumbent of Iguala and Cocula, Alonso de Maldonado, had 5,457 parishioners, one third of whom spoke Chontal, the remainder Nahuatl. In the twelve sujetos, only Chontal was spoken, but the Chontals understood sufficient Nahuatl to take confession because they spoke Nahuatl in the tianguis. Four or five Spaniards lived in Iguala, two of them married. The parishioners had built a hospital (now ruined), a school for the sons of the principales and some of the *macehuales* in Iguala, twelve churches in the sujetos, and presumably two more in Iguala and Cocula. Again, Indigenous officials were indispensable. In each sujeto two alguaciles and three or four *tepixqui* called the people to church, but they attended only if threatened with punishment. Maldonado earned 210 pesos, 150 paid by the Crown, 60 by the encomendera of Cocula.[60]

Taxco, the most important parish in the North because of its mining wealth, had four priests: Antonio Rivas, Alonso de Torquemada, Martin Rodriguez, and Joan de Tovar, who were responsible for the three *reales de minas* and their barrios, six cabeceras, and forty-four sujetos. The priests, who shared a salary of 470 pesos, ministered to 8,849 Indians, of whom 2,344 were in the reales, where 616 African slaves and 121 Spaniards also lived. This was the largest concentration of non-Indigenous population in Guerrero. There was one church and thirty-three chapels in the reales, and forty-five churches in the cabeceras and sujetos. In five decades, therefore, the Indigenous parishioners had built seventy-eight churches and chapels, a very substantial commitment of labor. Although this parish had the largest number of priests in all of Guerrero, the fathers still depended on Indigenous officials. The clerics complained that this was not a satisfactory way to manage church affairs, since the Indigenous officials "are tyrants and rob the poor *macehuales*, imposing on them excessive costs and monetary fines, to fund their drinking sessions, which are excessive, and an offence before God."[61] As Taylor's classic study notes, such accusations were common, underlining a general Spanish concern with Indigenous drunkenness, which reflected different cultural attitudes to drinking. Spaniards drank wine with meals and avoided obvious inebriation, while Indians drank on appropriate occasions only, but then perhaps to stupor.[62]

This sample of parishes in the Tierra Caliente and the North illustrates several facets of the activities of the secular clergy in sixteenth-century Guerrero. Parishes were large, their Indigenous population dispersed and multilingual. Priests were too few, even in Taxco, to minister effectively to the Indigenous population. Moreover, the priests lacked the languages to preach to and hear confession from those Indians who did not speak Nahuatl. Therefore, they relied heavily on Indigenous assistants, which created opportunities to join the ranks of village officialdom, as we will discover when we come to the Indigenous response to Spanish colonization. Moreover, since the teaching of the doctrine was spread very thinly, Indigenous understanding of the faith may have been skin deep, as the reluctance of parishioners of Iguala and Cocula to attend church suggests. Their priest, Alonso Maldonado, not a man who liked his parishioners, claimed that they were lazy and had to be forced to attend church in the cabecera de doctrina, especially (not unreasonably, one suspects) at sowing and harvest times.[63]

Haskett's study of the priests of the Cuernavaca and Taxco regions notes that the Nahuas had venerated their priesthood in precontact times and were predisposed to transfer this respect to the Spanish clergy. While many Spanish priests were responsible and benevolent, others levied excessive charges, demanded payments or services to which they were not entitled, or mistreated Indians. Such behavior scandalized Indigenous people, especially the nobility, since they expected priests to match the standards of personal propriety that had generally characterized the precontact priesthood.[64] The reports of the two archbishops tell us of priests who earned the respect of their flock but are equally frank about those whose character and conduct did not merit the approval of their parishioners. Archbishop Moya y Contreras reported, for example, that Martín Rodríguez of Taxco spoke Nahuatl and "is one of the best priests of this archbishopric," and that his colleague Joan de Ayllon spoke both Otomí and Nahuatl and gave "a good account of himself." Diego Núñez de Cabrera in Tetipac was an honest man who set a good example. Less satisfactory were Pedro Ynfante of Iguala, "a stupid man who knows little," and Hieronimo de Villanueva in Noxtepec, who had been known to be involved with women but now seemed to be living alone and honestly. Joan Pardo de Herrera, priest of Zumpango, spoke adequate Nahuatl, but treated his Indigenous parishioners harshly and was avaricious.[65]

A dramatic example of a priest abusing his authority to ill-treat the Indigenous population is the case of Gaspar de Tejeda, priest of Tlalcozautitlán, 1568–1570. Tejeda insisted that the Indians of Mezquitlán attend mass in Tlalcozautitlán, a round trip of 10 leagues (46 kilometers). The faithful of Mezquitlán complained to the Audiencia in Mexico City, which instructed the local corregidor Diego Díaz del Castillo, the illegitimate son of the conquistador Bernal Díaz del Castillo, to investigate. Diego instructed his interpreter and scribe, Juan de la Calle, a young Mestizo, to inform the people of Mezquitlán that they need not travel to mass nor pay fees to the priest. Tejeda promptly imprisoned de la Calle and the principales of Mezquitlán to compel them to denounce Díaz del Castillo to the Inquisition. Unfortunately for Tejeda, when the case came to court his witnesses testified that he had forced them to bear false witness. The Indians complained that Tejeda compelled them to spin cotton without paying them. It also emerged that Tejeda had brought previous cases against Spaniards before the Inquisition in Tlaxcala and Oaxaca. In both cases the Inquisition ruled against the priest.[66]

Tejeda's profiteering at the expense of his parishioners was not unique. Another notable example was García de Almaráz of Teloloapan, who testified on Tejeda's behalf, and who, according to Moya y Contreras, "is held to be greedy and does not want to stay in this land, but to return home, when he can get the means."[67] According to Díaz del Castillo, Almaráz, who "resembles a huckster rather than a priest," committed a number of abuses, such as demanding a fee for confession, obliging the Indians to buy maize and poor quality communion wine from him at inflated prices, and traded in a variety of goods, such as *mantas*, cacao, cheese, knives, shoes, and horses.[68]

Some priests amassed substantial wealth. One such was Garci Rodríguez, who had substantial mining interests. Rodríguez had been the incumbent of Teloloapan in 1559. From 1560 to 1566 and again 1578 to1600, he was in Taxco.[69] By 1575, aged fifty-five, he had been in New Spain for forty years. His archbishop reported that "he knows little grammar, speaks Nahuatl . . . is rich and has no benefice; he sets a good example, although somewhat avaricious."[70] By 1542 he was already a sufficiently prominent mineowner to sign a petition protesting the mining ordinances issued by Lorenzo de Tejada.[71] Rodríguez operated a mining company with several associates and in 1580 was allocated Indigenous labor to build houses and a refining mill. The construction caused a dispute with two Indigenous pueblos, Noxtepec and Tetipac. The mineowners won the case, pulling strings in Mexico City and alleging that the properties were the private property of the priest.[72]

Between December 22, 1610, and February 6, 1611, the bishop of Tlaxcala, Fray Alonso de la Mota y Escobar, visited twenty-six parishes in the Costa Chica, Montaña, and Center, to confirm 5,748 adults who had received baptism but had not yet been confirmed.[73] His report touches on some of the themes observed in the North and Tierra Caliente

Figure 29. The church of Ahuatepec Pueblo, near Chiepetlán, in the Montaña, photographed in 2010. The church is of a simple design and lacks the bell tower that was a symbol of municipal prestige to which pueblos aspired. Photograph courtesy of Alejandro Morales.

by Archbishops Montúfar and Moya y Contreras such as the variable quality of the clergy, abuses of clerical authority, and priests engaged in commercial activities. However, de la Mota y Escobar also commented on aspects of Indigenous society and religious observance in the region.

Here the priests were also spread thin over large parishes. For example, the bishop described the journey from Altixtac to Zapotitlán de Tablas as an "appalling six leagues" (28 kilometers) and the same distance from Ayutla to Chacaltitlan as "foul." To the problem of distance and bad roads was added the sheer number of parishioners. For example, Mota y Escobar confirmed 643 in Zitlala and 902 in Olinalá, both in a single day. It is not surprising that the Indians' understanding of and commitment to the faith was variable and sometimes shallow. While Fray Alonso considered that the congregation of San Luis had been taught their doctrine well, in Tlacoapa the people were uncouth, badly instructed, and

Figure 30. The ruined church of San Pedro Petlacala in the Montaña, with its restored bell tower, photographed in 2010. The church would once have been of a more elaborate design than the church of Ahuatepec. Photograph courtesy of Alejandro Morales.

flatly refused to be confirmed. The parishioners of Zapotitlán de Tablas similarly refused confirmation, even when the bishop excused them the substantial expense of providing candles.[74]

As to the quality of the religious, the secular priest of Olinalá was good and the Indians "admirable and well dressed." In San Luis (de los Yopes), where the bishop preached the mystery of the Epiphany, he received a good report of the priest. However, in Huamuxtitlán the parish priest obliged the Indians to supply his meals, which was not allowed, and he did not speak Nahuatl. The Indians rejoiced when the bishop replaced the incumbent with a Nahuatl speaker and told them they need not feed their priest. In Mochitlán the Indians complained about their priest and asked for the return of Father Hernando Carreño. The priest of Tixtla was accused of overcharging. The bishop ordered him to repay the excess charges and gave the Indians the scale of fees. Here, too, the Indians requested the return of Carreño, who had been suspended but had paid his penalty. The bishop admonished the priest of Apango regarding "a certain woman concerning with whom he has a bad reputation."[75]

The Asian trade in Acapulco was the commercial temptation in this region. On December 22, 1610, Mota y Escobar found that the Augustinian friars of Alcozauca had gone to Acapulco, leaving their flock with no priest. The bishop hinted darkly "but this is the least of the harm they do." The friar of Tlapa was also in Acapulco trading in cochineal and Asian goods. Worse still, the friar provided young girls to the Indian Domingo de Tovar, a man considered idolatrous and wicked who spent tribute money on himself. The friar of the monastery in Totomixtlahuaca was also absent in Acapulco. The bishop stated that it was not this friar's duty to sell China trade merchandise at immoderate prices to the Indians nor to buy cochineal from them at less than its real value. Not all Augustinians profited from the Acapulco trade, since the incumbent of Quechultenango was so poor that the bishop declined to stay there to spare the father the expense of feeding him. However, the friars were not alone in profiting from the Acapulco trade, since "The Indians [of Tixtla] are rich because they sell all they can raise, harvest and sow at very good prices, both to the passengers and to the muleteers who travel to and from the port." Similarly, the people of Apango lived well from the sale of maize, poultry, fruit, and hiring horses to drovers en route to Acapulco.[76]

The strong presence of Augustinians was but one of the differences that distinguished the Costa Chica from other regions. In this region, the epidemics of the sixteenth century and the importation of slaves had changed the demography. For example, in Ayutla the bishop preached to Spaniards, Mestizos, and Mulattos, as well as Indians and "confirmed 570 children of God of all colors." In contrast, he met only one Black inland, in Tixtla. In San Luis (de los Yopes) the Indians were well-to-do *ladinos* (Spanish speakers), most of whom cultivated cacao and cotton. Mota y Escobar joined in a fiesta, giving the mortal blow to a bull. The cacique of San Luis Acatlán, Don Domingo de los Ángeles, also spoke Spanish. He treated the bishop with elaborate courtesy "in the manner of the caciques of old," offering him a gift of a cotton bed canopy made by his daughters and a little cacao. With great modesty, he beseeched Fray Alonso not to offend him by refusing a humble gift. The bishop reciprocated with gifts of a fine shirt, some conserves, and five cornelians.[77] Don Domingo's manner recalls the formal exchange of gifts described in the narratives of precontact migration to the Montaña.[78] Two days later, the impoverished cacique of Sochitonala, not to be outdone, offered another bed canopy and a larger quantity of cacao. The bishop thanked him but declined the generous gift.[79]

The early colonial economy and social control of Indigenous labor and tribute rested to a great extent on three pillars: the encomienda, which supplied resources and labor; royal ordinances that sought to regulate labor, commerce, and injurious activities; and the church, whose duty was to evangelize and discipline the Indigenous population. However, Louise Burkhart's studies of evangelization have demonstrated that the Spanish friars relied on Indigenous assistants to help them communicate Christian concepts, and to cast Christian rhetoric in Nahua conceptual and linguistic terms. Consequently, "despite the incorporation of many Christian elements, the belief system of the majority of Nahuas remained essentially untouched."[80] Thus, it is not surprising that elements of what Spanish clerics might have considered idolatry persisted in colonial Indigenous Christianity.

Hernando Ruiz de Alarcón's treatise of 1613–1629 confirms that an array of Indigenous religious practices and rites persisted in Guerrero, despite a century of preaching the Gospel. For example, *ololiuhqui*, a hallucinogenic plant, was still taken to give Indians the powers of the *nahualli*, who could transform into an animal, such as an eagle, snake, or caiman. Ruiz de Alarcón identified a repertoire of spells used, for example, to sleep well, collect honey, hunt animals, or recover from illness. Some spells had been committed to alphabetic writing, thus preserving pre-Hispanic beliefs with the help of a new European (Christian) technology. The zealous priest's reports of similarities between Christian beliefs and Indigenous practices confirm Burkhart's insights that Christian practice was absorbed into a Nahua cultural framework. For example, the Indians had a precontact habit of saying a prayer similar to compline at bedtime. Indians had visions in which they saw Indigenous figures but also the Virgin Mary or God. Even Indigenous church officials retained pre-Hispanic beliefs and practices. For example, Miguel de Escobar, cantor of Tlaxmalac, kept hidden in his home three idols inherited from his ancestors. Ruiz de Alarcón was also concerned that Indigenous beliefs and practices were contaminating other racial groups. In the North there were "many cattle ranches where many Mulattos, Indians and base individuals" were carrying with them a certain root as protection against being injured by bulls. Spaniards were accused of serious crimes on the grounds of allegations based on Indigenous beliefs.[81]

Indigenous individuals found guilty of prohibited religious beliefs were not considered *gente de razón* and were, therefore, exempt from the severe punishments meted out to Spaniards and other "people of reason" by the Inquisition. A principal preoccupation of the judgements of the Inquisition 1563–1597 was to find and punish Jews who were considered to be heretics. This was the crime for which Tomás de Fonseca Castellanos, a Portuguese merchant and mineowner in Taxco and Oaxaca and cousin of the Portuguese mineowner Jorge de Almeida, was tortured and tried. Two judges voted to sentence him to attend mass, foreswear the Jewish faith, and pay a fine of 300 pesos, but the third believed he should be set free. In 1596 Fonseca was arrested again with three Portuguese merchants in Tlalpujahua, a mining town. Fonseca was tortured again, and all his assets were confiscated. A less wealthy Taxco resident accused of being a Jew was the mule driver Gonzalo Hernández de Hermosilla. His punishment was two hundred lashes and five years in the royal galleons. In 1574 Beatriz Hernández, a vecina of Taxco, was declared guilty of bigamy and of being a Jew. She received two hundred lashes and was exiled from New Spain for six years.[82]

Even the most prominent families could be tainted by rumors of Judaism. Luis Carvajal el Mozo was the nephew of Luis de Carvajal y la Cueva, el Viejo, governor of the province of Pánuco. Accused of Jewish practices, Luis sought refuge in his uncle's distant home, and later in the residence of Jorge de Almeida, a merchant and owner, with his brother-in-law Antonio Díaz de Cáceres of a mine and a refining mill in Taxco. However, Luis was eventually arrested and, under torture, denounced many others as Jews. He was also accused of defrauding the Crown of taxes due on silver mined in Taxco. His cousin Almeida prudently fled to Spain in 1591. Fate was less kind to Luis: He was executed with members of his family in Mexico City in 1596.[83]

Judaism was not the only heretical threat to authority in unruly Taxco. In 1564 the Englishman Guillermo Calens was accused of Lutheranism, sentenced to two hundred lashes, to wear distinctive penitential clothing, and to serve ten years in the galleons. Another Englishman accused of Lutheranism, Juan Gre, was sentenced to only eight years in the galleons, but one judge suspected that Gre had not understood the charges and ordered that he be tortured again. His sentence was later confirmed. Even priests could be accused by the Inquisition. In 1563 Father Diego de Soria of Taxco was tried but absolved of all charges.[84] Soria was subsequently judged by his archbishop to be a bad, avaricious priest.[85] Almost all the Inquisition's judgements related to Guerrero in the sixteenth century concerned Taxco. Clearly, heretical beliefs and transgressive behaviors were considered a threat to the wealth generated by the mines. A few judgements concerned Acapulco, the other significant economic pole of the region. Hernando Carreño, the priest suspended from his duties in Mochitlán and Tixtla in 1611,[86] was cleared of charges against him in Acapulco in 1585.[87] A Mulatto couple in the port, Mariana and Antón Hernández, were convicted of bigamy in 1594.[88] In 1592 the commissary of the Inquisition in the port seized goods from the cargo owned by the Portuguese *converso* Antonio Díaz de Cáceres, under a judgement of the Inquisition in Mexico City.[89]

4.5. Invasion, Colonization, and Evangelization: Conclusions

With the exception of the stubborn resistance of the Yopes, which lasted a decade or more, organized military opposition to the Spaniards and their Indigenous allies evaporated quite quickly. No doubt there were smaller local acts of defiance that were not documented. Although the invaders moved quickly through the regions of Guerrero, Spanish complaints about the difficult terrain suggest that there must have been many places that they simply passed by or could not reach. Resistance could be as simple as lying low or getting out of the way.

Military penetration was accompanied by Europeans seeking opportunities for enrichment, as they moved quickly into areas that promised rewards. The presence of the newcomers varied in the different regions of Guerrero. Royal officials and clergy were much more numerous in the mining areas of the North and the nearby Tierra Caliente. There were more encomenderos on the Costa Grande, Costa Chica, and Tierra Caliente than in other parts of Guerrero, although, as we shall see, the richest encomiendas in other areas were controlled by fewer powerful individuals.[90] Mineowning, and related activities, of course, were concentrated in the North around Taxco. As early as the mid-1520s, the first target was gold mining in the Zacatula region. The coastal gold boom would prove to be short lived, but several features of the colonial modus operandi would be essayed here and implemented later in other parts of the region, such as an intense demand for labor, the importance of credit, networks of personal relations, legal devices such as powers of attorney to facilitate dealings, and the significant role of livestock.

The representative of colonization with whom the Indigenous peoples of Guerrero would perhaps have most prolonged contact from the 1530s onward were the friars and secular priests. The church and its furnishings replaced the temple and the symbols of precontact religious beliefs and practices, although the "idols" did not entirely disappear, and the Indians fashioned their own version of the Catholic faith from the teachings of their clergy. The faith was not dispensed only, or perhaps principally, by European priests, but by Indigenous church officials. Indeed, despite the rapid introduction of new institutions, a new ordering of society, and a devastating series of epidemics that in extreme cases wiped out entire communities, the new colonial society was not solely the results of European impositions, but by means of innumerable acts, the Indigenous communities of Guerrero themselves participated in the making of a new society and helped to determine the outcomes.

CHAPTER FIVE

Power, Adaptation, Resistance, and New Institutions

The Response of the Indigenous Communities of Guerrero, 1521–ca. 1600

The population units with which the incoming Spaniards had to transact were not uniform, since the size and political-administrative organization of Guerrero's Indigenous polities was variable. The Chontal kingdoms, as the Spaniards termed them, of the North and Tierra Caliente were many and small. They spoke the same language and had certain shared beliefs and cultural practices, but they did not have a linguistic-ethnic solidarity and frequently went to war with other Chontal polities.[1] Pre-Hispanic lineage continued to be a source of authority and pride after the Spanish invasion. For example, Don Diego Osorio, the Chontal governor of San Simón Oztuma in 1575, traced his ancestry back to Amalpilli, who had ruled the community before 1460.[2] A much larger and more complex polity in the Montaña, Tlapa-Tlachinollan, was governed by lineages that can be documented as far back as 1300.[3] Later, Spanish administrative-political arrangements would closely reflect the structure of the Tlapa-Tlachinollan polity.

The Spaniards divided the population of New Spain into categories of people (known as *castas*) whose obligations and rights differed. The Indigenous inhabitants became "Indians." However, they did not regard themselves as a homogenous category. The most obvious aspect of their heterogeneity was the number of languages they spoke, traces of migrations that had been a feature of Mesoamerican Guerrero for many centuries.[4] For many communities the migration that was the origin of their settlement and the circumstances of its foundation were the basis of their identity and sense of community. Indigenous identity was closely tied to the local community, not to a wider linguistic or ethnic group. Indeed, Indigenous people from other communities were as much outsiders and potential threats as were the Spaniards. The Europeans who first entered Guerrero in 1521 were yet another set of intruders, with whom the leaders of Indigenous communities would negotiate a new accommodation to absorb selected Spanish norms and concepts into their native mold, as had been the practice for many centuries.[5]

From a legal point of view, the Indians lived in *repúblicas de indios* separated from towns where Spaniards, Mestizos, Blacks, Mulattos, and *chinos* (Asians of various ethnicities) lived, but in practice, the castas were never really separate. For example, in 1550 Juana de Zúñiga complained that Spaniards and two Mestizos were selling "wine" to the Indians of her encomienda of Coyuca and Acapulco. The authorities prohibited such sales and decreed punishments of 100 lashes for Mestizos and 100 pesos for Spaniards, apparently to little effect since in 1551 Spanish and Mestizo vagabonds were accused of trading with and harassing the Indians of Xicayán.[6] In 1552 the viceroy ordered the alcalde mayor of Zumpango to protect the Indians of Chilapa from abuses committed by the Mestizo merchant Burgueño.[7] In 1592 Mestizos and Mulattos were forbidden to spend more than three days in Pungarabato, in the Tierra Caliente.[8]

5.1. Demographic Change

The Indigenous population of Guerrero had to cope with many factors that disrupted their lives in the sixteenth century, but the most devastating was the mortality caused above all by disease, but also by forced labor and profound social dislocation. On the Costa Grande the "Relación de la Villa de Zacatula" noted in 1580 that "because of the epidemics, and the ways of life transplanted by the Europeans, the natives are fewer every day."[9] The "Relación de Xalapa, Cintla y Acatlán" reported in 1582 that the Indigenous tributary population of this area of the Costa Chica previously exceeded 225,000, a clearly exaggerated figure considering that the total precontact population of Guerrero was, at most, about 780,000, but now only 2,017 tributaries remained. Nevertheless, the latter figure represents a reliable enough indicator of reality.[10] In the North the "Relación de Iguala y su Partido" stated that 30 years ago, 6,000 vecinos lived in the town, but now there were only 840 tributaries, a decline attributed to work in the Taxco mines and disease.[11] The district of Ajuchitlán in the Tierra Caliente was said to be one of "few Indians. It had many more in times past: they have diminished, and they diminish every day."[12]

While it is clear that the Indigenous population declined precipitously in the sixteenth century, the data are fragmentary and not easy to interpret. The best source is the work of Danièle Dehouve,[13] but there are several reasons to treat the data with caution. Spanish population data counted only the number of Indigenous people required to pay tribute; that is, married adult males, bachelors, and widows. Children were not counted. Moreover, the size of an Indigenous family unit varied considerably. Von Mentz calculates that in the region of Cuauhnáhuac (Cuernacava) there were communities in which the family unit could average between 3.8 and 4.2 individuals, and in some cases as many as 5.4, 7.0, or 8.3.[14] The Indigenous elites, experienced in tribute collection,[15] were perfectly capable of manipulating census data to reduce the burden of Spanish tribute and thus maintain their own incomes. On the other hand, encomenderos and royal officials had good reasons to exaggerate the tribute paying population. Moreover, Indians could escape tribute obligations by going into hiding or seeking employment in the mines. In short, population data are indicative of trends, but by no means are they precise. Whatever the uncertainties of the sources, Indigenous mortality created a shortage of labor that was in part compensated for by the importation of African slaves and, to a lesser extent, of enslaved and free Asians.[16]

The population data clearly indicate significant differences between the regions of Guerrero. Simply put, the coast experienced the most severe decline in population. For example, from 1569 to 1580 the tributary population of the Tierra Caliente increased slightly from 2,526 to 2,889, hardly significant, but not indicative of a sharp reduction. In the North, population in the same period declined from 5,706 to 4,710, and in the Taxco area from 5,198 to 3,698. In the province of Tlapa, the tributary population rose from 5,151 in 1548 to 5,404 in 1570, and then declined sharply to 3,924 in 1588, 2,918 in 1599, and 1,936 in 1623.[17]

Census data for the three parishes of the diocese of Michoacán on the Costa Grande of Guerrero in the 1680s confirm a radical demographic shift. The 1,132 Indigenous residents aged 7 or more represented 64 percent of the population. There were also 626 non-Indigenous individuals, consisting of 209 Mulattos, 128 Spaniards, 72 Mestizos, 88 Blacks, 77 Asians, and 52 whose ethnicity was not specified. This heterogeneous population was not evenly distributed. The Indigenous population lived mostly in a small number of pueblos with few or no non-Indigenous neighbors, while most of the non-Indigenous lived on haciendas and ranches.[18]

TABLE 5.1. CENSUS OF THE POPULATION OF THE COSTA GRANDE AGED SEVEN YEARS OR MORE IN THE DIOCESE OF MICHOACÁN IN THE 1680S				
Population	Zacatula	Petatlán	Tecpan & Atoyac	Total
Indian	109	46	977	1,132
Spanish	6	60	62	128
Mestizo	0	38	34	72
Mulatto	0	38	171	209
Black	0	88	0	88
Asian	0	38	39	77
No data	0	0	52	52
Total	115	308	1,335	1,758
% Indian	95%	15%	73%	64%

Source: Carrillo Cázares, *Partidos y padrones*, 333–47. Census dates: Zacatula, 1680; Petatlán, 1681; Tecpan and Atoyac, 1683.

The demography of the six parishes of Acapulco in the late eighteenth century suggests a still more radical shift in the structure of the population: 433 Indigenous families and 524 of castas, of whom 400 were Mulattos and *pardos*, 113 chinos, and 11 Spaniards.[19] The data for the Costa Grande stand in stark contrast to those for the Montaña concerning the population toward the end of the eighteenth century. In the ten parishes of Tlapa, there were 7,869 families of Indigenous tributaries, but only 393 castas (374 Mestizos and 19 Spaniards), of whom 375 lived in just two parishes, Tlapa and Olinalá. Thus, the Montaña remained a distinctly Indigenous region.[20]

Dehouve's analysis similarly demonstrates a severe population decline on the tropical Costa Chica, especially when compared to the cooler zones inland. The reasons are not clear. Variable criteria for counting the population, movements of population to escaped forced labor, and disease outbreaks that were particularly severe on the coast may have been factors. The annual decrease on the coast was 9 percent. According to Dehouve's calculations, between 1519 and 1548 the cumulative reduction was 97.8 percent. From 1548 to 1570, the Indigenous population of the Costa Chica recovered somewhat, increasing more than 12 percent in Azoyú, 30 percent in Copalitech, 32 percent in Ometepec, and 33 percent in Xocutla. Nevertheless, in other parts of the Costa Chica, the decline continued. As a result, the Costa Chica, as a whole, suffered another 27 percent reduction.[21]

TABLE 5.2. CENSUS OF THE POPULATION OF THE TIERRA CALIENTE AGED TEN YEARS OR MORE IN THE DIOCESE OF MICHOACÁN IN THE 1680S

Population	Ajuchitlán	Cutzamala	Pungarabato	Zirándaro	Total
Indian	483	184	339	547	1,553
Spanish	10	4	30	35	79
Mestizo	3	33	17	25	78
Mulatto	129	19	0	9	157
Black	0	0	45	2	47
Total	625	240	431	618	1,914
% Indian	77%	77%	79%	89%	81%

Source: Carrillo Cázares, *Partidos y padrones*, 347–68. Census dates: Ajuchitlán, 1683; Cutzamala, 1682; Pungarabato, 1682; Zirándaro, 1681.

Meanwhile, from 1548 to 1570 the population of Tlapa and its subordinate cabeceras increased by 7.3 percent, in Huamuxtitlán and Olinalá by 10 percent, and in Chilapa and Tlalcozautitlán in the Center by 22.7 percent.[22] Thus, the demographic history of the coast in the sixteenth and seventeenth centuries is one of a steep decline of the Indigenous population, which was partially replaced by an influx of African, Asian, and mixed-race population, while the Montaña remained strongly Indigenous, with the exception of a modest Mestizo population in two parishes. Dehouve summarizes the long-term effects of the changes caused by Spanish colonization in Tlapa in the sixteenth century:

> The Tlapa region . . . during the entire colonial period was among the least populated zones of New Spain, and the most remote from the main centers of mining and agricultural production of the country. Contrary to the almost classic view which describes colonial rural Mexico as the scene of incessant struggles between Indian communities and haciendas, the region of Tlapa was practically spared from the development of large agrarian properties. Therefore, the economic integration of the Indian population into the colonial world was principally through small-scale production destined for the market.[23]

Small-scale production for the market would characterize the Indians of the region until the twentieth century.[24] This region, which had actively participated in the society of Mesoamerica for centuries, would be remote from the cultural and economic currents of the colonial period. Here the Indigenous languages of the ancient kingdom of Tlapa-Tlachinollan would survive, while in the mining region of the North, the ancient Chontals would become a minority in their own homeland before the sixteenth century had ended, their language disappearing completely not long afterward.[25]

The Spaniards considered the Tierra Caliente a rather inhospitable region—a land of rugged mountains, hot and dry from October to May, with a rainy season from mid-May to early October—but nevertheless the precontact population here was denser than on the coast, although less dense than the Montaña.[26] Data from the 1680s demonstrates that in Tierra Caliente the remaining Indian population was numerically and proportionally larger than on the coast, although the area was by this time quite sparsely populated. In Cutzamala district, all the Spaniards and Mestizos, and over half the Mulattos, lived at mines or on haciendas. Just one Spaniard, four Mestizos, and five Mulattos resided in Cutzamala itself, and three Mestizos in Tlachiapa. In Pungarabato district, all the Spaniards, Mestizos, and Blacks lived on haciendas and livestock ranches. In Zirándaro district, more than two-thirds of Indians lived in three settlements where no non-Indian lived, while all the non-Indigenous lived in the cabecera. In sum, the majority of the Indigenous population lived in separate locations from the non-Indigenous parishioners.[27]

5.2. Negotiations

After the defeat of the Mexicas in 1521, the conquistadors and the Crown faced the challenge of controlling a large, dispersed Indigenous population. Crown revenues must be secured, and Indigenous labor and resources were required. The expeditious solution was to govern the Indians with the cooperation of their existing rulers and structures of government and, thus, to benefit from and expand the alliances with Indigenous rulers that had enabled the defeat of the Mexicas and other hostile Indigenous groups. In sixteenth-century Guerrero the Spaniards found an Indigenous elite that was experienced in the administration and collection of tribute and the management of labor. This expertise was invaluable in the first decades of the colonial period. The Spaniards reciprocated by allowing the Indian nobility to retain its privileges, tribute, and authority.²⁸ Thus, the Indigenous nobility of Guerrero faced a choice: negotiate and accommodate as Noxtepec had done or resist as the Yopes had done.

In the Postclassic many of Guerrero's ethnic polities had negotiated alliances with the Mexicas, which provided them with a powerful ally to whose authority they might appeal in the event of a dispute with a neighboring altepetl. Disputes continued into the colonial period. A case with a long history was that of Tetipac, Cacalotenango, and Noxtepec, whose dispute over land was adjudicated by Axayácatl (1469–1481) and by Ahuítzotl (1486–1502) with differing results, depending on the state of the alliances at the time. The dispute arose again in the early colonial period when Juan de Cabra, encomendero of Noxtepec, relocated Tetipac to the territory of Noxtepec to facilitate his mining interests.²⁹

Negotiations concerning matters that affected the community continued to be an important function of the Indigenous lord, now termed a cacique or governor. Mayacat and his brother Tacatecla,³⁰ nobles of Tixtla and sons of the precontact ruler Aixpotetle, both opposed and collaborated with their encomendero Martín de Ircio. In 1531 they appealed to the Audiencia to complain of Ircio's excessive tribute demands and were granted a reduction of the amounts due. Then a few years later, they successfully disputed in the Audiencia, with Ircio's help and to their and his benefit, sujetos claimed by Zumpango and its encomendero Diego Jaramillo. The documents in this case suggest that precontact animosities between Tixtla and Zumpango motivated Mayacat and Tacatecla's actions.³¹ In 1547 the rulers of Noxtepec renegotiated, through their interpreter Juan Gallego, the tribute they paid to Juan de Cabra. In 1558 they appeared again before the Audiencia, this time together with representatives of Pilcaya, to negotiate a further reduction of tribute owed to Cabra's widow María de Herrera.³² In 1550 Pedro, Alonso, Andrés, and Tomás, principales, and Francisco and Bartolomé, alcaldes of Olinalá in the Montaña, appeared before Viceroy Mendoza, with Miguel and Juan, principales of the estancia of Malazingo, and Andrés, principal of the estancia of Chauango, to declare that they had agreed to a modification of their tribute with Alonso de Aguilar y Córdoba. Mendoza emphasized that Aguilar was not entitled to anything further and, in particular, he was no longer entitled to any services or food.³³ Thus, in short order, the Indigenous elites had learned to transfer their roles as negotiators for their communities from the court of the Mexica tlatoani to the Audiencia and the viceroy.

5.3. Adapting the Tools of Indigenous Government: The *Pinturas* Under Spanish Rule

One of the tools of Indigenous government was the pinturas, or pictographic documents, adapted from the Postclassic documents created by the *amatlacuilo*, "painter on paper." The Spaniards saw in these documents an equivalent to the alphabetic documents with which Spain ruled New Spain.[34] The amatlacuilo continued to paint amendments to existing documents or to create new ones designed for their new context, for the Indigenous rulers soon realized that the Spaniards accorded great importance to written documents, used to record tribute, administer justice, for property deeds—in short, matters of any significance. The new Indigenous documents were rooted in the pictographic tradition but were adapted with Nahuatl or Spanish glosses using the Latin alphabet. As early as 1532, three judges of the Audiencia of Mexico wrote to Empress Isabella, reporting that the Indians had seen that some corregidores who had stolen from them had rightly been punished or removed from office. Furthermore, the Indians understood through the teaching of Christian doctrine that the king cared for them. The correspondents noted approvingly that the Indians well understand that, if the corregidor does them any wrong, they will come to complain, even traveling long distances, and in his presence they dare to complain in words and with the pinturas that they bring, which should be considered very significant considering how obedient they had been up to now.[35] Soon after this, New Spain's newly installed viceroy Antonio de Mendoza established specific procedures for Indians in the courts, which encouraged the use of new-style pinturas in the Spanish legal and administrative system.[36]

A good number of codices and lienzos from Guerrero record the ways in which Indigenous caciques defended their rights and the rights of their communities, documented their history (at times with mythical elements), administered their tribute obligations, or defended themselves from abuses. These documents speak to the changes to the lives of the Indians, but also to how they both persisted with their traditions and modified their procedures and social structures to face new challenges.

The Chontal elite of the Tierra Caliente seems to have adapted quickly to the Spanish legal, ecclesiastical, and administrative system to defend their communities against abuses by civil or ecclesiastical officials. For example, in 1558 Teloloapan, Ixcatlan, Tutultepec, Oztuma, Alahuiztlán, and their sujetos filed a dossier of more than 143 folios of evidence of complaint against their priest, Rodrigo Ortiz. Most of the folios were in alphabetic writing, but five of the documents were pinturas painted by different Indigenous scribes on *amate* and European paper. Explanatory glosses in Spanish were added by other scribes. The pinturas were used as an aide-mémoire for Indigenous witnesses. Ortiz was accused of charging more than the official church fees and of using coercive practices to enforce payment, such as refusing to hear confession or give extreme unction. The complaint also alleged that Ortiz demanded more food than was his due, selling the excess in the Taxco mines. According to the Indians, the priest did not light the candles in church so that he could sell them, did not pay Indian bearers, and sexually abused women during confession.[37]

The documents in the case reveal various aspects of the administrative and judicial processes in which the Chontals, Nahuas, Ixcucas, and Tuxtecas of the pueblos participated, before and soon after the conquest. The Indians recorded in Postclassic glyphs precisely what the priest was due and what he actually charged. For example, there were glyphs of fish, each with the *pantli* glyph to denote the numeral twenty. Indians are depicted in profile, some with the pantli glyph, others with a circular glyph that seems to denote pesos. This system proved a remarkably effective means of administering the demands of Spanish civil and ecclesiastical administrations. Documents written in pictographic form were as acceptable to Spanish officials as those written in Nahuatl using Latin characters. The former rulers and other members of the Indigenous elite now styled themselves in Spanish categories as alcaldes, alguaciles, or principales. There were entirely new church offices, such as *fiscal* or bell ringer. Witnesses of lower social status included Indigenous merchants and tamemes. There were also new symbols, such as a church, weights, and a scale, and a Black person with curly hair. Women testified concerning sexual abuse. Some Spaniards, residents of nearby ranches, and salt works were also witnesses. Thus, justice was, like Indigenous government and iconography, a hybrid of Spanish and Indigenous practice. The verdict in the case has not survived, but most of both Indigenous and Spanish witnesses supported the accusations against Ortiz.[38]

Another function of colonial pictographic documents was to manage community finances. For example, the codices of Oapan, Tecuiciapan, and Teteltzinco in the Center, all made about 1557, and another document from Oapan created between 1547 and 1554, record the payments due to Indigenous municipal officials. From 1547 to 1554,

TABLE 5.3. PAYMENTS TO MUNICIPAL OFFICIALS OF OAPAN EVERY EIGHTY DAYS, 1547–1554			
Official	Pesos	In kind	Other
Don Gaspar, governor	3	1 turkey, 120 cacao beans	1 jícara of fish and 20 eggs every Friday and Saturday. 5.5 fanegas of cotton thread and cultivation of fields of maize (0.5 hectare), chile (70 square meters), and cotton (1.5 hectares) annually
Miguel, alcalde	2		
2 majordomos	2		
Source: Noguez, "Tres documentos pictográficos sobre tributación indígena."			

the municipal administration of Oapan consisted of a governor, Don Gaspar, an alcalde, Miguel, and two majordomos, whose remuneration is summarized in table 5.3. The payments to Don Gaspar surely followed a pattern and periodicity of tribute accustomed by a Postclassic ruler, a periodicity that also applied to tribute due to encomenderos in the first few decades of the colonial period. After 1550, tribute assessments increasingly set aside a portion of a community's tribute in a chest, which was locked with three keys held by three officials who were responsible for accounting for expenditures on community needs, such as a fiesta, church ornaments, or tribute. Oapan's contributions were every 80 days 800 mantas and 14 pesos, and annually the cultivation of 3,445 square meters of maize, 1,653 square meters of chía, and 1,653 square meters of cotton. Thus, thirty years after the Spanish invasion, the ruling elite of Oapan held offices with Spanish titles and managed new institutions, but the governor continued to receive the perquisites of a Postclassic tlatoani.[39]

The Nahua iconography of the Oapan codex, made in 1557, portrays Don Gaspar in the guise of a Postclassic tlatoani. He is barefoot and wears what seems to be a turquoise diadem and a *tilma* (cape); there is a *petate* (Nahua *petlatl*, a woven mat), and he sits on a *tepotzoicpalli* (a seat of woven reeds with a backrest). Nevertheless, the nature of Don Gaspar's tribute had changed: the cash element had doubled but no longer was he due the cultivation of his fields nor payment in food, as table 5.4 shows. Ten principales, presumably elders or some other members of the local elite, had been added to the community payroll. The contribution to Oapan's community expenses was now ten pesos for the saint's day fiesta, and an Indian man and woman worked in the town's community building. In Tecuiciapan there were five principales, one who received every eighty days 2 pesos and 120 cacao beans, two who received

TABLE 5.4. PAYMENTS TO MUNICIPAL OFFICIALS OF OAPAN, TECUICIAPAN, AND TETELZINCO EVERY EIGHTY DAYS, CA. 1557

Official	Community	Cash	Other
Don Gaspar, governor	Oapan	6 pesos	Services of Indian man and woman
Alcalde	Oapan	4 pesos, 4 tomines	
Escribano	Oapan	1 peso	
2 majordomos	Oapan	1 peso	
2 principales	Oapan	2 pesos	
5 principales	Oapan	1 peso	
1 principal	Oapan	4 tomines	
2 majordomos	Tecuiciapan	1 peso	
1 principal	Tecuiciapan	2 pesos	120 cacao beans
2 principales	Tecuiciapan	1 peso	
2 principales	Tecuiciapan	4 tomines	
2 majordomos	Tetelzinco	1 peso	
1 principal	Tetelzinco	2 pesos	100 cacao beans
2 principales	Tetelzinco	1 peso	

Source: Noguez, "Tres documentos pictográficos sobre tributación indígena."

1 peso, and two only 4 tomines. In addition, two majordomos were paid 1 peso, the fiesta cost 6 pesos, and two Indians worked in the *casa de comunidad*. There were a further seven officials in Tecuiciapan and five in Tetelzinco.[40] Thus, in 1557 no fewer than twenty-five individuals were on the municipal payroll and even the modest-sized altepetl of Tecuiciapan and Tetelzinco paid seven and five officials, respectively.

Don Gaspar's annual income ca. 1557, 27 pesos, was meager compared to a priest's salary of 100–200, but it was substantially more than that of senior principales, who were due 9 pesos a year, and of the most junior principal who received a mere 2 pesos and 2 tomines. An Indigenous alcalde, a new official with an imported Spanish title, was paid 20 pesos and 2 tomines annually, more than double the most senior principal and three-quarters of Don Gaspar's earnings. The escribano (scribe) was paid the same as a principal of the second rank. As for the Indians who labored in the community's fields or repairing houses, their weekly earnings were 1 tomín plus their food, or 6 pesos if they worked forty-eight weeks of the year. Thus, by the late 1550s, the hierarchy and prestige of Oapan's elite had begun to be changed by new offices introduced by the Spanish colonial administration.[41]

Pinturas had an important function as records of the boundaries of a pueblo's land. However, while Spanish documents defined landed property for purely legal purposes, Indigenous territorial records meant much more, for they told, with pride and careful attention to detail, the history of the settlement. They generally asserted the antiquity of the community and its identification with important, possibly mythical, figures who were the founders. The lineage of the local ruler and other members of the elite was often recorded. These documents report the participation of the Indians in a new Spanish legal and administrative system, while asserting traditions deeply rooted in pre-Hispanic times.[42]

One document that carefully delineates the land of a community is the *Mapa de Tepecoacuilco*, probably made in 1576 in connection with a dispute over land with the Indigenous communities of Oapan, Tlaxmalac, and possibly others. The cause of the dispute may have been the division of the territory controlled by the cabecera of Tepecoacuilco. The map, some portions of which are now missing, survives as three fragments stuck on brown paper whose dimensions are 1.13 by 1.02 meters. It was painted in color on amate paper by a draughts person trained in the Indigenous tradition. It depicts, very accurately compared to modern maps, features such as rivers, various sujetos of Tepecoacuilco, and neighboring Indigenous communities, identified by glyphs that consist of the sign for *calli* (house) topped by an identifying glyph. Parts of the document that contained Spanish glosses have been lost. Fragment 2 refers to Spanish encomenderos and Fragment 3 names two Spanish persons, one of whom, Pedro Moran, may have been a judge. The care with which Tepecoacuilco's territory was delineated speaks of the importance of the land. The naming of Spanish individuals and officials suggests their involvement in the dispute, but exactly to what extent is impossible to determine.[43]

The rulers of Malinaltepec availed themselves of a degree of ambiguity to increase the antiquity of possession of their community's land. The town possessed two lienzos. *Lienzo 1* was made possibly as late as the eighteenth century, and in any case before 1743, during a land dispute with neighboring Zitlaltepec, which was eventually settled by a formal possession ceremony in 1804 or 1805. A document dated 1743 in the municipal offices of Malinaltepec states that *Lienzo 2* is a copy of *Lienzo 1* painted by Bartolomé de Souza, a painter from Tlapa. Another document, dated 1740, held by the municipality, refers to a document that related events of Tuesday, March 6, 1556, which by then had been lost. The 1740 document includes a Spanish text, said to be a translation of the Nahuatl text of the sixteenth-century document, which enables a reconstruction of that document. Geographic features such as hills topped by crosses that designate the boundary markers of Malinaltepec's land are linked by footsteps (barefoot or shod). Topographical features (such as rivers and hills), roads, agricultural activities, and flora and fauna are depicted. The lienzos portray historical data from 1556 but also from the eighteenth century. The sixteenth-century caciques of Malinaltepec are present, but also the eighteenth-century alcalde mayor of Tlapa and another Spaniard of the same century, all there to confirm possession of Malinaltepec's land. The village church is dated 1520, which is clearly impossible.[44] However, what was important was not chronological precision but the assertion of the antiquity of a significant community institution and, thus, of the land, before the conquest of Tenochtitlan, even though by the eighteenth century the community's boundaries were not the same as in the sixteenth century. Since antiquity of possession was very significant in the Spanish legal system, the lienzos recognized the need to establish ancient possession, thus adapting an Indigenous form of documentation to colonial legal requirements.

5.4. Rulers and Power: Change and Continuity in Village Government

Just as Indigenous inhabitants of Guerrero adapted themselves and their traditions to colonial ways of recording land possession and history, in the sixteenth century they accommodated change when confronted with new Spanish governmental structures and jurisdictions in their communities. It is likely that the Indians considered Spanish officials to be equivalents of a Mexica calpixqui, military governor, or other Mexica nobility dispatched to Guerrero.[45] On the whole, the Mexicas interfered little in the government of subject polities beyond matters such as tribute. However, Guerrero's Spanish officials operated at a considerable distance from their superiors in Mexico City. Distance enabled abuses such as forced labor in the mines or coercive commercial practices. Not infrequently, encomenderos and mineowners were also officials serving the colonial bureaucracy, a powerful combination that facilitated the exploitation of the Indigenous people. Nevertheless, Crown officials dispensed justice at the local level and the Indians proved determined to assert their rights and defend their interests before them.[46]

Until the middle of the sixteenth century, new governmental structures modified the powers of Indigenous rulers but did not deprive them of authority or traditional perquisites. In 1549, for example, the *juez de comisión* Miguel de San Bernardino ruled that don Juan García, the Indigenous governor of Iguala, was entitled to receive every eighty days 45 small, thin mantas and 10 pesos of *oro común*; every forty days 4,800 cacao beans, 10 turkeys, 5 fanegas of pumpkin seeds, 5 fanegas of chile, and a block of salt; daily 2 candles and the services of 3 Indians; and annually the cultivation of a field 200 x 400 *brazas*.[47] This was probably similar to the tribute received by don Juan's Postclassic predecessors.

By 1550 new arrangements for the government of Indigenous repúblicas de indios came into force. The Indigenous community was no longer, from a strictly legal perspective, the domain by right of inheritance of the successor to the precontact rulers, the *señor natural*, entitled to tribute and services, but instead was governed by a *cabildo* of salaried officials elected from the village nobility. As in so many aspects of life in sixteenth-century New Spain, local practice did not conform to the formal policies of the royal government for quite some time. In many cases the established lineage retained traditional perquisites by controlling the elections. Nevertheless, the new structures of governance could be used to challenge the established elite. For example, elections did not always go to plan. Between 1575 and 1590, three or four different individuals claimed the right to rule Huamuxtitlán. Moreover, a corregidor or encomendero might interfere in elections, perhaps allied to an Indigenous faction. And if a descendant of an established lineage was elected, the sole legal entitlement was a salary, even if power could be abused to demand additional benefits. In short, the very nature of authority in the Indigenous communities had changed formally and to some extent in practice.[48]

For example, Oztuma, a Chontal altepetl, traced its ruling lineage back to Amalpilli, who died about 1460, Cuculetecuhtli (1460–?), Tetzauhtecuhtli (?–1487), Nochtecuhtli (ca. 1487–1488), Ahuehuetecuhtli (ca. 1488?–?), and Michtecuhtli (?–1519). Viceroy Martín Enríquez appointed as governor 1579–1585 a descendant of this lineage, don Diego Osorio. However, by 1593 don Diego was no longer governor, although he retained his social status, and no doubt a fair amount of influence, as cacique and principal. Don Diego certainly protested the loss of his standing and rights, alleging that the *regidores* and alcaldes had not paid him his governor's salary. However, his lineage remained prominent in Oztuma, for a descendant, don Luis Osorio, was governor in 1642.[49]

In the Montaña, Indigenous rulers managed to retain their privileges for longer than elsewhere. The office of governor was created in 1548, but after 1550 the number of officials increased, adding to the post of governor cabildo officials such as alcaldes, regidores, and alguaciles. In Huamuxtitlán, no fewer than twenty individuals held public offices in 1579. The introduction of officials of the cabildo, usually appointed from the principales and the church, gradually affected changes to the structure of government and power. However, the Spaniards refrained from directly attacking the power of the Indigenous nobility. The Indigenous elite recalled the local nobility of Iberia, and it suited Spaniards to leave in place the traditional nobles, who therefore received a portion of tribute, while their subjects continued to cultivate their land and care for their livestock. The cultivation of the governor's land continued in the Montaña until the mid-eighteenth century. In 1579 in Tlapa, the governor received an annual salary of 60 pesos. Other principales, exercising authority as municipal officials, such as alcaldes, regidores, or alguaciles, received 20 pesos. The governor of Huauchinango received 100 pesos and a governor who preserved the title of cacique could be paid up to 150 pesos (the equivalent of a good priest's salary).[50]

In the precontact era, Indigenous rulers combined administrative-political functions, such as tribute collection, negotiating relations with other polities, and declaring war, with sacred functions as the intermediary between the Indians and their gods. To some extent precontact rituals continued in modified form, sometimes to the present day. Furthermore, newly introduced Catholic feast days provided new sacred occasions for señores naturales to assert their authority and to demand payment, and perhaps to hold a banquet for fellow notables. Priests relied on Indigenous assistants, such as an *alguacil de doctrina* (a "constable" who enforced church attendance), a fiscal (who managed church assets), an escribano (notary or scribe), a *topile* (who carried out lower level supervisory functions), cantors, musicians, and bell ringers to carry out many church functions, as the studies of Lockhart and Haskett have demonstrated in the Valley of Mexico and Cuernavaca.[51] Cocula, in the valley of Iguala, had eight cantors and two alguaciles de doctrina.[52] The church created, parallel to civil municipal government, a second Indigenous hierarchy of prestige and privileges. Those who held church offices did not necessarily hold civil posts and vice versa (although sometimes the two overlapped), so new opportunities for prestige and power were created.

In some communities, disease eliminated entire lineages. The "Relación de Iguala y su Partido" reports that by 1579 all the señores naturales had died. Two alcaldes and other officials, whose authority was legitimized by election, not by lineage, collected tribute and administered justice. Nevertheless, there were still "lesser *principales*... who have their land and ranches, and Indians who serve them and recognize their status." The most senior noble, Alonso de Santiago, a youth of twenty-three years, had married the daughter of the governor don Francisco González. In Oapan, don Agustín de Ircio, who had adopted the last name of the powerful encomendero Martín de Ircio, was a grandson of the señor natural. He had married the daughter of principal Miguel de Mendoza, who had adopted the last name of the viceroy, but since don Agustín had not yet reached the age of majority, his father-in-law ruled in his stead. Don Miguel was "a good Indian dressed in Spanish style, who rides a horse with a saddle and bridle for which he has permission." Here the adoption of Spanish elements of prestige was combined with a last tenuous link to the lineage of Oapan.[53]

The powers of Postclassic rulers and other members of the elite were not immune from challenges, such as internal factional contestation, especially when succession was at issue or a rival leader of a neighboring polity attacked or, in the latter decades of the Late Postclassic, the Mexicas or the Tarascans invaded. Challenges and disruptions to traditional power had certainly occurred under the Mexicas, as the rebellion against Tlapa-Tlachinollan's alliance with the Mexica between 1468 and 1474 indicates.[54] Thus, new Spanish laws and governmental structures may not have been welcomed (certainly not by the Yopes, as their fierce resistance showed), but they were not unprecedented. Nevertheless, Spanish colonialism introduced important changes to the legal role and functions of Indigenous rulers, which affected their powers and privileges, even if they managed to preserve many of them in practice. The sacred function of rulership was inevitably changed with the appointment of a foreign priest to lead religious rituals. True, the Spanish priests were spread thinly, and the clergy relied on Indigenous assistants who might be members of the established elite or sometimes a parvenu from the lower social ranks. Nevertheless, a reluctance to adopt the new faith is evident in certain sources.⁵⁵ The duties and perquisites of Indigenous rulers were formally defined in exclusively secular terms, as were the salaries that rewarded municipal offices. The señores naturales might still be the most powerful individuals in their community but within the new structures dictated by their new rulers. Demands for tribute or services, which were customary but now illegal, at the very least provided grounds to challenge a ruler's authority.⁵⁶

The epidemics of the sixteenth century disrupted even the long-lived lineages of the province of Tlapa. When the cacique and governor of Tlapa died in May 1551, the succession required the approval of the viceroy.⁵⁷ By 1565 the successor, don Gerónimo de Guzmán, was referred to as cacique and governor of Tlapa, no longer of an entire province. That year, when the heirs of the encomenderos Bernaldino Vázquez de Tapia and Beatriz de Estrada claimed their tribute rights before the Real Audiencia, don Gerónimo appeared in court to claim his right to tribute from 186 Indians in 7 barrios and sujetos of Tlapa. The Audiencia ruled against him, instead allocating 23 pesos and 5 tomines to be retained for community expenses.⁵⁸ Thus, don Gerónimo's authority, that he claimed as of right, was constrained by the powers of the viceroy and the Audiencia in Mexico City. The royal government could also intervene to appoint a new ruler. A rather dramatic example occurred in Yguala (now Igualapa), a sujeto of Tlapa, in 1551, when an Indian principal and governor murdered his wife and fled. Viceroy Velasco appointed one don Miguel as the new governor.⁵⁹

The señores naturales also faced challenges from below as the case of Tixtla and Mochitlán illustrates. Mochitlán was a sujeto of Tixtla and, therefore, subordinate to don Martín Mayeque, cacique of Tixtla. In 1550 don Martín and some principales of Tixtla sold three parcels of land to Martín de Ircio, a sale confirmed by a "decree of [His Majesty] in the presence of the justice of Zumpango." The sale was clearly not to the liking of all residents of Tixtla, since in March 1551 Pedro Pacheco, the Spanish alcalde mayor of Acapulco, reported that Indians of Tixtla had "maliciously" tilled land belonging to Ircio that they had not worked for thirty years. Pacheco rejected the Indians' claim to the land. By September 1551 don Martín faced opposition from "some disorder and trouble" in Mochitlán, whose residents alleged that he had imposed excessive tribute. Diego Pardo, encomendero of Cacahuatepec and a mineowner on the Costa Chica, had been tasked with investigating the affair, but when he was unable to do so the viceroy instructed an Indigenous official, don Tomás de Tapia, governor of Tepeaca, to resolve the matter. Subsequent events suggest that don Martín had indeed exceeded his authority. Two years later, don Tomás returned to ensure that Indians whose tribute was being collected by the governors of Oapan, Tixtla, and Mochitlán were restored to their encomendero Martín de Ircio to enforce his previous order, which had been ignored, and to appoint new governors. Thus, one Indigenous governor, acting as an agent of the royal government in Mexico City, had clipped the wings of another.[60]

Elites who were reduced to receiving only a salary sought ways to recover their accustomed perquisites, which in some cases met resistance. In 1551 the governor of Olinalá in the Montaña was accused of collecting taxes from market traders, although none had been levied previously. In 1579 eleven Indigenous officials in nearby Huamuxtitlán were accused of demanding a minimum salary double the legal amount, and of requiring the community to cultivate their fields, guard their livestock, and spin cotton.[61]

The royal government sometimes protected the privileges of Indigenous rulers, including female members of the Indian elites. Thus, in September 1552 don Martín, the Indigenous governor of Cuytlacinchitlan in the jurisdiction of Taxco, was ordered to allocate to doña Catalina, a daughter of the deceased governor don Estevan, some of the services that had been her father's due, specifically the cultivation of a field of maize and the repair of her house.[62] In 1551 Viceroy Velasco issued a diplomatically even-handed ruling in a dispute between don Juan, the governor of Tetipac, and don Domingo, a principal of a sujeto called Ystlauaca, who claimed that his settlement was not, in fact, subject to Tetipac because his forebears had not paid tribute to don Juan's ancestors. Velasco ruled that Ystlauaca was a sujeto of Tetipac, but ordered both communities to build a church, each with its own priest, and a jail, and appoint an alcalde and two alguaciles to collect tribute, which should be placed in a chest locked by three keys and be used to pay the priests' salaries. Both don Juan and don Domingo were to receive the produce of a field of maize measuring 150 square brazas and a field of beans 50 brazas square. Don Juan was granted an annual salary of 70 pesos, and four Indians, paid 4 reales per month, were to serve in his house. Don Domingo received a salary of 50 pesos and four Indians for his domestic service.[63] Thus, both rulers emerged from their dispute with privileges and incomes confirmed, and the communities of both were to possess those important symbols of prestige in the colonial era, a church and their own priest, yet don Juan was recognized formally as being the superior of don Domingo.

A particularly notable case of an Indigenous elite whose privileges endured and developed under Spanish rule is that of the Moctezuma family of Chilapa, the product of an intricate network of Postclassic and sixteenth-century marriages between ruling families in the Valley of Mexico and noble lineages of Chilapa. For example, in 1522 the Indigenous ruler of Chilapa was Antonio Isquinantzin, son of Omocatzin, tlatoani of Xochimilco, and through his father's line descended from Axayácatl, Mexica tlatoani of Tenochtitlan. Isquinantzin had married into a Chilapa noble family, and his son, Agustín de Chilapa, reinforced the family's connections to great Indigenous lineages by marrying an Indigenous noble woman who could trace her ancestry back to Nezahualcóyotl, fifteenth-century lord of Texcoco. The Crown recognized Agustín's rights as cacique of Chilapa and the privileges that corresponded to that rank, including rights to land and tribute from several communities, some of them distant from Chilapa. In 1569 the *cacicazgo* was said to generate the substantial sum of 1,000 pesos in tribute alone. In the seventeenth century, Agustín's grandson married a daughter of Antonio de Ordaz Villagómez, the third member of the Ordaz family to hold the encomienda of Chilapa. A later seventeenth-century marriage to a Spanish woman resulted in the entailment of the family's holdings as a *mayorazgo*, which ensured primogeniture and prevented any alienation of the family's assets. These arrangements endured until 1823. Thus, a well-documented Indigenous noble lineage combined with marriages into elite Spanish families to create a powerful and enduring noble line in Chilapa.[64]

The appointment of Indigenous church officials further altered the hierarchy of prestige and privileges in Indigenous pueblos. Church officers were, for example, exempt from tribute and forced labor.[65] Late Postclassic veneration of the temple and its priests was inherited by the church, the parish priest, and his officials. The church was a symbol of the community's identity. The cabecera that did not maintain its church to the appropriate standard risked losing its status and authority. The priest, whose income depended on the ability of his flock to pay fees, could be a valuable ally in resisting unwanted exactions.[66] Some priests earned the respect of their parishioners. In 1633 the cabildos of Tenango, Atzalan, and Hueyztaca, near Taxco, told the archbishop that their priest Manuel Rodríguez de Ugarte was an esteemed and pious cleric. In 1636 Father

Pedro Serón Saavedra, a son of local Indigenous nobles, was highly thought of in Cacayotlan and Tlacotecapan for his piety and ability to speak Nahuatl. Others, such as Gaspar de Tejeda, priest of Teloloapan, Ixcateopan, and Atenango, were execrated for their abuses.[67]

The involvement of Spanish officials and encomenderos in the affairs of Indigenous communities further introduced changes to local government and hierarchies of power and prestige. The balance of power was unequal, but Indians soon learned to use administrative and legal processes to their advantage. For example, in 1552 the viceroy commissioned the corregidor of Iguala to investigate complaints that the Indians of Huitzuco lodged against the encomendero Isidro Moreno. The following year the governor of Tepecoacuilco investigated whether the cacique, governor, and majordomo of Huitzuco and Moreno's administrator were correctly administering tribute.[68] In the 1580s and 1590s, a complex dispute erupted among three factions in Huitzuco that involved neighboring pueblos, two encomenderos and the corregidor. The main bone of contention was control of *cascalote*, a bark used to tan leather. Moreno's heir, Bernardino de Casasola, owned livestock and mines, where leather was in demand. He supported a group in Huitzuco that opposed the ruling elite. Casasola also usurped Indigenous land and cut cascalote from trees that were not his. The ruling group, allied with Indigenous merchants, opposed Casasola and his faction. Another faction entered the fray when the Indians of Aguacaucingo made their own complaint to the Spanish authorities. Meanwhile, Mayanalán and Tlaxmalac, supported by their encomendera María de Cisneros, filed complaints against Casasola, alleging that his livestock had damaged their crops. In 1592 the viceroy appointed Juan de la Cruz, a principal of Metepec, to resolve the case.[69] This complicated affair demonstrates the difficulties that a governor and principales of a república de indios could encounter in managing their subjects, factionalism, and relations with neighboring communities, especially if Spanish interests were also involved.

Olinalá, in the Montaña, was another example of a Spanish encomendero interfering in the affairs of a pueblo, in this case violently. In 1556 Gonzalo Díaz de Vargas, the alguacil mayor of Ciudad de los Ángeles (Puebla), reported that the administrator (and cousin) of Alonso de Aguilar y Córdoba, who had lived in Olinalá for fourteen years, was accused of killing three Indians, of forcing six señores naturales from the offices they held, usurping the lands of three entailed estates, and collecting more tribute than was due. Díaz de Vargas reinstated the señores naturales, returned the misappropriated land, and obliged Aguilar to repay the excess tribute. The record does not indicate whether the administrator was punished for the deaths of the Indians.[70] Abuses committed by encomenderos were frequently brought before Spanish officials and courts throughout New Spain.[71] A less violent case that illuminates the complex ethnic and social mixing of sixteenth-century New Spain involved the cacique of Tecamama on the coast. The encomendero of that place complained that the cacique had married his daughter to a Spaniard and had given to his daughter a cacao orchard and other community property.[72]

Thus, by the end of the sixteenth century, the structure and nature of government in Guerrero's Indigenous communities had changed in some fundamental respects. Yet, despite the extinction of many lineages, local rulers had retained significant aspects of Indigenous traditions and practices. At the same time, they learned to utilize the new administrative and legal structures to defend their interests and those of their communities. They also sought permission, in the second half of the century, to add to the remaining elements of their pre-Hispanic identity symbols of Spanish practice and prestige such as wearing European-style clothing and riding a horse.[73] Furthermore, they assimilated into community life two significant new institutions: the caja de comunidad and the cofradía.

5.5. New institutions: *Cajas de Comunidad* and *Cofradías*

In the sixteenth century the Spaniards introduced two institutions that would be of great importance in Indigenous communities in following centuries: the caja de comunidad and the cofradía. When alguacil mayor Gonzalo Díaz de Vargas, whom we last met investigating ill-treatment of the Indians of Olinalá, visited nearby Papalutla in 1556 to reassess tribute, he added a new element. The Indians were to cultivate a field whose production would contribute half a tomín to community funds for each of 220 tributaries. He added a stipulation that was characteristic of many assessments after 1550.

> [The money] was to be placed in a chest, supervised by the governor, an alcalde and a majordomo, in which there shall be a book of accounts of all transactions, and with that they shall fund the church and the priests, and they shall meet the other expenses of

the república, without asking of the maceguales [commoners] anything else for any reason and the food they give to the corregidor and passing Spaniards shall be purchased from there and whatever they are given and paid for it shall be put back in the chest and properly accounted for, and let them know that every year they must account for this by means of inspection or however [the] Viceroy should require.[74]

Similar assessments varied, often substantially, in the amount contributed to community funds (table 5.5).

It is clear that the communities of the Costa Grande, severely decimated by epidemics, had little capacity to accumulate funds for community purposes. In the Montaña, on the other hand, much larger sums were paid into the caja. Certainly, half a century later, the caja de comunidad of Tlapa had a healthy surplus of 1,500 pesos, despite its income being reduced to 500 pesos per annum, no doubt because of population decline.[75] The caja de comunidad first appeared in the Montaña between 1551 and 1555. Here sources of funds for the caja included sugar cane grown on irrigated land, and some communities owned sugar mills. Another source of income was cattle or renting out land for pasture. In the long term, the increase in community funds would pay for improvements of the church and of community buildings. The cajas also financed fiestas or official banquets and legal expenses to defend community interests.[76] Gibson notes that in the Valley of Mexico, cajas paid for important expenses such as the salaries of Indigenous officials, religious festivals, and masses.[77] Haskett's study of Cuernavaca observes that community funds paid for public buildings and for litigation, which often emptied the caja.[78] In the Oaxacan Mixteca, the caja was funded from community land to pay for needs such as constructing and adorning church buildings, feasts, and tribute payments.[79]

In 1570 Archbishop Alonso de Montúfar noted the emergence of that other new institution in Guerrero, the cofradía.[80] Cofradías were religious associations that paid for significant costs incurred by their members (*cofrades*) and the community, such as funerals and fiestas. The cofradía became significant to the Indigenous population sufficiently early in the sixteenth century that Náhuatl had a loan word, *conflades*, for the term *cofrade* by 1549.[81] Cofradías were important throughout New Spain. The Nahua annalist Chimalpahin's accounts of elaborate processions of Nahua, Spanish, and Mulatto cofradías in late sixteenth- and

TABLE 5.5. TRIBUTE PAID INTO THE *CAJA DE COMUNIDAD* IN INDIGENOUS COMMUNITIES OF GUERRERO, 1558–1569

Region/Community	Year	Amount
COSTA GRANDE		
Achancaleca	1558	30 fanegas of maize
Chipila	1559	1 peso and 6 tomines, 1 fanega, and 9 zelemines of maize
Citlaltomahua	1559	2 cargas of cacao
Guaitlaco	1559	1 peso and 2 tomines paid in cacao beans
Petatlán	1559	3 pesos and 4 tomines paid in cacao beans
Puchutla	1559	9 pesos and 1 1/2 tomín, 7 fanegas, and 9 almudes of maize
Zuitla	1559	1 peso and 6 tomines paid as cacao beans
MONTAÑA		
Papalutla	1556	13 pesos and 6 tomines
Tlapa	1565	1001 pesos and 9 granos
CENTRE		
Huitziltepec	1566	26 pesos and 6 tomines
Mochitlán	1566	159 pesos and 2 tomines
Tixtla	1566	297 pesos and 4 tomines
Zumpango	1565	442 pesos, 2 tomines, and 9 granos
NORTH		
Iguala	1565	192 pesos and 2 tomines
Tenancingo	1564	215 pesos and 5 tomines
Tenango	1564	543 pesos and 6 tomines
Tenango	1566	51 pesos
Tululuava	1567	145 pesos and 6 tomines
Tululuava	1569	121 pesos and 4 tomines
Tuzantla	1566	93 pesos and 9 granos
TIERRA CALIENTE		
Ajuchitlán	1567	223 pesos and 1 tomín
Ajuchitlán	1569	280 pesos
Coyuca	1559	2 cargas of cotton and 13 cotton mantas, 1 manta of 4 piernas, 100 fanegas of maize
Coyuca	1567	111 pesos and 4 tomines
Cutzamala	1567	43 arrobas and 12 1/2 libras of cotton
Zirándaro and Guayameo	1566	57 pesos and 2 tomines

Sources: *El libro de las tasaciones*; Paso and Troncoso, *Epistolario de Nueva España*, vol. 11, 1570–1575, 119.

early seventeenth-century Mexico City demonstrate the importance of the cofradía in the social and religious life of the city.[82] The Cofradía del Santissimo Sacramento of Tula accepted both Indigenous and Spanish members, providing a Christian burial and masses.[83] The appeal of the eighteenth-century Congregación de la Buena Muerte in Mexico City to its Nahua and Creole members lay in its festivities and religious pageantry.[84] In the northern mining town of Zacatecas, the Cofradía de la Vera Cruz served a function quite different from the sodalities of central and southern New Spain. Here the cofradía unified a diverse, uprooted migrant population, and acted as a substitute for the nobility and community governance they had left behind.[85]

In Tetelzinco, a barrio of Taxco, there were two cofradías: the Cofradía de la Santa Veracruz was already active in 1561, and the Cofradía de Nuestra Señora was founded in 1565 or perhaps earlier. In 1581 two more cofradías were reported: Santísimo Sacramento y Nuestra Señora and Disciplinantes. Tepecoacuilco had just one cofradía. In Coyuca on the Costa Grande, on the other hand, the Archbishop reported that the Cofradía de Nuestra Señora was suspended for lack of donations.[86] The cofradía was never immune from interference or embezzlement by Indigenous nobles or Spanish priests, but, nevertheless, in parts of Guerrero, as capital accumulated, it became an institution that contributed to financial stability and community cohesion.[87] The enduring vigor of the cofradía in Guerrero attests to Lockhart's observation that the institution was better developed on the periphery than in central Mexico. A few were established early, but the expansion of sodalities began in the latter part of the sixteenth century.[88] During the seventeenth century the cofradías of the Tierra Caliente would become owners of livestock, some of them in considerable numbers. For example, by the final decades of the century, the Cofradía de Nuestra Señora de la Purificación in Apaxtla owned 698 beef cattle and 134 horses and colts. Santo Cristo in Alahuiztlán possessed 450 beef cattle. In Totoltepec, Nuestra Señora de la Concepción owned some 200 beef cattle and 5 horses, and the Cofradía de la Virgen had 20 mares, 5 horses, and 6 she-mules. In Teloloapan the Santo Entierro had 77 beef cattle and 7 horses, while the cofradía of the church of Santa María Oztuma owned 40 cows and 25 bullocks.[89]

By the late eighteenth century there were several cofradías and hermandades (brotherhoods, whose purpose and functions were essentially the same as the cofradía) in the jurisdictions of Taxco and Iguala in the North and Tixtla in the Center. In the Taxco area ten pueblos had some kind of religious association, which generally owned livestock and/or land. In Iguala's jurisdiction there were cofradías in Cocula, two or three in Huitzuco, of which one had 810 pesos and 6 reales in cash. In Mayanalán the cofradía owned 50 head of livestock, and the cofradía in Tepecoacuilco had a ranch of *ganado mayor* with 156 head of livestock. Tlaxmalac's cofradía had 783 pesos and 7.5 reales in a chest. Xochipala also had a cofradía. In Tixtla's jurisdiction there were two hermandades in San Francisco Ahuelicán, one in Santa María de la Concepción Amayotepec. Chilpancingo had three or four cofradías and three hermandades. The Cofradía del Santísimo Sacramento had the substantial sum of 2,000 pesos in cash. There were religious associations in Santiago Dos Caminos. An hermandad in Santa Ana Mochitlán owned 40 head of beef cattle. In the parish of Marcos Ocacingo there were no fewer than eight cofradías or hermandades, and eight also in San Agustín Oapan. San Juan Tetelcingo had three hermandades, and San Martín Tixtla two hermandades and four cofradías, one of which owned 500 head of livestock and capital of 1,652 pesos. In Zumpango there were three or five hermandades, one of which had 2,000 pesos in cash, and two cofradías, with cash of 1,000 and 1,300 pesos.[90]

In the Montaña the cofradías were founded by priests in the seventeenth century, but by the eighteenth century they operated largely independently. Between 1690 and 1736 the cofradías were administered by a small group of Indians, caciques, or principales, Spaniards or Mestizos, and, on occasion, an Indigenous woman.[91] Members of these groups could use the funds of the cofradía for their own benefit. However, from 1750 sodalities were more democratically managed for the benefit of the entire community, a process that was accelerated by separations of pueblos, which thus escaped the jurisdiction of the cacique in their former cabecera. The cabildo nominated officials of the cofradías, which had become quite wealthy. The history of the cofradías of the Montaña thus differed from those in the North and Tierra Caliente. They also operated a different funding model, involving themselves actively in commerce. Some Montaña cofradías raised and sold mules, traded soap purchased in Puebla, or manufactured textiles using cotton bought on the coast. There were good years and bad, but in general profits were large—from 37 percent to more than 100 percent. The cofradías also owned livestock as they did in other areas.[92] Much less is known about cofradías on the coast, but they did exist. For example, in 1719 the cofradía of Coahuayutla owned 170 head of beef cattle and some horses.[93] However, since by the eighteenth century very few Indigenous pueblos remained on the coast, the coastal cofradías cannot have been significant as institutions that bolstered Indigenous communities as they did elsewhere, especially in the Montaña and Tierra Caliente.

The florescence of the cofradía in Guerrero was a later development than the caja de comunidad. This was generally true of the development of the cofradía in other regions of New Spain. In Oaxaca some sodalities had been established in the 1570s and 1580s, but many more were founded in the second half of the colonial period.[94] In Cuernavaca there were four Spanish and three Indigenous cofradías by the late seventeenth century. By the eighteenth century there were several more.[95] Similarly, in the Valley of Mexico, some cofradías were founded in the sixteenth century, but for the most part sodalities were a development of the seventeenth century and later.[96] In the northern mining town of Zacatecas, three Spanish cofradías and a cofradía for Indigenous members who had migrated from other parts of New Spain were founded in the 1560s. More Indigenous sodalities followed in the seventeenth century. Female members were admitted from the sixteenth century, but it is not clear whether women performed any official roles.[97]

In Guerrero both institutions would become fundamental and cherished aspects of Indigenous communities and would have important implications for the region's long-term future in the later colonial period. By the second half of the eighteenth century, the caja de comunidad, to which each Indian contributed one and a half reales annually, was a significant source of capital accumulation from which compulsory or "voluntary" loans were demanded by the government. Since they were funded only by Indians, the cajas were entirely Indigenous institutions, while cofradías could be Indigenous, non-Indigenous, or a combination of the two. The cajas abounded and were wealthiest where numerous cofradías flourished, notably in the Montaña, Center, and Tierra Caliente. These two institutions financed community needs (fiestas, religious services, community buildings, sometimes feeding the hungry), stimulated important sectors of the local economy, and contributed to the cohesion and sustenance of the community. Their capital attracted the greedy attentions of priests, merchants, and civil officials. Communities fiercely resisted attempts to misappropriate funds. When government demands for loans became more pressing, the Indigenous communities became ever more hostile. Where the cofradías and the cajas were wealthy, such resentments were a factor in Indigenous support for the independence movement in Guerrero.[98]

TABLE 5.6. *CABECERAS, SUJETOS*, AND TRIBUTARY POPULATION IN GUERRERO, CA. 1548, ACCORDING TO THE *SUMA DE VISITAS*

Region	Cabeceras	Cabeceras that had sujetos	Sujetos	Tributaries
Costa Grande	56	8	10	6,961
Costa Chica	30	15	85	4,171–4,294
Montaña	15	13	95	14,171
Centre	8	4	41	4,225
North	11	8	56	6,556
Tierra Caliente	10	10	208	13,263

Source: García Castro, *Suma de visitas de pueblos*.

5.6. Restructuring Territory and Jurisdictions

Indigenous rulers governed polities of varying sizes and complexity, whose precontact structures both shaped the new jurisdictions and were changed by them as the colonial regime took hold. Indigenous leaders dealt with two or three formal jurisdictions: first came the encomenderos, allocated tribute from towns soon after the defeat of the Mexicas, then a local Crown official, a corregidor or alcalde mayor who administered Crown policy, dispensed justice, and collected Crown tribute. To these non-Indigenous power holders were added the clergy, who played a significant part in Indigenous life. In parts of Guerrero the regular orders managed ecclesiastical affairs, independently of the bishop, but by the end of the sixteenth century, secular priests who answered to a bishop ministered to most parishes. The number of clerics required to minister to the Indigenous population was substantial. Therefore, the Spaniard with whom the majority of Indians had most of their dealings was the priest or friar.

In Late Postclassic Guerrero, the territory ruled by an Indigenous leader was not always contiguous with fixed boundaries, but rather it was commingled in the territory of others. A victorious ruler customarily acquired land and labor from a community vanquished in war. This was contrary to the Spanish understanding of a territory with defined boundaries, but initially the Spaniards administered the Indigenous population by establishing jurisdictions based loosely on their understanding of Indigenous territories. However, the Spaniards soon changed boundaries to meet their needs, breaking up or reorganizing the territories of some communities. An encomienda might correspond to a single pre-Hispanic altepetl, or to two or more of them, or it might divide an altepetl. For example, when Cortés assigned Noxtepec and Pilcaya to Juan de Cabra, he combined into a single unit two previously independent Chontal communities.[99] The encomienda of Blas de Monterroso included Oztuma and Alahuiztlán, Chontal polities defeated and punished by the Mexica for rebellion, and Acapetlahuaya, a frontier military settlement founded by Mexica colonists to reinforce Mexica control.[100] Moreover, the Spanish imposed multiple jurisdictions that covered different but overlapping territories. An encomienda was subject to the authority of its encomendero, but also to a civil official whose jurisdiction might embrace several encomiendas. The Indians of the encomiendas would also be subject to an ecclesiastical jurisdiction whose boundaries differed from that of the encomienda and the civil official. Thus, the Indians were obliged to obey and pay tribute or tithes to a variety of authorities.

Moreover, the territorial organization and hierarchical structure of the Indigenous pueblos varied considerably by region, as table 5.6 indicates.

The coast was divided into three civil provinces: Zacatula (most of the Costa Grande, plus Motines in Michoacán), Acapulco (the eastern end of the Costa Grande and part of the Costa Chica), and Igualapa (most of the Costa Chica). By midcentury the Costa Grande was a region of predominantly small villages. For example, Ehancaleca was said to have "no more than nine Indian workers." In Mitla there were only 8 tributaries, in Cigua 11, Piquitla 25, Petatlán 40, Ystapa 53, and Tequepa 80. Of 57 pueblos, 25 had fewer than 100 tributaries, 21 between 100 and 200. Only 4 had a sizeable tribute-paying population: Huytalota 313, Lacoaba 500, Texupa 556, and Ayutla 807.[101] In 1570 the Costa Grande was an alcaldía mayor divided into 11 corregimientos.[102]

On the Costa Chica there were also villages with tiny populations by midcentury: Copalitech 14 tributaries, Potuctla 28, and Quahuitlán 30. The largest population centers were Azoyú with 245 tributaries, Xicayán 300, Xochistlahuaca 307, Ometepec 340, Tiquipa 400, and Çacaltepeque 550.[103] The first corregimientos were in Citlaltomahua and Xocutla, near Acapulco. In the 1530s a corregidor was appointed for Xalapa, Cintla, and Acatlán, a jurisdiction that in 1560 included the large cabeceras of Igualapa, Ometepec, and Xochistlahuaca. The corregidor of Nexpa, appointed in 1540, ruled the former Yopecingo. In

1550 this jurisdiction became the alcaldía mayor of Acapulco, although in 1560 its seat moved to Acamalutla. After 1580 it expanded to include Citlaltomahua and Anecuilco. By 1600 civil administration on the Costa Chica was divided into two alcaldías mayores, Acapulco and Igualapa.[104]

In the Montaña the hierarchy of the former Kingdom of Tlapa-Tlachinollan was the foundation on which civil administration and encomiendas were built. The *Suma de Visitas* listed twelve cabeceras, including Tlapa. These formed a single encomienda, which yielded riches in tribute to the Crown, and two powerful individual encomenderos. However, to the north, Huamuxtitlán was removed from the jurisdiction of Tlapa to assign it in encomienda to Bernaldino Vázquez de Tapia. In the 1520s Tlapa fell under the jurisdiction of the Spanish town of San Luis. In 1532 Tlapa became a corregimiento until 1550, when it was incorporated into the alcaldía mayor of Zumpango. About the same time Olinalá and Huamuxtitlán were merged into the alcaldía mayor of Minas de Ayoteco.[105] Thus, mining interests determined the location of civil administration. Separations of cabeceras were not the only changes in Tlapa's jurisdiction. In some cases, a sujeto became a cabecera and some cabeceras were demoted to the status of sujeto. For example, Olinalá acquired the status of cabecera when it was assigned in encomienda to Alonso de Aguilar y Córdoba, while Quiauhteopan, an important altepetl under Mexica rule, was reduced in rank.[106] An additional factor that characterized the Montaña in the sixteenth century was that two ecclesiastical jurisdictions applied here: the friars of the regular orders and the archdiocese of Tlaxcala (later Puebla).[107]

In the Center the *Suma de Visitas* recorded a small number of cabeceras with sujetos: Chilapa, Zumpango, Tixtla, Tlalcozautitlán, and Puchutitlán. Chilapa and its 21 estancias and 2,911 tributaries was assigned to the influential encomendero Diego de Ordaz. The encomendero of Tixtla, Martín de Ircio, was also a powerful figure. The *Suma* records very few sujetos of Tixtla and a small population of tributaries, but this was clearly an underestimate since in the 1530s Ircio stated, in a document connected with a legal dispute with Diego Jaramillo concerning some sujetos that Ircio claimed for his encomienda, that his lost income was 6,000 *ducados* annually, a figure that implies a substantial tributary population. A document of 1582 reports that Tixtla had fourteen sujetos, even after epidemics had decimated the population.[108]

In the North the *Suma* identifies the following: Acamixtlahuaca, Atenango, Coatlán, Cocula, Hueyistac, Iguala, Noxtepec, Taxco el Viejo,

Tenango, Tepecoacuilco, and Tetipac. Some of these had substantial populations: Iguala 1,540 tributaries and Tepecoacuilco and its dependent cabeceras 2,229. Taxco el Viejo and its ten sujetos counted 523 tributaries. The *Suma* omits Huitzuco, which in 1579 was reported to have eleven sujetos, as well as Tlaxmalac (ten sujetos) and Mayanalán (four sujetos). Thus, the picture painted in the *Suma* is incomplete, but taking into account data from other sources, the cabeceras of the North were larger in population terms than those of the Costa Grande, but smaller than those of the Montaña and Tierra Caliente.[109] Tepecoacuilco, which had been an important Mexica tribute center that administered a substantial territory, was reported in 1569 to control thirty-six sujetos, with a total population aged over twelve years old of 3,317, of whom 568 lived in the cabecera. The priest Joan Martinez told his archbishop: "The governor and *alcaldes* of this pueblo of Tepecuacuilco, which is the cabecera, manage and govern all these Indians, they dispense justice in all matters, and if anybody feels aggrieved, they appeal to the corregidor of Iguala."[110] In each of the thirty-six sujetos there was an alguacil and a tequitato who governed the Indians.[111] Like Tlapa, Tepecoacuilco ruled a hierarchical network of settlements capable of managing a considerable volume of tribute and labor.

According to the *Suma*, in the Tierra Caliente there were ten cabeceras, all of which had sujetos or barrios. Cutzamala and its thirteen sujetos had a population of 3,606 tributaries, sizeable for midcentury. Pungarabato and its thirteen sujetos counted 2,109 tributaries. For Oztuma and its eleven sujetos, 800 male tributaries were reported, living in 299 houses. Teloloapan and its thirteen sujetos registered 1,500 male tributaries in 736 houses. The *Suma* notes that Ixcapuzalco had 14 barrios and a total of 903 houses, but it does not state the population. If the proportion of adult males to houses was the same as in Teloloapan or Oztuma, Ixcapuzalco's male tributaries would have numbered 1,840–2,416. In Tetela there were fifteen sujetos and 1,488 tributaries.[112]

Allowing for gaps and inconsistencies in the data, the *Suma de Visitas* provides a midcentury snapshot of Guerrero that reveals disparities in population density and political-administrative structures, a pattern that was essentially the political geography of the Late Postclassic. These were the foundations that shaped the options of Indigenous governance open to the Spanish colonizers. However, the geography of the Indigenous communities of Guerrero during the sixteenth century was subject to substantial change due to territorial disputes and internal contestation.

5.7. Territorial Disputes, Factionalism, and the Separation of Pueblos

The bellicose conflicts between altepetl that had been a feature of the Late Postclassic continued in more legalistic fashion under Spanish rule. For example, in 1550 the corregidor of Ajuchitlán was dispatched to investigate a dispute concerning land boundaries between Pungarabato on one side and Cuyceo and Coyuca on the other. In 1552 Pungarabato was in dispute with Cutzamala, Coyuca, and Ajuchitlán, this time over saltworks, and was also involved in a disagreement concerning control of the people. A group of residents of Ajuchitlán had moved to Pungarabato, whose rulers complained in 1551 that the corregidor of Ajuchitlán had failed to take action to stop a principal from there from harassing vecinos of Ajuchitlán who had sought refuge in Pungarabato.[113] The following year the viceroy commissioned Miguel García, principal of Santiago, to investigate a conflict between Cuetzala and Apaxtla, also in the Tierra Caliente, concerning the ownership of land and houses, a spring of water, and a saltworks.[114] There were several similar disputes in the North. In 1551 Lorenzo de Luna, principal of Chiautla, was sent to Tlaxmalac and Tepecoacuilco to investigate a conflict over land boundaries. A month later Tepecoacuilco was in dispute with Zumpango over control of two sujetos, therefore over both land and people.[115] In November of the same year, the viceroy ordered an investigation of another dispute. Cuetlajuchitlán accused Huitzuco of seizing some of its land.[116] In 1552 Atenango claimed three sujetos controlled by Cuetlajuchitlán.[117] Similarly, on the Costa Chica, in 1548 the Audiencia ruled in a dispute over boundary markers between Guatepeque, Acatlán, and Cuylutla, and in 1549 the markers were formally confirmed by the authorities. Nevertheless, the disagreements among these Indigenous communities rumbled on into 1552. Guatepeque and Guypichila accused people from Cuylutla of fishing in its rivers and cutting firewood and torch pine from its forests.[118] Also, in 1552 Teyate and Xicayán disputed possession of land.[119]

This sample from only four years suggests that such disputes were frequent and numerous. Similar quantities and intensity of disputes were ubiquitous in New Spain as a few examples of other regions demonstrates. In the Oaxacan Mixteca, neighboring the Montaña of Guerrero, Terraciano classified disputes into external matters involving neighboring communities or non-Indigenous individuals and internal disagreements in which cabildos or village factions challenged caciques or other native individuals. Intercommunity disputes were an ancient tradition that were moved by colonial reorganization in the sixteenth century from the battlefield to the offices of Crown officials or the courtroom.[120] Taylor notes that in the Valley of Oaxaca, Indians fiercely defended their lands by force or litigation, but that in the sixteenth century, Spaniards were not greatly interested in land there, so disputes with Europeans occurred later in the colonial period.[121] By the eighteenth century in the Basin of the Tepalcatepec in Michoacán, adjacent to Guerrero's Tierra Caliente, Indigenous towns were left with communal lands that were rented out, and many Indigenous cofradías had cattle ranches. Disputes generally concerned nonpayment of rent, disagreements over ownership once a lease had expired, or access to water, which was important in a region of irregular rainfall.[122] In Cuernavaca, next to Guerrero's North, rental not only of farming land but of houses, lots, and market space were subjects of disputes. Cases also concerned matters such as usurpation of private land, boundary disputes, water rights, damage caused by Spanish livestock, or labor obligations in the Taxco mines.[123]

Some disputes presaged a process that accelerated in subsequent centuries: the "separation of the pueblos." Separation involved sujetos seeking formal sanction of independence from their cabecera, a process that was triggered in part by administrative decisions. A pueblo that had been a political-administrative center in the Late Postclassic could have its status confirmed by being recognized as a cabecera. However, some cabeceras were demoted to become sujetos, which implied a loss of status, privileges, and salary for the local rulers, while some sujetos were promoted to cabecera, increasing elite salaries and privileges. Stephanie Wood's study of the separation phenomenon in the Toluca region identified several factors that promoted corporate independence. Separation and micropatriotism were characteristic of Mesoamerican communities and were expressed in the early colonial period by the pursuit of cabecera status. Other motivations were the entitlement to a town site and other community holdings, political and religious autonomy, and general community pride and prestige. In the later colonial period, the pursuit of corporate autonomy was sought by hacienda and mining communities that had no history as precontact settlements nor as sujetos of a cabecera.[124]

Separation was especially significant in the Montaña since this was the region with the most complex hierarchy of cabeceras and sujetos in Guerrero. Around 1570 Tlapa and its 11 subordinate cabeceras controlled 112 sujetos (see table 5.7). The hierarchy was unchanged until the

TABLE 5.7. *CABECERAS* AND *SUJETOS* IN TLAPA PROVINCE, CA. 1570

Cabecera	Tributaries	Sujetos	Average distance between cabeceras and sujetos (km)	Notes
Tlapa	885	19	22.4	
Atliztaca	244	8	9.6	Cabecera near Tlapa
Caltitlán	679	20	17.9	Cabecera near Tlapa
Atlamajac	1088	12	16.9	Cabecera near Tlapa
Yguala	448	6	11.2	Cabecera near Tlapa
Ychcateopan	280	6	28.0	Cabecera near Tlapa
Petlacala	194	8	14.0	Cabecera near Tlapa
Chiepetlán	254	5	6.3	Cabecera near Tlapa
Tenango	242	7	25.7	Cabecera near Tlapa
Azoyú	159	9	17.7	Costa Chica
Totomixtlahuaca	390	6	18.2	In the sierra
Cuitlapan	301	6	15.1	In the sierra
TOTALS	5164	112		

Sources: Gutiérrez Mendoza, "La organización político-territorial del 'Reino' de Tlapa," 326–27; Dehouve, "Historia del municipio en la Montaña," 102–6.

1570s and 1580s, when caciques whose status was under threat initiated separation to preserve their status. For example, in 1575 Cualác refused to contribute tribute to Olinalá. In the same year Atlamajac and Atlixtac separated from Xochihuehuetlán by electing their own governors, elections that were repeated in 1579 and 1580, despite the opposition of Tlapa, the ultimate cabecera. These early cases signaled the start of a long-term process, through which caciques of the Montaña restructured the administrative-political organization of the region. Over the colonial period, separation converted the former domain of Tlapa-Tlachinollan into small municipalities. This process occurred very early and rapidly on the Costa Chica where pueblos that had been part of Tlapa-Tlachinollan's domain were assigned as individual encomiendas, effectively separating them at a stroke. Here only one separation occurred later in the sixteenth century: Cochoapa separated from Ometepec to become subordinate to Igualapa.[125]

A separation occurred in the Center in 1550 when the principales of Tixtla declared that they agreed with the wish of their sujeto Mochitlán that its tribute should be assessed separately.[126] Similarly, in the North, also in 1550, Tlamacazapa, Azala (Atzcala), and their cabecera

Taxco el Viejo disputed the tribute that each should contribute to the overall assessment of 1,000 pesos and 500 fanegas (23,000 kilograms) of maize. Tlamacazapa succeeded in escaping its share of this substantial amount to be assessed independently.[127] Thus, one motive for separation was for a pueblo to be responsible for its own tribute. Equally, cabeceras might seek control of a sujeto to spread the cost of tribute over a larger population. Such seems to have been the case of Comala, a sujeto claimed by Acaucingo and Tenango in 1553.[128] In the Tierra Caliente in 1585, teniente de corregidor Joan de Sandoval ruled, in the case of San Gaspar Sacatlan, a sujeto that sought separation from Oztuma, that Agustín Pérez, Domingo Ramírez, Juan López, Sebastián Tamina, and Melchor Hernández, "indios mandones" of San Gaspar, should obey the instructions of the governor and regidores of Oztuma, on pain of two hundred lashes.[129]

Conflicts and rivalries of the Late Postclassic could lead to dissension between pueblos in the colonial period. In the case of Oztuma and Acapetlahuaya, language and community history could lead to such conflicts. For example, in 1579 Oztuma, a Chontal town proud of its lineage, reported to Captain Lucas Pinto, author of "Relación de Ichcateupan," that its rulers had defied the Mexicas, a decision they paid for with their lives. Nevertheless, Chontal rulers continued to govern Oztuma and claimed that Acapetlahuaya, a Mexica settlement, was one of its sujetos. The Indians of Acapetlahuaya, however, asserted that under Mexica rule they had never paid tribute but instead were responsible for guarding the fortress of Oztuma. Indeed, they claimed that the neighboring altepetl had paid tribute to Acapetlahuaya, which was now an independent cabecera with its own sujetos, alcalde, and regidor.[130]

Similarly, the Mexicas of Cuetzala told Pinto a very different story from the version given to him by their Chontal neighbors. Their ancestors had migrated from the Valley of Mexico and asked the Chontals for land, a request that was firmly refused. The migrants settled on a hill and sustained themselves by hunting and eating maize given by their neighbors. They lived peacefully until Tenentzingo and Cocula demanded that they be paid tribute, a demand that Cuetzala rejected. Then Cuetzala lost many warriors in a war with Coatepec. Cuetzala requested assistance from Tenochtitlan, which sent two armies. The second defeated Coatepec and destroyed its houses. Moctezuma appointed a calpixqui to govern Cuetzala. Subsequently, Cuetzala defeated the Chontals of Apaxtla and went to war with the Chontals of Tenepatlan.[131]

However, the Chontals of Apaxtla, a sujeto of Cuetzala, told a very different story:

> They said that they are the ancient residents of the land, and that the Mexicans who came from Cuetzala came to ask that for the love of God they be given land to live on, which they [Apaxtla] gave them with good will, afterward they [Cuetzala] rose up against them [Apaxtla], and so, they [Cuetzala] defeated them and became lords of the land, and therefore the Mexicans consider themselves their [Apaxtla's] governor.[132]

The Chontals of Tenepatlan, also a sujeto of Cuetzala, told a similar tale of how the Nahuas of Cuetzala repaid the generosity of Tenepatlan by subjecting them to Cuetzala's rule.[133] Beneath these narratives lay the clear seeds of separation of the Chontal sujetos from their Nahua cabecera. A similar pair of competing narratives has been reported in the Oaxacan Mixteca, close to the Montaña of Guerrero. Documents, two primordial titles and a map, ostensibly written in the 1520s and produced as evidence in a 1690s territorial dispute between a Nahua town and a Mixtec community, tell different narratives of the "original conquest" of Oaxaca. The Nahuas asserted that they entered Oaxaca at the invitation of Zapotecs and defeated the Mixtecs long before the advent of the Spaniards. The Mixtec account paints the Nahuas as bellicose newcomers defeated by the Mixtecs, but nevertheless generously treated at the request of Cortés.[134]

Bernardo García Martínez observes that the Spanish redefinition of space precipitated separation.[135] Yet there were several motives for separation, among them historic conflicts between different polities, the competition between factions to control the posts of local government, the loss of cabecera status or the increase in status of a sujeto, displacements of population that resulted from congregaciones, movements of population in order to avoid tribute or other exactions such as the construction, maintenance, or adornment of a church in a distant cabecera, or alternatively the construction of a church in a sujeto that, therefore, no longer wished to contribute to the cabecera's church. While the process of separations was driven by Indigenous interests, a further reorganization of Indigenous settlements, known as congregaciones, was carried out by the viceregal government according to Spanish, rather than Indigenous, priorities.

5.8. Congregaciones and Resettlements

Bishop Vasco de Quiroga undertook the first relocations of the Indians into fewer settlements in Michoacán from the 1530s to 1547, followed by resettlements carried out by friars in other regions. Two later periods of congregaciones were organized by the viceroyalty, the first from 1557 to 1564 by Luis de Velasco the elder, the second initiated by Viceroy Gaspar de Zúñiga y Acevedo in 1590 and carried out from 1603 to 1625. The motive for congregations was essentially that the dispersed settlement pattern of Indigenous communities, which was further accentuated by the decline of the Indigenous population, was inconvenient for several Spanish interests. The friars and bishops promoted congregaciones to facilitate evangelization and the collection of tithes. A more concentrated population was easier for Crown officials to administer and eased the collection of tribute, as it did for encomenderos. Congregaciones also left more land vacant for Spanish agriculturalists and livestock ranchers.[136]

Lockhart notes that in central Mexico the high degree of nucleation of Indigenous altepetl made large-scale population movements much less imperative than in peripheral areas.[137] Wood's study of the Toluca region generally confirms Lockhart's conclusion, but notes that determined resistance frustrated relocation to sites considered unsuitable by the Indians.[138] In the eastern Tierra Caliente of Michoacán, a considerable number of resettlements during the sixteenth century facilitated evangelization, Spanish agriculture, tribute collection, and access to Indian labor. They also caused conflicts, especially over landownership.[139] In the Sierra Norte of Puebla, the religious congregaciones resulted in greater concentration of population units, which further centered administrative-political functions in the cabecera, and the removal of cabeceras from inaccessible hilltop sites. The seventeenth-century relocations moved communities from pre-Hispanic sites to colonial locales, destroying churches and houses in the process. Some Indians resisted by simply fleeing the new site and later returning to their original homes, and some sujetos refused promotion to the status of cabecera.[140]

The sixteenth century was a time of demographic upheaval and tumultuous changes for the Indigenous peoples of Guerrero. Some changes were violent and brutal, especially the suppression of Yope resistance by Vasco Porcallo in 1531. Porcallo, who imprisoned 1,000–2,000 Yopes and distributed them to his men as slaves, was imprisoned for excessive use of violence.¹⁴¹ While the Yopes resisted with force, other groups simply escaped, fled, or hid. Many did not experience armed violence, but rather the cruelty of forced labor, which could be as deadly as combat. Nevertheless, some Indians found in the labor of the mines opportunities to earn their livelihood and to escape tribute obligations. Mining was a significant factor in population movements in Guerrero. Relocations were also the result of formal processes of resettlement. Some were organized by the religious to facilitate evangelization, others by government to control the population and, hence, tribute collection.

The congregaciones of the Costa Grande took place in the context of an exceptional collapse of the population and a growing Spanish interest in acquiring land for livestock to cultivate cotton, cacao, or coconut palms. A famine in 1588 further devastated the Indigenous population. Evangelization drove the first resettlements, organized by Friar Juan Bautista Moya between 1553 and 1560. Another wave of congregaciones occurred between 1595 and 1606, although some pueblos were allowed to return to their original site in 1607. Two cases suggest that the process of congregation did not always run smoothly. In 1603 the priest of Yanhuitlán, Rafael de Trejo, had requested that the population of the district be concentrated in Yanhuitlán because an epidemic was killing twenty to thirty Indians a day. However, the viceroy suspended the process until he received a further report from the alcalde mayor of Zacatula. In 1614 the priest of Tecpan, Nicolás Resendi, informed the viceroy that his order of 1613 that the Indians of the district, who were few in number, should be concentrated in the cabecera to facilitate their religious instruction and public works on the church and an inn at Tecpan had not been carried out. The viceroy ordered the immediate implementation of the resettlement. Some groups, and even entire pueblos, did not wait to be moved but simply took charge of their own destiny and left the coast for good. These movements of population, combined with *mestizaje* and the importation of African and Asian labor, came close to eliminating the Indigenous character of the Costa Grande. By the eighteenth century, Nahuatl and Cuitlatec were spoken only in four pueblos of the Costa Grande.¹⁴²

The collapse of the population and pressure from livestock owners to acquire land shaped the congregaciones of the Costa Chica. Settlements were moved by livestock owners as well as by officials. Livestock owners took land from Cintla, Quetzalapa, Santa Catarina, and Tlacolula. Some Indigenous groups moved to places where they could cultivate land to escape hunger. Some Indians avoided relocation by fleeing, hiding, or moving only to return later. Others of their own accord sought protection in larger towns, such as Ometepec, whose population consequently remained stable despite the ravages of disease. Viceroy Velasco the younger ordered the congregación of the area in 1594. However, the Indians could still resist and protect their interests to some degree. Cosoyoapan, a sujeto of Xochistlahuaca, was relocated to the cabecera in 1600. However, Ometepec attempted to appropriate Cosoyoapan's crop land and orchards, so the Indians of Cosoyoapan reoccupied their land, building houses and churches on two sites. Ometepec, on the other hand, was unsuccessful in resisting the demolition of some houses and chapels to reorganize the town on Spanish lines. The general effect of the resettlements and congregaciones was to move the Indians away from the coastal plain to be replaced by livestock and a predominantly *Afromestizo* population.[143]

In the Montaña between 1570 and 1590, relocations for religious reasons, driven particularly by Augustinian friars, were an important factor in the ways in which the congregaciones played out. Cabeceras were consolidated around monasteries and churches to facilitate evangelization. A sujeto whose location was convenient for ministering to dispersed settlements distant from an existing cabecera could be elevated to the status of cabecera de doctrina. On the other hand, some sujetos ceased to exist. Between 1564 and 1571 the *Códice de Totomixtlahuaca* records at least seventeen subject communities, but after 1570 only ten remained. Some subordinate communities were congregated into Tlapa, but the newcomers found that Tlapa's principales had monopolized the irrigated land, leaving them no land to cultivate. They returned to their original locations, where it was difficult for the Spaniards to control them and count them for tribute purposes. Thus, the first episode of relocations in the Montaña did not change the dispersed settlement pattern fundamentally. Rather, it was an adjustment for Spanish administrative purposes.[144]

A second program of congregaciones began in 1598 during the administration of Viceroy Gaspar de Zúñiga to concentrate in fewer locations the Indigenous population, much reduced by epidemics in 1576–1581 and 1590. The Augustinian friars opposed these relocations since they had chosen the locations of churches and monasteries based on the existing settlements, which were conveniently located for their purposes. The case of Totomixtlahuaca indicates that rivalry between the Augustinians and the secular clergy played a part in the congregaciones.

In 1621 the viceroy refused the Augustinians permission to build a monastery in Totomixtlahuaca, which already had a secular assistant priest. The Augustinians' plans were opposed by the Indigenous communities of Malinaltepec, Zitlaltepec, Huehuetepec, Huehueyotlahuaca, and Huancoquitengo. The program was halted in 1604 and addressed only settlements that were in very inaccessible locations. Those who wished were allowed to return to their original settlement. Nevertheless, the congregaciones had some long-term effects. In the sierra, the population of the parishes of Totomixtlahuaca, Metlatónoc, Atlamajac, and Zoyatlán increased as did, except for Totomixtlahuaca, the number of sujetos. However, the number of sujetos and the population decreased in the jurisdictions of Tlapa, Alcozauca, Atlixtac, Olinalá, and Huamuxtitlán, where some settlements were left uninhabited, their churches in ruins.[145]

In the Center, church and civil relocations brought about some significant changes. These were not driven solely by Spanish interests; Indigenous concerns also played a part. The increasing significance of the Mexico City–Acapulco road was an especially important factor. In 1604 don Francisco de Balverdi informed the viceroy that relocation of San Francisco Ocamatlán and other towns that provided passage across the Balsas should be reconsidered because the crossing was very difficult.[146] In 1533 Chilapa was moved to the site of a monastery, about 1 kilometer from the town's original location. In 1603 a program of congregaciones was ordered to concentrate eleven communities with a population of 447.5 tributaries in Chilapa (population 778 tributaries) and its sujeto Zitlala (204.5 tributaries). Many settlements appealed against their relocation and the program was not completed as planned. For example, in 1604 Azacualoyan was ordered, with three of its sujetos, to move to Zitlala, but its residents successfully argued that they would rather stay in Azacualoyan where they had family and friends. San Jerónimo Palatlán also successfully appealed relocation to Zitlala on the grounds that the climate of Zitlala was too hot and that they should be moved to Azacualoyan, which was only a league distant and where the friars of Chilapa could minister to them. Thus, Azacualoyan preserved its autonomy and control of its population. Similarly, Xocutla and six of its sujetos with a total population of two hundred vecinos resisted being moved to Quechultenango, which would greatly reduce its status, and successfully argued that the sujetos should be moved to Xocutla, whose site was more suitable. Also in 1604, Santa Mónica Tlapeulapa opposed relocation to Quechultenango, preferring a move to Zitlala, only two leagues away. Tlapeulapa contended that Quechultenango's land was infertile and too far (twelve leagues) from the fields of maguey from which they made ships rigging (important for the Acapulco trade and therefore for Spanish interests). They preferred to move to Zitlala, only two leagues distant. San Martín Huitzcuaucingo's residents, on the other hand, successfully argued that they should relocate to Quechultenango rather than Chilapa.[147]

Since Zumpango's importance waned with the decline of mining, in the second half of the sixteenth century five of its estancias were moved to Tixtla. The rest were congregated in 1603, and the only surviving settlements were Zumpango, Yzquiapa, and Chilpancingo. The latter would grow in importance because of its location on the Acapulco road and eventually would separate from Zumpango's jurisdiction in 1629, a decision confirmed in 1693.[148] Tixtla was an important cabecera in the Center, with three subordinate cabeceras under its purview by about 1569 to 1571: Apango and Atliaca, with four sujetos each, and Yacapicatlán with three. Three settlements succeeded in resisting their relocation to Tixtla in the congregaciones of 1591–1604 by arguing that they had good, irrigated land at their original site. Three more opposed relocation to Zumpango. For instance, Atliaca appealed to Spanish mercantile interests, arguing that its location on the Acapulco road made relocation undesirable. However, Yacapicatlán failed to prevent its relocation to Tixtla around 1605, but in 1623 it was reported that some residents had built huts and cultivated land belonging to Yacapicatlán without permission.[149]

In the North, congregaciones and epidemics created open spaces where Spaniards could acquire land, legally or otherwise. Congregaciones here were influenced by two significant competing economic interests: the mineowners of the Taxco area and the mercantile and agricultural and livestock interests of Tepecoacuilco and the Iguala Valley. The Taxco mineowners sought labor and control of maize production in the valley, while the landowners and merchants of Tepecoacuilco and the Iguala Valley resisted control by mining enterprises. In October 1693 the viceroy appointed the encomendero of Huitzuco, the mineowner and landowner Bernardino de Casasola, to plan the congregaciones of Huitzuco, Zacango, and Atenango. However, a faction of Indians in Huitzuco opposed Casasola's appointment and in 1594 succeeded in persuading the viceroy to withdraw it. In the first decade of the seventeenth century, Melchor de Tornamira, the encomendero of Tepecoacuilco, began to accumulate land in areas left depopulated by the congregation of the town's sujetos. In the following decade merchants of Mexico City and Texcoco and the Jesuit College of San Pedro and San Pablo acquired land in the Iguala Valley.[150]

Congregaciones, epidemics, and labor exactions radically reorganized the Indigenous settlement pattern, as consideration of some population statistics indicate. Iguala was relocated to a site designed on a grid plan with a church and four neighborhoods, each with a chapel. Around 1550 it had some 5,400 tributaries, but by 1579 only 1,040. In Tepecoacuilco the reverse occurred: 2,290 in 1550, 5,000–6,000 by 1579. Meanwhile, Huitzuco's population remained stable: 600 in 1550, 520 around 1579.[151] Relocations in this region met some resistance. In 1604 it was reported that people from Santa María Concepción Palutla, congregated in Tepecoacuilco, left to set up home in San Cristóbal Mezcala, left vacant by moving its inhabitants to Tepecoacuilco.[152] Long-term residents of Tlaxmalac complained in the same year that newcomers who had taken refuge there from congregaciones ten or eleven years ago had driven established residents from their homes.[153]

In the Taxco area, the population unsurprisingly was moved for the convenience of mining. From 1590 congregaciones shifted Hueyistac and Cacahuamilpa from land they had cultivated before the arrival of the Spaniards. Disputes over land that originated in the Late Postclassic were now complicated by the interference of mineowners. For example, Tetipac, Pilcaya, Noxtepec, Coatlán, and Tenango's ancient conflict over land revived in the 1550s and 1560s, stimulated in part by the mineowner Luis de Castilla who settled Tarascans for his mining operations on land claimed by Tetipac. Furthermore, Tetipac claimed Tenango was collecting tribute from these newcomers. In the 1590s the Spanish authorities decided to resolve the dispute by means of congregation, starting with Pilcaya in 1594, followed by Tetipac being moved to a site near Noxtepec, the third location that Tetipac had occupied in seven decades. In 1539 at its original site its residents had built a church, which would have made the first relocation particularly distressing. About 1567 Tetipac had been moved to a new site where fray Joan de la Peña, son of the encomendero Joan de la Peña Vallejo, had built a chapel. He claimed that Tetipac had not received the sacraments at its former site for three years. These and other movements of population disrupted Indigenous landholding, leaving land free to graze livestock needed for mining.[154] Indigenous resistance could be sufficiently stubborn that Spanish authorities went to the extreme of threatening to hang governors of pueblos that resisted congregación.[155] In the end, however, powerful Spaniards, mineowners, encomenderos, government officials, and members of influential families were able to acquire land.[156]

In the Late Postclassic, Indigenous communities held land for a variety of purposes: land tilled by commoner tenants, land of village officials cultivated by commoner sharecroppers, fields whose produce funded war, temples, or some other community purpose. The sixteenth century altered this pattern of land use and set in motion acquisition by Spanish interests. Indigenous communities, much reduced in population by the end of the century, did not lose all their land. Community land continued to be cultivated for collective purposes, to fund churches and cofradías, and to finance municipal government through the caja de comunidad. The Indigenous elites were able to retain some land, which was cultivated for them by commoners, as well as some privileges and services. Thus, communal activities, with recognizable roots in precontact practices, were combined with new patterns of landownership and use driven by new interests—mining, agricultural and livestock exploitation, and associated commercial activities—with unprecedented intensity.[157]

In the Tierra Caliente epidemic disease and the congregaciones of 1594–1604 reduced the number of sujetos, as was the case of Ajuchitlán, whose twenty sujetos recorded in 1550 were reduced to just two by the early seventeenth century. A curious consequence of congregación in Ajuchitlán was that the Indians protested that it left untended a rose bush whose flowers were used to decorate the community's churches. The viceroy ordered that one house be left standing so that two or three persons could tend the roses. In Coyuca by midcentury, the *Suma de Visitas* recorded seven sujetos with 1,902 tributaries, but the "Relación de Ajuchitlán y su Partido" of 1579 counted twelve sujetos and only 350 tributaries. Coyuca had only 47 tributaries in 1603 when the 134.5 tributaries in its twelve sujetos were congregated in the cabecera. Pungarabato's sujetos were reduced progressively during the century: thirteen about 1550, down to seven in 1579, of which five with 80.5 tributaries were congregated in 1603 and 1604, leaving in situ only two sujetos. Cutzamala had thirteen sujetos around 1550 with a total tributary population of 3,706. By 1579 the number of sujetos had apparently increased to twenty-one, but the population had fallen to 813 tributaries. The church congregated the population of Guayameo into eleven barrios (internal neighborhoods of the cabecera) by 1565–1571, but then the congregación of 1603 merged Guayameo with Zirándaro and relocated ten sujetos to create a town of 275.5 tributaries.[158]

The congregaciones of 1590–1611 stripped Chontal Oztuma of its status as cabecera and promoted the Nahua settlement of Acapetlahuaya to cabecera. In this area the congregaciones relocated a dispersed population, much reduced by the epidemics, for the convenience of the priests, to remove Indians from land to graze livestock, to control saltworks, and to provide labor for work in the mines. These changes sometimes met resistance and on occasion were violently accomplished. Some congregated villagers returned to their homes, to be returned by the livestock owners to where they had been congregated. Where once there had been only Indigenous settlements, pueblos with a mixed population of Spaniards, Mestizos, Blacks, Mulattos, and some Indians emerged.[159] The data suggest a severely reduced population in the region, much moved around to leave land vacant for livestock and other Spanish enterprises.

5.9. Power, Adaptation, Resistance, and New Institutions: Conclusions

In the eight decades that followed the arrival of Spanish colonizers in Guerrero, the Indigenous communities of the region underwent substantial changes, changes that shaped their long-term future, many of which had consequences that can be traced over succeeding centuries to modern times. The most devastating transformation in human terms was the appalling mortality that afflicted every community in the region. This, combined with the admixture of European, African, and Asian newcomers, substantially altered the balance of Indigenous and other ethnicities differentially in the six regions of Guerrero. The Costa Grande and Costa Chica became characterized by Afromestizo communities with cultural features derived from Africa.[160] The Montaña, in contrast, remains the most Indigenous region of the modern state.[161]

New institutions and jurisdictions of municipal, civil, judicial, and religious governance, at the formal level, were modeled on Iberian practice, but the Indigenous peoples were able to modify the new structures to incorporate precontact ways of conducting the community's life. The offices of the cabildo and the church as often as not were filled by descendants of precontact village elites, and new institutions such as the caja de comunidad and the cofradía funded important functions such as festivals and the defense of the community's rights from the depredations of Crown officials, corrupt priests, and other Spaniards, or, indeed, other Indigenous towns. Precontact rivalries and disputes were now settled in Spanish courts rather than on the battlefield or by appealing to the tlatoani of Tenochtitlan or the cazonci. The Catholic church replaced the temple, but like its precontact predecessor, the town's church became a chief focus of community loyalty and pride, a sentiment as important in colonial times as it had been in the Late Postclassic and no doubt earlier. These would be features of Indigenous communities throughout the colonial period.

Guerrero's Indigenous peoples would contend with other factors introduced by the Spanish colonizers. The encomienda would become part of the tribute obligations of Indian villages. New Spanish forms of land tenure and use would fill vacant spaces left by depopulation but would also both come into conflict with Indigenous interests and offer new opportunities, such as Indigenous ownership of livestock. The new mining economy would affect the North and the Tierra Caliente in particular but would be a factor in all regions of Guerrero in the sixteenth century, if only for a period. And, most particular to Guerrero, from 1565 Acapulco would become the port through which the Spanish empire traded with Asia. It is to these factors that we turn next.

CHAPTER SIX

Encomiendas, Encomenderos, and Guerrero's Indigenous Communities

The Spanish invasion of Mexico was privately financed by a small group of adventurers who naturally sought a return on their investment and seigneurial privileges. The Crown had no intention of rewarding them from the royal treasury, so another way to remunerate the conquistadors was required. The solution was the encomienda. The term *encomienda* originated in the Spain of the Reconquista, where it signified a temporary grant of sovereignty over a territory. In the Caribbean colonies, an encomienda grant gave a conquistador the right to Indian labor to produce food and mine gold. The encomienda in New Spain was a third variant: an allotment of Indians who provided tribute (originally in kind, later in cash or a mixture of the two) and labor to the encomendero. In return, the encomendero was, in theory, obliged to care for the welfare and religious instruction of the Indians, an obligation frequently honored in the breach. Crucially, the encomienda granted no property rights and was not heritable unless the Crown conceded limited inheritance for one or occasionally more generations. Cortés wasted little time in distributing encomiendas to his loyal lieutenants until the Crown asserted more control over the institution through the Audiencia and the viceroy. As an answer to an urgent problem, the encomienda was an important institution in the first half of the sixteenth century, its importance gradually diminishing after 1550 as the Crown appropriated encomiendas, although some lasted well into the seventeenth century.[1]

6.1. The Regional Distribution of the Encomienda

Counting the number of encomiendas in Guerrero is not an exact science. Data for the early years especially are at times sketchy and contradictory. Moreover, the encomienda was not immutable. It might be divided

TABLE 6.1. REGIONAL DISTRIBUTION OF *ENCOMIENDAS* IN INDIVIDUAL HANDS IN GUERRERO IN THE SIXTEENTH CENTURY

Region	Number of encomiendas	Number of encomenderos	Encomenderos who were vecinos of the region
Costa Grande	15–16	23	12
Costa Chica	7–12	19	1–2
Montaña	3	7	0?
Center	4	10	0?
Norte	9	13	0?
Tierra Caliente	10	22	1
TOTAL	48–54	94	14–15

Sources: García Castro, *Suma de visitas de pueblos*; Gerhard, *A Guide to the Historical Geography of New Spain*; González Leal, *Relación secreta de conquistadores*; "Relación de méritos y servicios del conquistador Bernardino Vázquez de Tapia"; Himmerich and Valencia, *The Encomenderos of New Spain*; Icaza, *Diccionario autobiográfico de Conquistadores y Pobladores*; *El Libro de tasaciones de pueblos*; Scholes and Adams, *Documentos para la historia del México Colonial*; and various other works cited in the bibliography.

or the communities that comprised it might be changed. The latter was especially the case on the Costa Chica. An encomienda could be assigned to a single individual or shared by two or more. Encomiendas could also be inherited, although this was not always the case, and the inheritance was sometimes disputed. When an encomienda was reassigned or when the holder died, it might revert to the Crown, temporarily or permanently. The Crown assigned encomiendas to itself from the beginning, and in one case in Guerrero (the large encomienda of Tlapa) shared it with individual encomenderos. Table 6.1 counts primary holders, the first member of each family to receive an encomienda. Since encomiendas often changed hands, there were more primary encomenderos than there were encomiendas. Heirs are not counted.

About half of Guerrero's encomiendas were on the coast. Most were small. Slightly more than half the encomenderos of the Costa Grande were, for varying periods of time, resident in Zacatula because Zacatula was an early hub for military and mining operations along the Pacific coast and for exploration of the route to Asia. In no other region of Guerrero did this many encomenderos take up residence, even temporarily. On the other hand, the Montaña had only three encomiendas, but they were large and profitable. The first encomenderos here were powerful figures. Hernán Cortés himself briefly held Tlapa, for instance. The Center was another area of few, but profitable, encomiendas. Zumpango was the first

TABLE 6.2. REGIONAL DISTRIBUTION OF CROWN *ENCOMIENDAS* IN GUERRERO, CA. 1548, ACCORDING TO THE *SUMA DE VISITAS*

Region	Number of encomiendas	Tributaries
Province of Zacatula (Costa Grande)	42	5,183
Costa de la Mar del Sur (Costa Chica)	19	2,107–2,172
Montaña	12	9,370
Center	3	292
North	5	3,064
Tierra Caliente	3	3,879
Total	84	23,895–23,960

Notes: The Province of Zacatula and the Costa de la Mar del Sur do not correspond exactly to the Costa Grande and the Costa Chica. They include parts of modern Michoacán and Oaxaca respectively. The figure for the Montaña, where the Crown shared its encomiendas with individuals, differs from that in table 6.1 because the *Suma de Visitas* classifies cabeceras dependent on Tlapa as separate encomiendas. García Castro assigns some encomiendas to regions according to criteria different from those used in this study.

Source: García Castro, *Suma de visitas de pueblos*.

silver mining site in New Spain. Mining boomed there in the 1520s and 1530s, but over time the Acapulco–Mexico City road was what made this area attractive. In the North there were nine encomiendas, all attractive for being close to Taxco and other mines of the Silver Province. In the Tierra Caliente there were only ten encomiendas, but they were sizeable. This was an area with a precontact history of mining (copper and gold) that also produced salt and, like the Montaña, had a substantial population that was well organized for tribute collection. The Tierra Caliente was also within easy reach of the mines of the Silver Province.

There were also several royal encomiendas that paid tribute to the Crown. The Crown reserved some encomiendas for itself from the beginning and acquired others from individuals, whether on the death of the holder or for some other reason, particularly in the second half of the sixteenth century. By comparing the regional distribution of Crown encomiendas (table 6.2) with those in individual hands (table 6.1), we can reasonably deduce some of the rationale behind Crown policy. The bulk of Crown holdings were on the coast, probably because this was a region that produced cotton and cacao, but above all it was a region of gold placers before the discovery of richer silver deposits inland. Furthermore, Guerrero's coast was the base for seeking the return route to Asia. The

TABLE 6.3. VALUE OF ROYAL TRIBUTE FROM GUERRERO IN JANUARY 1560, AFTER DEDUCTION OF THE *DIEZMO*

Region	Number of encomiendas	Value of tribute in pesos
Costa Grande	40	3,588
Costa Chica	4	800
Montaña	1	1,000
Centre	0	0
North	9	5,380
Tierra Caliente	3	2,320
Total	57	13,088

Notes: The figures differ from those in table 6.2 because the 1560 document classifies encomiendas differently, and because some encomiendas reverted to the Crown or were reassigned to individuals. No tribute was reported for Atenango (North).

Source: "Tributos de pueblos de indios."

Crown held several encomiendas in the Montaña, including Tlapa, the richest in all Guerrero, of which, however, it had a minority share, the rest being held by especially influential families. Crown holdings in the Center were few, and the most productive, such as Tixtla and Zumpango, were in the hands of powerful individuals. Crown encomiendas in the North and Tierra Caliente were also few. Powerful mining interests held the best encomiendas here. Clearly, in 1548, the Crown was not yet in a position to deprive influential encomenderos of their entitlements.

The distribution of royal encomiendas in Guerrero reflected the structure of the Indigenous communities at the time of the Spanish invasion. On the Costa Grande the polities were relatively numerous and small. In the Montaña the ancient polity of Tlapa formed a large, hierarchically organized unit with a sizeable population, most of which was incorporated into a single encomienda. In the Tierra Caliente the encomiendas were also relatively large. Encomiendas in the North incorporated, in the main, long-established Chontal polities. In general, the settlements of the Costa Chica, Center, Montaña, North, and Tierra Caliente were more hierarchically complex than those of the Costa Grande.[2]

Accordingly, as tables 6.3 indicates, in 1560 the Crown had a substantial number of small encomiendas on the Costa Grande, but their yield was poor: only thirteen paid 100 pesos or more. Xaputiqua paid the most (420 pesos). Two paid only 20 pesos each. There was still a little gold in the coastal placers: Of the ten Crown encomiendas in New Spain that delivered gold to the King's coffers, seven were on the Costa Grande. The Crown encomiendas on the Costa Chica were few and small. By 1560 the Crown controlled some valuable encomiendas in the North: Iguala (1,175 pesos) and Taxco el Viejo (1,200 pesos). In Tierra Caliente, Ajuchitlán was worth 1,550 pesos. The richest encomienda in Guerrero was Tlapa (4,000 pesos, of which the Crown received 1,000). In 1560 the total Crown income from tribute (after the *diezmo*) was 152,075. Thus, Crown encomiendas in Guerrero represented only 8 percent of Crown tribute income.[3]

Until about the middle of the century, tribute from Crown encomiendas close to mining centers was used to support mining operations. Thus, the Crown insisted that its encomiendas provide supplies and labor for the mines of Taxco. For example, Teulistaca, near Taxco, was required to deliver clothing made of agave fiber, honey, beeswax, maize, beans, chile, salt, and copal, and to provide twenty workers in the mines. The demand for labor was dropped in 1551 to be replaced by a payment of 490 pesos and 4 tomines, and the harvest of a plot of land to be delivered to Taxco.[4] Similarly, in 1546, Tuzantla was required to deliver a variety of tribute items: maize, beans, chile, jícaras, 400 pairs of sandals, salt, cooking vessels, *comales*, *chicovites* (a kind of basket), 2 loads of melons, and every eighty days, 300 mantas and 2 *cargas* of fish delivered to Mexico City and food for the tribute administrator. Tuzantla was also obliged to cultivate and harvest cotton to be delivered to Mexico City. In 1546 the tribute was simplified: forty workers in the Coantepeque mines, chile, and beans. The mineworkers were to be treated as the regulations specified and to be fed by the mineowner. The labor requirement was dropped in 1549.[5] The Crown issued many decrees and instructions to ensure the well-being and good treatment of the Indians, most notably the New Laws of 1542. However, the king's good intentions were persistently contradicted by his demands to increase the royal revenues.[6]

In 1535 the royal government of New Spain spent 69 percent of tribute income on the salaries of the officials responsible for collecting it. If this figure remained true in 1560, the net value of the royal encomiendas of Guerrero was only 4,057 pesos.[7] According to a 1536 document, Crown income from seventeen encomiendas in Guerrero was 7,358 pesos, while officials' salaries amounted to 3,549 pesos (48 percent of income). In some cases (e.g., Pantla and Zolcoaca on the Costa Grande) salaries consumed all the tribute, and in others very little remained (e.g., Zacatula, Cinagua, and their district yielded a miserable net 21 pesos). Other encomiendas were more profitable, though still relatively modest on a net basis: Iguala yielded 370 pesos and Ajuchitlán 592. Chilapa, temporarily in the Crown's possession after the death of the encomendero Diego de Ordaz, netted 838 pesos. All in all, the 1536 report confirms that the encomiendas of the coast were poor, and those of the Montaña, Center, North, and Tierra Caliente were more profitable.[8]

Thus, the encomiendas that the Crown had been able to reserve for itself by about 1560 yielded a modest income for the royal coffers. In general, powerful individuals retained control of the better encomiendas, especially inland, until the end of the sixteenth century and in some cases into the seventeenth. The encomenderos of Guerrero were a privileged group who secured access to the resources of the encomienda in areas that seemed to offer opportunities in terms of precious minerals or of tradeable commodities such as cacao, cotton, or salt. Once an individual had secured an encomienda, the objective was to leverage the free resources provided by tribute in new enterprises. The encomenderos often sought partners for their new enterprises, which were not without risk. A selection of case studies of the commercial practices that were developed reveals the role that the encomienda played in capitalizing and creating the first fortunes of sixteenth-century Guerrero.

6.2. The Encomenderos of Guerrero

i. The Coast

Few of the encomenderos of the Costa Grande seem to have been figures of particular social or political importance, the exceptions being Juan Rodríguez de Villafuerte (Mescaltepec), the founder of Zacatula; Diego Jaramillo (Citlaltomahua), who also had the encomienda of Zumpango, an early center of silver mining; and governor and treasurer of New Spain Alonso de Estrada (a share of Coyuca), who also held part of Tlapa.[9] A number of encomiendas lapsed in the 1550s and 1560s, but some continued in private hands until the end of the century. The potential of gold placers and livestock raising were principal attractions of encomiendas here. For example, Alonso Martín de Jerez, the powerful encomendero of Toliman, was a resident of his encomienda and of Zacatula from at least

1525. Jerez avoided risky mining ventures that attracted other Spaniards to the coast. Toliman provided capital for his two principal enterprises, livestock and money lending. By 1528 he was raising substantial numbers of pigs to supply pork to mineworkers. He was also well connected with powerful figures of the day, such as Hernán Pérez de Bocanegra, an encomendero and landowner in Michoacán and Mexico City, who had significant official positions and social connections in the capital. Another associate was Juan de Burgos, encomendero in the Tierra Caliente and a Taxco mineowner.[10]

On the Costa Chica some encomiendas were larger than those of the Costa Grande and some of the encomenderos were well connected. For example, Gutierre de Badajoz used tribute to fund his mining and agricultural enterprises and had a network of personal relationships. He was encomendero of Nexpa, which he bought in 1531, of Tacolula and Huhuetlan, and he had encomiendas in Veracruz. He arrived in the Indies in 1512 and had been a mineowner in Santo Domingo before leading the capture of Tlatelolco and joining Vasco de Porcallo's campaign in Yopecingo. He married a daughter of Francisco de Orduña, a significant fellow encomendero on the Costa Chica. Badajoz combined his encomienda with slave owning and mining on the Costa Chica and in Chilapa. Nexpa provided Badajoz with cash (50 gold pesos every eighty days) and fed and clothed one hundred slaves in his Chilapa mines. In 1550 the cash was changed to 10 pesos of gold dust and 40 gold pesos, and thirteen Indian workers for his cacao plantation were added to the obligation to maintain Badajoz's slaves. Part of the tribute was to be delivered to Chilapa and part to Mexico City. In 1554 the tribute was changed to 78 pesos of oro común per year and twelve Indians for the cacao plantation, who were to be paid 8 *reales* per month. Food and clothing for the slaves was removed, as was delivering tribute to Mexico City. The payment of gold dust seems to have continued until July 1555, when it was commuted to 9 silver reales per peso of gold. In September 1555 Nexpa's obligations were simplified to 130 pesos of oro común every four months and cultivation of a planting of maize, and in 1557 to 125 pesos of oro común and a smaller planting of maize.[11]

Badajoz's commercial interests included two mining companies formed in 1525, one with Bernaldino Vázquez de Tapia, the powerful encomendero of a share of Tlapa and of Huamuxtitlán, the second with Gregorio Dávila. In 1527 Francisco de Junquera and Gonzalo Bazán appointed him attorney to collect debts owed to them. Badajoz was a lender and a debtor: In 1528 Rodrigo de Baeza owed him 75 pesos for 200 fanegas of wheat, the Costa Chica encomenderos Pedro Nieto and Cristóbal de Mafra owed him 150 pesos for a horse, and Badajoz owed 100 pesos to Juan de Montejo.[12] He owned land near Tacuba, given to him in 1528 by the cabildo of Mexico City, which also gave him a large vegetable garden with water rights for irrigation in 1547. He owned a livestock ranch in the mining region of Temascaltepec.[13] The cases of these coastal encomenderos included several themes of the new colonial economy: the encomienda as a source of capital, the importance of slave labor and mining, the association of livestock with mining, and networks of personal and family relationships.

ii. The Montaña

Throughout the century, the Montaña was a region of comparatively rich encomiendas held by exceptionally powerful figures. There was little or no direct Spanish involvement in mining in the Montaña, but some encomiendas in the region financed mining in Ayoteco, in what is now southwestern Puebla. An Audiencia report of 1533 considered Tlapa, the largest encomienda of the Montaña, to be a very rich tribute province, yielding 800 pesos of gold dust every eighty days.[14] This was later reduced to 80 pesos every eighty days, 100 jars of honey, 13 blocks of beeswax, and meals for the jurisdiction's corregidor and alguacil. In 1552 the obligation to supply gold dust was replaced with 320 *maravedís* of silver, an indication that the gold placers of the region were exhausted. By 1565 the value of the combined shares of Tlapa's tribute was 5,334 pesos, 4 tomines, and 9 *granos* of silver, and 2,667 fanegas and 3 almudes (122,693 kilograms) of maize.[15] In 1597 Tlapa had the largest tributary population (2,918) of any encomienda held by individuals in Guerrero, and the Montaña region accounted for 26 percent of all Indians who paid tribute to individual encomenderos. By the end of the century, Tlapa was held by scions of influential families, Bernardino Vázquez de Tapia, also encomendero of Huamuxtitlán, and doña Beatriz de Estrada. Another powerful figure, Viceroy Luis de Velasco the younger, was encomendero of Malinaltepec.[16]

The first holder of Tlapa was none other than Hernán Cortés[17] until the first Audiencia removed it from him as part of efforts to limit his power and resources. The Audiencia reassigned Tlapa to Francisco de Ribadeo, who already had encomiendas elsewhere. Then Alonso de Estrada, royal treasurer and, from 1524 to 1529, governor of New Spain, assigned himself a share of Cortés's holding. Estrada's heirs were his daughter Beatriz de Estrada and her husband, the politically and socially prominent don Francisco Vázquez de Coronado, encomendero of Cutzamala in the Tierra Caliente and Teutenango in the valley of Toluca. Vázquez de Coronado and Estrada's daughter Isabel de Luján married Bernardino de Bocanegra, a member of another wealthy and well-connected family with encomiendas and land in Michoacán and Temascaltepec among its many interests.[18]

In 1528 Alonso de Estrada assigned to Bernaldino Vázquez de Tapia, who had received Huamuxtitlán from Cortés, Ribadeo's quarter of Tlapa. The Huamuxtitlán encomienda provided fifty Indigenous workers for Bernaldino's mines in Ayoteco. Vázquez de Tapia was also encomendero of Churubusco, near Mexico City. In 1529 the first Audiencia removed Churubusco from him in return for another quarter of Tlapa, but in 1534 he produced the decree that had granted him Churubusco and successfully reclaimed it from the second Audiencia.[19] Vázquez de Tapia was a veteran of Cuba, Panama, Yucatán, Tlaxcala, Cholula, and Tenochtitlan who received a coat of arms from the king. He was close to Cortés, although they later became enemies. He twice traveled to Spain as *procurador a la corte* to represent conquistadors' interests before the King. He was a perpetual regidor of the cabildo of Mexico City, which gave him several prime plots of land in the city. When he returned from Spain in 1530, he brought with him five nieces and secured them all strategic marriages: with Antonio de Carvajal, a well-connected procurador a la corte and owner of livestock; Bernardino de Albornoz, a holder of several posts and recipient of special commissions; Juan de Valdivieso, a conquistador and encomendero; and Juan de Burgos and Antonio de la Cadena, both office holders in Mexico City and mineowners in Taxco. Bernaldino's son and heir, Bernardino, married Luisa de Castilla, daughter of the wealthy mineowner don Luis de Castilla. Bernardino's funeral in Mexico City in 1606 was a notable event attended by important figures.[20] The fortune of the Vázquez de Tapia family was built on its encomienda and commercial interests in Guerrero and elsewhere, and also a network of relations that included other men whose fortunes depended in part on their activities in Guerrero. The patriarch Bernaldino proudly summed up his career: He had been a regidor of Mexico City for twenty-two years, appointed by

His Majesty, the first and longest serving holder of that office. Moreover, "I have always had many servants and a quantity of horses and arms of all sorts, so that if the natives should rebel or if the governor or *oidores* should instruct me, I could serve anywhere."[21]

iii. The Center

The Center was another area of profitable encomiendas and powerful encomenderos. In 1597 five encomiendas remained in individual hands. In Chilapa there were 2,794 tributaries, in Tixtla 1,120, in Tlalcozautitlán 867, in Oapan 773, and in Mochitlán 440. Together these grants represented 39 percent of the tributary population of Guerrero that had not reverted to the Crown.[22] The initial economic opportunity in the Center was the silver mines in Zumpango,[23] but by the century's end, the region's strategic position on the Mexico City–Acapulco road was the principal source of business.

In 1526, Diego Jaramillo, who was also encomendero of Citlaltomahua on the Costa Grande, acquired Zumpango on the death of its holder.[24] Certain items of Zumpango's tribute were specifically designated to be delivered to Jaramillo's mining enterprise: every twenty days ten jars of honey; twenty chickens; twenty jars, comales, and cooking pots; twenty small bricks; ten stewing pans; mining tools (ten gold pans and ten baskets); and a quantity of gold and clothing. Five fields cultivated for Jaramillo by the tributaries yielded forty cargas (3,680 kilograms) of maize and twenty (1,840 kilograms) of beans, as well as chía and chiles, probably food for mineworkers. Further quantities of honey and beeswax were delivered to Mexico City every eighty days. The obligation to deliver clothing was later replaced by twenty Indians working in the mines. In 1555, when the production of the mines had declined, the tribute was limited to 400 pesos and thirty cargas of maize per year.[25]

The encomendero of Tixtla, Oapan, Huitziltepec, and Mochitlán was Martín de Ircio, brother-in-law of Viceroy Mendoza and future father-in-law of Luis de Velasco the younger. Ircio had campaigned in Pánuco, Colima, and Yopecingo. He was a partner with other Spaniards of the Cerro de San Martín mine in Zumpango[26] and in 1552 is recorded as having slaves working in the mines.[27] Dorantes Carranza remarked that the progeny of this family was very illustrious. Three grandsons bore the Velasco name (two of them members of the Order of Santiago). Another grandson, Juan Altamirano, owned a mine and a refining mill in Sultepec. The family of one of Ircio's sons-in-law, Marshall Carlos de Luna y Arellano, was very prominent. Moreover, when Ircio died in 1569 his heir was none other than his son-in-law Luis de Velasco the younger, a future viceroy. Ircio's encomienda was the foundation of a very diversified enterprise: Indians and slaves worked the mines; he produced silk near Tixtla; he had a sugar mill; he owned horticultural land; and he raised pigs and cows.[28]

In 1531, when Tacatecla, a principal who represented his brother Mayacat, "lord of the pueblo of Tistla," appeared with other Tixtla nobles before bishop Fray Juan de Zumárraga in Mexico City, the bishop's ruling provided a partial list of Tixtla's tribute. We have already encountered Mayacat as an ally of Martín de Ircio in a 1531–1561 court case, but on this occasion the rulers of Tixtla complained that Ircio's administrators had demanded excessive tribute "on account of which they are tired and vexed." Bishop Zumárraga ordered that the tribute be reduced. The records list items that Mayacat and his people continued to supply: gold, beeswax, cotton textiles, honey, the cultivation of maize, all delivered to the mines, as well as Indians to work there.[29] The tribute, as amended in 1543, was the most complex and largest set of demands recorded in Guerrero (table 6.4), which called on the experience of Tixtla's rulers in administering tribute since precontact times. Tribute gave Ircio supplies, equipment, and labor to support various enterprises (mining, sugar, livestock, silk), tradeable textile products, and food for his household. One gains the impression that he was a demanding and imperious character.

In short, the formula that applied to the Montaña repeated itself in the Center—powerful, well-connected men acquired lucrative encomiendas that formed a cornerstone of diversified enterprises, in which mining and livestock frequently were major factors.

iv. The North

In the North the encomienda was tightly linked to the mining economy as a source of essential supplies and labor. A good example of this is Isidro Moreno, a conquistador who received encomiendas in two promising areas: Huitzuco in the North and Utatlan in Tierra Caliente. Moreno managed his enterprises in a hands-on manner. He was resident in Utatlan, where there were mines, and established his son in Huitzuco, close to

		TABLE 6.4. TIXTLA TRIBUTE, 1543	
Every 20 days	Every 80 days	Annually	For Ircio or his administrator
5 fanegas of beans	10 petticoats	2 maize fields, 4 varas by 20 brazas	3 turkeys
15 chickens	10 shirts	15 marcos of silver (untaxed)	3 hens
1 taleguilla of cacao	2 fine petticoats	60 petticoats for slaves	65 eggs
5 jars of honey	2 fine shirts	60 shirts for slaves	A jícara of fish on Friday
30 Indian workers	5 striped mantas	60 mantas for slaves	Tortillas for servants
	2 damask bed hangings	60 mástiles (maxtlatl?) for slaves	Half a fanega of maize
	2 coverlets	60 small canopies	2 Indians for the horses and two for the house
	2 sheets the size of 4 piernas	20 shirts	1 turkey
	2 pairs of tablecloths	20 undershorts	1 basket of maize
	40 small canopies the size of 2 brazos	60 gold pans	20 eggs or fish on Friday
	20 jars of honey	20 Indians for the house and the animal pens	
	20 large jícaras		

Source: *El libro de Tasaciones*, 490–91.

Taxco. He was also given a housing plot, horticultural land, and "a piece of land" in Mexico City by the cabildo. Huitzuco had been a mining area in pre-Hispanic times, vesting his encomienda with access to skilled labor. In addition, Moreno had a gang of mineworkers in Tehuilotepec near Taxco.[30] Huitzuco's tribute obligations included twelve sheets of gold every eighty days, the cultivation of two fields to feed Moreno's slaves in the mines, and twenty Indigenous mineworkers. In addition, Huitzuco delivered honey, salt, chile, beans, maize, petticoats, mantas, and thirty-one blocks of beeswax (used to make candles to light mine shafts) and was obliged to feed and clothe a slave who shepherded Moreno's sheep. The tribute was reduced in 1538 but, in return, the number of mineworkers increased to thirty and the cultivation of fields to feed Moreno's slaves continued. In 1550 the obligation to supply workers was removed, but the requirement to supply foodstuffs and salt (essential for refining metal ore) to the mines continued.[31]

After Moreno died about 1564, his son Bernardino Moreno de Casasola expanded his father's livestock enterprise, acquiring in 1567 a ranch of 1.5 caballerías (66 hectares) between Tepecoacuilco and Tlaxmalac. In the following two decades, Moreno de Casasola enlarged his holdings, but this triggered a dispute with Tlaxmalac and Mayanalán, which were supported by their encomendero Mateo Vázquez de Cisneros. His opponents accused Moreno de Casasola of ordering a Black and some Indians to burn down houses in Tlaxmalac. Despite these challenges Moreno de Casasola expanded his enterprises. He bought cascalote (a tanning agent) from the Indians of Huitzuco, which suggests that he either ran a tannery himself or supplied tanneries. He also attempted to influence elections of Indigenous town officers in Huitzuco. In 1590 he tried, but failed, to acquire the encomienda of Atenango. He continued his father's mining business in Tehuilotepec, and in the 1590s he was appointed by the viceroy to prospect for new mines. The family continued to hold Huitzuco until 1643.[32] Such a long tenure suggests that the family had influence in the royal government. The encomienda provided early-stage finance and resources for the family's mining enterprises and the diversification of their enterprises, whether legal or not.

Juan de Cabra, who had been in Cuba in 1519 and participated in the conquests of Tenochtitlan and Yopecingo, received the encomienda of Noxtepec and Pilcaya, where silver mines were located. Cabra was one of the founders of Taxco. The Mexico City cabildo gave him plots of housing land as early as 1524 and 1527, and in 1542 a horticultural plot, all located in the capital.[33] Like some other Taxco mineowners, Cabra's first mining ventures were on the coast of Guerrero and Michoacán, using resources from Noxtepec and Pilcaya. When Cabra's focus shifted to the Taxco area, his encomienda supplied Indigenous laborers and fed his slaves.[34] Cabra became a significant figure in mining circles in Taxco and Zacualpan, where he had mines and refining mills. In 1551 he joined nineteen other mineowners to petition against Lorenzo de Tejada's mining ordinances. His daughter married another mineowner, Nicolás Chamorro. Cabra died about 1557, sufficiently wealthy to bequeath a large legacy to finance the marriages of poor orphaned girls. His widow, María de Herrera, married Francisco Ramírez Bravo, who thus acquired the encomienda and mines. In 1582 Ramírez Bravo wrote to a friend in Spain that he had purchased from the estate of a deceased rival the richest seam in the area to date. The purchase cost him the large sum of 12,500 pesos, which was evidently worth every peso since the mines he possessed by marriage and his new mine yielded 2,000 pesos or more every week. Strategic marriages such as that of Cabra's daughter or of Ramírez Bravo were a common feature of the mining society of the Silver Province.³⁵

The first encomendero of the sizeable encomienda of Tepecoacuilco, Juan de la Torre, was fortunate to inherit the headquarters of a Mexica tribute province and, thus, a well-established system of tribute collection.³⁶ Tepecoacuilco is a good example of how the encomienda, agriculture, livestock, mining, and a network of personal relations were keys to the accumulation of wealth and the emergence of some of the most powerful families in sixteenth-century Guerrero. De la Torre had been in Hispaniola with his brothers Luis and Alonso before the trio participated in the conquest of Tenochtitlan. They were cousins of treasurer Alonso de Estrada, a valuable sociopolitical connection. Furthermore, Juan was favored by Cortés, who gave him four encomiendas in various regions, among them Tepecoacuilco. Cortés appointed Juan regidor of Mexico City in 1525 and 1528. He was alcalde ordinario there in 1526, 1527, and 1532, and was one of three men appointed to welcome the first Audiencia in 1528. In short, the family relations of Juan and his brothers and their friendships tell us that these were influential men. Juan married Isabel de Tovar, daughter of the holder of several encomiendas. He died in 1535, but before then Tepecoacuilco had been reassigned to Hernando de Torres, a veteran conquistador who had arrived in the Indies in 1513 and had fought alongside Cortés in Tenochtitlan.³⁷

Hernando de Torres, like Juan de Cabra, was one of those who started his mining career on the coast. In 1527 and 1528, he was recorded as owning a mining venture and about 100 slaves in Coyuca on the Costa Grande and had 500–600 pigs in Colima. Torres had also incurred debts, the largest consisting of 800 pesos owed to Hernán Cortés for purposes that the source does not disclose. To avoid imprisonment for this debt, Torres pledged a horse, his houses in Mexico City, his slaves, and his livestock. His acquisition of Tepecoacuilco seems to have eased his debt problems, since when he married Juana de Loaysa in 1538, he gave her a substantial dowry of 2,500 pesos in urban property, gold, and silver.³⁸

Following Torres's death around 1546, his widow, Juana, married Antonio de Almoguer (also spelled Almaguer) in 1548. This was a strategic marriage for both. Almoguer, who had been secretary to the viceroy 1537–1542, was a vecino of Puebla where he had commercial interests when he married Juana. The marriage enhanced his wealth and influence by giving him access to a lucrative encomienda in a region that was experiencing a mining boom. Encomiendas did not automatically pass to widows, so Juana secured Tepecoacuilco and an influential husband at the same time. The couple's daughter Bernardina de Torres married the powerful Taxco mineowner Pedro de Osorio. Osorio held a mine and a refining mill in Taxco and, like Juan de Cabra, signed the petition against Tejada's mining ordinances. Potentially, when his mother- and father-in-law died, Tepecoacuilco would provide Osorio with invaluable resources for his mining enterprises.[39] Perhaps unsurprisingly, when Juana de Loaysa died in 1553, the inheritance of Tepecoacuilco became a matter of dispute between Almoguer and his son-in-law, who eventually won out.[40]

Osorio did not enjoy the fruits of his legal victory for long, however, since he died in 1556, leaving many debts. One of his creditors, Juan Martínez del Gajo, who lived in Spain, appointed Juan Rodríguez Zambrano and Álvaro Zambrano to collect Osorio's debts, but his attorneys reported disappointing news. Within days of her husband's death, Bernardina had married Luis de Godoy, a relative of treasurer don Juan Alonso de Sosa and of the wealthy and influential Taxco mineowner don Luis de Castilla. This, again, was a highly strategic marriage. By marrying Godoy, Bernardina acquired powerful family members to protect her from creditors. Her husband acquired a rich encomienda and Osorio's other assets. Meanwhile, a frustrated Zambrano explained to Martínez del Gajo that his debt was uncollectable.[41] Thus, the enterprises acquired and founded by Hernando de Torres, and further elaborated by his heirs, combined the familiar elements of encomienda, mining, slaves, livestock, debt, personal connections, and strategic marriages.

v. Tierra Caliente

Since the Tierra Caliente was in the metallurgical zone of Mesoamerica, its mining potential attracted several powerful encomenderos, and, indeed, the early encomenderos found a number of mines and used the tribute of their encomiendas to support mining enterprises. However, mining here was short lived and the encomenderos of Tierra Caliente switched their tribute resources to Taxco and other reales de minas of the Silver

Province. Nevertheless, a few of the encomiendas of the region were the foundation of the future fortunes of several wealthy individuals and their families.

In 1533, Coyuca, originally granted to the conquistador Guillén de Loa,[42] was reassigned to Pedro de Meneses, who had been a page to Cortés. His brother Bernardino de Meneses had been close to another powerful conquistador and archrival of Cortés, Nuño de Guzmán. Pedro held several official appointments. He was inspector of the Southern Sea and, in 1561, was alcalde ordinario and *tenedor de bienes de difuntos* (guardian of the goods of the deceased) of Mexico City, and, in 1562, *alcalde de mesta* (justice of the cattle owners' guild). He was favored with several land grants: in 1526 a house plot in Mexico City; in 1542 two estancias (3,512 hectares) for livestock near Coyuca; a further 1,756 hectares, also for livestock between Coyuca and the mining town of Sultepec; and land for an inn on the road to Puebla. In the 1540s Meneses purchased from Francisco Ramírez an interest in the encomiendas of Çicoac in modern Veracruz state and of Sultepec that cost him 3,700 "pesos de mynas." Like other wealthy encomenderos, Meneses was well connected. His first wife, Ana de Agüeros, was the daughter of a member of the royal household. Each of Meneses's four daughters respectively married an official of the Audiencia and *familiar* (roughly, constable) of the Inquisition, an encomendero and alcalde of Mexico City, a wealthy corregidor, and another alcalde of Mexico City. Meneses played an active part in New Spain's politics, defending his own interests and those of the conquistadors and encomenderos in general. He testified against the Second Audiencia, complaining that they had reduced tribute. He accused the friars of Tulancingo, where he also had an encomienda, of imprisoning Indians and freeing slaves. In 1552 he wrote in strong terms to the king, accusing corregidores and alcaldes mayores of depriving encomenderos of their Indians.[43]

The earliest extant tribute assessment of Coyuca enjoyed by Meneses included obligations to cultivate land and to harvest maize, chiles, and beans, and to supply salt. The tribute also included clothing, probably for slaves. These requirements were later reduced to supplying thirty Indians to work in the mines of Amatepec in the modern state of Mexico, foodstuffs, and clothing. In 1542 the labor obligation was increased to forty Indians to work in the Acayo mines and, in addition, salt, cooking vessels, mats, fish, chickens, and the cultivation of land, the

TABLE 6.5. INITIAL TRIBUTE OF GUAYAMEO AND ZIRÁNDARO			
Every 8 days[1]	Every 10 days[2]	Every 60 days	Annually
200 cargas (18,400kg) of maize	25 mantas	5 cargas of small canopies	Field of maize
10 cargas (920kg) of beans	25 mástiles (maxtlatl?)	1,150 jícaras	Field of beans
10 cargas of chile	25 shirts	200 small blocks of beeswax	
10 taleguillas of salt	100 pairs of sandals	6 cargas of cotton	
10 taleguillas of piñol			

Notes:
1. Delivered to the Coyuca mines.
2. For the slaves of the Amatepec mines.

Source: *El libro de Tasaciones*, 190–92.

harvest to be delivered to Acayo. Additionally, every thirty days twenty Indian bearers were to transport copper to Mexico City. Thus, Coyuca's tribute provided resources for Meneses's mining ventures. Further tribute assessments in 1553 and 1559 removed the obligation to work in the mines. In 1567, a year after Meneses's death, as was the general trend in the second half of the sixteenth century, the tribute was simplified: 557 pesos and 4 tomines and 223 fanegas (10,258 kilograms) of maize.[44]

The tribute of Gil de Benavides's encomienda Guayameo and Zirándaro was, likewise, funneled into his mining and commercial enterprises. Benavides was an ambitious man who used his personal relations for his own benefit, sometimes in a decidedly treacherous manner. Bishop Fonseca, president of the Consejo de Indias, had him appointed treasurer of Hispaniola and arranged for him to be given a contract to explore the Southern Sea. In Nicaragua and Honduras, Pedrarias Dávila had him imprisoned by Cristóbal de Olid, but after negotiating his release, Benavides murdered Olid over dinner, a crime for which he avoided prosecution, perhaps by means of influence in high places. Benavides then moved to New Spain where his brother Alonso de Ávila had encomiendas, including Guayameo and Zirándaro. While Alonso was in Spain, Viceroy Mendoza himself assigned Alonso's encomiendas to Benavides instead, over the objections of the attorney of the Audiencia. Mendoza also gave Benavides a house plot in Mexico City and later granted land to his widow.[45]

The tribute obligations of Guayameo and Zirándaro were notably onerous in comparison to those of other grants to Guerrero's encomenderos (table 6.5). A modified assessment of this tribute obligation, carried out in 1544, a year after Benavides's death, required delivery to Mexico City every four months of three cargas of mantas and eighty painted jícaras, honey, salt, and twenty fish. The tribute to be delivered to the Coyuca mines listed cotton, sandals, shirts, undershorts, mantas, petticoats, and the harvest of three fields of maize. In addition, Benavides's administrator at the mines was to receive weekly seven chickens, four fish, three cargas (276 kilograms) of beans, three cargas of chile, six *taleguillas* of salt, four *xicobitos*, and every fifteen days twelve stewing pots, twelve mats, and fifteen jícaras. Finally, four Indians were to work in the mines and four for Benavides's administrator. In 1557 the tribute was simplified to six cargas of clothing every six months and the cultivation and harvesting of some 13,800 kilograms of maize. In 1566 the tribute was much reduced, presumably because of population decline: 350 silver pesos and 5 fanegas of maize.[46]

The Benavides family became wealthy and well connected. Despite his unscrupulous past, Benavides married well to Leonor de Alvarado, a daughter of the conquistador Pedro de Alvarado, second only to Cortés. The couple were godparents to the eldest son of the wealthy encomendero and landowner Hernán Pérez de Bocanegra. Their son Alonso de Ávila, well-known for his lavish taste in attire, similarly married well, to María de Sosa, daughter of Treasurer Juan Alonso de Sosa, in whose house the couple lived. The second son, Gil González de Ávila, married the daughter of a conquistador and encomendero.[47]

In 1538 Juan de Burgos[48] sold Cutzamala and Teutenango in the Valley of Toluca to Francisco Vázquez de Coronado, who already had encomiendas elsewhere and was yet another well-connected encomendero in Guerrero. He arrived in New Spain in 1525 in the retinue of Viceroy Mendoza and was son-in-law of Royal Treasurer Alonso de Estrada. Like other Guerrero encomenderos, he formed a relationship with the influential Bocanegra family, in this case by marrying one of his daughters, Isabel de Luján, to Bernardino Pacheco de Bocanegra. Another daughter, Marina Vázquez de Coronado, also wed into the Bocanegra family. Aside from his famous quest from 1540 to 1542 for the legendary Seven Cities of Cíbola, Vázquez de Coronado held several important positions: in 1535 inspector of silver mines; 1538–1544 governor and captain general of New Galicia; 1538, 1539, 1542, and 1545–1554 regidor of Mexico City.[49]

Cutzamala's initial tribute roll clearly illustrates the linkage between tribute and mining activities during the tenure of Burgos (table 6.6). This was a substantial and complex schedule of tribute obligations. Most items were specified to be delivered to the mines or for slaves, and those that were not, such as clothing and salt, were almost certainly required for mine work, probably in Taxco, since later tribute rolls specified delivery there. By 1538, at the time Vázquez de Coronado took over, labor had become a more significant factor than clothing: The medium-sized clothing was replaced by a requirement to dispatch forty Indigenous workers to the mines of Taxco. A further modification in 1544 reduced the tribute in exchange for the assignment of a further forty workers in these mines. However, in 1554 the labor obligation was replaced by twenty cargas comprised of twenty cotton mantas each four times per year. In 1560, when Vázquez de Coronado's son-in-law Bernardino Pacheco de Bocanegra had inherited the encomienda, the tribute of Cutzamala was reviewed. The wording of the assessment is confusing, but it seems that, over Bocanegra's objections, tribute was fixed annually at twenty cargas of twenty mantas per carga and half a fanega of maize per tributary. In 1567, at the request of the Indigenous leaders of Cutzamala, the tribute was assessed at 340 arrobas and 12 1/2 pounds of cotton thread or pinked thin cotton cloth, of which 271 arrobas were due to the encomendero, the remainder to be kept in the caja de comunidad.[50] As in so many other encomiendas, tribute demands were much less onerous by midcentury, making it much less critical in supporting the mining economy than it had been in its earlier stages.

The conquistador Francisco Rodríguez de Magariño was assigned an encomienda comprised of the altepetl of Chilacachapa, Cuetzala, and Tlacotepec. The resources supplied by the encomienda formed part of a network of mining enterprises that would turn the Magariño family into powerful oligarchs in Guerrero. The "Relación de Ichcateupan" reports that Cuetzala grew maize, chile, and squash on irrigated land near the Balsas River. Other crops included chía, purslane (an edible leafy vegetable), jícamas, fruits, and a little cotton. Deer, turkeys, chickens, and quail were abundant. Cuetzala also produced salt. All these products would be useful in the gold mine that Magariño discovered 2 leagues (9 kilometers) from the core of his encomienda, although mining production was short lived. Tlacotepec's products were similar, including salt, much in demand in the mines, and timber. Another gold mine was discovered here, but similarly did not produce for long. Sources do not record whether the Indians of Cuetzala and Tlacotepec worked in the local mines, but we do

TABLE 6.6. INITIAL TRIBUTE OF CUTZAMALA			
Clothing	Foodstuffs	Plots of land cultivated	Other items every 80 days
12 cargas large clothing	2,000 cargas of maize for macehuales*	Accustomed plantings of chile, beans, cotton*	140 taleguillas of salt
12 cargas medium clothing	100 cargas of beans for macehuales*	One plot of "native melons"	100 jícaras
600 mantillas for slaves every 80 days	200 venequenes of chiles*	Two plots of maize	Unspecified pottery

* Items to be delivered to the mines.
Source: *El libro de tasaciones*, 158.

know that subsequently tributaries from Cuetzala worked in the Taxco mines (51 kilometers away) as part of their obligations.[51]

Chilacachapa, Cuetzala, and Tlacotepec were strategically located close to significant mining zones and were a source of supplies that played an important role in the early stages of Magariño's enterprises. He had a refining mill in Taxco and his son Juan Enríquez had 4 caballerías (175 hectares) of land and a refining mill near Temascaltepec. Juan Enríquez inherited from his father an entailed estate valued at 25,000 pesos, with an annual income of 3,300 pesos. These were substantial sums indeed in sixteenth-century New Spain. Like many another son of a prominent encomendero, Juan married well, to Polonia de la Serna, daughter of Alonso de Aguilar y Córdoba, a mineowner and encomendero of Olinalá and Papalutla in the Montaña. Another son, Gaspar Ortiz de Magariño, had mines and refining mills in Taxco.[52]

6.3. Conclusions

The value, function, and economic utility of encomiendas to their Spanish overlords varied considerably by region within Guerrero. Investors in gold mining were attracted initially and briefly to the coast, Zacatula and the Costa Grande especially, but also the Costa Chica. The encomiendas of the Costa Grande were comparatively small, but they provided initial resources for mining enterprises or for livestock raising, agricultural enterprises, and moneylending that supported mining activity. The Montaña was a region of large, remunerative encomiendas assigned to extremely influential family dynasties. Some encomiendas here financed mining in nearby Ayoteco, but the holders of Tlapa, the most remunerative in all of Guerrero, needed to do little more than await the regular deliveries of tribute. In the Center the encomiendas helped to finance early silver mining in Zumpango, but the long-term value of encomiendas by the late sixteenth century lay in their strategic location for traffic to Acapulco. Here again the encomenderos were powerful figures. In the North and Tierra Caliente, the encomienda was, above all, a source of goods and labor critical for the early stages of development in the mining boom of the Silver Province. Some of these encomenderos were among the wealthiest figures of the early colonial period.

CHAPTER SEVEN

Land, Agriculture, Livestock, and Commerce

Guerrero's Emerging Economy

Until the mid-sixteenth century, the encomienda was the principal institution that enabled Spanish colonizers to access Guerrero's resources, to exploit the labor of the Indians, and to capitalize their early commercial ventures. As the Indigenous population plummeted, and as the Crown gradually reappropriated encomiendas in the second half of the century, Spaniards turned their attention to exploiting land and resources themselves, sometimes directly through owning land for livestock or agriculture, sometimes through mechanisms such as the forced use of Indigenous labor (the repartimiento de indios) or the compulsory sale of goods (the *repartimiento de efectos*).[1] The extent of the ownership of land, whether by legal grants of land or by illicit usurpation of Indian land, and the purposes to which land was put varied in the regions of Guerrero.

7.1. The Coast

There is evidence of the introduction of livestock near Zacatula as early as 1525–1528,[2] but nothing is known about the ownership of the land on which they were raised. Certainly, by 1543 the realities of the mining decline in Zacatula led to the issue of the first land grants there (table 7.1). With the caveat that we lack a complete study of landownership throughout Guerrero, and particularly in the Tierra Caliente, more landowners are recorded on the Costa Grande in the sixteenth century than for any other region of Guerrero: sixty-one, compared to seven on the Costa Chica, three in the Montaña, eleven in the Center, twenty-seven in the North, and twelve in the Tierra Caliente. Of the sixty-one grants made on the Costa Grande for a total of up to 72,900 hectares, sixteen were

TABLE 7.1. LANDOWNERS ON THE COSTA GRANDE, 1543–1598

Year	Name	Location	Area	Ha.
1543	Francisco de Salcedo	Cihuatlán	2 caballerías	88
	Francisco de Salcedo	Pochutla	1 estancia	780 or 1,756
1544	Diego Ruiz	Zacatula	1 caballería	44
	Juan Campuzano	Zacatula	1 caballería	44
	Gerónimo Ponce	Zacatula	1 caballería	44
1548	Juan Alonso de Vargas	Costa Grande	1 huerta de cacao	?
1550	Juan Sánchez	Pichique	1 estancia para ganado mayor	1,756
	Juan Gallego	Coyuca	1.5 caballerías para cacahuatal	66
	Pedro Ruiz de Guadalcanal	Coyuca	?	?
1551	Diego Ruiz	Zacatula	1 caballería para sembrar	44
	Diego Ruiz	Zacatula	1 sitio de estancia	780 or 1,756
	Diego Ruiz de Mendoza	Tepuctepeque, Zacatula	1 estancia para ganado	780 or 1,756
	Juan Campuzano	Zacatula	1 caballería	44
	Gerónimo Ponce	Zacatula	1 caballería	44
1555	Juan Gallego	Pochutla	1 estancia	780 or 1,756
	Tristán de Arellano	Pochutla	1 estancia	780 or 1,756
1557	Francisco Villegas	Chietla	2 caballerías	88
1563	Francisco Vargas	Zacatula	2 caballerías	88
1567	Antonio Pedraza	Tecpan	1 caballería	44
	Francisco Muñoz	Tecpan	1 estancia + 1 caballería	824 or 1,800
	Juan Rade de Mendoza, Diego Villanueva and Juan San Pedro	Huiztlan	1 estancia + 1 lagunilla	780+ or 1,756+
	Juan de Santa Fe	Chancaleca	1 estancia	780 or 1,756
c.1569	García de Albornoz	Coyuca	1 estancia de ganado mayor	1,756
1576	Juan Rodríguez	Ciutla	1 estancia	780 or 1,756
1577	Juan Alonso de Vargas	Chietla	2 caballerías	88
1579	Juan Díaz	Tecpan	2 caballerías	88
1581	García de Albornoz	Nexpa	1 estancia	780 or 1,756
	Martín Robles	Chacala	1 estancia	780 or 1,756
	Bernardino Lozada	Ciutla	1 estancia + 2 caballerías	868 or 1,844
	Pedro Yebra	Ciutla	1 estancia + 2 caballerías	868 or 1,844
1582	Pedro Hernández	Ciutla	1 estancia	780 or 1,756
	Matías Coronel	Ciutla	1 estancia + 2 caballerías	868 or 1,844

TABLE 7.1. LANDOWNERS ON THE COSTA GRANDE, 1543–1598

Year	Name	Location	Area	Ha.
1582	Antonio Castrejón	Zacatula	1 estancia	780 or 1,756
	Francisco de Quevedo	Cachuatepec-Chietla	1 sitio de ganado	780 or 1,756
1583	Luis González	Ciutla	1 estancia	780 or 1,756
	Antonio Castrejón	Chietla	4 caballerías	176
	Hernando Ortega	Zacatula	2 caballerías	88
1584	Gómez Quintana	Zacatula	4 caballerías	176
	Antonio Castrejón	Coahuayutla	1 caballería	44
1585	Pablo Nacelo	Tecpan	2 caballerías	88
	García López	Tecpan	3 caballerías	132
	Francisco González	Petatlán	2 caballerías	88
	Antonio Correa	Petatlán	2 caballerías	88
	Ambrosio Bullón	Nexpa	1 estancia	780 or 1,756
1587	Gregorio Lara	Texupa	1 estancia	780 or 1,756
	Alejo Castrejón	Petatlán	4 caballerías	176
	Juan Ruiz	Zacatula	1 caballería	44
	Felipe Guzmán	Atoyac	1 estancia	780 or 1,756
1589	Pueblo de Atoyac	Atoyac	1 estancia	780 or 1,756
	López Escalante	Pochutla	1 estancia	780 or 1,756
	Pedro Portes	Nexpa	1 estancia + 1 potrero	780+ or 1,756+
1590	Diego Angulo	Tecpan	1 estancia	780 or 1,756
	Cristóbal Hernández	Cacalutla	1 estancia	780 or 1,756
1591	Leonés Tizuro	Zoitlan	2 caballerías	88
	Fernando Santorio	Nexpa	3 caballerías	132
1592	Gaspar Canízares	Tecpan	1 estancia + 2 caballerías	848 or 1,844
	Fernando Santorio	Nexpa	2 estancias	1560 or 3,512
	Gutiérrez de Chávez	Nexpa	2 estancias	1560 or 3,512
	Melchor Ruiz	Ciutla	1 estancia	780 or 1,756
	Andrés Cebreros	Ciguatlán	1 sitio ganado mayor + 2 caballerías	1,844
	Diego Morán	Tecpan	1 estancia	780 or 1,756
	Pueblo de Pochutla	Pochutla	1 estancia	780 or 1,756
	Andrés Cebreros	Tecpan	1 caballería	44
1598	Gómez de Quintana	Tecpan	2 sitios ganado mayor	3,512
	Pueblo de Coatlán	Coatlán	1 estancia	780 or 1,756
TOTAL				38,722 or 72,902

Sources: García Izcabalzeta and García Pimentel, *Descripción del Arzobispado de México*, 148, 150; Gerhard, *Síntesis e índice de los mandamientos*, 584–86; Labarthe R., "Provincia de Zacatula," 100–101; Zavala, *Libros de asientos*, 79–80.

issued from 1550 to 1557, and thirty-seven more between 1581 and 1598. The grants were made to fifty-two Spaniards, of whom only three were encomenderos in the region, and to three self-governing Indigenous towns (Atoyac, Coatlán, and Pochutla). For example, the encomendero of Coyuca and Huitlaluta, Diego Ruiz, a conquistador of Tenochtitlan and vecino of Zacatula, received three grants totaling two *caballerías* (agricultural land, approximately 44 hectares) and an estancia for cattle in 1544 and 1551. Juan Alonso de Vargas, encomendero of Tecpan, conquistador of Zacatula, and resident there until 1555, was granted two caballerías in 1548. In 1581 García de Albornoz, heir to an encomienda by marriage to the daughter of the encomendero and conquistador Rodríguez de Villafuerte, was given an estancia in Nexpa. Albornoz already owned, since at least 1569, a cattle ranch 18 kilometers from Acapulco, where he employed Indians and ten slaves. He also owned an estancia near Coyuca, cacao plantations, and a fishing enterprise, which employed Indigenous labor, twenty slaves, and two Spaniards. Several grants were made to vecinos of Zacatula who were not encomenderos, such as Juan Campuzano and Gerónimo Ponce, grants totaling two caballerías each in 1544 and 1551, and Juan Gallego 1.5 caballerías to cultivate cacao (1550) and an estancia for livestock (1555). Others were not recorded as vecinos of Zacatula; for example, Antonio Castrejón received three grants (1582, 1583, and 1584), one for an estancia and two totaling five caballerías, and Juan Rade de Mendoza, Diego Villanueva, and Juan San Pedro shared an estancia and a small coastal lagoon in 1567. Francisco González, who in 1537 was owner with two partners of sixty slaves, was granted two caballerías near Petatlán in 1585.[3]

Land grants were conditional. For example, in 1563, to retain possession of his land, Francisco Vargas was obliged to cultivate most of his holding and to make it available after the harvest for communal grazing. He was not to keep any livestock other than those necessary for cultivation, and he could not sell his land for four years. He was specifically prohibited from transferring title to any church, monastery, or clergy.[4]

Specific data concerning Spanish landowners on the Costa Chica are much more partial (table 7.2). Bernaldino del Castillo raised cattle and had a cacao plantation on his encomienda of Igualapa.[5] Another encomendero, Gutierre de Badajoz, had a cacao plantation at Nexpa that required thirteen Indians to tend the trees and was said to be large enough for twenty thousand trees.[6] The grant given to Diego de Ordaz

TABLE 7.2. LANDOWNERS ON THE COSTA CHICA IN THE SIXTEENTH CENTURY				
Year	Name	Location	Area	Ha.
1550	Bernaldino de Castillo	Igualapa	Cacao plantation	?
1552	Bernaldino de Castillo	Coatepec, near Xalapa	2 caballerías or 1 estancia	88 or 780 or 1,756
1553	Diego de Ordaz Villagómez	Nexpa	2 caballerías	88
1556	Tristán de Luna y Arellano	Pochutla	?	?
1560	Tristán de Luna y Arellano	Pochutla	?	?
1560	Gutierre de Badajoz	Nexpa	Cacao plantation	?
1582	Pedro de Castro	Nexpa	1 estancia de ganado mayor	1,756
TOTAL				1,932 or 2,624 or 3,600+

Sources: Aguirre Beltrán, *Cuijla*, 44; Álvarez, *Diccionario de conquistadores*, 1:122–24, 2:290; Gerhard, *Síntesis e índice de los mandamientos*, 578; Miranda, *El tributo indígena*, 194; "Relación de Xalapa, Cintla y Acatlan," 286.

Villagómez, heir to the encomienda of Chilapa and a resident of Puebla, permitted him to plant trees and other crops but prohibited cattle.[7] Tristán de Luna y Arellano, a member of a wealthy and well-connected family, had two plots of land for unspecified purposes at Pochutla.[8] Pedro de Castro was reported to have a cattle ranch near Nexpa.[9] According to Widmer, there were more than fifteen cattle ranches in the Igualapa area in 1580.[10]

A considerable portion of land, legally owned or not, on the Costa Grande and the Costa Chica was used to graze pigs, sheep, and cattle. Tomás Pérez, a Spanish sailor who had sailed the coast from Panama to Acapulco, and one of the authors of the "Relación de Xalapa, Cintla y Acatlan," reported in 1582 that there were good pasture lands on the Costa Chica that could supply meat for the ships in Acapulco and added that the area was rich in fish.[11] By the late 1530s Francisco Gutiérrez had cattle near his encomienda of Pochutla. By 1569 the cattle estancias in Pochutla and Huiztlán employed eight Spaniards and ten African slaves, and livestock began to cause problems for the Indigenous population. In 1581 the Indigenous community of Mexcaltepec complained that the livestock of Juan Rodríguez was damaging their crops, a complaint heard frequently in other regions of Guerrero and New Spain. This kind of conflict was only one of the drawbacks to raising livestock on the coast. Wild animals attacked the stock, and it often suffered from worms and poor husbandry.[12]

Another important element of the coastal economy was cacao. By midcentury eight cacao plantations were worked by Indigenous labor and seven Spaniards were mentioned as owners of cacao plantations: Juan Vera, vecino of Petatlán, and six encomenderos, Alonso de Aguilar y Córdoba, Sebastián de Ébora, Antón Sánchez, Francisco Saucedo, and Alonso de Vargas on the Costa Grande and Bernaldino del Castillo on the Costa Chica.[13] Ébora and Vargas also received cacao as tribute from their encomiendas.[14] There were also Indigenous owners of cacao plantations. In 1583 royal officials confirmed the possession of plantations (presumably of cacao) that the Indian Francisco Jerónimo and his brothers owned near Mexcaltepec.[15] Indians met their tribute obligations by cultivating cacao themselves, but also by trading fish, tecomates, and maguey fiber sacks (used to transport goods) for cacao beans. At higher elevations, where cacao did not grow, Indians were obliged to trade for the cacao tribute required of them. Royal policy promoted cacao cultivation.[16] In 1560 the Crown received cacao tribute from ten royal encomiendas.[17] In 1582 the alcalde mayor of Zacatula was instructed to assist Francisco Martínez in the cultivation of his plantations.[18] Cultivation of cacao in the Zacatula, Igualapa, and Xicayán regions would continue into the late seventeenth century, despite competition from cheaper and higher quality cacao from Guayaquil that was first landed at Acapulco in 1595.[19]

Cotton was also a significant crop in the sixteenth century, especially on the coast and in the Tierra Caliente, but unlike cacao, which the Spaniards obtained both by direct cultivation and as tribute, cotton was sourced almost entirely from tribute. The value of cotton lay not in the unprocessed fiber but in the control of spinning, weaving, and distribution of the finished products. This was achieved by means of tribute and obliging Indians to spin and weave cotton, using official programs of forced labor or illegal compulsion. The province of Zacatula was an important source of Crown cotton tribute. In 1560, fifty-five pueblos in New Spain paid royal tribute in the form of cotton mantas, nineteen of which were in the province of Zacatula.[20] As had been the case of Mexica tribute demands in the Late Postclassic,[21] Guerrero's encomenderos received cotton tribute whether their encomienda was in a cotton-producing area or not. Communities in non-cotton-producing locations would have acquired fiber to meet their obligations by trade with the coast or perhaps Tierra Caliente.[22] When textile tribute was replaced in the 1560s with payment in maize, money, and, sometimes, cacao, Spaniards turned to Indigenous and royal officials and merchants to source cotton textiles. By the late sixteenth century, royal officials operated the repartimiento de indios, which, in this case, obliged Indians to spin and weave cotton in return for low rates of pay or for nothing. Indigenous officials and caciques became intermediaries in this system to supplement their salaries. Some twenty pueblos in the province of Zacatula wove cotton that was sold in central Mexico and Michoacán.[23]

After 1565 the Manila trade led to the importation of Asian crops and labor, the latter both enslaved and free. Many Asians passed through Acapulco on their way to masters in Mexico City, but a number stayed on the coast from Guerrero to Michoacán and Colima to work in the cacao plantations.[24] Asians brought with them skills that made the cultivation of the coconut palm an important aspect of coastal commerce. In 1569 Álvaro de Mendaña brought coconut seeds to the port of Salagua, Colima. Byproducts of the new coconut palm industry included *tuba*, a coconut wine popular in the Philippines, from which spirits could be distilled, and coconut fiber used to caulk ships. Another imported Asian crop was ginger, first introduced to New Spain in 1569 by the governor of the Philippines, don Guido de Lavezares. The encomendero Bernaldino del Castillo was said to have planted ginger seedlings on his land on the Costa Chica, and by the late 1580s the Asian Juan Rodríguez was growing ginger on the Costa Grande near Acapulco. Lavezares also sent seedlings of tamarind and pepper, but whether they were planted in Guerrero is not known.[25] It seems that coconut caught on more quickly than Spanish crops. Zacatula reported only oranges, melons, and cucumbers; Citlaltomahua oranges, limes, lemons, and sugar cane; and Xicayan oranges, limes, and grapefruit.[26]

The cattle and agricultural enterprises of the coast required labor. Indigenous labor was a constant concern of royal officials throughout New Spain. In 1553 Viceroy Luis de Velasco explained to Emperor Charles V that restrictions on the use of Indigenous labor and on the use of tamemes were gravely reducing income from the mines and other enterprises.[27] Spanish authorities sought to address the shortage of labor by means of officially sanctioned forced labor, the repartimiento de indios. As early as 1528 the emperor had instructed the Audiencia to investigate the potential of the repartimiento in the mines.[28] However, illegal exploitation of Indigenous labor was an equally early phenomenon. A 1528 document noted that encomenderos were improperly demanding labor services for their own profit and that other "Spanish Christians" were simply forcing Indians to work for them, to the detriment of food crops.[29]

Abuses of the repartimiento and illegal forced labor were reported on the Costa Grande. For example, in 1550, Gonzalo Gallego, encomendero of Huiztla, complained that his Indians were not paying their tribute because the teniente del alcalde mayor was forcing them to work for another Spaniard, Pedro Guerrero. Forced labor seems to have been common practice since a general injunction was issued to prevent the alcalde mayor of Zacatula province, other Spanish officials, Indigenous governors, and principales from forcing Indians to work as tamemes and obliging Indian women to carry out domestic tasks for the Spanish residents of Zacatula.[30] Viceroy Mendoza had ordered in 1536 that no tamemes were to carry merchandise in hot regions such as the Pacific coast, but the lack of alternative means of transport forced him to permit porters to carry moderate loads for short distances in return for pay.[31]

A partial solution for the labor shortages caused by mass deaths of the Indigenous population, a demographic disaster much lamented by Spanish officials, was found in African and Asian slavery.[32] The epidemics of the sixteenth century were the principal cause, but some Indians simply left the coast, and the congregaciones of 1553, 1560, and 1595–1606 further disrupted Indigenous society.[33] By the 1560s African slaves were indispensable on cacao plantations, and they soon outnumbered Europeans; in 1570 the population of Zacatula consisted of 150 Africans and only 70 Spaniards. The region was an attractive refuge for escaped Blacks and Mulattos,[34] who were a constant preoccupation of the authorities. Black men and women were accused of witchcraft and of possessing diabolical powers. Allegations included the ability to predict when galleons would arrive in Acapulco, curing the sick using magical powers and remedies, and the ability to fly. Black and Mulatto women were accused of dressing scandalously, causing the viceroy to issue an edict in 1598 forbidding them to wear gold, silver, or pearl jewelry and prohibiting them from wearing Castilian silk or Chinese velvet. Free Black women were allowed to wear Chinese taffeta and damask, but showy outfits were liable to confiscation. Black men were alleged to drink to excess and to be violent. They were also accused of having sexual relations outside marriage with Black women, although, since there were cases of Spaniards and Black men fighting over Black women, sexual immorality was not confined to Blacks. In 1600 plans for a revolt of African slaves in the shipyards caused alarm, but the threat was nipped in the bud by exiling the ringleaders to Peru.[35] A report in 1607 expressed concern about numerous runaway slaves who were attacking and robbing the royal warehouses in Acapulco.[36] Alarming reports of pernicious slave plots were not infrequent in New Spain, but they can be attributed more to stereotypical Spanish views of African slaves, exaggerated in regions where Blacks and Mulattos outnumbered Europeans, such as the coast of Guerrero, than to reality. In 1612 the historian and annalist Chimalpahin Quauhtlehuanitzin reported with wry amusement the great alarm caused by rumors of a plot hatched by "black renegades" in Acapulco to enthrone an African king and, among other nefarious plans, to marry comely Spanish women, including nuns. Twenty-eight Black men and seven women were hung to avert an outrage that was probably imaginary or at best an exaggeration of rumored events in far-off Acapulco.[37]

The importation of African slave labor changed the ethnic, linguistic, and cultural composition of the coast rapidly. Aguirre Beltrán's classic study of Cuajinicuilapa records the changes caused by Spanish colonization from the sixteenth century to the mid-twentieth. Gangs of African slaves were managed by African foremen. Thus, there were Blacks of higher status living in the area, even if they were still slaves themselves. By the mid-sixteenth century, a process of Indigenous-African mestizaje had begun, but complaints began to be heard of illegal and harmful activities of Blacks in Indigenous settlements. In addition to working as laborers or foremen, Africans were also cowboys who mixed with the Indians but could also be on hostile terms with them. Blacks were also sugar mill workers, mule drivers, and maroons who attacked Indigenous settlements.[38] Free and enslaved Asians worked on the livestock ranches and cacao plantations alongside Africans. The priests of the coast owned Asian as well as African slaves. Cases of Spaniards, other Europeans, and Mestizos who sought marriage with the widows of wealthy Indian landowners are evidence that some Indians prospered; for example, the república de indios of Coyuca gave some land to an Indian named Nicolás. In 1572, the Indians of the same town complained that Manuel Ríos, a Portuguese, had married Nicolás's widow, had a child with her to justify his claim to the property, and had then occupied more of Coyuca's land. When his Indigenous wife died, Ríos sold all the land to two Spaniards of Acapulco.[39]

TABLE 7.3. LANDOWNERS IN THE MONTAÑA IN THE SIXTEENTH CENTURY				
Year	Name	Location	Area	Ha.
1542	Bernaldino Vázquez de Tapia	Pazcala, provincia de Tlapa	1 estancia, 1 caballería	824 or 1,800
1544	Bernaldino Vázquez de Tapia	Xochihuehuetlán	sitio de estancia	780 or 1,756
1581	Torres de la Sierra, Juan de	Tlapa	Land for wheat	?
TOTAL				1,604 or 3,556+

Sources: Álvarez, *Diccionario de conquistadores*, 2:575–80; Jiménez García, "La nobleza indígena," 154; Zavala, *El servicio personal de los indios*, 201–2.

7.2. The Montaña and Center

The economic model in the Montaña and adjacent areas of the Center emphasized the seasonal rental of land for pasture from Indigenous communities rather than outright ownership of the land or simply grazing livestock without paying rent to anyone. Forced Indigenous workers managed animals introduced from Europe during the entire colonial period.[40] On a seasonal basis, after crops had been harvested, livestock owners in Oaxaca and Puebla grazed their animals on the pastures of so-called flying haciendas (*haciendas volantes*) of the provinces of Tlapa and Chilapa (the same model predominated in the Tierra Caliente). The carcasses were rendered to make fat to produce soap and candles, the hides were tanned for the leather industry, and the meat was dried or salted. Meat thus preserved would have been suitable for transportation to distant markets, and particularly for the long sea voyages from ports such as Acapulco. Throughout the colonial period and beyond up to 1910, enormous herds of 3,000 up to 300,000 cattle and other livestock grazed the region. In 1901 it was said of an absentee governor of Guerrero that his only connection with the state was the goats he bought in Tlapa.[41] Accordingly, although there were surely more landowners than the available data record, we find only two recipients of land grants mentioned in the literature, one of them the encomendero Bernaldino Vázquez de Tapia (table 7.3).

In contrast, with the exception of Chilapa, direct control of land was the commercial model of choice in the Center. Here the Zumpango mines, and subsequently Acapulco's trade, were the incentives for Spaniards to acquire land for livestock or the construction and operation of inns. As early as 1538, the testament of Spaniard Diego de León

TABLE 7.4. LANDOWNERS IN THE CENTER, 1539–1600

Year	Name	Location	Area	Ha.
1539	Martín de Ircio	Zumpango	Land bought from Zumpango	?
1550	Martín de Ircio	Uchistlan	Three plots of uncultivated land	?
Before 1551	Martín de Ircio	Coauquinea, near Tixtla	Livestock ranches	?
1551	Gonzalo Cerezo	Zumpango	A hacienda	?
1560	María de Mendoza	Near Tixtla, Atliaca and Muchitlán	2 sitios for an inn	?
Before 1567	María de Mendoza	On the plain of Mazatlán	1 estancia for cows	1,756
1567	Luis de Velasco	Coacoyula	1 sitio for an inn	?
1567	Luis de Velasco	Sutetepeque on Acapulco road	1 sitio for an inn	?
1567	Baltasar de la Serna	On the plain of Mazatlán	1 sitio de ganado mayor	1,756
1583	Joan de la Serna	On plains near Tixtla and Mochitlán	3 caballerías	132
1590	Pedro Sánchez Moreno	Near Zumpango	1 sitio de ganado menor	780
1593	Antonio Gómez	Tixtla, between Quacoyula and Mazatlán	1 sitio for an inn and 1.5 caballerías	66+
TOTAL				4,490+

Sources: Amith, "The Möbius Strip," 1134–35; Gerhard, *Síntesis e índice de los mandamientos*, 287, 289, 293.

recorded that he had five hundred sheep near Zumpango.[42] By 1543 the encomendero of Tixtla, Martín de Ircio, had a sufficient number of cows to require five Indigenous workers to manage them.[43] Some eight Spaniards were given grants of land for livestock or inns, among them notably powerful and influential individuals: Gonzalo Cerezo, a Taxco mineowner and encomendero of Cocula, and Martín de Ircio, María de Mendoza (sister of Viceroy Mendoza), and Luis de Velasco the younger, members of families connected by marriage.[44] The activities of this family in the sixteenth century had lasting repercussions in the Tixtla region. Ircio quickly acquired land, initially for the mining market in Zumpango, but soon traffic on the road to Acapulco would offer new opportunities. These early land acquisitions by interconnected Ircio-Mendoza-Velascos would later form part of a vast hacienda by the eighteenth century.[45]

While livestock was the most extensive Spanish enterprise in the Montaña and the Center, commerce was also a growing sector of their economies. In Tixtla and Mochitlán toward the end of the century, wheat and a variety of Spanish fruits and vegetables ("Relación de Tistla y Muchitlán" records seventeen varieties) were grown on irrigated land.

A similar variety was grown in Chilapa ("Relación de Tistla y Muchitlán" mentions twenty-three distinct crop types). Chilapa had become a center for commerce whose merchants sold wine and wheat flour to the Indians and traded Spanish goods for cacao on the coast. Merchants in Tixtla and Mochitlán acquired cacao from the coast in exchange for chickens, maize, mats, chile, and honey. Some merchants were said to buy 100,000 pesos worth of cacao or more. Whether such a large sum is correct or not, the report suggests substantial volumes of trade. Tlapa also became a commercial hub, exploiting its location on the road to Puebla and routes to the coast. The larger-scale merchants were Spanish, but Indigenous traders were also active, whether as merchants on their own account or as mule drivers.[46]

Among the new enterprises in the Montaña and the Center in the sixteenth century was cochineal, which was an important dye for textile workshops. By 1582 production was reported in Chilapa, and by 1610 in Huamuxtitlán, Olinalá, Tlapa, and Ahuacuotzingo. Although cotton could not be grown in the Montaña, in pre-Hispanic times its inhabitants had been skilled weavers of both everyday textiles and luxury items for elite wear.[47] Since wealthy Spaniards preferred to wear silk, sericulture was introduced to Guerrero—the earliest reference dates to 1543. However, as elsewhere in New Spain, after 1600, inexpensive Asian imports wiped out the domestic silk industry.[48] In the long run, those who profited most were livestock owners who rented community lands, the Spanish cochineal traders, or those who used the repartimiento de efectos.[49] This repartimiento enabled Spanish officials and merchants to extract products of commercial value (such as cacao, chiles, or pumpkin seeds) in compulsory exchange for goods for which the Indians had little or no need, such as cheap Chinese clothing, from Acapulco.[50]

7.3. The North

Land, legally, by means of *mercedes*, or illegally acquired, was essential for the mining economy. In the sixteenth century, twenty-nine mercedes (half the sixty-one on the Costa Grande) were granted, twenty-two or twenty-three of them in the Taxco area, the rest in the valley of Iguala. Almost half—thirteen—were for refining mills to process metal. Grants on the banks of rivers and streams ensured a source of power for refining the ore. In the early years Indigenous production of maize and other

TABLE 7.5. LANDOWNERS IN THE NORTH, 1542–1600

Year	Name	Location	Area	Ha.
1542	Luis de Castilla	Near Taxco and Tenango	1 caballería	44
	Juan de Manzanilla	Jurisdiction of Taxco	1 sitio de ganado	780 or 1,756
	Pedro de Sandoval	Near Taxco and Tenango	1 caballería	44
	Pedro de Sandoval	Acamistlahuaca	1 estancia	780 or 1,756
	Antonio de la Cadena	Jurisdiction of Taxco	1 caballería	44
	Antonio de Almoguer	Near Cinacantlan and Iguala	1.5 caballerías and a water source	66+
Before 1543	Alonso de la Serna	Jurisdiction of Taxco	Water mill to grind and smelt metal	?
Before 1543	Pedro de Ayala	Jurisdiction of Taxco	Water mill to grind and smelt metal	?
1543	Antonio de Almoguer	Near Cinacantlan and Tepecoacuilco	1.5 caballerías for Castilian trees and other things and water for a mill	66+
	Luis de Castilla	Jurisdiction of Taxco	2 sitios for water mill to grind and smelt metal	?
	Juan Alonso de Sosa	Jurisdiction of Taxco	1 sitio for water mill to grind and smelt metal	?
	Juan Jaramillo	Jurisdiction of Taxco	1.5 caballerías	66
c.1552	María de Cisneros	Tlaxmalac	1 estancia de ganado mayor	1,756
1567	Bernardino de Casasola	Near Tepecoacuilco and Tlaxmalac	1.5 caballerías	66
	Francisco Rodríguez	Near Huitzuco and Santiago	2 caballerías	88
1568–1580	Julián Ybañes Morillas	Jurisdiction of Taxco	1 sitio de ganado mayor	1,756
Before 1580	Pedro de Ledesma	Tenantzingo	1 sitio de ganado menor and other lands	780+
Before 1586	Diego Juárez Carrizales	Jurisdiction of Taxco	Water mill to grind and smelt metal	?
	Baltasar Pérez	Noxtepec	Mill for metals	?
	Francisco Ramírez Bravo	Noxtepec	Mill for metals	?
1586	[Diego] Antonio Velázquez	Noxtepec	Water for mill to grind metals	?
	Hernando de Ulloa	Noxtepec	Mill for metals	?
1589	Miguel de Perla [Perea?] [Pérez?]	Taxco el Viejo	1 sitio de ganado menor, 1 caballería	824
1590	Domingo de Salcedo	Huitzuco	1 sitio de ganado mayor, 1 caballería	1,800
c.1592	Isabel Pacheco	Santa María Tetelzingo	1 sitio for a mill	?
1592	Bachiller Joan Rodríguez [previously granted to Luis de Castilla]	Santa María Tetelzingo	1 sitio for houses, a labor gang, and refining mills	?
1593	Luis de Castilla	?	?	?
1590–1595	Martín de Herrera	Jurisdiction of Taxco	1 sitio de ganado mayor	1,756
Before 1599	Pedro Mártir de Castro el Mozo	Taxco el Viejo	2 caballerías, mines, refining mills, and vegetable garden	88+
TOTAL				10,803+ or 12,756+

Sources: Amith, "The Möbius Strip," 1109–12, 1115; Gerhard, *Síntesis e índice de los mandamientos*, 307.

foodstuffs was sufficient, but as mine production increased, land was acquired for food production. Many of the grants in the Taxco area were given in the 1540s to members of New Spain's elite. Thus, the chronology and character of land acquisition was quite different in the North to the coast, where land was directed to livestock or the production of cacao and cotton.[51]

The mercedes in the valley of Iguala were different in character from those close to Taxco. Three were given to the encomenderos Antonio de Almoguer (Tepecoacuilco), Bernardino Moreno de Casasola (Huitzuco), and María de Cisneros (Mayanalán and Tlaxmalac). These lands were for livestock, growing foodstuffs, and other enterprises, such as the harvesting of cascalote, used to tan leather, all supplies with an eager market in the mines to the north. These early grants did not impinge substantially on Indigenous land, since disease and later congregaciones left a good deal of land vacant. However, by the early seventeenth century, Spaniards acquired land by renting it from Indigenous communities or illegally occupying it. In the later colonial period, land in the valley would be acquired by Mexico City and Texcoco merchants and, eventually, by the Jesuits of the Colegio de San Pedro y San Pablo.[52]

The pigs, cattle, sheep, and goats introduced into the valley of Iguala grazed land that had never been fenced. Nothing prevented livestock from eating Indigenous crops. Although land grants in the sixteenth century were not numerous, the numbers of livestock were more significant. For example, in 1590, Domingo de Salcedo received 1,800 hectares near Huitzuco, but his livestock had been grazing the area long before he received legal title to the land. Also, in 1590, the corregidor of Iguala was instructed to have livestock removed from the lands of Cocula and to oblige the owner to pay compensation for damages. By this time the Indigenous communities had also entered the livestock business. In 1591, Tetipac had 400 sheep on community land that would otherwise have been left vacant. In the seventeenth century, livestock raising would fund the cofradías and churches of the Indigenous communities.[53]

Honey had a long history in Guerrero, but the Spaniards introduced sugar cane, a crop that required a warm climate and plenty of water. Land suitable for sugar cane was found, for instance, near Cocula, Iguala, Huitzuco, and Tepecoacuilco, as well as in the Tierra Caliente around Teloloapan and Alahuiztlán. Small-scale production was also possible in the Taxco region. In these areas sugar production seems to have begun in the first years of the seventeenth century, after livestock raising had established itself, perhaps because it required substantial investments in sugar mills, which became viable once demand in the mines was sufficient. Just as they had seized the opportunities offered by cattle, some Indigenous communities cultivated sugar cane, a development opposed by the Taxco mineowners who complained that the sugar was used to produce strong liquor. Sugar mills were, therefore, controlled by licenses.[54]

The economics of landowning in the North were very different from the situation on the Costa Grande, where the end of the brief gold rush left relatively meager commercial opportunities. In the North, demand in the mining towns seemed insatiable. Moreover, demand was also growing in the cities of central Mexico, which were within easy reach of the valley of Iguala. Thus, although mining relied on the encomienda for inputs in the early years, later in the century the focus shifted to acquiring land to supply the demands of mining towns and cities. This set the scene for an enduring theme of colonial Guerrero, the tussle between mineowners who sought to control the production of crops and livestock in the valley of Iguala, and the merchant interests who would supply whichever market would pay the most.[55]

Mules were indispensable for transport since the only alternative was human bearers, who were subject to many legal restrictions to prevent their ill-treatment.[56] Taxco was fortunate that the valley of Iguala was suitable for raising mules. "Relación de Iguala y su partido" reported in 1579, "All around there are large savannahs or pasture where a large number of mules from the Tasco mines and elsewhere graze, getting very fat and it is very excellent for them."[57] A 1582 permit allowed the Taxco mineowners to keep mules in Iguala and Tepecoacuilco. However, raising mules could cause problems, as a 1582 order indicates: "Alonso and Diego Torres must remove the mules they have in Iguala for two months on pain of confiscation."[58]

7.4. Tierra Caliente

The livestock business in the Tierra Caliente was closely linked to mining. Meat was needed to feed workers, to produce leather to make a variety of containers such as bags used to carry ore-bearing rocks from the shafts to the surface, and tallow for candles to light underground mining works.[59] By 1542 encomendero Pedro de Meneses had land for cattle between Coyuca and Sultepec and in Tlalistaca, near the Coyuca mines.[60]

TABLE 7.6. LANDOWNERS AND RENTERS OF LAND IN THE TIERRA CALIENTE IN THE SIXTEENTH CENTURY

Year	Name	Location	Area	Ha.
1542	Pedro de Meneses	Between Coyuca and Sultepec	1 sitio	780 or 1,756
	Pedro de Meneses	Tlalistaca, mines of Coyuca	2 estancias	1,560 or 3,512
Before 1569	Baltasar Muñoz	Near Teloloapan	Land: purpose not known	?
	Pedro Muñoz	Near Teloloapan	Land: purpose not known	?
	Dr. Sedeño	Near Teloloapan	1 estancia de ganado menor	780
	Diego de Morales, tenant	Near Teloloapan	1 estancia de ganado menor	780
	Cristóbal de Escudero	Near Teloloapan	1 estancia de ganado menor	780
	Joan Tellez	Near Teloloapan	1 estancia de ganado menor	780
	Pero Gonzalez Barrientos, tenant	Near Teloloapan	1 estancia de ganado menor	780
	Francisco de Vera	Near Teloloapan	1 estancia de ganado menor	780
	Hospital of Xiquipilco	Near Teloloapan	1 estancia de ganado menor	780
	Don Francisco de Vitoria, "indio principal"	Near Teloloapan	1 estancia de ganado menor	780
1591	Pedro Salgado	Teloloapan	1 estancia de ganado menor, 4 caballerías, 1 pasture for horses	956+
TOTAL				9,536+ or 13,244+

Sources: Álvarez, *Diccionario de conquistadores*, 2:352–55; García Izcabalzeta and García Pimentel, *Descripción del Arzobispado*, 242; Von Mentz, *Señoríos indígenas*, 260.

In 1569 the priest Diego García de Almaráz listed six Spanish cattlemen in his parish, Teloloapan, who received grants of land for *ganado menor* (sheep, goats, pigs), and two tenants: Dr. Sedeño, fiscal of the Audiencia of Mexico, Diego de Morales of Toluca (tenant), Cristóbal de Escudero, Joan Tellez, Francisco de Vera, and Pero González Barrientos (tenant). In addition, Baltasar and Pedro Muñoz, sons of the Pedro Muñoz (or Núñez), known as the Maese de Roa, were given lands near Teloloapan (table 7.6).[61] Other livestock owners who were not granted land simply allowed their animals to invade and to graze on Indigenous lands. Such was the case in Alahuiztlán, which in 1599 complained that sheep belonging to Bartolomé del Águila and Pedro Salgado's cattle were damaging their community's holdings.[62]

Two of the landowners in the parish of Teloloapan mentioned by the priest García de Almaráz were Indigenous: The Indian principal, Francisco de Vitoria, received a grant for ganado menor, as did the hospital of the Indigenous community of Xiquipilco.[63] By 1579 the Indigenous towns of the Tierra Caliente had added to their traditional produce animals and crops introduced from Europe. Ixcateopan raised chickens and a few mares, suggesting that some breeding of horses took place, and cultivated sugar cane. Ixcapuzalco had purchased many horses from nearby ranches and harvested sugar cane and peaches. Sugar cane and some Spanish fruits such as oranges or quince were similarly grown in Alahuiztlán, Oztuma, Coatepec, Tlacotepec, and Utatlan, but sugar cane was not reported in Tetela, Cuetzala, Teloloapan, and Tututepec.[64]

The Tierra Caliente had two other resources that were important in the sixteenth-century economy, cotton and salt, which Indigenous communities produced for their own use and for trade. Cotton was grown in Tetela, Ajuchitlán, and Ixcateopan (whose name derived from *ichcatl*, Nahuatl for cotton). Tlacotepec, Utatlan, and Acapetlahuaya grew no cotton, but acquired what they needed to satisfy their community's requirements for textiles and clothing from Tetela or Ajuchitlán. Cuetzala harvested some cotton, supplemented by acquiring more from Tetela.[65] Salt, which had been one of the resources that led the Tarascans and the Mexica to dispute control of the Tierra Caliente, became still more important in the sixteenth century since it was used to process metal ores— the processing of 920 kilograms of ore required 57.5 kilograms of salt.[66] Salt was produced in Ixcapuzalco, Alahuiztlán, Oztuma, and Cutzamala and, on a smaller scale, in Tlacotepec and Tetela.[67] Cotton and salt sustained the survival of pre-Hispanic networks of exchange while at the same time creating new networks geared to supplying the mining industry. Towns that lacked their own saltworks acquired it from sources in the region or traveled to the coast to acquire it. For instance, Indigenous merchants in Oztuma were active traders of salt to the mines and also traded salt for cotton. Similarly, the Indians of Ixcapuzalco and Oztuma sold salt, chickens, and maize to Zacualpan and Taxco, while Alahuiztlán supplied salt to Zacualpan, Taxco, and Sultepec. In other words, while the precontact pattern of trade continued, Spanish-owned mining operations opened new networks of exchange that could potentially benefit Indigenous communities in the Tierra Caliente.[68]

7.5. Conclusions

The character, extent, and economic functions of private landownership in the sixteenth century varied considerably by region. After an early boom of placer gold mining on the coast and a more precipitate decline of the Indigenous population than in other regions, Spaniards acquired land to raise cattle, grow cacao, and for coconut plantations. For lack of Indigenous labor, the importation of African and Asian slaves left an indelible ethnic and cultural mark on the coast, which survives to this day. The Montaña, on the other hand, witnessed much less direct acquisition of land, Spanish livestock owners, instead, grazing animals seasonally on rented or usurped land, using Indigenous labor. In the Center the Chilapa region followed the same model, but around Tixtla and Zumpango silver mining prompted Spaniards to acquire land, until production declined. Later in the century, traffic along the Mexico City–Acapulco road became the economic opportunity in this area, including the acquisition of land for inns along the highway. In subsequent centuries, these early acquisitions would form the basis of an enormous, landed estate.

The Taxco boom shaped landholding in the North. The demand for foodstuffs, meat, leather, and pack animals attracted Spanish investments in land in the fertile valley of Iguala. As in the Center, these holdings would be consolidated in later centuries into large estates. The market created by the Taxco mineowners was both a benefit and a problem for the landowners of the valley, since the mineowners used all their influence to attempt to keep prices for agricultural produce low. Around Taxco itself, much of the land was acquired for facilities necessary to process the ore disgorged by the mines and for essential supplies such as firewood and charcoal. Although the mines of the Tierra Caliente were small affairs compared to Taxco and other mining zones of the Silver Province, proximity to some of the most productive mines of the sixteenth century drove the economy and landowning here. Land was devoted to cattle ranches and agricultural production. Salt and cotton also found ready markets in the mines.

CHAPTER EIGHT

From Gold to Silver

The Mining Economy of Sixteenth-Century Guerrero

Mining was by far the main driving force of Spanish activities in New Spain in the sixteenth century, even after the discovery of the return route to Asia in 1565. Moreover, Guerrero was a very early focus of mining activity. Cortés dispatched expeditions to the coast in 1521, and by 1523 Zacatula was founded on the Costa Grande, followed by the Villa de San Luis on the Costa Chica in 1524.[1] In the Center the first substantial silver strike occurred at Zumpango, but this was overshadowed by the discovery in Taxco of the richest seams of silver in all New Spain until the mines of northern Mexico in turn eclipsed Taxco. Thus, an examination of sixteenth-century mining in Guerrero is important not just for the history of the region but also for an understanding of the organization of mining enterprises in the early years of the colonial period.

8.1. Zacatula

Mining required capital investment in equipment and sustenance of Indigenous mineworkers, which invariably involved sellers extending credit to buyers. Debt was, therefore, an essential element of mining from the beginning. For example, in September 1525 Antón Sánchez purchased mining tools on credit from Miguel Rodríguez de Guadalupe, vecino of Mexico City.[2] In 1528 Pedro García Moreno of Mexico City, a slaveowner and possibly an investor in mining himself, sold to the mineowner Felipe Navarro wine and clothing valued at 51 pesos on credit. Juan de Rodas owed García Moreno 100 pesos for an Indigenous slave named Juana, mining tools, and clothing. Alonso García, his debtor, appointed García Moreno to collect debts in Mexico City, as did Juan de Cartagena in the sizeable amount of 200 pesos.[3] Transactions paid for in hard cash were rare.

Ready and cheap access to labor was essential. Thus, in March 1527 Hernando de Torres, encomendero of Tepecoacuilco, and Martín Jiménez, a resident of Colima, formed a mining company, both investing Indigenous slaves and Indians from their encomiendas. The latter were theoretically free but, in fact, were forced laborers. Jiménez also invested 300 gold pesos. Neither partner dirtied his hands by working or overseeing operations in the mines, preferring to employ another Spaniard to do so.[4] In 1528 Juan de Cabra, encomendero of Noxtepec and Pilcaya near Taxco, who would later be a significant figure in mining there, agreed to contribute seventy Indigenous male and female slaves and encomienda Indians from distant Noxtepec to a mining company in Zacatula and Michoacán. His partner, Serván Bejarano, encomendero of Ocuylaconguantepeque in Michoacán, likewise contributed eighty slaves and half the labor provided by his encomienda.[5] It is probable that neither partner scrupulously fulfilled their obligations to care for their workers' spiritual welfare.

Alonso de Aguilar y Córdoba's contribution to the mining venture he established in 1528 with his partner Andrés Núñez was not encomienda labor, but food provided free of charge by a distant encomienda, Olinalá and Papalutla in the Montaña, for Núñez's one hundred Indigenous slaves, equipped with tools and gold pans. Once again, the partners employed an unnamed mineworker to supervise operations, in this case for a share of the gold. After paying this supervisor, tax—the royal quinto—and the costs of smelting, Núñez took 60 percent of the remaining gold and Aguilar 40 percent.[6]

The encomienda, thus, was a source of capital for many mining ventures in the region, but not all were financed in this way. In 1527 Hernando Gallego and Diego de la Muela formed a mining company and then bought seventy-two Indigenous slaves with their equipment (most sales of slaves in Zacatula included tools and gold pans) for 340 gold pesos. Next, Gallego purchased 124 fanegas (5,704 kilograms) of maize from Fernando de Jerez, of Mexico City, to feed the slaves. The total investment to start this mining venture was 402 pesos, a substantial sum.[7] In 1528 Andrés de Monjarrás and Blasco Hernández established a similar enterprise for a year to seek gold in Zacatula or elsewhere. Each contributed fifty slaves with their tools. Monjarrás was to maintain the slaves and the man hired to manage the venture, probably Pedro López Galbito, himself an owner of slaves in the Zacatula mines and therefore experienced in mining operations. The two partners shared the profits equally.[8] There were also mineowners who managed their slaves and mines themselves, probably on a small scale. One such was Juan Garrido, a Black or Mulatto, who owed Cristóbal López 107 gold pesos for slaves and tools, which he was unable to repay. López won a judgement for default in April 1528.[9]

The heyday of the Zacatula mining boom had waned by 1536–1538, when only one document relating to mining was registered. The 1537 testament of Tomás de Valverde records that, with his partners Francisco González and Baltasar de Palacios, he bought sixty slaves for 150 "or so" gold pesos. Valverde sent this sizeable number of slaves to Zacatula in the custody of Palacios, almost certainly for a mining venture.[10] As mining ended, the economic decline of the province of Zacatula continued throughout the sixteenth century. A sign of the times was the Spanish population of Zacatula, reduced from the 122 vecinos of 1523 to a mere 13 by 1580. Labor was scarce, as the author of the "Relación de la Villa de Zacatula" notes: "Because of the epidemics, and the ways of life transplanted by the Europeans, the natives are fewer everyday."[11]

8.2. Zumpango and Chilapa

According to the "Relación de las minas de Zumpango," Diego Jaramillo, the third encomendero of Zumpango, discovered silver there in 1534, but this cannot be correct because mineowners were already resident in 1533.[12] In his probanza de méritos, Francisco de Hoyos, who had been mining gold near the coast when Yope warriors attacked him and some other Spaniards, claimed that he had spent more than 2,000 pesos as a member of Vasco de Porcallo's 1531 campaign to pacify the Yopes, and then had been "one of the first to discover silver in Çumpango, which was the source of everything he had today."[13] If de Hoyos's boasts are to be believed, the mines may have been discovered in 1531 or 1532. However, Diego Curiel also claimed to have discovered the mines, while Rodrigo de Tamar affirmed that not only was he the first to discover the mine of Cerro de San Martyn in Zumpango, but also Cerro Rico in Taxco, and the mines of Nyxapa and Culiacán, which had profited the king substantially.[14]

By 1533 there were no fewer than forty-seven resident Spanish mineowners in Zumpango, who urged improvements to the road from Mexico City to the mines to supply them with wine, olive oil, vinegar, and other Castilian goods.[15] Thus, whoever was genuinely first to discover silver in Zumpango, many Spaniards soon went there in search of wealth. One such was Diego de Castañeda, who participated in military expeditions in Yopecingo and Motines. He was a silversmith and is said to have processed the first ore mined in Zumpango. Joan de Talavera also fought in Yopecingo with Porcallo, and he stated that he "had many mines for a long time in Çunpango, and paid many quintos to His Majesty." In 1536 Ruy López de Villalobos, alguacil mayor of New Spain, and Bernardino de Vargas subcontracted the work of looking for and registering mines in Zumpango to Antón de Rojas and Bartolomé Dávila.[16] Important encomenderos of the Coast and the Center owned Zumpango mines: Juan Rodríguez de Villafuerte (Costa Grande), Diego de Pardo (Costa Chica), Diego Jaramillo, Martín de Ircio, and Vasco Porcallo (Center).[17] However, by 1582, when Gonzalo Bazán, alcalde mayor of Zumpango, and the priest Francisco Moreno wrote the "Relación de las minas de Zumpango," only a few Indian laborers worked in the mines.[18]

Spaniards had also prospected for mines in Chilapa. However, in 1582 the relaciones of Chilapa and Tixtla reported that the gold that the Indians previously had panned for in the rivers was now exhausted. Chilapa's mines had produced a small quantity of silver, but this production was eclipsed by much richer mines in Zumpango and Taxco.[19] The lack of a sustained mining boom and the persistence of Indigenous structures of government would determine a very different colonial trajectory for the Center and for the adjacent Montaña where placer gold worked by Indians was the norm.

8.3. Tierra Caliente

Spaniards eagerly sought mines in this region, probably as early as the 1520s, and, as the "Relación de Ichcateupan" reports, a number were found but by 1579 were generally abandoned. For example, the encomendero Juan de Mansanilla had found a gold mine three leagues from Ixcapuzalco and had worked it intensively until Indian forced labor was prohibited and silver was discovered elsewhere. There was also a silver mine in the vicinity, discovered by Jerónimo Ruiz de Baeza, where mining continued.[20] A gold mine in Topila, a sujeto of Tlacotepec, attracted many to seek riches there, but now the mineworks lay idle.[21] In Tetela two copper mines had been worked "in ancient times," but likewise now were neglected.[22] Mining in Tetela resumed from 1580 to 1630 when the priest Joseph de Urizar invested in silver mining, although mercury turned out to be much more abundant than silver. However, although Tetela experienced something of a local bonanza, cattle raising, agriculture, and debt financed fluctuating levels of production.[23]

8.4. Taxco and Neighboring Mines

At the end of the sixteenth century, the Zacatula gold rush was merely a memory, and Zumpango was greatly diminished. However, the magnificent church of Santa Prisca, built in the eighteenth century with riches from the mines, testifies to the enduring importance of Taxco's silver in the history of Guerrero. Here the first great silver strikes in the Spanish empire created some of the great mining fortunes. Taxco would later be overshadowed by the mines of Guanajuato, Pachuca, Zacatecas, and San Luis Potosí, but this small town, not far from Mexico City, would be a key to the economy of much of Guerrero. And, as in Zacatula and Zumpango, it all happened at speed.

Taxco was located in a very different region from Zacatula. Here the silver lodes were not on a tropical coast, but in a cooler, drier mountainous terrain. In the mining zone, and a little to the south in the fertile valley of Iguala, were substantial Indigenous populations, in towns such as Taxco el Viejo, Noxtepec, Pilcaya, Tepecoacuilco, Huitzuco, Cocula, and Iguala. There were centuries old links—economic, political, cultural—with the valley of Toluca and the basin of Mexico. These had been provinces of the Mexica Empire for several decades, while the coast was conquered much later and was probably more loosely controlled.[24] To the west lay the Tierra Caliente and to the north the ancient kingdom of Cuauhnáhuac. In short, this was a fertile region with a population able to supply the inputs and labor required in Taxco's early mining years. Moreover, Taxco was in a wider zone of silver mines, such as Sultepec, Temascaltepec, and Zacualpan, which earned the region the name of the Silver Province. The sources of labor were very different in a northern mining settlement such as Zacatecas, where there were no local sedentary Indigenous peoples; free wage laborers were recruited from regions such as Michoacán, and African slaves played a minor and costly role.[25]

By 1579–1582 the population of Taxco was exceptional in Guerrero for its mix of Spaniards, slaves, and encomienda Indian workers, but, above all, many Indian wage laborers. Indeed, Taxco stood out not only when compared to other towns in Guerrero, but also by comparison to other mining centers of the Silver Province (table 8.1). The highest echelon of this society was occupied by some of the richest and most powerful individuals in New Spain.

TABLE 8.1. POPULATION OF MINING TOWNS OF THE SILVER PROVINCE, 1579–1582					
	Mines	Spaniards	Slaves	Encomienda Indians	Indigenous wage laborers
Taxco	30	150	600	200	2,300
Temascaltepec	30	50	250	100	150
Sultepec	10	50	50	250	
Zacualpan	5	50	150		150
TOTAL	75	300	1,050	550	2,600
Source: Zavala, *El servicio personal de los indios*, 3:300.					

8.5. The Mining Elite of Taxco

Many of the most prominent mineowners were absentees, preferring residences in Mexico City and visiting Taxco only when business required. Nevertheless, this area was home to the largest population of Spaniards in Guerrero, and whether absentee or resident, Taxco's mining elite consisted of a variety of actors. Among the investors and active participants in silver mining we find conquistadors, encomenderos,[26] high royal officials, and other figures of great influence in Mexico City and Spain, along with merchants, priests such as Garci Rodríguez,[27] and local royal officials.

The first silver deposits were discovered in 1524, but the man whose fortune was made by the first great strike, probably in 1530, was Luis de Castilla.[28] Castilla would become one of the most powerful and well-connected men of sixteenth-century New Spain. He was descended via a bastard line from King Pedro I, "the Cruel" or "the Just."[29] Luis married Joana de Sosa, sister of the Royal Treasurer Juan Alonso de Sosa, who also had mining interests in Taxco. The Castilla family was related to the powerful Pacheco de Bocanegra family, and Luis's daughters married very well. Royal Visitor Jerónimo Valderrama told the king in 1564 that the Castillas had close family ties to Viceroy Luis de Velasco. The previous viceroy had given legal protection to Castilla's mines, and Velasco granted land to Luis, his son Pedro Lorenzo, and his daughter Inés. Further grants of land followed to Luis and Pedro, as well as to Luis de Godoy, a member of Castilla's household, and to Gonzalo de León, a silversmith and servant of Luis. Several sons and a brother-in-law received encomiendas or were appointed to corregimientos. Even minor figures in the household were appointed to corregimientos; for example, Juan

Gutiérrez Bocanegra, who Valderrama dismissed as a mere "unmarried youth, of no merits."[30]

In his probanza de méritos asking favors of the king in the 1550s or 1560s, Castilla lamented that his encomiendas in Jalisco were insufficient to support him, despite being appointed to corregimientos.[31] Nevertheless, Dorantes Carranza emphasizes Castilla's influence in the highest circles, noting:

> He maintained a great household, as of a great lord, many horses, servants, arms, people and followers, with such flamboyance and all the splendour of a great personage; and such was the wealth he acquired from that Tasco mine, that he could afford all his heart wished for, because even the humblest kitchen vessels and other wares were of fine silver.[32]

In 1542 Castilla was alcalde mayor of Taxco when, it is said, an Indian called Miguel José discovered a lode richer even than the 1530 strike. Castilla used his power to seize the mine. He had another mine and a refining mill in Zacualpan.[33] In 1560 pictographic documents presented by the Chontals of Tetipac as part of their testimony in a legal case claimed that in 1540 Castilla had settled Tarascans on land that belonged to Tetipac and Tenango. Tetipac accused Castilla of establishing a refining mill on the land and the Tarascans of cutting firewood from their land to fuel the mill.[34]

Castilla employed the Indians of Iguala to build a water-driven refining mill and foundry in Taxco. In 1553 he complained that the Indians had not finished the work, although he had paid them most of their dues in gold pesos.[35] In 1583 he petitioned the alcalde mayor of Taxco to conscript Indigenous labor for his mines.[36] The most successful Taxco mining entrepreneurs had certain strategic advantages such as encomiendas, official posts, influence, personal or family connections with powerful people, and access to capital. Luis de Castilla had all of these in abundance.

Mining activity in Taxco, and debt to finance it, expanded rapidly. Before September 1536 Gaspar de Soria bought mines and thirty-six slaves from Diego de San Martín and Gregorio Yáñez de Burgos, a Mexico City merchant. Soria then sold the mines and two-thirds of two African slaves named Agustín and Gonzalo, with their tools, to Cristóbal de Cisneros for 2,500 gold pesos. Both these large transactions involved credit. Soria owed San Martín and Yáñez de Burgos 1,600 pesos (the price of thirty-eight slaves, including Agustín and Gonzalo). Cisneros agreed to repay this debt. He further owed the outstanding 900 pesos to Soria. In short, no cash changed hands.[37] Taxco mining debts could be sizeable. For example, in 1549 or 1550, the mineowner Pedro de Sandoval bought a hacienda where wheat was grown for the Taxco market from the oidor Lorenzo de Tejada for 48,000–60,000 ducados. Sandoval bought more than land in this transaction. He also acquired the protection of Tejada from his creditors to whom he owed 150,000 ducados.[38]

Yáñez de Burgos was very active in Taxco mining in the 1530s. His name appears in ten documents relating to mining, slaves, or other enterprises. He was one of the early mineowners and also a dealer in Indigenous and African slaves, the former in greater quantities than the latter. He extended credit and collected debts on behalf of other investors in the Taxco mines. He also invested in transport; for example, forming a company with the mule driver Fernando Bravo, who managed the mules while Yáñez sold the merchandise.[39]

Indian laborers were an indispensable input in the mines. In 1537 Pablo de Melgosa and Miguel Legazpi (who would command the fleet that sailed to the Philippines in 1565) agreed to hire from Martín de Zavala thirty encomienda Indians for a year to work in the Taxco mines, a form of forced labor that was not at all legal. Melgosa and Legazpi were well connected in Taxco mining circles: They had been tutors of Pedro Salcedo, son of the mineowner and encomendero Juan de Salcedo.[40] In 1536 Francisco Quintero de Zamora, encomendero of Tetipac, rented forty laborers for a year to the Taxco mineowner Juan Fernández for 550 gold pesos. In 1537 Hernán Pérez de Bocanegra formed a company for a year to rent sixty workers from his encomienda in Acámbaro, some 300 kilometers away, in the Taxco mines for 1,600 pesos.[41]

Food for slaves and animals was another significant input. In 1536 and 1537, of nineteen legal documents related to Taxco mining, five involved slaves.[42] In 1536 the bishop of Mexico City sold to Antón de Carmona "all the tithes of maize, beans and chile from 20 leagues around the mines of Çunpango and Tasco and Amatepeque." Carmona sold the foodstuffs on to Pedro Núñez at a price of 5 golden reales per fanega. Carmona also sold to Jerónimo de León 1,300 fanegas (59,800 kilograms) of maize, 100 (4,600 kilograms) of beans, and 100 of chile to be delivered to León's Taxco home. Carmona further delivered 1,200 fanegas (55,200 kilograms) of maize, 100 of beans, and 100 of chile to

Diego de Logroño's mines in nearby Sultepec.[43] As well as being a merchant, Carmona was a Taxco mineowner who purchased one hundred Indigenous slaves in 1528.[44]

Several Spaniards had mines in both Taxco and Sultepec, the most important mining centers of the Silver Province. In 1536 Royal Treasurer Juan Alonso de Sosa, who had mines in Taxco, and Hernán Cortés were partners in a Sultepec mine. Cortés owned a very productive Taxco mine, Cantarranas, where he made substantial investments in infrastructure. The workforce in the Sultepec mine consisted of two hundred Indigenous slaves (twenty from Cortes's cuadrilla in Taxco), eighty Indians de servicio, and twelve African slaves.[45] Cortés also owned a share in the Albarrada mine in Sultepec. Sosa was joint owner of another share in Albarrada with Diego de Logroño and the Cutzamala encomendero and Taxco mineowner Juan de Burgos.[46]

The elite of the mining towns also included royal officials, who in theory enforced royal decrees and ensured that the Indians were well treated. However, the official, who had bought his post, was motivated to ensure a good return on investment. In 1592 Rodrigo de Ávila paid a hefty 12,000 pesos for a post in Taxco, three times more than the same position in Guanajuato and six times more than in Temascaltepec. Only Pachuca commanded a slightly higher price, 12,600 pesos. When the alguacil mayor of Taxco died in 1595, Diego de Ocampo bought the post for 8,125 pesos.[47] These were substantial investments. Many of Taxco's officials were actively involved in mining. Francisco Termiño, teniente de alcalde mayor in 1572, was an investor in Sultepec mines. The family of Diego Santa Cruz y Aguilar, alcalde mayor in 1593, were silver traders and loaned money to mineowners in Taxco and Zacualpan. Diego's sister was Isabel Salcedo de Legazpi, whose last names suggest links to the Salcedo (encomenderos and mineowners) and Legazpi (mineowners) families. Juan de la Peña, who was alguacil mayor, bought silver from small-scale miners and had a shop in another mining town, Tecicapa.[48]

The principal beneficiaries of mining in Taxco were individuals, such as encomenderos and merchants, with access to the considerable resources that mining required and the credit to finance operations. Networks of powerful associates and family ties were indispensable as was influence with royal officials, including the highest levels of the royal administration in New Spain. These were individuals whose operations consumed great quantities of essential inputs.

8.6. Mining Inputs

In 1572 English merchant Henry Hawks enumerated the resources a mineowner needed: one hundred slaves to extract and crush the ore, mules and people to look after them, a refining mill, much firewood, quantities of mercury, great amounts of brine, and sufficient capital to cover many costs.[49] Some figures from 1597 offer a more detailed account of the human and physical inputs of the Taxco mines. There were sixty-one mineowners, more than any other mining town in New Spain (in Pachuca there were fifty-two, in Zacatecas thirty-four). Forty-seven refining mills were in operation (a further fourteen no longer functioned), with ninety-six engines (thirty-six driven by water, forty-five by horses, fifteen by men). They produced annually 49,610 quintales (2,282,060 kilograms) of metal. Only Zacatecas produced more (78,858 quintales). The Taxco mines employed 266 African slaves, 834 salaried Indigenous workers, 406 indios de repartimiento, and 436 mules. To feed workers and animals required 70,505 fanegas (3,243,300 kilograms) of maize. The mine shafts were lit by 2,294 candles, more than any other mine and 20 percent of New Spain's consumption. Processing the ore required 13,030 fanegas (599,380 kilograms) of salt and 1,171 quintales of mercury, more than any other mine in New Spain (Pachuca consumed 929 quintales). Mineowners complained frequently about the price of mercury and delayed payment. The mine and refinery owners of New Spain owed the Crown 1,375,738 pesos, 6 tomines, and 7 granos.[50]

Beeswax for making candles came principally from encomienda tribute for several decades. It seems likely that Indigenous candlemakers produced most, perhaps all, of the lighting required in the mines. A group of Indigenous candlemakers from Mexico City was resident in Taxco in 1550, and in the same year four Indians from Iguala and Huitzuco were given permits to make and sell candles of yellow beeswax.[51]

Ore was refined by heating it repeatedly, which required firewood and charcoal. Huitzuco, Taxco, and Tenancingo supplied firewood as tribute.[52] Royal officials made money in the firewood business. In 1551 the Indians of Cuetzala sought an injunction to prevent the alcalde mayor, whom they accused of forcing them to cut firewood for the refining engines and of forcing them to work without pay in the Taxco mines. In 1550 the viceroy issued an order to the alcalde mayor of Taxco to enforce ordinances to control the cutting of firewood in the woods of eleven pueblos in the Taxco region.[53]

The Indigenous communities of the region were involved in firewood and other enterprises related to mining. Around 1570, some residents of Pilcaya were reported to be merchants, others transported goods on horseback, while others "since they are close to the mines of Tasco and Zacualpa are in the business of selling charcoal and firewood and hay and timber." They also worked with honey, which sold for two tomines, the cuartillo, and raised a few chickens. Similarly, the people of Acamixtlahuaca sold charcoal, firewood, and hay, and hired themselves as laborers in the mines. In Tenango the residents were Tarascan newcomers who sold charcoal and firewood to the town's mines.[54] Indeed, cutting firewood was a pre-Hispanic trade, although for religious rites rather than for mining.[55]

Taxco was a boom town run in the interests of a powerful, ambitious mining elite, who were able to flout the law and their religious obligations. Encomenderos, mineowners, merchants, and royal officials—indeed some priests—came to Taxco to get rich.[56] But if rules meant little to the powerful, they were also honored in the breach by encomienda laborers, wages laborers, and Indigenous and African slaves. In this town most were on the make.

8.7. Ordinances, Disorder, and Environmental Harms

Taxco was the most important town in sixteenth-century Guerrero. It had an exceptionally diverse population and engaged in a wide range of activities compared to other settlements in the region. Silver made some fabulously wealthy, but it also created a boisterous society in which social and legal norms counted for little. Baptismal records for 1589–1600 mention thirty-two landowners who had slaves or gangs of Indigenous workers in Taxco. The population included mineowners, clergy, royal officials, swindlers, merchants, foremen, shopkeepers, butchers, bakers, and laborers. Some mineowners, such as Luis de Castilla or Gonzalo Cerezo, kept residences in Mexico City and visited Taxco when business required. However, prominent mining entrepreneur Gaspar Hernández built his home in Cantarranas and lived there with his wife, Luisa de Morales. In 1593 they were godparents of an Indian child and of a child of one of their hacienda workers. The future Golden Age dramatist Juan Ruiz de Alarcón was born in Taxco in 1580 or 1581, but his family soon moved to Mexico City where the children could be educated and enjoy the refinements of city life.[57]

This was a disorderly society in which heresies prosecuted by the Inquisition flourished, and where for two decades the civil authorities struggled to exercise control over illicit practices that proliferated in a society in which the pursuit of profit rode roughshod over the law. The problems that, from the Crown's point of view, beset Taxco are evident in the provisions of the ordinances issued in 1542 by Lorenzo de Tejada to address Taxco's social problems and criminality. Tejada focused on three broad areas: commerce, environmental impacts, and social control.[58]

Tejada's attempts to control commercial activities of Spanish merchants, humble workers, and Indians reflect the large profits available in Taxco. Key goods were scarce; above all salt, wheat flour, maize, olive oil, cacao, sugar, honey, fish, chickpeas, and beans all sold at high prices. Viceroy Mendoza considered the shortage of flour in Taxco and Sultepec to be one of the most significant problems of New Spain. Merchants were blamed for selling unnecessary goods to Indians and slaves on credit to be paid in silver stolen from the mines and smelted at home. One merchant had forty-one debtors, of whom sixteen were Indians. Tejada forbade Spanish merchants to come within four leagues of Taxco on pain of a fine and confiscation of goods. Merchants were specifically prohibited from buying maize elsewhere for sale in the mines. Sales to Indians and slaves were absolutely forbidden. Indigenous merchants were subject to similar restrictions, which suggests a substantial Indigenous trade in Taxco. Tejada also attempted to control the Sunday tianguis in the main plaza. To prevent Indians leaving work in the mines to become market traders, Indians were allowed to sell produce of their own land only. These restrictions probably served Tejada's personal interests, for the oidor had acquired, by means of dubious legality, considerable amounts of land to grow wheat and vines. Since flour and wine were much in demand, in expelling Spanish merchants from Taxco, Tejada may not simply have been protecting the Crown's interests but perhaps attempted to monopolize the Taxco market.[59]

The technologies used in Taxco were dangerous for the health of workers, their families, and society in general. The silver ore contained lead and arsenic, released when ore was heated using *soplillos*, small tubes through which workers blew to raise the temperature of the fire. Workers and slaves heated stolen ore at home, exposing themselves and their families to *engasamiento*, noxious fumes, to which the Spaniards attributed high infant mortality. Pollutants leached into the water supply. The ordinances restricted the work of pregnant women in refining mills, prohibited bathing children in water from the mills, and restricted the use of soplillos.⁶⁰

Tejada's ordinances attempted to control rapid deforestation caused by mining. One Spanish and six Indigenous forest guards, all carrying the rod of legal office, were appointed. The Indigenous guards were able to arrest Indians and Africans, to punish them with lashes, and to cut their hair. The Spanish guard was empowered to fine Spanish lawbreakers. The restrictions were repeated in 1550, which suggests that they had limited success. In fact, royal ordinances proved incapable of stopping deforestation. Production of 1 kilogram of silver required 1,168 kilograms of charcoal, the product of cutting 15.45 cubed meters of wood, which in turn felled 6,332 cubed meters of forest land. One calculation estimates that between 1558 and 1804 timber covering 193,650 square kilometers was felled in New Spain for mining purposes. Taxco, in short, had the dubious distinction of being the place where large scale deforestation began, to spread later to other mines of New Spain as far north as Durango and Sonora.⁶¹

The mining boom attracted a motley array of characters to Taxco. Spaniards dreamed of great riches, free Indians could earn a wage and avoid paying tribute or dabble in small-scale commerce. Labor was permanently scarce, so the great preoccupation of mineowners and officials alike was to control labor and disruptive behavior. Tejada's ordinances lamented the presence of "vagrants, petty thieves and marginal types of all sorts," and the ever-present risk of heresy and Jews. Indians, Blacks, and Mulattos were obliged to work in the mines, and Spanish vagrants were expelled from Taxco.⁶² Tejada's ordinances confirm that competition for workers was intense. Mineowners lured indios naboríos away from their labor gangs. Although Tejada forbade this practice, laborers found other ways to profit from the opportunities available in Taxco. Tejada attempted to prevent free and slave workers from stealing ore by prohibiting them from processing it, and anybody found with silver for which tax had not been paid was to be expelled from Taxco.⁶³

Numerous ordinances were issued prior to and after Tejada's regulations in the sixteenth century, which suggests that the practices that Tejada attempted to control were impossible to eradicate. In 1547 the sale of wine to Indians and Blacks was prohibited. Within a radius of eight leagues (37 kilometers) of Taxco, wine could be sold only in a tavern in the house of the alcalde mayor at permitted times. Spaniards linked drunkenness to witchcraft. Drunken Indians were said to transform into "tigers and lions." Regulations of 1571, 1573, and 1574 expressed similar concerns. Mulattos and Indians in Taxco were to be registered. To secure Indian labor in mining and for public works competition between mineowners to employ workers was to be regulated. To ensure supplies of salt, maize, and other essentials, and to control their prices, sales within a radius of eight leagues were to be controlled.[64]

In 1575 new ordinances issued by Dr. Lope de Miranda, oidor of the Audiencia of Mexico, addressed familiar concerns. Intense competition for scarce labor continued. Workers devised means of maximizing their earnings. For example, Indigenous laborers who were working under the *tequio* system of community work hired themselves to two or three employers without any formal contract. They added rock, slag, or earth to the ore to exaggerate their production. Indigenous workers returned to the mines at night to remove ore from the pillars of rock that held up the roof of the shafts, causing them to collapse. Miranda prohibited this practice and ordered workers to remove debris that obstructed the shaft. The *diputados de minas* further reported that workers stole mercury. Miranda banned the mineowners' practice of *sonsaque*, payment of wages in advance to lure workers away from another employer. Miranda's reports of detrimental labor practices suggest that Indigenous workers were able to use their negotiating power to their advantage. Miranda also addressed familiar themes of social control: Indian, Mulatto, and Black vagabonds were to be registered and obliged to work in the mines or be expelled from Taxco. He also attempted to regulate harmful commercial practices, such as those of hucksters who bought salt cheaply from saltworks to sell it at inflated prices in Taxco. The problems addressed by Miranda and his predecessors persisted, since in 1590 Viceroy Velasco again prohibited illegal use of Indian labor and the theft of ore.[65]

In short, the wealth that flowed from sixteenth-century Taxco made enforcement of regulations difficult if not impossible. The mineowners certainly considered that Tejada's edicts did not go far enough, since in 1551 twenty of them signed a petition criticizing his ordinances. They claimed that thirty-eight mineowners who had gangs of slaves had debts of 450,000 pesos and that only two mines were profitable. They complained about superfluous goods in the shops, such as silk, linen, and woolen textiles, about hucksters profiteering in essential supplies, especially those needed to refine ore, and of thieving Indigenous vagabonds. The mineowners recommended that four *diputados* be appointed annually to assist the alcalde mayor to enforce regulations concerning prices and labor. The signatories included influential figures such as encomendero Juan de Cabra, Luis de Castilla, and Pedro de Osorio, encomendero and alcalde mayor of Taxco.[66]

8.8. Conclusions

Almost immediately after the defeat of the Mexicas, the Spaniards extended their search for precious metals to most corners of Guerrero. The placer gold of the Pacific coast lured many to Zacatula, where some of the principal themes of sixteenth-century mining ventures were soon apparent: the encomienda as a source of labor and resources, slavery, credit to finance costly mining operations, the formation of partnerships to pool resources, and the importance of networks of personal and familial connections. For a time Zumpango in the Center seemed destined to be a significant focus of silver mining, but as the sixteenth century drew to a close, Taxco had become by far the most significant economic center in Guerrero. Mines in northern New Spain would generate much more wealth in years to come, but, as the place where the first big silver strikes of New Spain occurred, Taxco was a laboratory where commercial models and regulations were developed and tested. In the context of Guerrero, Taxco's wealth and the power of its elite would shape the history of Guerrero beyond the sixteenth century. The only place that could rival the economic power of Taxco in the region was Acapulco, but the port of the fabled Manila Galleon would not rise to prominence until more than three decades had elapsed since Luis de Castilla took possession of the first rich seam of Taxco silver. The Taxco-Acapulco axis would from then on be the determining factor that shaped the economic and social geography of Guerrero until our own times.

CHAPTER NINE

The Lure of Asia

Acapulco and the Manila Galleon

In 1610 Bishop of Tlaxcala Fray Alonso de Mota y Escobar reported that friars and Indians alike in the Montaña were engaged in the Philippines trade, begun some thirty-five years before. In a few decades Acapulco, the former shell mound by the bay, had become the most important place in New Spain when the galleon arrived. The trade in Asian goods, which had transformed the economy of New Spain, would also transform the spatial organization of Guerrero, with profound consequences for the region.[1]

9.1. The Search for the Return Route

The designation of Acapulco as the official port for trade with Asia was the result of a strategic imperative of the Spanish Crown and persistent exploration. In 1493 a papal bull divided the world between Spain and Portugal, an arrangement confirmed in the Treaty of Tordesillas. Spain violated the treaty twice. Ferdinand Magellan's expedition (1519–1522), which rounded the Cape of Good Hope to reach the Pacific, was the first breach. Although Magellan was killed in the Philippines, Sebastián del Cano captained the *Victoria* home to Spain by the route that under the treaty was the preserve of the Portuguese. The second contravention occurred when Spain colonized the Philippines. The search for a route to that archipelago that avoided the Cape of Good Hope was a paramount concern of the Crown that proved costly in lives and ships.[2]

The last expedition to sail from Spain, in 1525, was a failure that sowed the seeds of later success. Two friars, both knowledgeable seafarers, were key figures in this voyage. Juan García Jofre de Loaisa commanded the fleet, and the Augustinian Andrés de Urdaneta, an outstanding pilot, was the navigator. The expedition ended in disaster, as Hernando de la Torre informed the king on June 11, 1528. The captains, the treasurer, the accountant, and other officials all died. However, Urdaneta, who survived and sailed home on a Portuguese ship, wrote a detailed account of the voyage and began to plan another route.[3]

From 1527 New Spain became the base for the search for a route to the Western Isles. However, Acapulco did not play an important part in the search until 1565. The 1527 fleet commanded by Álvaro de Saavedra left from Zihuatanejo on Guerrrero's coast. This voyage, too, ended in failure but carried a germ of success since once again Urdaneta was one of the pilots. Only Saavedra's ship reached the Philippines, but it failed to find a return route to New Spain. Once again, the surviving Spaniards (Saavedra died at sea) were taken to safety in Europe by the Portuguese.[4] Another expedition left Puerto de Navidad in 1542 under Ruy López de Villalobos. After calling at several islands and fighting with hostile natives, hunger forced Villalobos to anchor in Portuguese territory in 1545. He attempted a return to New Spain, but after five months admitted failure and returned to a port from which the Portuguese carried to Europe the surviving Spaniards in 1546.[5]

These expeditions had not succeeded in returning to New Spain because they had not found the favorable prevailing winds and currents that would carry them to the Pacific coast. By the mid-sixteenth century, the search for the fabled route was a resounding failure, and Acapulco was not in the running to play a part in future efforts. To make matters worse, the poor condition of the Mexico City–Acapulco road was considered a major obstacle to the efficient transport of stores to the port. Navidad, Salagua, and Huatulco seemed more likely sites for Asian ventures.[6] However, an unexpected bonus of consecutive failures was that Spanish mariners, cosmographers, and pilots had accumulated knowledge of what did not work. One such, Urdaneta, had a new plan. He would be the key to the selection of Acapulco as the Crown's monopoly port for the Asian trade.

When the king wrote to Viceroy Velasco ordering him to prepare ships for an expedition to the Philippines, he enclosed a letter appointing Urdaneta as the pilot of the expedition. Urdaneta had written convincingly to the king outlining his plan, noting that Acapulco was a much better port than Puerto de Navidad. Its climate was healthier, and it was closer to Mexico City, which facilitated provisioning. On November 19, 1564, the fleet, commanded by Miguel López de Legazpi, left Puerto de Navidad. When it reached Cebú in the Philippines, the miraculous appearance of an image of the Christ child, dressed Flanders-style, was taken as a good omen to found the first Spanish settlement in the islands, Nombre de Jesús.[7]

Urdaneta set sail from the Philippines for New Spain on June 1, 1565, sighted Alta California on September 26, 1565, and sailed on to Acapulco. Although he had conceived of the ultimately successful return route, Urdaneta suffered the disappointment of not being the first to accomplish it. A dispatch boat (*patache*) that became separated from his fleet in a storm had reached the islands and returned to Puerto de Navidad on August 9.[8] A report published in Barcelona in 1566 told the public:

> This dispatch boat has now arrived here carrying ginger, cinnamon, gold dust, an arroba of precious shells colored gold and white, gold jewelry, wax, and other samples of what can be found in those lands, and many baubles and other very fine things.[9]

Nevertheless, Urdaneta's great accomplishment was to precisely calculate the optimal return route that Spanish ships would sail for the next 250 years. A comparison of maps that chart Saavedra's two failed attempts and Urdaneta's successful route clearly demonstrates the key to success that Fray Andrés had correctly judged, learning from the failures of previous expeditions. Saavedra had headed northeast from the Philippines in the direction of the Sandwich Islands but had stopped short of crossing the Tropic of Cancer, failing to catch favorable winds and currents, and he was forced to return to the Philippines. Urdaneta, in contrast, crossed the Tropic and continued on a northeasterly course eventually reaching longitude 40 degrees, then on a southeasterly course to Baja California, and south to Acapulco. This route caught favorable winds and the west-east currents of the North Pacific Drift.[10]

Nevertheless, the journey from Manila to Acapulco lasted a minimum of three months and could take as long as six to reach land. Storms, shipwrecks, pirates, and diseases claimed many lives. Seventeenth-century records attributed almost 49.5 percent of deaths to drowning, 12 percent to enemy action, 2 percent to accidents, and 1 percent to shipwrecks. No cause of death was recorded for 35.5 percent of cases, but disease clearly played its part given the conditions on board.[11]

Figure 31. *Vista del Puerto y parte de la Ciudad de Acapulco, sacada desde su Hospital* (View of the Port and part of the City of Acapulco, seen from its Hospital), 1791, José Cardero (1776 – 1811). Ink and sepia wash on paper, 35.2 cm x 60 cm. Cardero was a member of the Malaspina expedition. Archivo del Museo Naval de Madrid, AMN Ms.1726 (51).

9.2. Short- and Long-term Consequences of the Asian Trade in Guerrero

The Philippines trade, as well as shipping to Guatemala, Panama, and Peru, imposed a variety of labor obligations on the Indigenous peoples of Guerrero, and not only on the coast. In 1590 the corregidor of Iguala, almost 300 kilometers inland, was ordered to instruct the residents of Huitzuco, Cocula, and other pueblos to provide services to soldiers en route to Acapulco, while Mayanalán was required to supply provisions and other requirements. The following year, the corregidor made similar demands of Teloloapan, in Tierra Caliente.[12] In 1591 Viceroy Velasco issued an order requiring a very particular service from those who lived along the Acapulco route to the mule driver Juan Fernández, who was transporting the king's personal property from Mexico City. The communities where he rested for the night were to provide two bearers the next day to carry the monarch's *aguafuerte* (nitric acid), used to assay the royal gold. Loading the corrosive substance on mules was considered too dangerous. The bearers were paid one tomín per day.¹³

Labor demands on the coast were onerous. The port's operations required buildings for customs, accounting, stores, and offices. Indigenous labor also built a church, a Franciscan monastery, and a guesthouse. Indigenous workers ensured the provision of supplies for the operations of the port and shipping. Wood and pitch, cotton textiles, salt, meat from the coastal cattle ranches, and fish were all required. Trade required specific materials. For example, in 1592 the alcalde mayor of Acapulco was instructed to have the Indians make 1,000 petates to be delivered to Huatulco. Indigenous labor loaded and unloaded the galleons. In 1595 thirty Indigenous laborers were required to unload a ship. A very specific requirement arose in 1579: the formation of a Mulatto and Indian militia to ward off the attacks of Francis Drake, the first of several English pirates to threaten the port.¹⁴

The impacts of the Acapulco trade were felt also by Indigenous people, Mulattos, and Blacks beyond the mountains of Guerrero, as Chimalpain recorded. In 1613, for example, 150 forzados (forced laborers) considered wrongdoers or vagabonds were marched in chains from Mexico City to Acapulco to sail to the Philippines. Chimalpain recorded the alarm caused by Flemish and English pirates in 1615. More amicable was the arrival of Japanese traders in 1610 and of a Japanese embassy en route to Spain and the Vatican in 1614.¹⁵ By this time, Asian arrivals of many nationalities were already a familiar sight on the Pacific coast. The first may have arrived on Urdaneta's ship in 1565 or perhaps in 1570. In the course of 250 years, according to one estimate, some 100,000 chinos, as the Spaniards termed all Asians, settled in New Spain, some free, many slaves. A good number settled on the coast from Acapulco, Tecpan, Coyuca, San Miguel, Atoyac, Zihuatanejo, and Zacatula in Guerrero, as far as Navidad and Colima. In Acapulco, Asians were laborers and craftspeople in the shipyards and later were among those who built the Fort of San Diego. Asian slaves also worked on coconut plantations. Although formally prohibited to bear arms, by 1590 some chinos helped to defend the coast, and by the eighteenth century they had formed their own militia. From the late 1500s, chinos lived alongside Indians in Coyuca. The Indigenous inhabitants were ruled by their elected governor, while an alcalde mayor governed the chinos.¹⁶

Reports of friars engaged in the trade in 1610 tell us that Asian goods soon reached markets inland. In the long term, Asian items and social practices became part of the culture of Guerrero. In 1791 the Malaspina expedition reported cockfighting, imported from Malaysia, in Acapulco. *Charape*, tuba sweetened with unrefined sugar, was a popular drink. Even humble homes had the odd piece of Chinese porcelain. Tixtla, some 140 kilometers distant, traded its unrefined sugar, petates, fodder, and fruits in Acapulco for cacao and Asian textiles. Asian goods also adorned the homes of Chilpancingo. Tamarind trees from Asia grew 275 kilometers to the north in Iguala and today line the plaza of the modern city. The women of eighteenth-century Iguala wore petticoats of Indian cloth and Chinese silk stockings. In Taxco shops sold Asian silks and cottons.[17]

In colonial Guerrero the arrival of the Manila Galleon and the trade fair, which attracted thousands of people and mules, defined the main artery that linked Guerrero to central Mexico. Merchants arrived from all parts of New Spain: Mexico City, Puebla, León, Querétaro, Morelia, Zamora, Sayula, Oaxaca, and Tehuantepec.[18] The great tide of traders opened commercial opportunities: inns and the sale of food, crossings by raft of the rivers, mule driving, and a modest local participation in the Asian trade. Thus, Acapulco joined Taxco as the second economic pole of colonial Guerrero.

9.3. The Royal Road to Acapulco and the Reorientation of Space in Guerrero

The royal Acapulco–Mexico City road was ill named, for it was really a track some 72.5 leagues (334 kilometers) long. Sixteenth- and seventeenth-century travelers' accounts paint a vivid picture of its defects and dangers. Precipices and crossings of the Papagayo on rafts put at risk merchandise and lives. Some passes were so narrow that only one mule train at a time could use the road. The journey lasted thirteen to sixteen days at a daily speed of 21–26 kilometers.[19] The royal road was not efficient or very fit for transporting galleon-loads of Asian goods. A calculation for the eighteenth century estimates the cost of transporting a load of cacao from Acapulco to Tepecoacuilco at 18 percent of the value of the cargo; to reach Veracruz cost 60 percent.[20] Nevertheless, until the second half of the eighteenth century, Acapulco was the official port for all communication with the Philippines, Central America, and Peru. Through Acapulco passed viceroys, officials, clergy, soldiers, merchants, prisoners, and great loads of silver.[21]

The Acapulco road broadly followed an ancient pre-Hispanic route through the Montaña. Colonial commerce required a deviation through

Tepecoacuilco. However, as so often in sixteenth-century Guerrero, mining demanded another detour from the ancient route. In 1533 the Zumpango mineowners petitioned the king to divert the road in their direction. From there the route led south to Chilpancingo. Thus, the demands of colonial commerce and mining redrew the ancient route.[22] The Mesoamerican route that for centuries had carried people and resources between the coast and central Mexico via Tlapa and the Montaña would become of secondary importance from the sixteenth century onward. In contrast, although precontact Chilpancingo had participated in regional and supraregional exchange, it had never rivaled Tlapa,[23] but now things changed. In the 1580s Chilpancingo was still a mere estancia of Zumpango. However, although Chilpancingo had no mines, its location was strategic. Roads that converged here connected with Tlapa via Quechultenango, with the Costa Grande across the Sierra Madre, with Tierra Caliente by Tlacotepec, and farther afield with Puebla, Morelos, and Mexico City. However, by far the most important factor was the town's location on the Acapulco road. Chilpancingo's population increased during the seventeenth century. In 1639 its Indigenous residents were exempted from tribute because they provided important services to travelers to Acapulco. The Indigenous elite were permitted to own "mules to carry goods, deal and trade, in all seeds and produce as permitted by Royal Decrees." The success of Chilpancingo's efforts to separate from Zumpango, granted in 1639 and confirmed in 1693, signaled the town's stature. The long-term effects of the rise of Chilpancingo are evident from eighteenth-century population data. In 1743 Chilpancingo recorded only 353 Indigenous families, but some 900 non-Indigenous persons. Half a century later Chilpancingo's 1,866 non-Indigenous residents formed a very heterogeneous group: farmers, livestock owners, tanners, cobblers, masons, carpenters, tailors, weavers, embroiderers, workers, mule drivers and their servants, messengers, militia, officials, merchants, and owners of ranches and farms.[24] In short, the route of the royal road transformed the spatial organization and geography of Guerrero.

9.4. Merchants and the Acapulco Trade Until the Early Seventeenth century

From the start, the profits of the Philippines trade did not benefit Acapulco, and those who conducted it stayed there only the time necessary to conclude their business. The riches of the Acapulco trade accrued to Asian traders in Manila and to wealthy merchants of New Spain and Peru. Although costly sumptuary items arrived on the galleons, the bulk of the goods were low-cost items for the mass market of the Spanish Americas. The galleons' cargoes were a problem that the Crown and the frustrated merchant houses of Spain would never be able to contend with, for the Asian traders undercut their Iberian rivals and rapidly adapted their goods to satisfy American tastes.

Trade with the Philippines took some years to gather pace after 1565. Viceroy Martín Enríquez informed the king on April 28, 1572, that the merchants of New Spain were reluctant to participate in the China trade since the terms were not yet settled.[25] Another letter, on December 5, 1573, suggests that trade had begun to pick up but was still disappointing. Two ships from the Philippines had brought for the king 136 gold *marcos* and some other precious things. However, a cargo of 280 quintales of cinnamon was of little value in New Spain. Enríquez added that the ship carried "silks of different colors, damasks, satins, and delicate fabrics, and some gold and a quantity of mantas of white and colored cotton, and a quantity of wax, of porcelain and other baubles, such as fans, sunshades, desks, and some thousand small boxes."[26]

A report dated in Mexico City on January 11, 1574, informed the king that three vessels from the Philippines had arrived in Acapulco with a cargo of 448 marcos of gold of different assay values, 712 "pieces of all sorts of silk," 312 quintales of cinnamon, 22,300 items of porcelain, 11,300 mantas of cotton worth 22,600 pesos, wax valued at 13,950 pesos, cotton thread worth 5,768–6,680 pesos, and many other trifles whose value was not known.[27] Viceroy Enríquez had written to the king on January 9, 1574, presumably referring to the same three ships, giving a damning evaluation of the cargo:

> It is all worthless and damaging for trade rather than beneficial: because all [the ships] brought are some very wretched silks, most of them containing threads of grass, and some false brocades and fans and porcelain and writing desks and small painted boxes . . . and in payment for this they [the Asians] take away gold and silver, they are so acute that they want nothing else. I am told that they took over 14,000 ducados in gold and silver from the islands; and if this is not corrected, they will always be the winners, although if the Spaniards who trade there were businessmen, they would also reject what they bring and would try to select what is valuable and put the trade in order.[28]

Enríquez's report summed up the trade's dilemma. Asian merchants accepted only gold and silver for merchandise that consisted principally of inexpensive items for the mass market with which the merchant houses of Spain could not compete rather than sumptuary goods. Ideal conditions for silk production and superior technology gave Chinese producers a competitive advantage, although substantial quantities of Philippines goods were also shipped to Acapulco. Mexico City merchants profited from the trade in goods shipped from Spain to Veracruz and at the same time had agents in Manila to benefit from Asian trade, while Lima merchants maintained agents in Acapulco, Mexico City, and Manila. The profits from trade with the Americas accrued to Spain's Asian competitors and the merchants of Mexico City and Lima.[29] Competition from Asian textiles so alarmed the Andaluz merchants that for almost two centuries they lobbied unsuccessfully to change Crown policy.[30]

As early as 1574, Guido de Lavezares, governor of the Philippines, wrote to Felipe II that the Chinese "continue to increase their commerce each year."[31] In 1582 Gonzalo Ronquillo de Peñalosa reported to the king that he had imposed "three per cent as duties on both importations and exportations of the merchandise of both Spaniards and Chinese. A freight charge of twelve pesos per *tonelada* is also imposed. Considering their large profits, these duties are very moderate."[32] The Spanish houses had to contend with a considerable array of Asian competitors. Merchants from Japan, Macao, and Siam were early traders in Manila. Rival Portuguese merchants shipped goods to Acapulco from Manila as early as 1570. The clerics of Manila were also early participants, trading to support church work.[33]

The only textile recorded in a cargo dispatched from Manila to Acapulco in 1570 was mantas. More than a thousand pieces of porcelain were on board. The cargo also included utilitarian items required in New Spain, such as canvas, cables, bronze, lead, and padlocks. A 1572 cargo included a foremast, sails, cables, and 400 pieces of fine porcelain. Chinese porcelain dated to between 1573 and 1620 has been excavated in the Zócalo of Mexico City, confirming the early presence of porcelain in the trade. In 1575, 712 bales of silk and 22,300 pieces of fine gold-decorated China and other porcelain wares arrived. By 1588–1591, a wider variety of textiles began to appear—silks, figured satins, black and colored damasks, brocades, and assorted other fabrics.[34]

A study of the cargoes of nineteen ships from 1573 to 1640 provides an overview of the first phase of the Philippines trade. The variety

TABLE 9.1. PERCENTAGE OF TAXES PAID BY LARGE, MEDIUM, AND SMALL SHIPPERS IN ACAPULCO, 1590–1659

Decade	% Large	% Medium	% Small
1590–1599	67.0	27.2	5.8
1600–1699	54.1	35.1	10.8
1610–1619	64.1	29.0	6.9
1620–1629	71.2	9.5	19.3
1630–1639	87.1	11.3	1.5
1640–1649	71.4	25.9	2.7
1650–1659	85.3	13.5	1.2

Source: Hoberman, *Mexico's Merchant Elite*, 40.

of textiles was enormous. The workshops of New Spain bought fine silk thread from Choguey to manufacture cloth locally. Indian cottons, Philippine *mantas de Ilocos*, and Chinese silks were inexpensive compared to Spanish equivalents. Chinese manufacturers soon produced European-style taffeta, velvets, ribbed silks, and brocades at competitive prices. All manner of European clothing arrived, such as breeches, shirts, doublets, stockings, skirts, waistcoats, and capes. The Chinese shipped items for the home, such as cushions, coverlets, bedspreads, tablecloths, carpets, rugs, and painted pillows from Bengal, some for the luxury market. Luxury sets of bed linen cost 315–400 pesos. Ecclesiastical vestments and decorations for the church were of grand style, as were trappings for horses to display the rider's wealth.[35]

The quantity of porcelain increased in the second half of the seventeenth century, but already in 1602, a cargo of 4,000 plates arrived. Some of the porcelain was destined for the wealthy households of New Spain—in 1597 the inventory of possessions of Isabel de Luján, encomendera of Cutzamala in Tierra Caliente, included twenty items of Chinese porcelain, plates, and coats of arms. Imports also included metalwork, arms, marble crucifixes, figures of saints and the Christ Child, precious stones, and jewelry. Furniture included writing desks, Japanese coffers, tables, and beds. *Biombos* (Japanese screens), first documented in 1598, became indispensable in wealthy homes. Furniture arrived filled with "trifles": stockings, jewelry, ribbons, buttons, and beads.[36] In sum, the merchants who traded through Manila quickly adapted and widened their range of goods to cater for both the wealthy and the masses of the Spanish Americas.

Data concerning the *almojarifazgo* (customs duty) paid by Mexican merchants loading goods from the Philippines to Acapulco from 1590 to1659 record that large, medium, and small investors participated in the trade but that large investors dominated it. Between 1590 and 1599, 120 merchants loaded goods worth less than 1,500 pesos, 83 imported merchandise valued at 1,500–7,000, and 43 large-scale investors shipped goods worth more than 7,000 pesos. Between 1600–1609, 11 percent of shippers were large-scale, 33 percent medium, and 50 percent small. However, the percentage of taxes paid by large shippers demonstrates that they dominated the trade (table 9.1).[37]

One New Spanish merchant who became fabulously rich was don Baltasar Rodríguez de los Ríos. In 1592 he was a founder of *Consulado de México*, the merchants' guild. He owned a ship that plied the Southern Sea and another for the Atlantic trade. Such was his influence that a royal decree, signed in Barcelona in 1585, gave him permission to send a ship laden with Asian goods to Peru, and in 1591 Viceroy Manrique issued him another such license.[38] If Juan Rodríguez de Figueroa, Esteban Rodríguez de Figueroa, Álvaro Rodríguez de Figueroa, and Diego Rodríguez de Torres, who invested heavily in the Philippines trade in 1595 and 1596, were relatives of Baltasar, the family was a big player in Asian commerce.[39] In 1618 Baltasar's properties in Mexico City were valued at 125,000 pesos. He used his wealth to buy influence in New Spain and the Philippines. He loaned 54,000 pesos in merchandise to the alguacil of the Inquisition of Manila, and the enormous sum of 161,200 pesos to the cabildo of Mexico City. His money and influence talked at the highest levels.[40] Baltasar died in 1620 and was buried in a tomb of the Monastery of Saint Augustine, where only the elite of New Spain found their final resting place and where he had funded a chapel. He left substantial legacies to several religious institutions in Mexico City and had funded a chapel to bury his parents in the church of his hometown in Spain.[41]

An investor in the Philippines trade whose career was much more picaresque was the Portuguese converso Antonio Díaz de Cáceres, a Taxco mineowner and a merchant who traded in several mining towns. Antonio arrived in the Americas in 1561, and by 1583 he was wealthy and well connected. He extended credit to his commercial associates; for example, to Cristóbal Gómez, an unknown quantity, and the sizeable sum of 4,000 pesos to his brother-in-law Jorge de Almeida. In December 1589, Antonio fled to Acapulco to escape the Inquisition. There Dr. Palacios,

Antonio de los Cobos, and Almeida were his partners in a ship with a crew of 450 men, loaded with wine, olives, and silver, as well as an unregistered contraband cargo. Twenty-five passengers paid 50 pesos each for the journey. The ship foundered in the port of Cavite in the Philippines, suffering 400 pesos of damage. Antonio was accused of smuggling contraband and was imprisoned twice by the Portuguese. Nevertheless, he returned to Acapulco with a cargo of silk, copper tools, Chinese porcelain, a variety of small items, and 300 quintales of unregistered iron or gold (accounts differ). However, in Acapulco an official of the Inquisition searched the ship to confiscate the dowry of Antonio's wife, which he had invested in the cargo. Further problems ensued. Crew members demanded payment of some 2,500 pesos, and a rival ship owner demanded that Antonio's ship be sold to settle these debts. He was accused of selling damaged merchandise and of goods missing from deliveries. Guarantors demanded their money. Out of cash, Antonio paid up in porcelain and eventually departed for Mexico City.[42]

In Acapulco itself the Philippines trade offered opportunities to trade in supplies for the galleons. From 1570 to 1580, García de Albornoz, encomendero, landowner, and livestock rancher on the Costa Grande, was contracted to supply meat and fish. He had a contract to supply biscuit but lost it to Francisco Pérez Payán in 1576. In 1576 Juan and Melchor Pérez de Soto were suppliers of lead and Baltasar and Salvador Apelo of salt pork.[43] However, most ships' supplies came from further afield. In 1645 biscuit, kidney beans, chickpeas, beans, lentils, cheese, and pipes were sourced in Puebla.[44] Guerrero merchants participated in Asian trade, but their share of the business seems to have declined over time. By 1775, 1776, and 1778, some 117 merchants invested in the Acapulco trade. Fifty-three came from several parts of Guerrero, of whom thirteen invested 67–200 pesos, twenty-four 240–930 pesos, fifteen 1,100–4,500 pesos, and one 20,000 pesos.[45]

In sum, while the port offered commercial opportunities to suppliers on the coast and inland in Guerrero, most of the profit from the galleons was made by traders in Puebla and wealthy Mexico City merchants. The very traders who stored Spanish merchandise shipped to Veracruz in their warehouses were simultaneously importing Asian goods so inexpensive that they forced the Spanish merchants to lower their prices, but to no avail. The power of the Mexico City merchants was a constant theme of complaint from Spaniards in the Philippines who could not match the deep pockets of their American rivals.

TABLE 9.2. SPANISH POPULATION OF THE PHILIPPINES	
Years	Population
1571–1579	600
1580–1589	250
1590–1599	500
1600–1609	650
1610–1629	500
Source: García Abasolo, "Problemas para gobernar un imperio," 14.	

9.5. The Acapulco Trade Seen from the Philippines

If the permanent population of Acapulco was remarkably small, the number of Spaniards who occupied the New Spanish colony in the Philippines was also tiny and vastly outnumbered by the Chinese. One estimate of the Spanish population is summarized in table 9.2.

In 1594 don Luis Pérez Desmariñas, interim governor of the Philippines (he held this office after the untimely death of his father, the governor don Gómez Pérez Desmariñas), wrote to Felipe II. Don Luis complained that the *paganos sangleyes* ("pagan *sangleyes*"), as the Spaniards termed the Chinese, were making off with the money and business of the state as well as the Manila Galleon trade, profits that should accrue to the Spaniards.[46] In 1589 Friar Juan Cobo painted a very different picture. The Chinese merchants in Manila were not many, but there were large numbers of sailors, fishermen, and workers. The Chinese did all the work and built all the Spaniards' houses.[47] In 1590 Friar Domingo de Salazar estimated the Chinese population to be 6,000–7,000.[48] A 1588 census reported a larger Chinese population, 750 Spaniards and 10,000 Chinese, and a 1603 census was starker still: 600 Spaniards, 20,000–25,000 Chinese.[49] Relations between the two groups were unstable. For example, in 1593 Chinese oarsmen mutinied, a violent uprising during which don Luis Pérez Demariñas's father was killed.[50] There were more Chinese uprisings in 1603, 1639, and 1662. Fires in 1594 and 1628 and earthquakes in 1645 and 1654 suggest that the Spanish foothold in the Philippines was fragile.[51]

In 1565 a list of supplies and manpower urgently needed in Cebú underlined the delicacy of the Spanish occupation. A variety of artillery, arms, and military equipment was needed, as were tools, paper, a long list of foodstuffs, including salt, sugar, and wine, as well as materials to build galleys. Specialists were also required: twelve artillerymen, three hundred soldiers, twelve carpenters, two blacksmiths with their forges and tools, and twelve Blacks to work with them. Also needed were a maker of arquebuses, two locksmiths, a surgeon, a doctor, a royal ropemaker already waiting in New Spain, and shipyard workers.[52] It is clear that without the Chinese the Spaniards could not prosper. The Chinese understood this very well; the price for their cooperation was the payment of large quantities of silver.

In the first years, although Acapulco was officially the only authorized port, ships sailed from the Philippines for other ports in the Americas. Don Gonzalo Ronquillo de Peñalosa, governor of the islands, informed Felipe II in 1581 that he had dispatched a ship to Peru since he had been informed that the Asian trade was important for the progress of that region. In 1582 don Gonzalo was thinking of sending another to Panama.[53] In 1586 Dr. Santiago Vera, bishop of the Philippines, and forty-eight other Spaniards signed a memorandum complaining that the merchants of New Spain had agents in Manila, funded with such large quantities of silver that the residents of the city could not compete. The signatories requested that only resident Spaniards be permitted to trade with the Chinese.[54] The cabildo of Manila, likewise, complained of competition from New Spain,[55] and complaints continued in subsequent years.[56] In 1590 the king ruled in their favor, prohibiting New Spain's merchants from sending money or agents to Manila and from establishing companies there.[57] The royal decree proved to be a dead letter since the complaints continued. In 1598 Dr. Antonio de Morga, lieutenant governor, claimed that officials who arrived from New Spain were relatives of or connected with the viceroy, were in fact little more than traders, and that they removed goods on board the galleon belonging to Philippine residents to make room for their own.[58] Francisco de Tello, president of the Audiencia of Manila, reported that Peruvian and New Spanish merchants were so wealthy that they dominated the trade. In 1599 he repeated his accusations, which the royal attorney Hierónimo de Salazar y Salcedo corroborated.[59]

Several reports emphasized how cheap the Chinese goods were. In 1586 two royal officials wrote of the poor quality of the textiles, alleging that even the finest contained little silk. However, they were so cheap that buyers in New Spain bought them in preference to Spanish textiles, even though Spanish producers had reduced their prices.[60] In 1587 Vera informed the king that in June more than thirty large Chinese vessels, crewed by more than one hundred men, had arrived with a great quantity of merchandise, horses, and cows. Although Chinese prices were low, their profits were high.[61]

TABLE 9.3. SHIPPERS FROM MANILA, 1591	
Don Fray Domingo de Salazar, bishop	15 bales and 33 cases
Santiago de Vera, president of the Audiencia	60 bales and 29 cases
Pedro Herrandez, for licenciado Rojas, previously accountant of the Audiencia, and now counsellor	19 bales and 4 cases
Don Antonio de Rribera Maldonado, accountant	52 bales and 20 cases
Licenciado Ayala, attorney	27 bales and 17 cases
The Dean of the Cathedral, in the Sant Felippe and Juan Pablo's vessel	13 bales and 7 cases
Estevan Gonzales, canon of the cathedral	5 bales and 3 boxes
Licenciado Herver del Corral, inspector of the Audiencia	28 bales and 1 case
The cathedral schoolteacher	6 bales
Father Cervantes	3 bales and 6 cases
Curate Juan Gutiérrez	2 cases
Father Rodrigo de Morales	3 bales
Father Crisanto de Tamayo	2 bales
Benito Gutiérrez, priest	2 bales

Source: "Register of merchandise carried in the ship 'Sant Felippe,' Manila, 04/06/1591," in Blair and Robertson, *The Philippine Islands*, vol. 8.

Despite protesting their exclusion from the trade by merchants based in New Spain and their agents in the Philippines, the Spaniards of Manila participated in the Acapulco trade from the bishop and the president of the Audiencia to the humble schoolmaster or priest. In 1591 the notary of mines and registrar of goods of Manila, Juan de Cuellar, recorded the shippers of the galleon *Sant Felippe* (table 9.3).

Thus, the merchant houses of Mexico City had a presence at both ends of the Asian trade, in Manila and Acapulco. However, Manila was not the only axis of the Acapulco trade since ships sailed with Asian goods to Central America and Peru, returning with Peruvian merchandise.

9.6. Acapulco, Central America, and Peru

The control of the Philippines trade through a monopoly port was intended to maximize royal tax revenues and restrain competition with Spanish goods. However, the Crown never exercised effective control of the Asian trade, and Acapulco was never absolutely the only port involved. The scale of profits generated by Asian goods in the Americas proved cronyism, corruption, and contraband unstoppable. In the first two decades, after the first successful return journey from the islands, the interests of New Spanish and Peruvian merchants, not the Crown, decided the routes, the commercial networks, and mercantile practices of the Asian trade.

In the 1580s and 1590s, numerous royal decrees were issued to control the trade. However, a decree of 1593 suggests that the decrees were not successful. The trade with Asia had increased substantially, while trade from Spain had declined.[62] In 1582 the governor of the Philippines was reprimanded for permitting ships to sail to Peru in 1580 and 1581. The viceroy of Peru was ordered to prevent the sale of the cargoes. Ships were forbidden to sail to the Philippines from Peru. In 1588 the king reminded Viceroy Villamanrique that he was not to permit any shipments of Asian merchandise from New Spain to Peru.[63] A decree of 1593 absolutely prohibited commerce between New Spain and Peru, Tierra Firme, and Guatemala, and forbade merchants from the latter three regions to trade with the Philippines.[64] Nevertheless, friendships with royal officials and contraband could overcome any obstacle the Crown placed in the way of the powerful merchant interests of New Spain and Lima.[65]

From early on, trade between New Spain and Peru was driven by surpluses in South America. Peru's huge silver production ensured that Lima merchants were well capitalized. Huancavelica could ship mercury to New Spain's mine and refinery owners in quantities, and at a price that Almadén in Spain could not match. Conditions in Peru were much more favorable than those of New Spain for producing olives, olive oil, and wine, which found a ready market in New Spain. Even cacao, a quintessentially Mexican crop for centuries, was produced at a better quality and a lower price in Guayaquil and shipped to Acapulco and, occasionally, to Huatulco and Zihuatanejo. In return New Spain's merchants offered Asian goods, especially inexpensive textiles and fabrics made in the workshops of Mexico City and Puebla, or cloth and thread for the workshops of Guatemala and Lima. Surplus imports from Spain were trans-shipped from New Spain to Peru. New Spain's merchants benefitted from multiple sources of capital and goods, having the only authorized port for trade with Asia and profits from smuggling carried out through Acapulco or other ports.[66]

According to Crown policy, Peru should conduct trade with Spain only at the Portobello fair on the Isthmus of Panama. However, the demand for Asian goods undermined all efforts to maintain Portobello's intended monopoly. Asian goods flowed south liberally through Acapulco, but also other unauthorized ports linked to a network of illegal distribution. Ships sailed from Zihuatanejo and Huatulco to Sonsonate, Acajutla, and Realejo in Guatemala, to Panama, Guayaquil, Esmeralda, Puerto Viejo, and Manta in South America, and finally El Callao in Peru.[67] For example, in 1573, 1,500 quintales of Peruvian mercury arrived in Huatulco aboard the *San Sebastián*.[68] By the 1590s Huatulco had become a preferred port for illegal shipments of Asian merchandise to Peru.[69] In the same decade galleons arriving from Manila restocked with provisions at Salagua, Colima, and Navidad before continuing to Acapulco, a perfect cover for landing contraband.[70] From the first decade of the seventeenth century, Peruvian ships anchored at Huatulco, Zacatula, and Zihuatanejo. For example, in 1610 two ships from Peru were seized with agents of Lima merchants on board, with gold and silver to be traded with New Spain's merchants.[71]

Pierre Chaunu's classic study of the Philippines trade demonstrates that the funds that flowed into the royal coffers in Manila exceeded those of Acapulco. He concludes that the real center of the trade was Manila and that Acapulco was no more than a point of transit for the funds that flowed from Spain to the Philippines.[72] Mariano Bonialian's research shows that Chaunu's work missed the clandestine movements of merchandise and capital. Acapulco's trade was, in fact, a major component of a complex network of commerce involving all the Spanish Americas. The goods and silver that passed through Acapulco (a good part of it contraband) constituted a vigorous American trade with Asia, controlled by merchants in Lima and Mexico City, where the demand in the two viceroyalties drove a significant amount of intercolonial commerce that was not registered in official figures.[73]

9.7 Conclusions: The Future of Acapulco

The Crown's preoccupations are clear from a compilation of royal decrees from 1593 to 1736: to control who traded in the Philippines and in Acapulco; to regulate the goods that could be traded; to restrict the number of galleons and their capacity; to prevent Peru from trading directly with the Philippines; and to collect taxes and eliminate fraud. The Crown also had strategic and imperial motives: to secure the prosperity of the Philippines colony and defend Spanish commercial interests in Asia against Dutch, Portuguese, and English competitors.[74] However, the mercantile houses of New Spain and Peru eluded royal controls. A letter of 1566 observes that "the Mexicans are very proud of their discovery, which they believe will make them the center of the world."[75] From the beginning, the colonization, government, and evangelization of the Philippines was a New Spanish enterprise that placed Acapulco at the heart of a global commercial network.[76] Nevertheless, the Crown showed no interest whatsoever in the well-being of Acapulco and its residents.[77]

The monopoly role of Acapulco, punctuated by trade fairs when the Manila galleons arrived, imposed severe limits on its economic development. The arrival of two galleons a year did not justify more than modest investments in the port. Data concerning the legal arrivals of ships in nineteen years between 1591 and 1622 record only 134 vessels that entered the port. No doubt, illicit arrivals swelled the figures. Nevertheless, Acapulco's shipping volume was very sickly compared to the 400 or 500 vessels per year that entered Veracruz.[78]

A traveler dazzled by tales of the legendary Manila Galleon perhaps imagined a resplendent city. However, in June 1595 the Italian merchant and explorer Francesco Carletti penned this unflattering assessment:

> There are no more than perhaps twenty houses for Spaniards, made of interwoven branches and held together with mud and roofed with straw, with no ceiling, like a hut, which are used only when the ships arrive from the Philippine Islands or Peru . . . *almost nobody lives there* since it is a very unhealthy place and swampy.[79]

About 1628 or 1629, Fray Antonio Vázquez de Espinosa acknowledged that the climate was hot and sickly but praised Acapulco's safe port. The population was small: up to seventy Spanish vecinos and a similar number of Mulattos, free Blacks, and slaves. However, a fort and a Spanish garrison governed by a Castellan appointed by the king, an alcalde mayor who dispensed justice, and royal officials, including an accountant and a treasurer who administered the Crown's business and collected taxes on Asian trade, were all favorable signs of Spanish civilization.[80]

A little more than two centuries later, Alexander von Humboldt disparaged the port: "The population of this wretched city, inhabited almost exclusively by men of color, increases to 9,000 souls when the China galleon arrives; but usually it does not exceed 4,000."[81] Eighteenth-century figures suggest that Humboldt's 4,000 inhabitants were an overestimate. In 1743, only eleven Spanish families lived in Acapulco, alongside four hundred morenos, pardos, and chinos, plus four companies of militia composed of the same ethnic mixture and a battalion of Spanish soldiers.[82] By 1790 the population of the port, excluding nearby villages, was 229 families, a total of 996 individuals. Nine families were Spanish, three Indian, five Asian, and 212 "mulattos of all the *castas*."[83]

The expedition of Alessandro Malaspina provides a detailed portrait of the port in 1791.[84] The well-to-do lived in brick houses with tiled roofs, but the bulk of the population lived in homes of adobe, branches, and palm leaves, which were frequently destroyed by heavy rains. The majority were poor or of modest income. A few shopkeepers were more comfortable economically. The relatively wealthy were merchants, militiamen, and landowners. The humbler households possessed vessels made from gourds, clay cooking pots, a few pieces of Chinese porcelain, a metate, and a hammock with a canopy to ward off insects. Royal officials lived in Acapulco only during the fair, after which they left the administration of the port to their assistants, who were mostly Mulattos.[85] Thus, for ten months of the year, the affairs of the gateway to Asia were managed by descendants of slaves.

During the trade fair the locals rented out their houses. From Tixtla and Chilapa came onions, garlic, chickpeas, eggs, chickens, fine tableware, sweet potatoes, fruits, and vegetables. Consumption increased with the arrival of the galleon: 268 live and 99 salted beef cattle, 169 pigs (live and salted), 5,244 kilograms of beans, 69,552 kilograms of rice, 67,344 kilograms of wheat flour, 31,823 kilograms of sugar, 42,320 kilograms of unrefined sugar, 174,432 kilograms of maize, 9,430 kilograms of cheese, 31,740 kilograms of bananas, and 13,248 kilograms of *ocote* (torch pine) for lighting.[86]

Corruption at the fair, already evident in the sixteenth century, continued unabated. According to an analysis by Arcadio Pineda, an officer in the expedition, in the previous six years the Crown had been cheated of revenues amounting to 1,519,063 pesos. The flows of money and goods provided tempting motives for fraud and general corruption. Mapmaker José Espinoza y Tello calculated that the value of trade at the fair in 1791 was 1,890,706 pesos.[87] However, the Acapulco trade had already seen its best days. The Bourbon reforms of 1750 introduced free trade in the colonies. The galleons still sailed but arrived half-laden or full of merchandise for which demand had collapsed. San Blas and El Callao were authorized to trade with Manila. Much of the trade between Acapulco and Peru disappeared. The Guayaquil cacao trade became Acapulco's main business.[88] The wars of independence gave the Manila trade its coup de grace in 1815.

Concluding Observations

The tale of Guerrero's history told here began some 9,000 years ago with a meal of maize in a rock shelter in the Iguala Valley. In subsequent periods, the Indigenous communities of the different ecological and resource zones of the region invented ways to prosper, to accomplish notable cultural achievements, to exchange ideas with other regions of Mesoamerica, and to craft governing arrangements that by the Postclassic varied from the small polities of the Costa Grande to the hierarchical realm of Tlapa-Tlachinollan in the Montaña. During the final eight decades of the sixteenth century, Guerrero's native peoples contended with mass death, the reorganization of their communities, the imposition of new institutions such as the encomienda, the corregimiento, the cabildo, and the Catholic church, and found themselves obliged to labor in Spanish enterprises. Yet, even in these daunting circumstances, as they had during their long Mesoamerican history, Indigenous peoples called on their ancient cultures and resources, while they incorporated and refashioned unfamiliar structures of municipal government and new commercial and trading arrangements into communities that mixed the ancient and the new. Exactly how these processes turned out owed much to regional context as it had in Mesoamerican times. The Guerrero that emerged in New Spain by 1600 owed much to its deep past.

A key factor in understanding the trajectory of the Indigenous communities of Guerrero over many centuries is the variety of resources that existed in different zones of Guerrero's rugged terrain. We know that ecological diversity was a significant driver of the development of Postclassic Mesoamerican commerce and society.[1] However, this study has demonstrated that the great diversity of ecological zones and, therefore, of resources in Guerrero had still more far-reaching consequences over the long term, since the Late Archaic and especially from the Early Formative. Archaeological evidence points to the movement of marine shells, cotton, cacao, and probably salt along routes of exchange from the coast through the Montaña and Center and on to Morelos and central Mexico, which coincide with the locations of Olmec-style rock art and sculpture and regional traditions such as Mezcala stone sculpture and Xochipala figurines and early use of the corbelled arch. In other words, the peoples of Guerrero made pan-Mesoamerican contributions to Formative culture and, at the same time, in central-northern Guerrero fashioned their own regional variant of Formative lifeways. The exchange of goods and ideas stimulated the emergence, in Guerrero's terms, of sizeable Formative population centers such as Teopantecuanitlán, Cuetlajuchitlán, and Ahuináhuac, which processed and redistributed materials from the coast, the Montaña (polished stone), and from their own region (cinnabar, mica, iron, and onyx). Further to the west in the Tierra Caliente the Balsas Valley served similar exchange and redistributive functions for the Costa Grande and between Michoacán and central Mexico. Cotton, cacao, and salt were products of this ecological niche. Guerrero was also abundant in metals, which were found in all regions: placer gold on the coast and in the Montaña; silver and placer gold in the Center; tin, copper, iron, silver, and placer gold in the North; and copper, gold, and silver in the Tierra Caliente.

While one might consider the Formative to have been something of a golden era for Guerrero, the region's contributions to and participation in Mesoamerican developments did not end there. In the Classic, Guerrero's rulers absorbed cultural influences from Teotihuacan and Monte Albán rather than making major contributions to wider Mesoamerican ideas, but they also integrated local iconography and ideas into Classic material culture and, in the case of monumental sculpture, for example, continued to express concepts independently of the two great cities of the Classic. From the later Classic, the advent of metallurgical methods added new commodities to the goods that Guerrero traded with other regions. Archaeological data do not allow us to trace the fluctuations and changes in exchange that surely occurred over the long centuries between the Late Archaic, Formative, and the Late Postclassic, but continuing evidence of contacts with central Mexico and Oaxaca during the Classic, and documentary testimony of the significance of products transported between differing ecological zones in the Late Postclassic, confirm the continuing importance of the movement of goods and ideas.

Population, settlement patterns, and political organization unsurprisingly echoed configurations of ecological resource zones and exchange. Late Archaic coastal settlements were early participants in obsidian commerce in exchange for the region's resources, but the Formative archaeological record tells us that larger, more prosperous settlements formed inland where they could control routes of exchange. By the Classic and the Postclassic, the Montaña was one of the regions where population concentrated, and where in the fourteenth and fifteenth centuries, Tlapa-Tlachinollan formed a polity of a complexity and size unmatched in Guerrero before the Mexica and Tarascan incursions. The cases of Cototolapan, also in the Montaña, and of Oapan in the Center are further examples of smaller hierarchical Postclassic polities that formed along routes of exchange in the east. The North and the Tierra Caliente were, by contrast, regions of small but vigorous and often combative realms, while the coast was more thinly populated by predominantly smaller political units, with the exception by the late Postclassic of pugnacious Yopecingo, a confederation of states that seem to have prospered from skilled working of metals and precious stones and trade in tropical goods.

Thus, communities of varying size, complexity, political-administrative capabilities, and cultural traditions confronted the incursions on the western fringes of Guerrero of the Tarascans and, throughout the region, of the Mexicas, and after 1521 of the Spaniards and their Indigenous allies. The Mexica empire in Guerrero was not the dominant iron fist of Tenochtitlan's propaganda.[2] Mexica control was variable, sometimes imposed by brute force or the threat of force and the introduction of colonists from other areas, in other cases by negotiation and accommodation, and sometimes the intruders were fiercely resisted. Those rulers of communities that fell under the sway of the Mexicas or the Tarascans worked with officials of the lords of Tenochtitlan or Tzintzuntzan, and administered the tribute they were required or had negotiated to pay.

When new intruders arrived from Spain, the rulers of the region's communities called upon their skills in negotiations, alliance building, and tribute administration to fashion, with differing degrees of success, a new future for themselves. For the creation of New Spain was not simply the story of the imposition of a new order by the Spaniards. To the contrary, Indigenous peoples absorbed new institutions and practices—the cabildo, the Catholic church, the cofradía, and the caja de comunidad, for example—and interpreted and fashioned them in the light of their own traditions to make them part of their own communities, much as they had done in precontact times. The evidence, over the *longue durée*, demonstrates that the Indigenous communities of Guerrero possessed what Matthew Restall terms the "native vitality" with which the Indigenous peoples of New Spain responded to the Spanish colonial enterprise, and which numerous historians have demonstrated, initially in the Valley of Mexico and subsequently in other culture areas.[3] As this study has demonstrated, a marriage of archaeological and historical data over an exceptionally long term enriches our understanding of Guerrero's Indigenous societies and explains, at least in part, the differing outcomes of the Spanish invasion and early colonial changes instituted by the new Crown government.

Our study of the early decades of the creation of New Spain in the sixteenth century has demonstrated that the outcomes varied across the different geographic and ecological zones that constituted Guerrero. The extent to which precontact communities were successful in retaining languages, cultural characteristics, land, and other community and economic assets varied substantially, as a review area by area demonstrates. The coast, a region of relatively small polities at the time of the Spanish invasion, was an early target of Spanish operations for three principal reasons: Zacatula, which as the tribute province of Cihuatlán, supplied gold tribute to the Mexica, became the center of operations for placer gold mining on the coast of Guerrero and Michoacán; military expeditions to quell the combative Yopes; and the search for a return route to Asia. The encomienda here was generally a small-scale poor affair, and the majority of the numerous encomenderos were less wealthy and influential than those who acquired larger and richer encomiendas in other parts of Guerrero. The Zacatula gold rush turned out to be ephemeral, and it was not until 1565 that Andrés de Urdaneta resolved the puzzle of a sea route from Manila to Acapulco. The marine shells that had been so prized in precontact times were now worthless. However, when the gold ran out, the main attractions of the coast for Spaniards were cacao and grazing for livestock (cotton was mostly produced by Indians and in the later colonial period by Mulatto sharecroppers, but Spaniards profited by controlling its sale) and a few Spanish fishing enterprises. The Spaniards sought to acquire land for cultivation and especially for grazing. Cotton and cattle were mainstays of the coastal economy throughout the colonial period.[4] Meanwhile, the epidemics of the sixteenth century brought more severe mortality to the coast than to inland regions, to which should be added Yope deaths caused by war. The solution to resultant labor shortages was the importation of African and Asian labor. Those whom the census data described as Indian were concentrated in a few towns, the remainder of the coast being populated largely by Blacks and Afromestizos. Except for some areas of the Costa Chica where more Indian villages survived than on the Costa Grande,[5] native languages disappeared. Acapulco, in particular, benefitted little from being the official port for Asian trade and became a distinctly Mulatto town, except when the annual arrival of the Manila Galleon swelled the population. In short, for the precontact inhabitants of the coast and their descendants, the sixteenth century was generally disastrous.

To the north of the Costa Chica, the story of the Montaña was completely different. The structure of the Postclassic domain of Tlapa-Tlachinollan developed along ancient routes of exchange, its established ruling lineages were left largely intact by the Mexicas, and Tlapa had become a tribute center. The region was occupied by a substantial population well organized to meet tribute demands. The resources that attracted Spanish attention to the Montaña were not the cotton warriors' suits, greenstone, or rubber recorded in the Mexica tribute rolls, but placer gold which had been paid in tribute to Tenochtitlan, land for seasonal grazing of newly introduced livestock from Puebla, an existing administrative structure to collect tribute, and labor and skills, particularly for the manufacture of cotton clothing. While epidemics brought death to the Montaña as they did elsewhere, the mortality, though dreadful, was less severe than on the coast. The encomiendas here were few, large, and allocated to powerful individuals. Gold could be extracted by tribute, so there was no need for the hefty investments in mining that mineowners had to finance elsewhere. Similarly, cotton could be spun and woven for tribute or by forced labor, and cattle could be grazed on land left vacant after the harvest under the hacienda volante system. Moreover, the axis of Guerrero's key commercial route, which had carried trade through the Montaña in precontact times, moved eastward from the Montaña to the Center to cater to the needs of mining in Zumpango and, subsequently, of the Acapulco trade. Consequently, in the Montaña most land remained in the hands of Indigenous communities or individuals throughout the colonial period.[6] The population of the Montaña attracted not only the attention of encomenderos but also of the Augustinian order. As a result, there were more friars here than in other areas and fewer secular clergy. Royal officials were less numerous, presumably because the administrative capacity of the Indigenous elite and the absence of lucrative mining required and attracted fewer office holders. Blacks and Mulattos, who were a feature of the coastal population, were almost entirely absent in the Montaña, and mestizos and Spaniards were few.

The Montaña remained predominantly Indigenous, and its people were left, relatively speaking, to their own devices for much of the colonial period. The prosperity of the caja de comunidad from the mid-sixteenth century, and the cofradía from the seventeenth century, sustained the community finances of the Montaña in stark contrast to the coast, where these institutions were scarce and much poorer. From at least the mid-sixteenth century onward, the Indigenous peoples of the Montaña produced a particularly rich array of pictographic documents (in Spanish terms *pinturas*), surely evidence of a pervasive precontact written culture that was deployed in the colonial period to defend the interests of ruling elites and their communities.[7] Some of these documents continue to be an indispensable and a treasured part of contemporary community rituals. Although the Spanish changes to administrative jurisdictions removed some towns from the control of Tlapa, and programs of congregación instituted some changes to the settlement pattern of the region, the greatest change to Indigenous municipal government, the separation of pueblos, was brought about by Indigenous communities themselves.[8] The Indigenous languages of this region continued to be spoken throughout the colonial period. In modern times, the Montaña is the principal region in which the Indigenous languages of Guerrero have survived. In 2000, twenty-nine municipalities exceeded the state average percentage (13.87 percent) of speakers of Indigenous languages. Eighteen of these municipalities were in the Montaña, five in the nearby Center, four in municipalities of the Costa Chica that had once formed part of the polity of Tlapa-Tlachinollan, none on the Costa Grande, two in the North, and none in Tierra Caliente. In sum, the Montaña's precontact history furnished the communities of the region with political and cultural resources that enabled them to defend their interests and to maintain a substantial degree of autonomy.

The Center was part of the zone in which Mezcala-style sculpture and Xochipala figures were produced and where the corbelled arch, clavos, and quesos were features of architecture. Deposits of marine shells in Chilpancingo document contacts with the coast. Like the Montaña, but on a smaller scale, this was a region ruled by a hierarchy of lineages capable of meeting substantial tribute demands, which attracted powerful encomenderos. Indigenous rulers both stood up to and worked with encomenderos to ward off excessive tribute demands and maintain control of the population and their own power and privileges. In addition, the Center held two other significant attractions for Spaniards: the first substantial silver mines discovered in Guerrero at Zumpango and a strategic position on the favored route from Mexico City to Acapulco. To the east around Chilapa, Spanish interest in land concentrated on livestock raising, adopting the hacienda volante system as in the Montaña. However, around Tixtla and Zumpango Spaniards acquired land to supply the mines in Zumpango and to build inns catering to travelers to Acapulco. In the sixteenth and seventeenth centuries, Spanish landholding did not involve a sizeable transfer from Indian to European hands, but in the eighteenth century an enormous estate was formed. Spanish merchants in Chilapa, Tixtla, and Mochitlán traded with the coast, but Indian traders also engaged in commerce with the coast, as their ancestors had no doubt done, and sold goods and services to travelers to Acapulco. The place in the Center that was most transformed because of its strategic location on the Acapulco road was Chilpancingo, which in the seventeenth century became a town of non-Indian residents engaged in a variety of enterprises; later, in 1813, the place where independent Mexico's first congress gathered; and in 1853 the capital of the recently formed state of Guerrero. Thus, the force of Spanish interests in the Center weighed more heavily there than was the case of the Montaña, but resourceful rulers, scribes, and traders helped the Indigenous communities find new ways to survive and, to some degree, to prosper.

In the North and the Tierra Caliente, mining interests held sway over all other considerations. In precontact times the salt, cotton, and cacao of the Tierra Caliente and the metals of both zones were exchanged, in return for resources traded with the coast, Michoacán, the Valley of Toluca, and Morelos. Here established Chontal (as well as Nahua, Cuitlatec, and Otomí) polities, in which family and lineage were the foundation of government and sumptuary goods the symbols of prestige and power, were long-established. Rulers performed important sacred functions. Ruling families forged marital alliances with one another but were also prepared to go to war for tribute or land, even against fellow Chontals. Under Mexica dominion Nahuatl became the lingua franca of Indigenous elites, who negotiated mutually beneficial arrangements with Tenochtitlan but, on occasion, rebelled against Mexica demands.

Once the Spaniards realized that the Taxco region was an exceptionally rich source of silver, mining interests dominated for Spaniards and Indigenous peoples alike. Spaniards acquired land in the Taxco region and in the fertile Iguala Valley to build facilities for their mines and to raise cattle and mules and grow crops to supply their laborers. Encomiendas of the North and the Tierra Caliente, whose beneficiaries were often mine-owners and influential individuals, supplied labor, clothing, and foodstuffs. Indigenous communities and individuals were not without agency, but their scope for autonomous activity was more constrained by powerful Spanish interests than was the case in the Montaña and the Center. Nevertheless, they proved adept at finding economic opportunities, preserving and refashioning their social structures. Indians in the North and the Tierra Caliente could profit from the supply of foodstuffs, salt, firewood, and other resources to the mines. Repeated regulations to keep Indian traders from selling their goods in Taxco suggest that tempting profits trumped the law. The population in the immediate vicinity of the mines was not nearly enough to provide the labor required by the mines. Workers were brought from Morelos, Michoacán, and elsewhere to meet their encomienda or repartimiento labor obligations in the mines, but Indians, from near and afar, also found free employment in the mines and refining mills where they had sufficient bargaining power to encourage mineowners to compete for their labor. They could also profit from refining metal stolen from the mines. Nowhere else in Guerrero were there so many Indians from other regions. The Taxco mines employed African slaves, but their numbers never constituted as high a proportion of the population, nor did they leave behind a permanent Afromestizo population as they did on the coast.

The Iguala Valley became the most important agricultural and livestock (cattle for meat, tallow, and leather, mules for transport) zone of Guerrero, and Tepecoacuilco was home to the most important Spanish merchant houses of the region. Tepecoacuilco had already been a major Mexica tribute collecting center. It now found itself in the advantageous position of sitting astride the route between central Mexico, Taxco's riches, and Acapulco's Asian trade. Merchants and encomenderos acquired land, and in the early seventeenth century don Melchor de Tornamira began to accumulate land that by the eighteenth century became the large Hacienda de Palula, later part-owned by the famous Taxco mineowner José de la Borda.[9] In the Tierra Caliente Spaniards acquired land, while others leased or temporarily rented it from Indigenous communities as haciendas volantes, joined in the seventeenth century by Indigenous cofradías, funded by raising cattle, which were surely evidence of continuing community vigor. Cattle raising remained a significant element of the Tierra Caliente's economy into the nineteenth and early twentieth centuries.[10]

While Tlapanec, Mixtec, Amuzgo, and Nahuatl continued to be spoken in the former territory of Tlapa-Tlachinollan into the twenty-first century, Chontal disappeared at an uncertain date but seems still to have been spoken in some places as late as 1685,[11] while Cuitlatec survived in ever-reducing numbers until its final extinction in the 1940s. The disappearance of a language did not, of course, equate to the complete extinction of a culture, as the persistence today of traces of the cult of the rabbit in the area once occupied by Chontal polities indicates.[12]

Guerrero's history as a region that for centuries participated fully in developments in Mesoamerica, and which in the early colonial period was the focus of intense Spanish interest and activity and vigorous Indigenous responses, poses a question for historians of the modern state. For it is a commonplace of studies of nineteenth- and twentieth-century Guerrero that the state was, and still is, marginal, "notably backward," and beset by "precarious communications."[13] A 1964 study judged that "the majority of the pueblos of the state have been isolated for centuries."[14] An assessment in 2000 concluded that, with the exception of the Autopista del Sol, linking Mexico City to Acapulco, Guerrero "continues to lack adequate routes of communication," and the majority of the state's population live in pueblos with a population of 5,000 or less and suffer from "high indices of deprivation."[15] How the once thriving culture of the region resulted in such a grim modern reality is a puzzle that awaits further research.[16]

Appendix 1

Weights, Measures, and Money

Units of Distance

Vara: 0.8 meter
Legua: 4.6 kilometers
Legua larga: 5.3 kilometers

Units of Area

Sitio de venta: 0.4 hectare
Fanega de sembradura: 3.6 hectares
Caballería: 44 hectares
Fundo legal: 101 hectares
Estancia or *sitio de ganado menor*: 780 hectares
Estancia or *sitio de ganado mayor*: 1,756 hectares

Units of Weight

Almud: 3.75 kilograms
Libra: 10.5 kilograms
Arroba: 11.25 kilograms
Fanega: 46 kilograms
Quintal: 46 kilograms
Carga: 92 kilograms

Units of Volume

Cuartillo: 1.9 liters
Almud: 7.6 liters
Fanega: 91 liters
Carga: 182 liters

Money

Maravedí: 1/34 of a *tomín/real*
Grano: 1/12 of a *tomín/real*
Real: 34 *maravedíes* or 12 *granos*
Tomín: 34 *maravedíes* or 12 *granos*
Peso: 272 *maravedíes* or 8 *tomines/reales*
Ducado: 375 *maravedíes* or 11 *tomines/reales* or 1.4 pesos
Castellano: 500 *maravedíes* or 15 *tomines/reales* or 1.9 pesos

Note: The peso here is the *peso de tepuzque*. There were also *peso de oro común* (1.1 pesos de tepuzque); *peso de oro ensayado* (1.5 pesos de tepuzque); *peso de oro de minas* (1.7 pesos de tepuzque); *peso de oro* (1.8 pesos de tepuzque).

Transport

The *carga* of a *tameme*: 23 kilograms
The *carga* of a mule: 130–200 kilograms

Sources: Amith, *The Möbius Strip*; Carrera Stampa, "El sistema de pesos"; Carrera Stampa, "El sistema Monetario Colonial"; González Claverán, *La expedición científica*; Millares Carlo and Mantecón, eds., *Índice y extractos*; Von Mentz, *Señoríos indígenas*.

Appendix 2

Rulers of New Spain, 1524–1603

Alonso de Estrada, gobernador (1524–1528, with interruptions)
First Audiencia (1528–1530)
Second Audiencia (1530–1535)
Antonio de Mendoza, viceroy (1535–1550)
Luis de Velasco, the Elder, viceroy (1550–1564)
Audiencia (1564–1566)
Gastón de Peralta, Marqués de Falces, viceroy (1566–1568)
Martín Enríquez, viceroy (1568–1580)
Lorenzo Suárez de Mendoza, conde de la Coruña, viceroy (1580–1583)
Audiencia (1583–1584)
Pedro Moya de Contreras, viceroy (1584–1585)
Álvaro Manrique de Zúñiga, Marqués de Villamanrique, viceroy (1585–1590)
Luis de Velasco, the younger, viceroy (1590–1595)
Gaspar de Zúñiga y Acevedo, conde de Monterrey, viceroy (1595–1603)

Appendix 3

Some Individuals Engaged in the Peruvian and Manila Trade with Acapulco, 1583–1601

Name	Year	Notes
Aguilar, Sebastián de	1599	Agent in Philippines of Diego Núñez de Campoverde. See also Álvaro de Castrillo.
Aguirre, Juan de	1598	Agent of Baltasar de Lorca and Diego Núñez de Campoverde to buy goods in Acapulco.
Alcalá Ugarte, Antonio de	1598	Lima merchant. Entrusted Alonso González de la Canal with 12,000 pesos to buy merchandise and ship goods to Lima.
Álvarez Altamirano, Pedro	1599	Lima merchant. Entrusted Juan Bautista de Astudillo with 3,460 pesos to buy in New Spain merchandise from Castile, China, and New Spain.
Arias, Juan	1598	Lima silk merchant. Appointed Elvira Rodríguez attorney for legal disputes and business in New Spain and China.
Ascencio, Antonia de	1601	Lima merchant. She and her husband, Sebastián Núñez de Aguilar, appointed mariner Antón Castillo Bohórquez attorney to collect from Pedro de Picavea, alcalde mayor of Acapulco, a debt of 5,000 pesos.
Astudillo, Juan Bautista de	1599	Resident of Lima. Agent in New Spain of Pedro Álvarez Altamirano.
Avendaño, Pedro de	1599	With Tomás de Zárate, attorney of Baltazar de Soria, to collect Chinese merchandise.
Castillo Bohórquez, Antón	1601	Mariner, representative of Sebastián Núñez de Aguilar and Antonia de Ascencio.
Cano de Nebrisa, Francisco	1597	Lima resident, agent in Acapulco of Francisco Ramírez Olivos.
Castrillo, Álvaro de	1596, 1599, 1600	Cargo register scribe (escribano de registro) in Acapulco. Agent of Juan Francisco Roque Forte in 1596, of Diego Núñez de Campoverde in 1599, and of Nicolás de Zavala in 1600. See also Diego Vázquez de Mercado, Miguel González Morón, and Sebastián de Aguilar.
Cerdán, Isabel	1597	Partner of Tomás de Solarana and Julián de Tudela.
Cervantes, María de	1599	Resident and merchant of Lima. Appointed Gerónimo de Pamenes attorney to buy merchandise in Acapulco and ship it to Lima.
Chaguya, Capitán Juan de	1584	Licensed to ship Philippines merchandise from Tehuantepec to Peru. Partner of Baltazar Rodríguez.
Cuellar, Juan de	1591	Notary of mines and cargo register in Manila, responsible for certifying the cargo of the galleons.
Díaz de la Barrera, Alonso	1600	Agent in Acapulco of Bernabé de Medina, and of Baltasar de Lorca.
Domínguez de Cepeda, Alonso	1599	Lima resident. Agent of Juan Rodríguez de Cepeda.

Name	Year	Notes
Encinas, Manuel de	1600, 1601	Resident of Acapulco. 1600, attorney of Antonio Ponce Terán and Francisco de Mansilla Marroquí. See also Simón Gutiérrez. 1601, attorney of Francisco de Mansilla Marroquí. 1601, attorney of Francisco Muñoz Zenteno. See also Diego Hernández "de Manila," Alonso Sánchez de Cuellar, Diego Hernández de Trebejo, Juan López de Mugaren, Ribero Sánchez, Bernardo de Venegas Vergara, and Juan de León Castillo.
García, Cristóbal	1601	Attorney in Lima of Ascencio de Mendarozquieta. See also Mateo Landa.
Girón, Gerónimo	1598	Merchant and public notary of the Audiencia of Lima. He entrusted Martín de Ribero Sánchez with silver to buy merchandise in China.
González de la Canal, Alonso	1598	Agent of Antonio de Alcalá Ugarte.
González Morón, Miguel	1596	Master of the Santa Margarita and La Visitación, agent of Juan Francisco Roque Forte. See also Álvaro de Castrillo and Diego Vázquez de Mercado.
González de Rosas, Cristóbal	1583	Resident of Lima. Passenger on the ship of Pedro Rodríguez. Agent of Blas Hernández to buy merchandise in the Philippines.
Gutiérrez, Andrés	1597	Lima merchant. Entrusted his agent, Lima resident Juan de Legarda, to purchase New Spanish and Chinese merchandise.
Gutiérrez, Simón	1600	Resident of Lima traveling to Acapulco. Attorney of Antonio Ponce Terán. See also Manuel de Encinas.
Hernández, Blas	1583	Lima merchant, public scribe, and scribe of the cabildo of Lima. He entrusted 1,000 pesos to Pedro Rodríguez to buy Chinese clothing and 2,000 pesos to Cristóbal González de Rosas to buy Philippines merchandise.
Hernández "de Manila," Diego	1600	Agent in Manila of Antonio Ponce Terán and of Francisco de Mansilla Marroquí. See also Manuel de Encinas.
Hernández Trebejo, Diego	1601	Attorney of Francisco de Mansilla Marroquí. See also Alonso Sánchez de Cuellar, Manuel de Encinas, and Juan López de Mugaren.
Hita, Alonso de	1600	Resident of Peru. Agent in China and Philippines of Pedro de Ortega de Sotomayor.
Landa, Mateo	1601	Attorney in Acapulco of Ascencio de Mendarozquieta. See also Cristóbal García.
Legarda, Juan de	1597	Lima resident. Agent of Andrés Gutiérrez.
León Castillo, Juan de	1601	Resident of Manila. Agent of Francisco Muñoz Zenteno. See also Ribero Sánchez, Bernardo de Venegas Vergara, and Manuel de Encinas.
Lorca, Baltasar de	1598, 1600	Lima merchant. 1598, partner of Diego Núñez de Campoverde. He entrusted 5,000 pesos to Juan de Aguirre, shipmaster, to purchase merchandise in Acapulco. 1600, he entrusted 11,531 pesos to Alonso Díaz de la Barrera for business in Acapulco.
Mansilla Marroquí, Francisco de	1600, 1601	Lima merchant. Regidor and general trustee (depositario general) of Lima. 1600, appointed Manuel de Encinas attorney to collect in Acapulco merchandise sent from the Philippines by Diego Hernández "de Manila." 1601, he appointed Alonso Sánchez de Cuellar and Diego Hernández Trebejo, of Lima, attorneys for the collection of debt and other business. Their agent in Acapulco was Manuel de Encinas and in Manila Juan López de Mugaren.
Medina, Bernabé de	1600	Lima merchant. He invested 12 bars of silver in trade in Acapulco.

Name	Year	Notes
Mendarozquieta, Ascencio de	1601	Lima merchant. He appointed as his attorneys Cristóbal García, resident of Lima, and Mateo Landa in Acapulco to receive merchandise from New Spain.
López de Mugaren, Juan	1601	Manila resident, attorney of Francisco de Mansilla Marroquí. See also Alonso Sánchez de Cuellar, Diego Hernández Trebejo, and Manuel de Encinas.
Muñoz Zenteno, Francisco	1601	Lima merchant, partner of Simón Rodríguez. They gave a letter of payment for 2,000 pesos to Bernardo Venegas de Vergara to bring Chinese merchandise from the Philippines. He also appointed Ribero Sánchez and Bernardo Venegas de Vergara of Lima, Manuel de Encinas, a resident of Acapulco, and Juan de León Castillo, a resident of Manila, attorneys to ship Chinese goods.
Neblino, Pedro	1599	Master of Nuestra Señora del Rosario. Agent of Baltasar de Soria to buy merchandise in the provinces of China.
Núñez de Aguilar, Sebastián	1601	Lima merchant. With his wife, Antonia de Ascencio, he appointed the mariner Antón Castillo Bohórquez attorney to collect from Pedro de Picavea, alcalde mayor of Acapulco, a debt of 5,000 pesos.
Núñez de Campoverde, Diego	1598, 1599	Important Lima merchant. 1598, partner of Baltasar de Lorca, he entrusted 12,000 pesos to Juan de Aguirre, shipmaster, to buy merchandise in Acapulco. 1599, he entrusted to Álvaro de Castrillo the receipt of merchandise shipped from the Philippines by Sebastián de Aguilar.
Ortega de Sotomayor, Pedro de	1600	Lima merchant. He entrusted money to Alonso de Hita, traveling to China and the Philippines, to buy merchandise.
Pamenes, Gerónimo de	1599	Lima resident traveling to Acapulco. Agent of María de Cervantes.
Ponce Terán, Antonio	1600	Lima merchant. He appointed Simón Gutiérrez, a Lima resident, and Manuel de Encinas, an Acapulco resident, attorneys to collect in Acapulco merchandise shipped from Manila by Diego Hernández "de Manila."
Ramírez Olivos, Francisco	1597	Lima merchant. He entrusted to his agent Francisco Cano de Nebrisa 20,000 pesos to buy merchandise from Castile, New Spain, and China in Acapulco.
Ribero Sánchez, Martín de	1598	Agent of Gerónimo Girón.
Rodríguez, Elvira	1598	Lima resident. Attorney in New Spain and China of Juan Arias.
Rodríguez, Pedro	1583	Agent for the purchase of Chinese clothing of Blas Hernández.
Rodríguez, Simón	1601	Lima merchant. Partner of Francisco Muñoz Zenteno. They gave a letter of payment for 2,000 pesos to Bernardo Venegas de Vergara to bring Chinese merchandise from the Philippines.
Rodríguez de Cepeda, Juan	1599, 1601	Lima merchant. 1599, he entrusted 16,293 pesos to Alonso Domínguez de Cepeda to buy merchandise in Acapulco. 1601, he gave a letter of payment for 5,486 pesos to Bernardo Venegas de Vergara, who traveled to Manila to buy merchandise.
Rodríguez [de los Ríos], Baltasar [Baltazar]	1584	Mexico City merchant. Partner of Capitán Juan de Chaguya. They loaded a ship in Tehuantepec with Philippines merchandise bound for Peru.
Rojas, Licenciado	1591	Former accountant and now counselor of the Audiencia de Manila. He shipped nineteen bundles and four chests of merchandise from Manila to Acapulco.

Name	Year	Notes
Roque Forte, Juan Francisco	1596	Lima merchant and secretary. He entrusted to Álvaro de Castrillo, scribe of Acapulco, and Miguel González Morón, master of the Santa Margarita and La Visitación, sailing from Lima, to collect from Diego Vázquez de Mercado, dean of the Cathedral of Manila, 2,000 pesos or more owed for Philippines merchandise.
Sánchez, Ribero	1601	Lima resident. Attorney of Francisco Muñoz Zenteno. See also Bernardo de Venegas Vergara, Manuel de Encinas, and Juan de León Castillo.
Sánchez de Cuellar, Alonso	1601	Attorney of Francisco de Mansilla Marroquí. See also Diego Hernández Trebejo, Manuel de Encinas, and Juan López de Mugaren.
Serna de Haro, Juan de la	1599	Lima merchant. Partner of Francisco de Soria. They invested in commerce in the provinces of China.
Solarana, Tomás de	1597	Lima merchant. Partner of Isabel Cerdán and Julián de Tudela.
Soria, Baltazar de	1599	Lima merchant. Appointed as his attorneys Tomás de Zárate and Pedro de Avendaño to collect from Pedro Neblino, master of the Nuestra Señora del Rosario, merchandise acquired in the provinces of China.
Soria, Francisco	1599	Lima merchant. Partner of Juan de la Serna de Haro. They invested in commerce in the provinces of China.
Tudela, Julián de	1597	Lima merchant, prosecutor, and secretary of the Lima Inquisition. Partner of Isabel Cerdán and Tomás de Solarana. He entrusted 400 botijas of Peruvian wine sent to Acapulco to Nicolás de Zabala, his agent in Mexico City.
Vázquez de Mercado, Diego	1596	Dean of the Cathedral of Manila, attorney of Juan Francisco Roque Forte. See also Álvaro de Castrillo and Miguel González Morón.
Venegas de Vergara, Bernardo	1601	Lima resident. He received a letter of payment for 2,000 pesos as agent of Francisco Muñoz Zenteno and Simón Rodríguez to buy Chinese merchandise. He received another 5,486 pesos from Juan Rodríguez de Cepeda to buy merchandise in Manila. Attorney of Francisco Muñoz Zenteno. See also Ribero Sánchez, Manuel de Encinas, and Juan de León Castillo.
Zabala, Nicolás de	1597	Agent in Mexico City of Julián de Tudela.
Zavala, Nicolás de	1600	Lima merchant. He appointed as his attorney Álvaro de Castrillo to collect debts in Acapulco. Probably the Nicolás de Zabala who was in Mexico City in 1597.
Zárate, Tomás de	1599	With Pedro de Avendaño, attorney of Baltazar de Soria, to collect Chinese merchandise.

Sources: Bonialian, *América española*, table 1.6; Blair and Robertson, *The Philippine Islands*, 8:239–40.

Appendix 4

Glossary of Place Names

Spelling in Text	Alternative Spellings	Current Name
Acapetlahuaya	Acapetlahuayan	Acapetlahuaya
Acuitlapán	Acuitlapam	Acuitlapán
Ahuacuotzingo	Aguacaucingo, Ahuacuatzingo	Ahuacuotzingo
Ajuchitlán	Asinchintlan, Asuchitlan, Axuchitlan	Ajuchitlán del Progreso
Alahuiztlán	Alahuistlan	Alahuixtlán
Alcozauca	Alcocauhcan	Alcozauca de Guerrero
Apaxtla	Apastla, Apastlan, Apaztla, Apaztlan	Apaxtla de Castrejón
Atenango		Atenango del Río
Atlamajac	Atlamaxac, Atlimaxaque	Atlamajalcingo del Monte
Ayutla		Ayutla de los Libres
Azala	Açala	Atzala de la Asunción
Azoyú	Açoyuque, Azoyoc, Azoyuc, Atzoyoc	Azoyú
Cacahuatepec	Cacahuatepeque	Cacahuatepec
Chiepetlán	Chipetlan	San Miguel Chiepetlán
Chilapa	Chilapan	Chilapa
Citlaltomahua	Citlaltomagua, Zitlaltomagua	
Coahuayutla	Coaguayutla	Coahuayutla de José María Izazaga
Cocula	Cocolan	Cocula
Cototolapan		Ruinas cerca de Cualác
Coyuca (Costa Grande)		Coyuca de Benítez
Coyuca (Tierra Caliente)	Coyucan	Coyuca de Catalán
Cualác	Cualac, Cuaulasyotepetl	Cualác
Cuauhnáhuac		Cuernavaca
Cuetlajuchitlán	Cuetlasuchutlan, Quitlasuchitlan	Querende (Cuetlajuchitlán)
Cuetzala	Cueçalan, Cuetzalan, Cuezala	Cuetzala del Progreso
Cutzamala	Cuçamala, Cuzamala	Cutzamala de Pinzón

Spelling in Text	Alternative Spellings	Current Name
Guayameo	Guaimeo, Guaymeo	Guayameo
Huamuxtitlán	Quamochtitlan	Huamuxtitlán
Hueyistac	Gueyystaca, Huistaca	Huixtac
Huitziltepec	Huiziltepeque	Huitziltepec
Huitzuco	Izuco	Huitzuco de los Figueroa
Huytalota	Huitaluta	/
Iguala	Yohuallan, Yoallan	Iguala de la Independencia
Igualapa	Ygualapa	Igualapa
Ixcapuzalco	Çicapuçalco, Itzcaputzalco, Tzicapotzalco, Tzicaputzalco	Ixcapuzalco
Ixcateopan	Escateupa, Ichcateopan, Ichcateupa, Ichcateupan, Iscateupa, Izcateupa	Ixcateopan de Cauahtémoc
Mayanalán	Mayanala, Mayanalan	Mayanalán
Mochitlán	Muchitlan	Mochitlán
Nexpa (Costa Grande)	Nespa	
Noxtepec	Nochistepeque, Nochtepec, Nochtepeque, Nonthepeque, Noxtepeque	Santiago Noxtepec
Oapan	Ohuapan, Ouapa	San Agustín Oapan
Ometepec	Ometepeque	Ometepec
Oztuma	Ostuma, Oztoma, San Simón de Oztuma	Ixtepec de San Simón
Petlacala		San Pedro Petlacala
Petatlán	Petlatlan	Petatlán
Pilcaya	Pilcayan	Pilcaya
Pungarabato	Pungarauato, Pungaravuato, Pungari-hoato	Ciudad Altamirano
Quechultenango	Quecholtenango	Quechultenango
Sochitonala	Xuchitonala	
Taxco	Tasco	Taxco de Alarcón
Taxco el Viejo	Tasco el Viejo, Tlachco	Taxco el Viejo
Tecpan		Tecpan de Galeana
Tepecoacuilco	Tepecoaquilco, Tepecuacuilco, Tepequaquilco	Tepecoacuilco de Trujano
Tetela		Tetela del Río
Tetipac	Teticpac, Teticpaque	Tetipac
Tixtla	Tistla	Tixtla de Guerrero
Tlacotepec	Tlacotepeque	Tlacotepec
Tlalcozautitlán	Tlacoçauhtitlán, Tlalcuçautitlan	Tlalcozotitlán
Tlamacazapa	Tamagaçapa, Tamagazapa	Tlamacazapa

Spelling in Text	Alternative Spellings	Current Name
Tlapa-Tlachinollan (precontact)		Tlapa de Comonfort
Tlapa (colonial)		Tlapa de Comonfort
Tlaxmalac	Tasmalaca, Taxmalaca	Tlaxmalac
Totomixtlahuaca	Totomistlauaca, Xotomistlauaca	Totomixtlahuaca
Tululuaba	Tululuava	
Tututepec	Tutultepec	
Villa de San Luis		San Luis Acatlán
Xalapa		Jalapa
Xicayán		Jicayán de Tovar
Xochistlahuaca	Suchistlahuaca	Xochistlahuaca
Ygualan (in the Montaña)		
Yopecingo	Yopeçingo, Yopitzinco	
Zacatula	Çacatula, Villa de la Concepción [de Zacatula]	Zacatula
Zirándaro	Çarandacho, Sirandacho, Sirandaro	Zirándaro
Zitlala	Citlala	Zitlala
Zumpango	Çumpango, Çunpango, Tzompanco	Zumpango del Río

Appendix 5

Glossary

Afromestizo: A person of mixed ancestry, one ancestor being African
aguafuerte: Nitric acid
ají: A chile pepper
alcalde: A judge, a member of a cabildo
alcalde de mesta: A judge of the cattle owners' guild
alcalde mayor: A Spanish official responsible for a district, including collecting Crown tribute and certain judicial functions (see also *corregidor*).
alcaldía mayor: The district administered by an alcalde mayor
alguacil: A constable, civil, or ecclesiastical, the latter termed an *alguacil de doctrina*
almojarifazgo: A customs duty or tax applied to imports and exports
altepetl: (Nahuatl) A term for a group of Indigenous settlements that form a self-governing whole
amate: Tree bark used to make Indigenous paper
amatlacuilo: (Nahuatl) An Indigenous "painter on paper," scribe
anahuatl: (Nahuatl) A pectoral
arriero: A muleteer, often also a small-scale merchant
artifact: A portable object used, made, or modified by humans

bachiller: A university graduate
ballcourt: An enclosed space used to play the ritual ballgame
barrio: A district or subdivision of a town
biombo: A screen, used to divide space in a room, originally imported from Japan
botijo: A ceramic vessel used to transport liquids
braza: A unit of measure, typically about 66 inches

caballería: A measure of land area, approximately 44 hectares. Usually refers to crop land, not grazing for livestock.
cabecera: A head town of an Indigenous municipality with authority over *sujetos* (see *sujeto*)

cabecera de doctrina: A head town of a parish
cabildo: A municipal council
cacahuatl: (Nahuatl) A cacao plantation
cacique: An Indigenous ruler
cactli: (Nahuatl) Sandals
caja de comunidad: A wooden chest used to store the funds of a community
calli: (Nahuatl) A house
calpixqui: (Nahuatl) A tax or tribute collector; a Mexica military governor
calpolli: (Nahuatl) A territorial-social unit of an *altepetl*; the inhabitants of that unit
cantor: A singer in church
casa de comunidad: A building where community officials meet, and community gathering are held
cascalote: A small tree or shrub (Caesalpinia cacalaco) whose bark, an excellent source of gallic and tannic acid, is used for tanning
castas: Racial categories used by the Spanish administration to classify the population of New Spain
cazonci: The ruler of the Tarascan polity
chalchihuite or chalchihuitl: (Nahuatl) Precious stone, often greenstone
charape: A fermented drink made from coconut (see *tuba*), sweetened with unrefined sugar, popular on the coast of Guerrero
chía: (Salvia hispanica) Produces edible seeds
chicovite: A basket used in mines to carry ore
chino: Literally a Chinese person, but in practice any Asian person
clavo: A conical stone with round head inserted into *tablero* walls, often carved with human faces
codex/códice: A folding pictographic book painted on *amate* or animal skin and, postcontact, often on European paper
cofrade: A member of a cofradía (see *cofradía*)
cofradía: A religious sodality or association
comal: (from Nahuatl *comalli*) A griddle
composición de tierras: Regularization of title to land in return for a fee paid to the Crown
conflade: (Nahuatl) A sixteenth-century loanword for cofrade, a member of a cofradía (see *cofrade* and *cofradía*)
congregación: Literally "congregation"; a forced relocation of a community to a new location, usually to concentrate Indigenous populations in fewer places, usually for administrative convenience
converso: A Jewish convert to Christianity
corregidor: A Spanish official responsible for a district, including collecting Crown tribute and certain judicial functions (see also *alcalde mayor*)

corregimiento: The district administered by a corregidor
cuadrilla: A labor gang in a mine

diezmo: A tithe or 10 percent tax
diputado de minas: A representative responsible for enforcing mining regulations

encomendero: An individual entitled to the proceeds of an *encomienda*
encomienda: A grant of Indians who paid tribute and provided labor and services to an *encomendero*; the area in which the Indians lived
engasamiento: Contamination by noxious fumes from heating metal ore
entrada: A military expedition of Spaniards against rebellious Indigenous people
epcololli: (Nahuatl) A hook-shaped ear ornament
escribano: A scribe or secretary to a Spanish official or priest
escribano de registro: A registrar of cargo in a port such as Acapulco
estancia: A settlement subject to a *cabecera*; also a cattle ranch; also an alternative term for a *sujeto* (see *sujeto*)

familiar: A constable of the Inquisition
fiscal: The most senior Indigenous official in a parish who assisted the priest

ganado mayor: Large livestock, usually cattle
ganado menor: Smaller livestock, usually pigs or goats
gente de razón: A person considered to be culturally Hispanicized and, therefore, capable of understanding Christian doctrine and punishable for heresy
gobernador: A governor of an indigenous municipality

hacienda volante: The practice of grazing livestock seasonally on rented or illegally occupied land as opposed to a hacienda or landed estate owned by the cattle rancher
hermandad: A religious brotherhood
hortelano: A gardener, usually a market gardener
huauhtli: (Nahuatl) Amaranth
huerta: A garden, horticultural land
huipil: (from Nahuatl *huipilli*) Woman's blouse

ichcatl: (Nahuatl) Cotton
icpalli: (Nahuatl) A seat made of woven reeds of an Indigenous ruler
indio mandón: A low-level Indigenous town officer
indio naborío: A free wage worker
indio de servicio: An Indian providing compulsory labor service

jícara pintada: A colorfully lacquered drinking vessel made from dried gourd
juez de comisión: A judge appointed to investigate a specific matter

ladino: A Spanish-speaking and acculturated Indian
lienzo: A pictorial document painted on cloth
longue durée: (French) A long period of time, frequently centuries

macehual/macegual: (from Nahuatl *macehualli*) An Indigenous commoner
maestre: Master, perhaps a distinguished person or master of a military order
manta: A length of cotton cloth
manta de Ilocos: A luxurious cotton bed covering made in the Ilocos region of the Philippines
mapa: A pictorial representation of the territory and important features of an Indigenous community, they usually defined territory precisely without using European scale cartographic conventions
marco: A coin equal to 68 reales or 8.5 pesos
maxtlatl: (Nahuatl) Loincloth
merced: Literally a favor, by extension a grant of land made by the Crown
mestizaje: biological or cultural miscegenation involving European and Indigenous Mexican peoples
Mexica: The term by which the people commonly known in English as Aztecs identified themselves
minero: mineowner

nahualli: (Nahuatl) An Indian with power to convert into an animal
ñuu: a Mixtec state equivalent to a Nahua *altepetl*

ocote: Torch pine, used for lighting
oidor: An Audiencia judge
ojos sin pupila: Literally eyes without pupils, used to describe a type of Olmec figurine
Olmec: Term applied both to a culture that flourished on the Gulf Coast of Mexico ca. 1200 BCE to ca. 300 BCE, but also to the style associated with that culture that had a much wider distribution
ololiuhqui: Turbina Corymbosa, whose seeds have a hallucinogenic effect
oro común: A lower-grade gold coin

pantli: (Nahuatl) The number 20 and the glyph signifying that number
pardo: A person of whom one parent was Black and the other White or Indian, or a person descended from such parentage
partido: A civil or parochial jurisdiction
patache: A dispatch boat, used to carry messages between larger ships in a fleet
petate: (from Nahuatl *petlatl*) Woven mat
piñol: (from Nahuatl *pinolli*) Flour made, for example, from ground maize or *chía*
pintura: Spanish term for an Indigenous pictographic document
poblador: Spanish term for a settler as opposed to a conquistador
potrero: A paddock, pastureland for horses
principal: Member of the Indian elite
probanza de méritos: A petition to the king requesting rewards for alleged services to the Crown
procurador a la corte: A Spaniard of New Spain chosen to represent the interests of New Spain's Spaniards at the royal court in Madrid
Provincia de la Plata: Literally Silver Province, a term coined in the 1530s to refer to the region of the mines of Taxco, Temascaltepec, Zacualpan, and Zultepec
pulque: A drink made from fermented agave juice
Purhépecha: Term preferred in contemporary scholarship and society to refer to the Tarascans and their descendants; speakers of the Purhépecha language (see *Tarascans*)

quachtli/cuachtli: (Nahuatl) An Indigenous cloak; by extension, cotton cloth
queso: Literally "cheese"; a circular stone used to make circular columns
quezquémetl: A form of stole
quinto: One-fifth tax on silver paid to the Crown

real [de minas]: A municipality dedicated to mining
Real Hacienda: The royal treasury
regidor: A member of a *cabildo* (see *cabildo*)
reino: Spanish term designating an Indigenous polity ruled by an Indigenous elite person
repartimiento de efectos: Compulsory sale of goods to Indians
repartimiento de indios: Allocation of compulsory Indian laborers
república de indios: an Indigenous political entity theoretically separate from Spanish municipalities

sangley: A term used by Spaniards in the Philippines to refer to the Chinese

señor natural: Literally "natural lord"; an Indigenous ruler by right of descent

sonsaque: The practice of mineowners paying Indigenous mineworkers in advance to lure them away from their existing employer

soplillos: Narrow tubes used to blow on a fire to raise its temperature to smelt metal, a practice of Indigenous origin

sujeto: An Indigenous settlement dependent on a *cabecera*

taleguilla: A small, cloth bag used in some circumstances as a measure of tribute, for example of salt

talud-tablero: A method of wall construction, with a sloping base (*talud*) topped by a vertical *tablero*

tameme: A human carrier or porter

Tarascans: Traditional term applied to the people of the Late Postclassic polity centered on Lake Pátzcuaro in Michoacán, with its capital in Tzinzuntzan (see *Purhépecha*)

tecoçahuitl: (Nahuatl) A yellow ochre pigment

tecomate: (Nahutatl tecomatl) A ceramic cup, jar, or vessel

tecpan: (Nahuatl) A house of an Indigenous ruler or noble

tenedor de bienes de difuntos: An officer of the Mexico City cabildo, guardian of the goods of the deceased

teniente de corregidor: The assistant of a corregidor

tepixqui: (Nahuatl) A ward leader in an *altepetl*; in colonial Iguala and Cocula, a church official

tepotzoicpalli: (Nahuatl) A seat of woven reeds with a backrest, indicative of high noble status of figures depicted in codices and lienzos (see also *tolicpalli*)

tequio: Community work

tequitato: (from Nahuatl *tequitlato*) A municipal tribute officer; also, an Indigenous church or civil official

terrrazguero: Sharecropper

teuctli: (from Nahuatl *tecuhpilli*) A lord or member of the high Indigenous nobility

tianguis: (from Nahuatl *tianquiztli*) Town market

tierras baldías: Abandoned or uncultivated land that could be acquired in exchange for a fee paid to the Crown

tilma: (Nahuatl) A cape

tlacatecuhtli: (Nahuatl) An Indigenous governor

tlacuilo: (Nahuatl) An Indigenous scribe or painter

tlatoani: (Nahuatl) An Indigenous ruler of an altepetl

tolicpalli: (Nahuatl) A high-backed seat of woven reeds of a lord (see also *tepotzoicpalli*)

tonelada: A ton

topile: (Nahuatl) A lower-level Indigenous church official who carried out supervisory functions

trompezón: A wall used to accumulate alluvial soil for cultivation in the Montaña

tuba: A fermented beverage made from coconut, it originated in the Philippines

vecino: A resident or homeowner of a Spanish town

xicolli: (Nahuatl) Sleeveless jacket

X-ray fluorescence: Method used to detect and measure elements that compose an artifact

yuhuitayu: In Mixtec society, a marital union of two dynastic lines to form a united polity

Notes

Introduction

1. For a map, Dehouve, *Entre el caimán*, 22.
2. Bonfil Batalla, *México Profundo*.
3. Ranere, Piperno, Holst, Dickau, Iriarte, and Sabloff, "The Cultural and Chronological Context."
4. Brush, "Pox Pottery." The date is debated as the reader will discover.
5. Grove, "Olmec Paintings of Oxtotitlan"; Russ et al., "Strategies for 14C Dating the Oxtotitlán Cave Paintings."
6. Martínez Donjuán, "Teopantecuanitlan, Guerrero"; Martínez Donjuán, "Teopantecuanitlán," *Primer coloquio*.
7. Manzanilla López, *La región arqueológica de la Costa Grande*.
8. Labarthe R., "Provincia de Zacatula."
9. For example, Smith, Ebert, and Kennett, "Human Ecology of Shellfish Exploitation."
10. Hepp, "La Consentida."
11. Voorhies, Kennett, Jones, and Wake, "A Middle Archaic Archaeological Site."
12. *El Libro de tasaciones*.
13. Millares Carlo and Mantecón, eds., *Índice y extractos*.
14. For example, Gutiérrez, "Expanding Polity"; Gutiérrez, *Catálogo de sitios*; Gutiérrez, *The Aztec Conquest*.
15. For example, see Dehouve's "Dos relatos sobre migraciones nahuas"; "Les Lienzos de Malinaltepec"; and *Quand les banquiers*.
16. See table 4.1.
17. For example, *El Libro de tasaciones*; García Izcabalzeta and García Pimentel, *Descripción del Arzobispado*.
18. See table 6.1.

19. Grove, "The Olmec Paintings of Oxtotitlan Cave."
20. For example, Martínez Donjuán, "Teopantecuanitlan, Guerrero"; Martínez Donjuán, "Sculpture from Teopantecuanitlan."
21. Niederberger, "Excavación de un área de habitación doméstica"; Niederberger, "Nácar."
22. See chapter 1.
23. Von Mentz, *Señoríos indígenas*.
24. Amith, *The Möbius Strip*.
25. For examples, Millares Carlo and Mantecón eds., *Índice y extractos*, 1:239; *Historia de Chilpancingo*, 81–86; Zavala, *Libros de asientos*; Paso y Troncoso, *Epistolario*, 4:148–49.
26. See table 4.1.
27. Sharer et al., "On the Logic of Archaeological Inference."
28. Yannakakis, *The Art of Being In-Between*.
29. Renfrew and Bahn, *Archaeology*, 481–89.
30. Dehouve, *Entre el caimán*, 29. Author's translation.
31. Davies, *The Aztec Empire*, 6.
32. Silverstein, "A Study of the Late Postclassic Aztec-Tarascan Frontier," 55–71.
33. Jiménez P. and Villela F., *Historia y cultura*; Dehouve, "Les Lienzos de Malinaltepec"; Oettinger and Horcasitas, "Lienzo of Petlacala"; Ramírez C., *El Códice de Teloloapan*. Codices of the Tierra Caliente of Michoacán suggest that there were more pictographic documents than the surviving texts. See Roskamp, *La Historiografía indígena*.
34. See, for example, Haskett, *Indigenous* Rulers.
35. The literature of the *Códices de Azoyú* is ample. See, for example, Vega Sosa, "El Códice Azoyú 1 y el Lienzo de Tlapa," 195–208; Gutiérrez, "The Expanding Polity," 155–232; Gutiérrez and Brito, *El Códice Azoyú 2*; Oudijk, "El Señorío de Tlapa-Tlachinollan."
36. Oudijk, "El Señorío de Tlapa-Tlachinollan," 80–82.
37. Pollard, *Taríacuri's Legacy*, 142; Roskamp, *Historiografía indígena*; Roskamp, *Historia, mito y legitimación*; Roskamp, *Códices de Cutzio y Huetamo*; Punzo Díaz, "Presencia tarasca."
38. The *Relaciones geográficas* were reports of the geography, resources, and population of New Spain. A questionnaire was to be completed by Crown officials in each jurisdiction. The quality of the data in the reports is variable since some officials were more diligent than others, and some reports have been lost. The questionnaire is in "Instrucción y memoria de las relaciones," 17–23.

39. Niederberger, "Nácar"; Velázquez-Castro, "The Study of Shell Object Manufacturing"; "Relación de Xalapa," 286; "Relación de Citlaltomahua," 118–21.
40. Schmidt Schoenberg and Litvak King, "Problemas y perspectivas."
41. For dating methods, Renfrew and Bahn, *Archaeology*, 131–76.
42. Michelet, "Apuntes para el análisis," 13–14.
43. Smith, "The Expansion of the Aztec Empire," 37–54.
44. Ranere, Piperno, Holst, Dickau, Iriarte, and Sabloff, "The Cultural and Chronological Context."
45. Coe, Snow, and Benson, *Atlas of Ancient America*, 101.
46. For a discussion of the terminology, see Espejel, "Reflexiones acerca del estado Tarasco," 73–78.
47. Spaniards designated as a cabecera (head town) what they perceived as the principal, ruling settlement of an altepetl. Other settlements that comprised the altepetl were termed sujetos (or estancias). In fact, as Lockhart, *The Nahuas After the Conquest*, 15–28, notes, this terminology misunderstood the *altepetl*, which was a unit of people who controlled a territory, not strictly a territorial unit.

Chapter One

1. Gemelli Carreri, *Viaje a la Nueva España*, 7–8, 13.
2. Cabrera Guerrero, *Los pobladores prehispánicos de Acapulco*, 15–24; Widmer, *Conquista y despertar*, 26–32; Gerhard, *A Guide to the Historical Geography of New Spain*, 39, 148, 393.
3. Gutiérrez, "The Expanding Polity," 31–87.
4. Gerhard, *A Guide to the Historical Geography of New Spain*, 111, 316.
5. Paradis, "The Tierra Caliente," 1–5; Armillas, "Expediciones en el occidente," 73–85.
6. Gerhard, *A Guide to the Historical Geography of New Spain*, 146.
7. Hirth, *The Aztec Economic World*, 6–12.
8. Gutiérrez, "The Expanding Polity," 32–43.
9. Voorhies, Kennett, Jones, and Wake, "A Middle Archaic Archaeological Site," 179–200; Kennett, Piperno, et al., "Pre-pottery Farmers on the Pacific Coast of Southern Mexico," 3401–11.
10. Hepp, "La Consentida." For more perspectives on early Pacific coastal communities: Cabrero G., "El modo de vida marítima," 183–92; Love, "Recent Research in the Southern Highlands," 275–328; Beekman, "Recent Research in Western Mexican Archaeology," 41–109.

11. Smith, Ebert, and Kennett, "Human Ecology of Shellfish Exploitation," 183–202; Kennett, Voorhies, Wake, and Martínez, "Long-Term Effects of Human Predation," 103–24.
12. Brush, "Pox Pottery."
13. Ebert, Dennison, Hirth, McClure, and Kennett, "Formative Period Obsidian Exchange."
14. Brush, "Pox Pottery," 194.
15. García Cook, "Las cerámicas más tempranas."
16. Voorhies and Kennett, "Reanalizando el 'Pox Pottery.'"
17. Smith, Ebert, and Kennett, "Human Ecology."
18. Ebert, Dennison, Hirth, McClure, and Kennett, "Formative Period Obsidian Exchange"; Paul Schmidt Schoenberg, e-mail to author, January 20, 2021.
19. González Quintero and Mora Echeverría, "Estudio arqueológico de explotación," 321–37. A similar site, El Embarcadero on the Laguna de Coyuca, was occupied through the Archaic and the Postclassic. By the Classic its inhabitants imported obsidian and used ceramics with influences from Teotihuacan, See Galeana Cruz, "Resultados preliminares . . . en El Embarcadero I." For sites at Pantla and Petatlán, see Jiménez García, Martínez Donjuán, and Arboleyda Castro, "Época prehispánica," 53–54.
20. Manzanilla López, "La investigación arqueológica de la Costa Grande," 115–20; Manzanilla López, *La región arqueológica de la Costa Grande*, 51–77, 86–99.
21. Manzanilla López, *La región arqueológica de la Costa Grande*, 110–15.
22. Manzanilla López, *La región arqueológica de la Costa Grande*, 109–33. I am grateful to Paul Schmidt for pointing out the year sign to me. The other example of monumental sculpture is the Bird Man at Villa Rotaria, near Tecpan. A Tláloc figure attributed to the coast by Manzanilla López is now known to have originated in the Center. See Schmidt Schoenberg and Padilla Gutiérrez, "William Niven y la Estela de Quechomictlipan." Other sites on the Costa Grande shared some or all the features seen at La Soledad de Maciel. For example, terraced habitational areas at Coyuca, San Jerónimo, and Atoyac, and ballcourts at La Yácata and Tecpan. Lobato, "El sistema de comunicación religiosa de Xihuacan," 181–82. Lobato cites three other sites on the Costa Grande with monumental architecture similar to Xihuacán: Xuluchuca (1100–1521 CE), El Zopilote (450–1521 CE), and Tierras Prietas (400 BCE–900 CE).
23. Pulido Méndez, "Datos para la historia arqueológica," 302–12.

24. Manzanilla López, *La región arqueológica de la Costa Grande*, 55–63, 66–69, 115, 124. The influence of Teotihuacan was particularly evident in ceramics at Acapulco and Zacatula-La Villita. At Coyuca de Benítez ceramics resembled Teotihuacan and Zapotec styles, and ceramics in Los Altos de Guatemala.
25. For the most detailed recent description of the site, see Reyes Àlvarez, "Piedra Labrada." Gutiérrez Mendoza, *Catálogo de sitios*, 333–54, includes numerous photographs of the sculptures. The latter estimated the size of the site to be at least 50 hectares and counted eighteen sculptures.
26. Gutiérrez Mendoza, *Catálogo de sitios*, 364–68. The site of Azoyú-Tenconahualle, covering some 43 hectares and consisting of platforms and plazas on low hills, is notable for an estimated 10,000 meters squared of stone paved plazas and other areas, as well as a large quantity of ceramics and sculptures. Gutiérrez Mendoza, *Catálogo de sitios*, 318–30.
27. Jiménez García, Martínez Donjuán, and Arboleyda Castro, "Época prehispánica," 114–16.
28. Litvak King, *Cihuatlán y Tepecoacuilco*, 85, 100, 108, 113–16, 130, 155.
29. Dehouve, *Quand les banquiers*, 77–82; Berdan, Blanton, Hill Boone, Hodge, Smith and Umberger, *Aztec Imperial Strategies*, 277–78.
30. Hirth, *The Aztec Economic World*, 164; Paradis, "The Tierra Caliente," 167–68; Williams, "The Ethnoarchaeology of Salt Production." Trade in salt between the Balsas Valley and the Costa Chica continued as late as the 1950s. Good, "Salt Production and Commerce in Guerrero."
31. Solís Ciriaco and Monterrosa Desruelles, "Malacological Material from Pezuapan's Archaeological Site," 34–40; Solís Ciriaco and Martínez Donjuán, "Specialized Shell Object Production at Teopantecuanitlan"; Manzanilla López, Talavera González, and Rojas Chávez, "Interpretaciones de la dinámica cultural," 283–93.
32. Manzanilla López, *La región arqueológica de la Costa Grande*, 70–77.
33. Urcid, "Pacific Coast of Oaxaca and Guerrero"; Ball and Brockington, "Trade and Travel."
34. Dewan and Hosler, "Ancient Maritime Trade on Balsa Rafts"; Hosler, "Ancient West Mexican Metallurgy."
35. See map in Dehouve, *Quand les banquiers*, 2.
36. Dehouve, *Quand les banquiers*, 3–6; Gutiérrez, "The Expanding Polity," 45–60; Gerhard, *A Guide to the Historical Geography of New Spain*, 321.
37. Altamirano, "Paisajes y Leyendas", cited in Niederberger, "Antiguos paisajes de Guerrero," 25. Author's translation.

38. Gutiérrez, "The Expanding Polity," 79–86.
39. Pérez Rodríguez, "Recent Advances in Mixtec Archaeology."
40. Gutiérrez, Vera, Pye, and Serrano, *Contlalco y La Coquera*, 95.
41. Ranere, Piperno, Holst, Dickau, Iriarte, and Sabloff, "Cultural and Chronological Context."
42. Vélez Calvo, "Etnohistoria," 153–61, 234–39.
43. Gutiérrez Mendoza, *Catálogo de sitios*, 1–313.
44. Gutiérrez, Vera, Pye, and Serrano, *Contlalco y La Coquera*, 16–95; Gutiérrez Mendoza, *Catálogo de sitios*, 27–30, 33–42.
45. Gutiérrez Mendoza, "Territorial Structure and Urbanism." On *ñuu* and *yuhuitayu*, see Terraciano, *The Mixtecs*, 102–5, 171–79.
46. Gutiérrez Mendoza, *Catálogo de sitios*, 16–69.
47. Gutiérrez Mendoza, *Catálogo de sitios*, 75–76.
48. Gutiérrez Mendoza, *Catálogo de sitios*, 191.
49. Dehouve, *Quand les banquiers*, 78–82; Rubí Alarcón, "La encomienda de la Montaña," 433–40.
50. Berdan, "Cotton in Aztec Mexico"; Weitlaner Johnson and Mastache, "Tejidos prehispánicos de Guerrero," 444, 450–53.
51. Widmer, *Conquista y despertar*, 169.
52. Niederberger, "Nácar"; Pye and Gutiérrez, "The Pacific Coast Trade Route of Mesoamerica"; Nuttall, "Chalchihuitl in Ancient Mexico," 87.
53. Rubí Alarcón, "Comunidades indígenas," 319–24; Widmer, *Conquista y despertar*, 94–112.
54. Gerhard, *A Guide to the Historical Geography of New Spain*, 316.
55. Amith, *The Möbius Strip*, 39.
56. Paul Schmidt Schoenberg, e-mail to author June 6, 2017.
57. Pérez Negrete, "Arqueología de Guerrero," 16–17.
58. Monterrosa Desruelles, "Proyecto Arqueológico Pezuapan."
59. Pérez Negrete and Arias Vázquez, "Proyecto de investigación y conservación"; Monterrosa Desruelles, "Proyecto Arqueológico Pezuapan"; Solís Ciriaco and Monterrosa Desruelles, "Malacological Material from Pezuapan."
60. Reyna Robles, *La Organera-Xochipala*, 297–98, 331–32. There is a sound argument that the archaeological model of the urban city, in contrast to the rural village, does not apply to the urban centers of Mesoamerica. Daneels and Gutiérrez Mendoza, eds., *El poder compartido*. Paul Schmidt considers La Organera to be a palace complex, not a city: e-mail to author October 7, 2021.

61. Schmidt Schoenberg, *Arqueología de Xochipala*; Schmidt Schoenberg, "Secuencia arqueológica de Xochipala." Schmidt was unable to measure the extent of all the ninety-three sites recorded.
62. Reyna Robles, *La Organera-Xochipala*; Reyna Robles, "La Organera-Xochipala, Guerrero." Reyna Robles notes that the porticoed palace structures of La Organera resemble the architectural models of the Mezcala sculpture tradition (see chapter 2.3).
63. Gerhard, *A Guide to the Historical Geography of New Spain*, 146, 252.
64. Ranere, Piperno, Holst, Dickau, Iriarte, and Sabloff, "The Cultural and Chronological Context."
65. Amith, *The Möbius Strip*, 37.
66. Martínez Donjuán, "Sculpture from Teopantecuanlitlan," 57–58; Martínez Donjuán, "Teopantecuanitlán," *Primer coloquio de arqueologia*.
67. Evans, *Ancient Mexico*, 191, 214, 221, 255.
68. Martínez Donjuán, "Teopantecuanitlan, Guerrero"; Martínez Donjuán, "Teopantecuanitlán," *Arqueología Mexicana*, 60–62; Martínez Donjuán, "Sculpture from Teopantecuanlitlan."
69. Niederberger, "Nácar," 186–87.
70. Martínez Donjuán, "Teopantecuanitlan, Guerrero"; Martínez Donjuán, "Teopantecuanitlán," *Primer coloquio de arqueologia*; Martínez Donjuán, "Los olmecas," 154–62; Martínez Donjuán, "Teopantecuanitlán," *Arqueología Mexicana*; Martínez Donjuán, "Sculpture from Teopantecuanlitlan"; Niederberger, "Excavación de un área de habitación doméstica"; Niederberger, "Nácar," 186–200. There are a ballcourt and corbelled arched tombs at El Frilojar, near Teopantecuanitlán, probably dating to the Classic. Paul Schmidt, e-mail to author, January 20, 2021.
71. Manzanilla López, "La zona arqueológica de Cuetlajuchitlán"; Manzanilla López, Talavera González, and Rojas Chávez, "Interpretaciones de la dinámica cultural"; Manzanilla López and Talavera González, "Cuetlajuchitlan." There are five other sites nearby.
72. This may indicate an architectural innovation in Guerrero, or perhaps the Teotihuacan dates should be earlier.
73. Paradis, "Ahuináhuac." The four sites contemporary with Ahuináhuac were La Organera-Tepecoacuilco, Cerro de los Muertos, Apantipán, and Tehuacatlipa. See Paradis, "Ahuinahuac," 90, for a map of sites in the Tepecoacuilco river region.
74. Cabrera Castro, "El Proyecto arqueológico 'Cocula'"; Cabrera Castro, "Arquitectura y sistemas constructivos," 98. Prehistoric, colonial, and postcolonial sites were identified.
75. Von Mentz, *Señoríos indígenas*, 73–102.

76. Niederberger, "Nácar," 178; Dehouve, *Entre el caimán*, 25.
77. Paradis, "Tierra Caliente," 119.
78. Niederberger, "Nácar," 178. Amith, *The Möbius Strip*, 33, 40, differs, emphasizing the hot dry climate and considering the river an obstacle to communication.
79. Paradis, "Tierra Caliente," 5, 118–24; Armillas, "Expediciones en el occidente," 74–75.
80. Armillas, "Expediciones en el occidente"; Lister, "Archaeology of the Middle Rio Balsas Basin," 67–78. Lister notes that the number of sites found supported a comment by Francisco Cervantes de Salazar, writing in 1558–1567, that the population of the region was once as numerous as bees.
81. Paradis, "Tierra Caliente," 52–81, 206–15. Paradis interpreted Amuco Abelino as an example of subsistence village life, which persisted while large urban centers flourished elsewhere. She began her work on Formative Ahuináhuac with similar assumptions, only to conclude that the site hierarchy there varied from simple encampments to urban centers such as Ahuináhuac. In retrospect, a similar interpretation may perhaps be applied to Amuco Abelino. Paradis, "Tierra Caliente," 275; Paradis, "Ahuináhuac," 80.
82. Silverstein, "A Study of the Late Postclassic Aztec-Tarascan Frontier."
83. Von Mentz, *Señoríos indígenas*, 55–58, 70–71, 81–82, 92–98. A survey in the Cutzamala valley recorded twenty-nine sites dated from the seventh to the sixteenth centuries CE. Moguel, "Exploraciones arqueológicas en el Valle del río Cutzamala." In the Presa de los Altos area, thirty-five undated sites have been identified Arana and Cepeda C., "Localización de sitios arqueológicos."
84. Silverstein, "A Study of the Late Postclassic Aztec-Tarascan Frontier," 133–35; Silverstein, "Un Estudio de la Frontera Azteca-Tarasca"; Silverstein, "La frontera mexica-tarasca," 47.
85. Maldonado, *Ofrendas*; Maldonado Cárdenas, "Las Paletas del Infiernillo"; González Crespo, *Patrón de asentamiento*. Further down the Balsas, between 1200 BCE and around 200 CE, small villages occupied the riverbanks. Inhabitants lived from agriculture, hunting, and foraging. Evidence of occupation in the Classic is scarce, but burials, shell objects, and ceramics attest human activities. In the Postclassic most houses were of perishable materials, sometimes with stone foundations. Ceremonial centers were constructed on rectangular platforms. Stuccoed stone buildings were very few. Figurines and copper objects became more abundant. Cabrera Castro, "El desarrollo cultural."

86. Paradis, "Tierra Caliente," 94, 165–66, 168, 177; Silverstein, "A Study of the Late Postclassic Aztec-Tarascan Frontier," 58, 72–73, 87–88, 106, 108, 110, 310–11; Maldonado, *Ofrendas*, 43–44, 223–26; González Crespo, *Patrón de asentamiento*, 21–22; Hosler, "Nuevos hallazgos sobre la metalurgia."
87. Pollard, "Recent Research," 356, 359, 363, 365; Maldonado, *Ofrendas*, 41–3; Silverstein, "A Study of the Late Postclassic Aztec-Tarascan Frontier," 304–10, 314. Paradis, "Tierra Caliente," 179–85, 262, describes early colonial routes of pre-Hispanic origin.
88. Weitlaner and Barlow, "Breve Nota," 30.
89. Berdan, "Economic Dimensions of Precious Metals."
90. Matos Moctezuma, "Los mexicas y el rumbo sur"; Matos Moctezuma, "Presencia del Sur." Mezcala sculptures were abstracted human figures or architectural models carved in polished stone (see chapter 2.3). The Templo Mayor offerings were human figures. González and Olmedo Vera, *Esculturas mezcala en el Templo Mayor*.
91. Ebert, Dennison, Hirth, McClure and Kennett, "Formative Period Obsidian Exchange"; Brush, "Pox Pottery," 149, found obsidian in Puerto Marqués in a context dated to 2940 ± 130 BCE; however, no obsidian was found at sites of similar antiquity in the Montaña which had no direct access to shells. Gutiérrez, Vera, Pye and Serrano, *Contlalco y La Coquera*, 95.
92. Solís Ciriaco and Martínez Donjuán, "Specialized Shell Object Production," 38–41.
93. Manzanilla López, Talavera González, and Rojas Chávez, "Interpretaciones de la dinámica cultural."
94. Solís Ciriaco and Monterrosa Desruelles, "Malacological Material from Pezuapan"; Grove, *Chalcatzingo*, 161–63.
95. For examples, see Matos Moctezuma, "Presencia del Sur," 148; Niederberger, "Nácar," 212–15.
96. Matos Moctezuma, "Los mexicas y el rumbo sur"; Matos Moctezuma, "Presencia del Sur"; Polaco Ramos, "Restos biológicos," identifies offerings of shells from the Pacific coast of Guerrero and Oaxaca, as well as fish, sharks, and other species that may have come from the Pacific coast.
97. Velázquez-Castro, "The Study of Shell Object Manufacturing Techniques." *Epcololli* is a Nahuatl term meaning "shell [eptli] hook [cuyulli/cuyolli/cololli]." Wood, "Nahuatl Dictionary." The ear

ornaments illustrated in Velázquez-Castro's study are roughly the shape of a letter *J*. I am grateful to a reviewer of my manuscript for clarifying the meaning of *epcololli*.
98. Widmer, *Conquista y despertar*, 59; Haskett, "Our Suffering," 449.
99. Restall, *Seven Myths*, 22–23.
100. Hosler, "West Mexican Metallurgy Revisited."
101. For a summary of the arguments, see Solar Valverde, Nelson, and Ohnersorgen, "Aztatlán: Una red de interacción en el Occidente de México," 17–19. Work at Huetamo, Michoacán, also suggests a later date. Punzo Díaz, Rangel, Ibarra, Zarco, and Castañón, "Revisiting the Archaeology of the Huetamo Area."
102. Hosler, "West Mexican Metallurgy Revisited," 186, 193; Hosler, "Ancient West Mexican Metallurgy."
103. Hosler, "Nuevos hallazgos sobre la metalurgia"; Hosler, "Excavations at the Copper Smelting Site of El Manchon."
104. Jiménez García, "Apuntes sobre la arqueología," 393–95.
105. Gutiérrez, "Negotiating Aztec Tributary Demands," 141, 147, 149, 151, 153, 154, 156–64.
106. Litvak King, *Cihuatlán y Tepecoacuilco*, 86, 90–96, 103–5, 156.
107. Hosler, "Sound, Color and Meaning"; Hosler, Lechtman, and Holm, "Axe-monies," 1–97, 99–103. Pincers were symbols of the state in the Tarascan empire. Priests wore quantities of them.
108. Maldonado, *Ofrendas*, 223–26.
109. For a settlement of full-time mineworkers in the Sierra Gorda of Querétaro, see Herrera Muñoz and Mejía Pérez Campos, "Minería prehispánica de Querétaro."
110. Coe and Coe, *The True History of Chocolate*, 35–104.
111. Maldonado, *Ofrendas*, 225–26; Jiménez García, "Materiales arqueológicos de orígen orgánico"; Paradis, "Tierra Caliente," 171–74, 177; Silverstein, "A Study of the Late Postclassic Aztec-Tarascan Frontier," 106; Gutiérrez, "Negotiating Aztec Tributary Demands," 151, 153, 156–57.
112. Castelló Iturbide, "El Maque," 98–100; López, *Crafting Mexico*, 201–27.
113. Litvak King, *Cihuatlán y Tepecoacuilco*, 90–96, 100, 108.
114. Hirth, *The Aztec Economic World*, 72, 143, 171–72, 249–52, 265–68; Haskett, "Our Suffering," 454–55. For barter and quasi-currencies in Aztec commerce, see Kurtz, "Peripheral and Transitional Markets," 694–95.

115. For an overview of finds in Guerrero, see Weitlaner Johnson and Mastache, "Tejidos prehispánicos de Guerrero." For spindles and textiles, Jiménez García, Martínez Donjuán, and Arboleyda Castro, "Época prehispánica," 114–16; Lister, "Archaeology of Middle Rio Balsas," 70–71; Cabrera Castro, "El Desarrollo cultural," 139–40.
116. Weitlaner Johnson and Mastache, "Tejidos prehispánicos," 450–53, 456.
117. Weitlaner Johnson and Mastache, "Tejidos prehispánicos," 444–47.
118. On the importance of cotton, see Berdan, "Cotton in Aztec Mexico."
119. Widmer, *Conquista y despertar*, 42–45, 49; Paradis, "Tierra Caliente," 165, 169–70, 175.
120. Gutiérrez, "Expanding Polity," 307–8.
121. Litvak King, *Cihuatlán y Tepecoacuilco*, 74, 90–96, 99–100, 108, 110.
122. Gutiérrez, "Negotiating Aztec Tributary Demands," 144–48, 151–58.
123. Paradis, "Tierra Caliente," 175.
124. Berdan, "Cotton in Aztec Mexico."
125. Berdan, "Cotton in Aztec Mexico," 239; Hirth, *The Aztec Economic World*, 171–72, 249–52. Berdan, and Anawalt, *Essential Codex Mendoza*, 2:217, note that a boatload of water cost one small cotton cape and an unskilled slave thirty large capes.
126. Townsend, "State and Cosmos," 34–35, 40–41, 55, 61.
127. Gutiérrez, "Expanding Polity," 116, 117–18, 123, 309, 357. For the censer, see Gutiérrez Mendoza, *Catálogo de sitios*, 161, 163–64. For the coast, Litvak King, *Cihuatlán y Tepecoacuilco*, 47. For the Tierra Caliente, Silverstein, "A Study of the Late Postclassic Aztec-Tarascan Frontier," 225.
128. Litvak King, *Cihuatlán y Tepecoacuilco*, 112–13; Silverstein, "A Study of the Late Postclassic Aztec-Tarascan Frontier," 225; Jiménez García, Martínez Donjuán, and Arboleyda Castro, "Época prehispánica," 116–17; Paradis, "Tierra Caliente," 172.
129. Tarkanian, and Hosler, "America's First Polymer Scientists."
130. Tarkanian and Hosler, "America's First Polymer Scientists," 482, 484–85; Gutiérrez, "Negotiating Aztec Tributary Demands," 152–53, 156–57.
131. Miller, "The Ballgame," 24; Gay, *Xochipala: The Beginnings of Olmec art*, 20–21; Griffin, "Xochipala: The Earliest Great Art Style," 308–9.
132. See, for example, Cabrera Castro, "Arquitectura y sistemas constructivos," 262–68. Gutiérrez Mendoza, *Catálogo de sitios*, passim; Reyna Robles, "La Organera-Xochipala, Guerrero," 45.

133. Good, "Salt Production," 1–14; Williams, "The Ethnoarchaeology of Salt Production," 402, 403, 409; Widmer, *Conquista y despertar*, 47, 49; Silverstein, "A Study of the Late Postclassic Aztec-Tarascan Frontier," 72–73, 84–88; Litvak King, *Cihuatlán y Tepecoacuilco*, 79–86.
134. Von Mentz, *Señoríos indígenas*, 48, 55–58, 63–67.
135. Litvak King, *Cihuatlán y Tepecoacuilco*, 102–3, 112–13, 117–18, 156; Jiménez García, Martínez Donjuán, and Arboleyda Castro, "Época prehispánica," 116–17; Paradis, "Tierra Caliente," 90, 94, 171, 174, 177.
136. Renfrew and Bahn, *Archaeology*, 357–90.
137. Hirth, *The Aztec Economic World*, 6–10.
138. Drennan, "Long-Distance Movement of Goods"; Drennan, "Long-Distance Transport Costs."
139. Litvak King, *Cihuatlán y Tepecoacuilco*, 99–112.
140. Hirth, *The Aztec Economic World*, 58–59, 272–79. For the quote, see page 272.
141. For the coast, see Brush, "Pox Pottery"; Ebert, Dennison, Hirth, McClure, and Kennett, "Formative Period Obsidian Exchange." For other regions, Lister, "Archaeology of Middle Rio Balsas"; Cabrera Castro, "El Desarrollo cultural"; Spinden, "An Ancient Sepulchre at Placeres Del Oro."
142. Solís Ciriaco and Martínez Donjuán, "Specialized Shell Object Production."
143. Neiderberger, "Nácar," 186–203.
144. Hirth, *The Aztec Economic World*, 270–94. On colonial commerce, Amith, *The Möbius Strip*, 341–61. Cuetlajuchitlán was another such Formative center. See Manzanilla López, "La zona arqueológica de Cuetlajuchitlán."
145. Maldonado, *Ofrendas*; Maldonado Cárdenas, "Las Paletas del Infiernillo."
146. Schmidt Schoenberg, "La Época prehispánica en Guerrero," 32–33; Padilla Gutiérrez, "La Cerámica blanco granular." Blanco granular is still made in Tulimán, Ameyaltepec, and San Agustín Oapan.
147. Meanwell, "Technical Requirements," 327.
148. Pulido Méndez, "Datos para la historia."
149. Silverstein, "A Study of Late Postclassic Aztec-Tarascan Frontier," 310–11, 314; Von Mentz, *Señoríos indígenas*, 55–61, 63–68. Albiez-Wieck, "Contactos exteriores del Estado Tarasco," 66–70, notes interaction between the Tarascan empire and Oztuma, as well as several other *altepetl* of the Tierra Caliente of Guerrero, which ignores what the historical literature regards as a hostile frontier.

150. Berdan, "Ports of Trade"; Berdan, "Aztec Merchants and Markets"; Gutiérrez, "Negotiating Aztec Tributary Demands."
151. Good, "Salt Production."
152. Kyle, "From Burros to Buses."

Chapter Two

1. Grove, "Olmec Horizons"; Grove, "Olmec Archaeology"; Diehl, "Olmec Archaeology After 'Regional Perspectives'"; Clark and Pye, "The Pacific Coast and the Olmec Question"; Blomster and Cheetham, *The Early Olmec and Mesoamerica*; Blomster, Neff, and Glascock, "Olmec Pottery."
2. Blomster, Neff, and Glascock, "Olmec Pottery."
3. Sharer et al., "On the Logic of Archaeological Inference."
4. Jiménez García, Martínez Donjuán, and Arboleyda Castro, "Época prehispánica," 35–50.
5. Jiménez García, Martínez Donjuán, and Arboleyda Castro, "Época prehispánica," 35–50; Martínez Donjuán, "Los olmecas"; Grove and Paradis, "An Olmec Stela from San Miguel Amuco"; Henderson, *Atopula, Guerrero and Olmec Horizons*.
6. Grove, "Olmec Archaeology," 85.
7. Sharer et al., "On the Logic of Archaeological Inference," 99. The exception is a stone head about 1 meter tall that bears similarities to the colossal heads of the Gulf but lacks their monumentality and aesthetic. Martínez Donjuán, "Sculpture from Teopantecuanitlan," 71–74.
8. Grove, "The Olmec Paintings of Oxtotitlan."
9. Schmidt, "Arqueología de Superficie," 15–16.
10. Russ et al., "Strategies for 14C Dating the Oxtotitlán Cave Paintings."
11. Evans, *Ancient Mexico*, 146–48; Coe and Koontz, *Mexico*, 67–68.
12. The jaguar was the alter ego of the ruler-shaman in many Mesoamerican societies. Evans, *Ancient Mexico*, 167.
13. Cabrera Guerrero, *Las Grutas de Juxtlahuaca*. For a comparison of the Juxtlahuaca and Oxtotitlán paintings, see Grove, "The Olmec Paintings of Oxtotitlan Cave," 29–31. The serpent and the plumed serpent, like the jaguar, were ceremonially and religiously significant. Evans, *Ancient Mexico*, 364–65.
14. Cabrera Guerrero, *Las Grutas de Juxtlahuaca*.
15. Gutiérrez Mendoza, *Catálogo de sitios*, 208–22.

16. Gutiérrez and Pye, "Los gobernadores de Techan"; Evans, *Ancient Mexico*, 259–60, 428 notes the ceremonial and sacred importance of caves throughout Mesoamerica.
17. Grove, *Chalcatzingo*, 25–27, 34, 110–11.
18. Pérez Negrete, Martz de la Vega, Rueda Robledo, and Aguilera Almanza, *De árboles cósmicos*. For examples of Guerrero's rock art, see Reyes Álvarez and Guerrero Gómez, *Geometrías de la imaginación*. For rock art in Acapulco, Manzanilla López and Mena Cruz, "Arqueología de la Punta Diamante"; Cabrera Gurerrero, "The Cave of the Bat"; Cabrera Guerrero, "Las pinturas rupestres de la Cueva de Pie de la Cuesta." For an example in Xochipala, see Reyna Robles, "Las pinturas de la cueva del Cerro Tláloc." For Tierra Caliente rock paintings and petroglyphs, Rodríguez Betancourt, "Desarrollo cultural en la región de Mezcala-Tetela del Río."
19. Matos Moctezuma, "Presencia del Sur." Mezcala sculpture was one of many offerings from Guerrero in the Templo Mayor of Tenochtitlan. Umberger, "Antiques, Revivals."
20. Gay, "Mezcala: herencia cultural."
21. Paradis, Bélanger, Raby, and Ross, "Le Style Mezcala," 203–8.
22. Gay, *Mezcala: Architecture*; Schávelzon, *Treinta siglos de imágenes*.
23. Reyna Robles, "Inspección arqueológica," 144; Gay, *Mezcala: Architecture in Miniature*, 19, estimates 20,000–25,000 pieces are in museums and private collections.
24. Paradis, Bélanger, Raby, and Ross, "Le Style Mezcala," 209–10; Paradis, "El estilo Mezcala," 65; Schávelzon, *Treinta siglos de imágenes*, 72–77. Mezcala sculptures have been found in context at Cuetlajuchitlán in the North, Las Vinatas and La Organera-Xochipala in the Center. Manzanilla López, Talavera González, and Rojas Chávez, "Interpretaciones de la dinámica cultural," 289–90; Reyna Robles, *La Organera-Xochipala*, 361; Reyna Robles, "Inspección arqueológica," 137–38, 142–45.
25. For a concise summary, González and Olmedo Vera, *Esculturas mezcala*, 15–26.
26. Castro, "El estilo Mezcala," 72–95.
27. Gay, *Mezcala: Architecture in Miniature*, 29–35. For an analysis of the manufacturing process, Monterrosa Desruelles and Melgar Tísoc, "Tecnología de cuentas," 4–6; Pineda Santa Cruz, "Análisis de huellas de manufactura."
28. Niederberger, "Nácar," 188–89.
29. Paradis, "Ahuináhuac."

30. Reyna Robles, "La cultura arqueológica Mezcala," 114–18; Schmidt Schoenberg, "Secuencia arqueológica."
31. Gay, *Xochipala*. See also Griffin, "*Xochipala*." Both include many photos.
32. Miller, "The Ballgame."
33. Reyna Robles, "La Organera-Xochipala, Guerrero," 43–44.
34. Schmidt Schoenberg, *Arqueología de Xochipala*, 213–21; Reyna Robles, *La Organera-Xochipala*, 323–32, 403–5.
35. Just, "Xochipala: Salvaging a Looted Culture." Thermoluminiscence dates include a wide range of uncertainty. At a maximum, Xochipala sculptures could date from 2380 BCE to 508 CE.
36. Paradis, "The Tierra Caliente," 252–54.
37. Martínez Donjuán, "Sculpture from Teopantecuanlitlan." For Monument 9 at Chalcatzingo, Grove, *Chalcatzingo*, 48, 50.
38. Martínez Donjuán, "Sculpture from Teopantecuanitlan"; Martínez Donjuán, "Teopantecuanitlan, Guerrero," 124–25.
39. Piña Chan, "Algunos sitios arqueológicos," 73–74.
40. Gutiérrez Mendoza, *Catálogo de sitios*, 333.
41. Urcid, "The Pacific Coast." For the decline of Teotihuacan and Monte Albán, Evans, *Ancient Mexico*, 270–74, 384–85.
42. Gutiérrez Mendoza, *Catálogo de sitios*, 333. Reyes Àlvarez, "Piedra Labrada," also reads the glyph as 10 Nudo and describes the figure in detail.
43. Díaz Oyarzábal, "La presencia teotihuacana"; Reyna Robles, "Esculturas, estelas y lápidas," 368. Nielsen, Jiménez García, and Rivera, "Across the Hills," 187–89, argue that the iconography of Classic stelae in Guerrero indicates that Teotihuacan exercised direct control in the region.
44. Reyna Robles, "Esculturas, estelas," 364–65.
45. Reyna Robles, "Esculturas, estelas," 359–60.
46. H. J. Spinden, "An Ancient Sepulchre at Placeres Del Oro," 34–37.
47. Cepeda Cárdenas, "Estela del Cerro de los Monos."
48. Nielsen, Jiménez García, and Rivera, "Across the Hills," 191–96.
49. Armillas, "Expediciones en el occidente," 80–81; Reyna Robles, "Esculturas, estelas," 366; Paul Schmidt, e-mail to author, January 20, 2021.
50. Gutiérrez, "The Cohimbre Stela."
51. García Payón, "Estudio Preliminar." For a recent study, Gutiérrez Mendoza, *Catálogo de sitios*, 6, 243–50.
52. Jiménez García, "Apuntes," 393–95.

53. Reyna Robles, "De la antigüedad"; Reyna Robles, *La Organera-Xochipala*, 31, 46–47, 50–51, 87–90; Reyna Robles and González Quintero, *Rescate arqueológico de un espacio funerario*; Martínez Donjuán, "Los olmecas," 160–61; Schmidt Schoenberg, *Arqueología de Xochipala*, 16–37, 91–97.
54. Reyna Robles, *La Organera-Xochipala*, 93–94, 405. For other sites, Paradis, "Ahuináhuac," 80–85; Reyna Robles, "La época Clásica," 225–27; Arana, *Proyecto Coatlan*, 144, 148–49.
55. Reyna Robles, "La cultura arqueológica Mezcala," 112–13; Schmidt, "Arqueología de superficie," 15.
56. Reyna Robles, *La Organera-Xochipala*, 44, 49–50, 300, 325–26, 337–38, 361.
57. Reyna Robles, "La cultura arqueológica Mezcala," 108–11; Schmidt, "Arqueología de superficie," 15; Schmidt Schoenberg, "La época prehispánica en Guerrero," 33–34.
58. Niederberger, "Nácar," 182, 198–99; Martínez Donjuán, "Los olmecas," 151–54.
59. Paradis, "Ahuináhuac," 94; Niederberger, "Nácar," 210–11; Reyna Robles, *La Organera-Xochipala*, 358–59; Silverstein, "A Study of the Late Postclassic Aztec-Tarascan Frontier," 224–25; Pulido Méndez, "Datos para la historia," 310–11; Gutiérrez, "The Expanding Polity," 92, 94, 111. Baby-face figurines have been found in the Tierra Caliente and on the Costa Grande. Jiménez García, Martínez Donjuán, and Arboleyda Castro, "Época prehispánica," 36.
60. Jiménez García, Martínez Donjuán, and Arboleyda Castro, "Época prehispánica," 69–73.
61. Oettinger and Horcasitas, "Lienzo of Petlacala," 15.
62. Sandstrom and Effrein Sandstrom, *Traditional Papermaking*, 12–15.
63. Armillas, "Expediciones en el occidente," 85; Litvak King, *Cihuatlán y Tepecoacuilco*, 54; Chadwick, "Archaeological Synthesis of Michoacán," 679.
64. For the distinction between a codex, a lienzo, and a mapa, see Wood, *Transcending Conquest*, 12, 158, note 11; Terraciano, *The Mixtecs*, 19–31; Hill Boone, "Manuscript Painting, 193–96.
65. Gutiérrez, "The Expanding Polity," 16–18; Dakin Anderson, "El náhuatl del Norte," 198, 311–17; Jiménez P. and Villela F., *Historia y cultura*, 111–14; Barlow, "El Palimsesto de veinte mazorcas," 97–110; Galarza, *Lienzos de Chiepetlan*, 25–67.

66. Gruzinski, *The Conquest of Mexico*, 1–70; Vega Sosa, "The Annals of Tlapanecs," 34–52; Oettinger and Horcasitas, "Lienzo of Petlacala," 50–60; Jiménez P. and Villela F., *Historia y cultura*, 36, 155, 173.
67. Villela F., "El Códice Panel de Chiepetlán," 133–46.
68. Dehouve, "Dos relatos sobre migraciones nahuas," 137–48.
69. Galarza, *Lienzos de Chiepetlan*, 25–67; Villela F., "El Códice Panel de Chiepetlán." For the similar case of Tlaquilcingo, Jiménez P. and Villela F., *Historia y cultura*, 45. For a convenient overview of migration to the Montaña, see Dehouve, "La migración, una tradición prehispánica."
70. Galarza, *Lienzos de Chiepetlan*, 25–67.
71. Galarza, *Lienzos de Chiepetlan*, 95–115, 117–19, 121–23, 167–79. *Lienzo III* is a genre of document known as a *título primordial*. These recorded a survey of borders but also included topics such as the first foundation, the coming of the Spaniards, and Christianity. Lockhart, *Nahuas and Spaniards*, 39–64.
72. Oettinger and Horcasitas, "Lienzo of Petlacala," 50–58. The current lienzo is a 1953 copy of an older original.
73. Jiménez Padilla and Villela Flores, "Rituales y protocolos de posesión," 94–112; Iwaniszewski, "De Nahualac al Cerro Ehécatl," 497–518. For a similar ceremony in Coachimalco, Jiménez P. and Villela F., *Historia y cultura*, 73–76.
74. Gruzinski, *The Conquest of Mexico*, 4.
75. On the enduring importance of lineage, see Oudijk, "El Señorío de Tlapa-Tlachinollan," 73–229; Jiménez García, "La nobleza indígena de la Montaña," 35–37, 115–19.
76. Gutiérrez and Brito, *El Códice Azoyú 2*; Gutiérrez, "The Expanding Polity," 4–24; Vega Sosa, "El Códice Azoyú 1 y el Lienzo de Tlapa"; Hill Boone, "Manuscript Painting," 181–92.
77. Oudijk, "El Señorío de Tlapa-Tlachinollan," 78–82. El Códice de Cualác also records lineages of Tlapa-Tlachinollan. Jiménez P. and Villela F., *Historia y cultura*, 128–32.
78. Vega Sosa, "El Códice Azoyú 1 y el Lienzo de Tlapa"; Vega Sosa, "The Annals of the Tlapanecs"; Vega Sosa, "La Ruta de Ahuitzotl"; Gutiérrez, "The Expanding Polity," 157–230; Gutiérrez and Brito, *El Códice Azoyú 2*, 19–20, 22–23, 74–78; Oudijk, "El Señorío de Tlapa-Tlachinollan," 103–70; Barlow, "El palimsesto de veinte mazorcas." Oudijk, "Señorío de Tlapa-Tlachinollan," 136–37, reading folio 24 of the *Códice de Azoyú 1*, together with folio 5 of the *Códice de Azoyú 2*, reads the Mexica lord's name as Insecto en el Agua and the ruler

of Tlapa-Tlachinollan as 4 Lluvia. The chronology and names of the last rulers of Tlapa-Tlachinollan discussed here are based on Vega Sosa, "Códice Azoyú 2 y Humboldt Fragmento 1," 24, 36, 57. Other studies read the names of rulers and the events differently. Gutiérrez and Brito, *Códice Azoyú 2*, 74–78, for example, state that Conejo was succeeded by Coyote-Abuelo. Oudijk, "El Señorío de Tlapa-Tlachinollan," 58–60, 159–65, offers the most complex and detailed reading. Conejo (whose Spanish name was Don Domingo Cortés Quapoltochin) succeeded Serpiente-Espina de Maguey in 1542, but his rule was interrupted by elite disputes, and he was temporarily replaced in office by Señor Agua. However, Conejo returned to power in 1544 after the death of Señor Agua.

79. Huerta Carrillo and Berthier Villaseñor, "Análisis y técnica de manufactura."
80. Hill Boone, "Manuscript Painting," 182–92.
81. For example, in Fol. 25 of the Códice de Azoyú 2 three mortuary bundles signal the incorporation of Yoallan into Tlapa-Tlachinollan's polity. Oudijk, "El Señorío de Tlapa-Tlachinollan," 139.
82. Gutiérrez, "The Expanding Polity," 3–13.
83. Evans, *Ancient Mexico*, 261–62, 281–86, 361, 469–72, 485–87, 510–14; Hassig, *Aztec Warfare*.
84. Hirth, *The Aztec Economic World*, 224–25.
85. Dehouve, *Entre el caimán*, 29–32; Vélez Calvo, "Etnohistoria," 164–340; Marino Flores, "Panorama étnica."
86. Dirección General de Estadística, *Quinto censo de población*; Hendrichs Pérez, *Por tierras ignotas*, 1:20, confirms the existence of a small group of Cuitlatecs in the 1940s and 2:130–246 describes Cuitlatec vocabulary and grammar.
87. Vélez Calvo, "Etnohistoria," 153–61.
88. Paredes Martínez, "Los pueblos originarios del oriente"; Vélez Calvo, "Etnohistoria," 164–70.
89. Von Mentz, *Señoríos indígenas*, 25–44, 313–14, 418–28. Chontal is one of several unclassified languages. Campbell, "Middle American Languages," 905, 947; Marino Flores, "Panorama étnica," 531–33.
90. Meza Herrera, "Yopes y tlapanecas."
91. Gutiérrez Mendoza, "La organización político-territorial," 326–57; Vega Sosa, "The Annals of the Tlapanecs."
92. Von Mentz, *Señoríos indígenas*, 40–41, 80–83.
93. Canger, "Los dialectos náhuatl de Guerrero."

94. Dehouve, "Dos relatos"; Dehouve, *Hacia una historia del espacio*, 26–45; Oettinger and Horcasitas, "Lienzo of Petlacala," 26–45.
95. Renfrew and Bahn, *Archaeology*, 194.
96. Love, "Recent Research," 279–80.
97. Servín Carlos, "La frontera multilingüe de la Tierra Caliente," 153.
98. Lockhart, *Nahuas and Spaniards*, 40–41.
99. Gerhard, *A Guide to the Historical Geography of New Spain*, 22–28.
100. Gerhard, *A Guide to the Historical Geography of New Spain*, 24–25.
101. Gutiérrez, "The Expanding Polity," 6–7; Gutiérrez, *The Aztec Conquest of the Kingdom of Tlapa*, 44; Gerardo Gutiérrez, e-mail to author, August 22, 2019.
102. Litvak King, *Cihuatlán y Tepecoacuilco*, 101–2, 110–11.
103. Dirección de Geografía, Meteorología e Hidrología, *Atlas Geográfico*, cites the figure of 64,458 kilometers^2 for the territorial extent of Guerrero. For the modern population, *XII censo general de población*. The definition of the Montaña is in Gutiérrez, "The Expanding Polity," 34.
104. Borah and Cook, *The Population of Central Mexico in 1548*, 109–15.
105. Borah and Cook, *The Aboriginal Population of Central Mexico*.
106. Vélez Calvo, "Etnohistoria," 164–70, 184–89, 210–21, 234–39, 259–63, 281–302. For a map of language distribution, Jiménez García, Martínez Donjuán, and Arboleyda Castro, "Época prehispánica," fig. 34.

Chapter Three

1. See chapter 1, section 1.1; Manzanilla López, *La región arqueológica de la Costa Grande*, 98–110.
2. See discussions of these sites in chapters 1 and 2.
3. Manzanilla López, *La región arqueológica de la Costa Grande*, 110–33.
4. González Crespo, *Patrón de asentamiento*; Maldonado, *Ofrendas*.
5. J. López, "Teotihuacan y el estado de Guerrero," 16–19; Díaz Oyarzábal, "La presencia teotihuacana"; Schmidt Schoenberg, "La época prehispánica," 29, 32–33; Jiménez García, Martínez Donjuán, and Arboleyda Castro, "Época prehispánica," 79–83, 116–17; Gutiérrez, "The Expanding Polity," 91–93, 115–23, 130, 309, 357, 359.
6. Nielsen, Jiménez García, and Rivera, "Across the Hills."
7. Gutiérrez, "The Expanding Polity," 123.
8. Reyna Robles, "Movimientos de población," 15–17.

9. Jiménez García, Martínez Donjuán, and Arboleyda Castro, "Época prehispánica," 95–97; Jiménez García, "Apuntes," 302–12, 393–96; Monterrosa Desruelles, "Proyecto Arqueológico Pezuapan," 1; Pérez Negrete, Martz de la Vega, Rueda Robledo, and Aguilera Almanza, *De árboles cósmicos*, 17; Maldonado, *Ofrendas*, 132.
10. Evans, *Ancient Mexico*, 418–19.
11. Gutiérrez, "The Expanding Polity," 11–12.
12. Gutiérrez, "The Expanding Polity," 6–7, 44, 51; Gutiérrez, *The Aztec Conquest*, 44; Gerardo Gutiérrez, e-mail to author, August 22, 2019.
13. Gutiérrez, "The Expanding Polity," 37–39, 230; Gutiérrez Mendoza, *Catálogo de sitios*; Gutiérrez Mendoza, "La Organización político-territorial," 324–26; Meza Herrera, "Yopes y tlapanecas," 397–400; Jiménez García, "Apuntes," 396–401.
14. Hassig, *Aztec Warfare*, 65–72.
15. Gutiérrez, "The Expanding Polity," 4–7.
16. Pérez Rodríguez and Heredia Espinoza, *La epopeya de la Mixteca*, 199–235.
17. Gutiérrez, "The Expanding Polity," 13, 157–94; Gutiérrez and Brito, *El Códice Azoyú 2*; Vega Sosa, "Annals," 50–52; Vega Sosa, "La Ruta de Ahuitzotl."
18. Gutiérrez, "The Expanding Polity," 211–12, 218, 221.
19. Vega Sosa, "La Ruta de Ahuitzotl," 508–9; Barlow, "Conquistas de los antiguos mexicanos," 218; Litvak King, *Cihuatlán y Tepecoacuilco*, 68–69.
20. Gutiérrez, "The Expanding Polity," 194–209; Vega Sosa, "Annals," 46–50; Gutiérrez and Brito, *El Códice Azoyú 2*, 100–108. The interpretation of the succession to Señor Lluvia summarized here is in Gutiérrez, "The Expanding Polity," 198–207. Other studies differ as to the exact events, rulers, and participants involved. According to Gutiérrez and Brito, *El Códice Azoyú 2*, 107–9, conflicts occurred under both Señor Lluvia and his successor Señor Serpiente de Turquesa. In this account, Señor Mono was a lord sacrificed in the course of annexing Atlamaxac (Atlamajac) and Ixcateopan. Vega Sosa, "Annals," 46–47, identifies Señor Lluvia as Lord Tláloc, who was succeeded by Lord Turquoise Serpent (no reference is made to Mono). Similarly, Vega Sosa, "Códice Azoyú 2 y Humboldt Fragmento 1," 29, records that Señor Serpiente de Turquesa succeeded Señor Lluvia. Oudijk, "Señorío de Tlapa-Tlachinollan," 136–41, offers yet another interpretation, based on close readings of the differences between the *Códice de Azoyú 1* and the

Códice de Azoyú 2. The agreement that Señor 4 Lluvia, ruler of Tlapa-Tlachinollan, reached with a Mexica envoy Señor Insecto en Agua, and succession problems after the death of 4 Lluvia, triggered internal conflicts in Tlapa-Tlachinollan. Señor 4 Lluvia's successor, Serpiente que se Quema (or de Fuego), was succeeded by Señor 3 Mono. Thus, the precise sequence of events in the history of Tlapa-Tlachinollan narrated in the *Códices de Azoyú 1 and 2* is subject to several interpretations.

21. Gutiérrez, "The Expanding Polity," 15–26.
22. Dibble and Anderson, *Florentine Codex*, 187. In contrast, Sahagún describes the Tlappaneca thus: "They are not speakers of a barbarous tongue; they speak Nahuatl. These are very rich." Ibid., 187.
23. Davies, *Los señoríos independientes*, 157–62.
24. Vélez Calvo, "Etnohistoria," 184–210; Meza Herrera, "Yopes y tlapanecas"; Jiménez García, Martínez Donjuán, and Arboleyda Castro, "Época prehispánica," 90–97; Vié-Wohrer, "Huellas del culto de Xipe Totec"; Widmer, *Conquista y despertar*, 153–55; Ball and Brockington, "Trade and Travel"; Gutiérrez, "The Expanding Polity," 94, 96–105; Dehouve, *Entre el caimán*, 34–36.
25. Gerhard, *A Guide to the Historical Geography of New Spain*, 39.
26. For an overall description of the site, Pérez Negrete and Arana Álvarez, "Proyecto arqueológico Tehuacalco," For the ballcourt, Moreno Hernández, "Excavación y restauración integral." For the settlement pattern, Román Ramos, "Primeras aproximaciones."
27. Gerhard, *A Guide to the Historical Geography of New Spain*, 39, 148–49, 393–94; Jiménez García, Martínez Donjuán, and Arboleyda Castro, "Época prehispánica," 95–97.
28. Jacobs Muller, *El Códice de Cualác*.
29. Megged, "Salvaging Recurring Themes."
30. Von Mentz, *Señoríos indígenas*, 25–102; Martínez Baracs, "Documentos en náhuatl de Oztuma"; "Relación de Ichcateupan."
31. Pollard, *Taríacuri's Legacy*, 169–70; Litvak King, *Cihuatlán y Tepecoacuilco*, 66–70.
32. Pollard, *Taríacuri's Legacy*, 133.
33. Pollard, *Taríacuri's Legacy*, 12, 26–27, 167–69; Paredes M., "Sistemas de intercambio."
34. Convenient summaries of the conquests of each tlatoani are in Berdan and Anawalt, *The Essential Codex Mendoza*, 2:14–25. See also Hassig, *Aztec Warfare*, 157–224; Davies, *The Aztec Empire*, 50–100; Barlow, "Conquistas."

35. Hassig, *Aztec Warfare*, 17–26, 208–11.
36. Berdan, Blanton, Hill Boone, Hodge, Smith, and Umberger, *Aztec Imperial Strategies*, 110–13, 115–50.
37. Litvak King, *Cihuatlán y Tepecoacuilco*, 68–70.
38. Von Mentz, *Señoríos indígenas*, 39–44.
39. Hassig, *Aztec Warfare*, 17, 21–26, 147–48; Berdan, Blanton, Hill Boone, Hodge, Smith, and Umberger, *Aztec Imperial Strategies*, 110–12.
40. Silverstein, "Aztec Imperialism."
41. Hill Boone, "Manuscript Painting," 181–92.
42. Umberger, "Aztec Presence."
43. Umberger, "Aztec Presence"; Silverstein, "Aztec Imperialism."
44. Berdan, "Economic Dimensions," 319.
45. Barlow, *The Extent of the Empire*, 8–22, 82–84.
46. Litvak King, *Cihuatlán y Tepecoacuilco*, 89–90, 99–102, 108. My figures are based on Litvak King's assumptions of agricultural productivity. In some cases our figures differ slightly.
47. Litvak King, *Cihuatlán y Tepecoacuilco*, 101–2, 109. Cihuatlán's tribute did not include bulky crops.
48. Anderson and Barlow, "The Maize Tribute of Moctezuma's Empire," 413–18, 420.
49. Berdan, "Cotton in Aztec Mexico."
50. Gutiérrez, "Negotiating Aztec Tributary Demands"; Berdan, "Aztec Merchants." According to Berdan, tribute stimulated exchange in local markets.
51. Berdan, Blanton, Hill Boone, Hodge, Smith, and Umberger, *Aztec Imperial Strategies*, 141–47. For the Mexica-Tarascan frontier, Silverstein, "Aztec-Tarascan Frontier"; and Silverstein, "La frontera mexica-tarasca." For the Yope frontier, Davies, *Los señoríos independientes*, 157–62, 215–24; and Vélez Calvo, "Etnohistoria," 189–96.
52. Silverstein, "Aztec-Tarascan Frontier," 326.
53. Silverstein, "Aztec-Tarascan Frontier," 104–26, 288–90.
54. Pollard, *Taríacuri's Legacy*, 109–32, for the quote, 122.
55. Hassig, *Aztec Warfare*, 208–11.
56. Pollard, *Taríacuri's Legacy*, 92. For a list of conquests and maps of the Tarascan state, 5, 8, 89, 91, 93, 94–98, 100, 117, 127. For a list of battles between the Tarascans and the Mexica, 169–70.
57. Pollard, *Taríacuri's Legacy*, 103.
58. Pollard, *Taríacuri's Legacy*, 122–28.

59. Silverstein, "Aztec-Tarascan Frontier," 108–25.
60. Silverstein, "Aztec-Tarascan Frontier," 120–21; Smith, Burke, Hare, and Glascock, "Sources of Imported Obsidian," 429–50. On the permeability of the Tarascan-Mexica frontier, see Albiez-Wieck, "Contactos exteriores del Estado Tarasco," 66–70.
61. Silverstein, "Aztec-Tarascan Frontier," 114.
62. "Relación de Sirandaro y Guayameo," 265. Author's translation.

Chapter Four

1. Von Mentz, *Señoríos indígenas*, 99–101. On Indigenous allies, Restall, *Seven Myths*, 46–51; and Oudijk and Restall, *Conquistas de buenas palabras*.
2. Reyes García, *Documentos manuscritos*, 187–92.
3. Restall, *Seven Myths*, 22–23.
4. "Relación de la Villa de Zacatula," 449–52; Widmer, *Conquista y despertar*, 59–61; Labarthe R., "Provincia de Zacatula," 62–78.
5. Widmer, *Conquista y despertar*, 60–62; Himmerich y Valencia, *The Encomenderos*, 120–21.
6. Paso y Troncoso, *Epistolario de Nueva España*, 2:29–33, 62; Widmer, *Conquista y despertar*, 153–56; Himmerich y Valencia, *The Encomenderos*, 211; Álvarez, *Diccionario de conquistadores*, 2:432–33. Pardo reported that the Yopes killed many "mexicanos" in Cuscotitlan and carried off 250 of them as prisoners. Perhaps these were Mexican allies who came to Guerrero with the Spaniards or, alternatively, settlers under Mexica rule sent to contain the Yopes.
7. Castrejón Díez, "Una ciudad minera"; Haskett, "Our Suffering."
8. "Relación de Sirandaro y Guayameo," 262; Millares Carlo and Mantecón, eds., *Índice y extractos*, 1:274; *Historia de Chilpancingo*, 81–84, 86. For Garrido and cases of other Black conquistadors, Restall, "Black Conquistadors."
9. Millares Carlo and Mantecón, eds., *Índice y extractos*, 1:32, 40, 80, 142, 177, 181, 183, 195, 239, 276; Ruiz Medrano, *Reshaping New Spain*, 265–97; Schwaller, *Partidos*.
10. Icaza, *Diccionario autobiográfico*; *Probanzas de méritos* were also submitted by Indigenous nobles, Oudijk and Restall, *Conquistas de buenas palabras*, 15–18.

11. Millares Carlo and Mantecón, eds., *Índice y extractos*.
12. The term *Provincia de la Plata* designated the mining districts of Temascaltepec, Zultepec, Zacualpan, and Taxco from the 1530s. García Mendoza, "La formación de grupos de poder," 19–20.
13. Schwaller, *Partidos*.
14. Millares Carlo and Mantecón, eds., *Índice y extractos*, passim.
15. For gold tribute, chapter 6; for livestock grazing, chapter 7. The case of Tlapa is an exception to the rule noted by Lockhart and Schwartz, *Early Latin America*, 100–101, that gold was mined by Indian slaves. On the other hand, as has been noted, coastal mining involved both slaves and encomienda labor.
16. See chapter 6.
17. "Relación de las minas de Zumpango," 196–97; Icaza, *Diccionario autobiográfico*, 1:92, 2:111, 196, 299–300, 329–30, 337; Paso y Troncoso, *Epistolario de Nueva España*, 3:148–49; García Mendoza, "La formación de grupos de poder," 228.
18. For examples of contracts concerning African and Indian slaves, see Millares Carlo and Mantecón, eds., *Índice y extractos*, 1:28, 45, 117, 119, 174, 175. For labor and slavery in the Taxco mines, see Von Mentz, *Señoríos indígenas*, 173–78, 295–305. See also chapter 8.
19. Simpson, *The Encomienda*.
20. Gibson, *The Aztecs Under Spanish Rule*, 223–30.
21. For landowning in the Taxco area, see Álvarez, *Diccionario de conquistadores*, 1:120–21; Amith, "The Möbius Strip," 1109–12; Gerhard, *A Guide to the Historical Geography of New Spain*, 309.
22. See, for example, *El libro de tasaciones*, 60–62, 146–49, 190–92. For landownership, Álvarez, *Diccionario de conquistadores*, 2:352–55; García Izcabalzeta and García Pimentel, *Descripción del Arzobispado*, 242; Von Mentz, *Señoríos indígenas*, 313–14, 359–60, 362, 364–65. Until more studies of land grants in this region are conducted, data on landholding in the Tierra Caliente will remain incomplete.
23. For the Montaña, Mota y Escobar, *Memoriales del Obispo de Tlaxcala*, 106–15. For secular priests, Schwaller, *Partidos*.
24. Schwaller, *Partidos*.
25. Gibson, *The Aztecs under Spanish Rule*, 81–92; Lockhart, *The Nahuas After the Conquest*, 46–47; Ruiz Medrano, *Reshaping New Spain*, 42–51, 95–116, 265–97; concerning Indigenous cabildos acting independently, see Lockhart, Berdan, and Anderson, *The Tlaxcalan Actas*, 14–16.

26. Ruiz Medrano, *Reshaping New Spain*, 90, 98–108, 111, 271, 274, 277, 286–88; Porras Muñoz, *El gobierno de la ciudad de México*, 234–38; Álvarez, *Diccionario de conquistadores*, 1:120–21, 126–28, 142–43, 168–69, 2:332–34; Gerhard, *Síntesis e índice*, 288; Bonialian, *La América española*, 141–43.
27. Millares Carlo and Mantecón, eds., *Índice y extractos*, 2:23.
28. *Procesos de Luis Carvajal*, 44, 152–53, 169–71, 309–408.
29. King, *Juan Ruiz de Alarcón*, 31–32. King notes also shopkeepers, butchers, and bakers.
30. Contreras, *Taxco en el siglo XVI*, 150–51.
31. Haskett, "Our Suffering," 454–55.
32. Von Mentz, *Señoríos indígenas*, 246–47; *El Libro de tasaciones*, 146–49, 158–61, 449–52.
33. Machuca, "El Arribo de plantas," 73–114.
34. Millares Carlo and Mantecón, eds., *Índice y extractos*, 1:208, 2:57.
35. Von Mentz, *Señoríos indígenas*, 297.
36. Mota y Escobar, *Memoriales*, 106–7; Haskett, "Not a Pastor"; Von Mentz, *Señoríos indígenas*, 130–36; Von Mentz, *Cuauhnáhuac*, 285–90; Litvak King, *Cihuatlán y Tepecoacuilco*, 101–2.
37. Vázquez de Espinosa, *Compendio y descripción*, 266–67.
38. Millares Carlo and Mantecón, eds., *Índice y extractos*, 1:78, 237, 241, 256, 261–63, 272, 275; Himmerich y Valencia, *The Encomenderos*, 113–14.
39. Millares Carlo and Mantecón, *Índice y extractos*, 1, 264; Himmerich y Valencia, *The Encomenderos*, 131, 190; "Relación de la Villa de Zacatula," 451–52.
40. Millares Carlo and Mantecón, eds., *Índice y extractos*, 1:237, 239, 241, 276.
41. Schwaller, *Partidos*; Millares Carlo and Mantecón, eds., *Índice y extractos*, 1:78, 135, 195, 206, 232, 262, 314, 320, 354.
42. Millares Carlo and Mantecón, eds., *Índice y extractos*, 1:183, 188–189, 217, 320.
43. Millares Carlo and Mantecón, eds., *Índice y extractos*, 1:45, 142, 181, 195, 241, 278.
44. Millares Carlo and Mantecón, eds., *Índice y extractos*, 1:282–83, 317. This Pedro López may have been the Pedro López de Alcántara who was an encomendero in Veracruz, a regidor in Puebla, and a magistrate in several towns. Álvarez, *Diccionario de conquistadores*, 2:310.
45. See 4.3. Martínez was probably a secular priest, although sources do not confirm this.

46. Widmer, *Conquista y despertar*, 78.
47. See 4.1.
48. Grijalva, *Crónica*, 36.
49. Grijalva, *Crónica*, 35–42; Dehouve, *Quand les banquiers*, 7; Dehouve, "Historia del municipio en la Montaña," 104–5.
50. Torres Aguilar, "Aculturación religiosa," 47.
51. Table 4.1.
52. Widmer, *Conquista y despertar*, 77–78.
53. Torres Aguilar, "Aculturación religiosa," 67–68.
54. Ortega Ortiz Montero, "Tetela del Río."
55. Schwaller, *Partidos*, 1–2, 18–30, 41–42, 46–51, 71–78, 87, 153–63, 234–41, 273–75, 303–14, 324–27, 332–36, 341–45, 416–21, 468–73, 489–92, 503–11.
56. García Izcabalzeta and García Pimentel, *Descripción del Arzobispado*, 242.
57. *Cartas de Indias*, 210–18.
58. García Izcabalzeta and García Pimentel, *Descripción del Arzobispado*, 241–48.
59. García Izcabalzeta and García Pimentel, *Descripción del Arzobispado*, 192–99.
60. García Izcabalzeta and García Pimentel, *Descripción del Arzobispado*, 96–101.
61. García Izcabalzeta and García Pimentel, *Descripción del Arzobispado*, 170–84.
62. Taylor, *Drinking, Homicide*, 34–45. European wine and brandy may have caused more serious social problems than pulque.
63. García Izcabalzeta and García Pimentel, *Descripción del Arzobispado*, 97, 99.
64. Haskett, "Not a Pastor." For a judicious survey of attitudes to priestly wrongdoing and exemplary conduct in the eighteenth century, see Taylor, *Magistrates of the Sacred*, 182–96 (see 183, 185–86, 195 for some examples from Guerrero).
65. *Cartas de Indias*, 210–11, 215.
66. Reynolds, *El Corregidor Diego Díaz*, especially 119–29.
67. *Cartas de Indias*, 213.
68. Reynolds, *El Corregidor Diego Díaz*, 46–48.
69. Schwaller, *Partidos*, 305–6, 309–14, 333.
70. *Cartas de Indias*, 213.
71. Gerhard, *Síntesis e índice*, 305–6.
72. Von Mentz, *Señoríos indígenas*, 133.

73. Mota y Escobar, *Memoriales*, 106–15. Priests could conduct baptism, but bishops carried out confirmation.
74. Mota y Escobar, *Memoriales*, 108, 109, 112, 115. Author's translation.
75. Mota y Escobar, *Memoriales*, 107–8, 110, 114–15. Author's translation.
76. Mota y Escobar, *Memoriales*, 106–7, 110, 113–14. For the bishop's comment about the friars of Alcozauca, 106, and about Tixtla, 113. Author's translation.
77. Mota y Escobar, *Memoriales*, 110–13. For the comment about Ayutla, 112, and about don Domingo de los Ángeles, 111. Author's translation.
78. For example, see 2.9.
79. Mota y Escobar, *Memoriales*, 111.
80. For the quote, Burkhart, *The Slippery Earth*, 192; and Burkhart, "Flowery Heaven," 89–90.
81. Ruiz de Alarcón, *Tratado de las idolatrías*, especially 23–34, 49, 53, 62–67, 73, 87–88, 94–97, 157–61. For the quote, 53. Author's translation.
82. *Libro primero de votos*, 27, 128, 134–35, 153–54, 157; Uchmany, *La vida entre el judaísmo*, 105, 442–43; *Procesos de Luis de Carvajal*, 44, 118–19, 147, 166, 309, 314, 336–40, 359, 390–93, 408.
83. King, *Juan Ruiz de Alarcón*, 26, 28, 30–31, 34; Uchmany, *La vida entre el judaísmo*, 2–53, 55, 57, 66, 76, 89–92; *Procesos de Luis de Carvajal*, 14, 40–44, 169–71, 309, 440–57; Adler, *Trial of Jorge de Almeida*.
84. *Libro primero de votos*, 6, 20, 38–41, 44–45, 158.
85. *Cartas de Indias*, 216.
86. Mota y Escobar, *Memoriales*, 120.
87. *Libro Primero de votos*, 121.
88. *Libro Primero de votos*, 167.
89. Cohen, "Antonio Díaz de Cáceres," 57–58.
90. Chapter 6.

Chapter Five

1. Von Mentz, *Señoríos indígenas*, 27–31. Conflict between communities was common in precontact Guerrero. For examples, "Relación de la Villa de Zacatula," 456; "Relación de Citlaltomahua y Anecuilco," 114–15.
2. Martínez Baracs, "Documentos en náhuatl de Oztuma," 270–71.
3. Gutiérrez and Brito, *El Códice Azoyú 2*.

4. Vélez Calvo, "Etnohistoria," 153–61.
5. For examples of the importance of local identity and the emergence of municipal government in the Chalco region, see Lockhart, *Nahuas and Spaniards*, 46–57; for Oaxaca, Restall, *Seven Myths*, 122–30; for Cuernavaca, Haskett, *Indigenous Rulers*, 60–85, 95–123, 125–45.
6. Gerhard, *Síntesis e índice*, 573–75. The term *wine* referred to many types of alcoholic drinks in sixteenth-century sources. We cannot know whether these merchants may have been selling wine made from grapes or some other fermented beverage such as pulque. The sale of wine to Indians was prohibited in ordinances of 1594, 1637, and 1640. Taylor, *Drinking, Homicide*, 38–39.
7. Gerhard, *Síntesis e índice*, 294.
8. Chávez Orozco, *Índice del Ramo de Indios*, 2:157.
9. "Relación de la Villa de Zacatula," 441–42, 449–51, 456.
10. "Relación de Xalapa, Cintla y Acatlán," 281–86.
11. "Relación de Iguala y su partido," 341, 345.
12. "Relación de Ajuchitlan y su partido," 30–32.
13. Dehouve, *Quand les banquiers*, 22–27; Dehouve, *Entre el caimán*, 53, 61, 67, 91–95.
14. Von Mentz, *Cuauhnáhuac*, 150–62.
15. Von Mentz, *Cuauhnáhuac*, 105–36.
16. Aguirre Beltrán, *Cuijla*, 52–64; Moedano Navarro, "Notas etnohistóricas"; Pavía Miller, "Mulatos, moriscos y negros"; Oropeza Keresey, "La esclavitud asiática."
17. Dehouve, *Quand les banquiers*, 22–27; Dehouve, *Entre el caimán*, 53, 61, 67, 91–95.
18. Carrillo Cázares, *Partidos y padrones*, 333–47.
19. Dehouve, *Entre el caimán*, 92–94.
20. Dehouve, *Entre el caimán*, 91–95.
21. Dehouve, *Quand les banquiers*, 17–21, 314–15. Dehouve's sources are the "*Relación de Xalapa, Cintla y Acatlán*" and García Castro's *Suma de Visitas*. The questionable figures for 1519 in the "*Relación*" make precise calculations unreliable, but the stark comparison between the Costa Chica and the Montaña (the latter based on a wider range of sources) is credible.
22. Dehouve, *Quand les banquiers*, 17–21, 316–17.
23. Dehouve, *Quand les banquiers*, xvi. Author's translation.
24. Dehouve, *Quand les banquiers*, xvi–xvii. Author's translation.
25. Von Mentz, "Aproximaciones," 52–54.
26. See 2.10.

27. Carrillo Cázares, *Partidos y padrones*, 347–68. Data for the population of Alahuiztlán in 1789 give a similar picture of this Tierra Caliente parish. The priest reported 760 Indian families (all Nahuatl speakers, some of them bilingual) and only 26 families that were not classed as Indian. All of the latter lived either in Alahuiztlán itself or in a subordinate rancho. Taylor, *Magistrates of the Sacred*, 316.
28. For cases of Indigenous communities fashioning their versions of municipal government under Spanish rule, see Lockhart, Berdan, and Anderson, *The Tlaxcalan Actas*; Haskett, *Indigenous Rulers*, 95–123; García Martínez, *Los pueblos de la Sierra*, 65–105.
29. Von Mentz, *Señoríos indígenas*, 40–41, 92–98, 156–71.
30. I am grateful to a reviewer who informed me that Tacatecla seems to be a corruption of Tlacatecatl, a noble title adopted by surviving high nobles in the colonial era.
31. *El libro de tasaciones*, 489–91; Megged, "Salvaging Recurring Themes," 397. In 1561 the case was settled in Ircio's favor, but Jaramillo's widow won on appeal to the Council of the Indies.
32. *El libro de tasaciones*, 272–73.
33. *El libro de tasaciones*, 275–76.
34. Lockhart, *The Nahuas After the Conquest*, 40, 326–27, 445–46, 449; Gruzinski, *The Conquest of Mexico*.
35. Paso y Troncoso, *Epistolario*, 2:209–10, 221. Author's translation. The quote is on page 210. The letter was signed by licenciados Salmerón, Alonso Maldonado, and Ceynos.
36. Ruiz Medrano, *Mexico's Indigenous Communities*, 33–37.
37. Ramírez C., *Códice de Teloloapan*.
38. Ramírez C., *Códice de Teloloapan*; Jiménez P. and Villela F., *Historia y cultura*, 115–17. For studies of Indigenous municipal offices, Lockhart, *Nahuas and Spaniards*, 28–47; Gibson, *The Aztecs Under Spanish Rule*, 166–93; Haskett, *Indigenous Rulers*, 95–123.
39. Batalla Rosado, "Códice de Ohuapan II." Another example of tribute paid to the caja de comunidad is the 1567 assessment for Cutzamala: 43 arrobas and 12 1/2 libras of cotton thread or pinked cotton. *El libro de tasaciones*, 158–61. For the caja de comunidad, see Gibson, *The Aztecs Under Spanish Rule*, 126, 185, 198–99, 213; and Haskett, *Indigenous Rulers*, 62–65. Lockhart, *The Nahuas After the Conquest*, 22–38, notes that the Spaniards saw the altepetl as a core settlement (cabecera) with subordinate sujetos, while the Nahua conceived it as composed of equal units, which all should be represented.

40. Noguez, "Tres documentos pictográficos," 10–11.
41. Noguez, "Tres documentos pictográficos," 10–11.
42. A good overview of the Indigenous documents of Guerrero is Jiménez P. and Villela F., *Historia y cultura*. The same authors' "Rituales y protocolos" examines documents that legitimated Indigenous possession of land and rituals of possession. Amith, *The Möbius Strip*, 70–115, examines the interplay between Spanish legal concepts of property and Indigenous traditions. For a broader discussion of the almost four hundred mapas produced in New Spain between 1570–1630 to claim ownership of land, to control local tribute, and to preserve economic privileges of elites, see Leibsohn, "Colony and Cartography."
43. Bittmann Simons, "Further Notes"; Ramírez Celestino, "El mapa de Tepecuacuilco." There are several other mapas made to assert rights over land; for example, the *Lienzo de Totomixtlahuaca*, late sixteenth century; the *Mapa de Santiago Zapotitlán* (1537, original now lost); the *Mapa de Tecomatlan e Ixtapa* (1585). Jiménez P. and Villela F., *Historia y cultura*, 139, 154, 165.
44. Dehouve, "Les Lienzos de Malinaltepec," 109–39.
45. Berdan, Blanton, Hill Boone, Hodge, Smith, and Umberger, *Aztec Imperial Strategies*, 122–35, 152–59; Gutiérrez, "Negotiating Aztec Tributary Demands," 142–43.
46. On corregidores and alcaldes mayores, see Gibson, *The Aztecs Under Spanish Rule*, 81–97; Borah, *Justice by Insurance*, 149–52.
47. Gerhard, *Síntesis e índice*, 299.
48. Dehouve, *Quand les banquiers*, 112–15. For the case of Huamuxtitlán, see Dehouve, "Les élites indiennes," 18. For an overview of change and continuity in indigenous rule, see Haskett, *Indigenous Rulers*. Lockhart concluded that Nahua governors initially took on much of the prestige and powers of a tlatoani, but that later in the sixteenth century, considerable changes took place in the highest office of an Indigenous municipality, although some change was more superficial than real, and dynastic succession and long-term tenure later reasserted itself. *Nahuas After the Conquest*, 30–35.
49. Martínez Baracs, "Documentos en náhuatl de Oztuma," 270–71, 275.
50. Dehouve, "Les élites indiennes." In Tlaxcala dynastic rulers sat on the cabildo and retained residual power but were not governors, and they could be challenged by regidores. Lockhart, Berdan, and Anderson, *The Tlaxcalan Actas*, 2–3, 7–8.

51. Dehouve, *Entre el caimán*, 86–87; Dehouve, *Quand les banquiers*, 167–68; García Izcabalzeta and García Pimentel, *Descripción del Arzobispado*, 132–34. On Indigenous church officials in other regions, see Lockhart, *The Nahuas After the Conquest*, 206–18; Haskett, *Indigenous Rulers*, 114–20.
52. Von Mentz, *Señoríos indígenas*, 123–24.
53. "Relación de Iguala," 348, 352. See 352 for the quote. Author's translation.
54. Gutiérrez and Brito, *El Códice Azoyú 2*, 100–108.
55. For example, Ruiz de Alarcón, *Tratado de idolatrías*; Mota y Escobar, *Memoriales*, 109, reports the Indians of Tzapotitlan (now Zapotitlán Tablas) and Tlacoapa flatly refused to be confirmed.
56. Dehouve, "Les élites indiennes." Lockhart, *The Nahuas After the Conquest*, 132, argues that Nahua nobility were the authors of a "great and for a time successful scam of extolling their privileges and sweeping their duties under the rug that hoodwinked Spanish authorities into thinking they had been exempt."
57. Gerhard, *Síntesis e índice*, 289. Problems also occurred in the succession of the rulers of Tlapa-Tlachinollan in the Postclassic. Oudijk, "El Señorío de Tlapa-Tlachinollan," 122–23, 140, 158–59.
58. *El libro de tasaciones*, 511–13.
59. Zavala, *Libros de asientos*, 368.
60. Gerhard, *Síntesis e índice*, 287, 289, 290, 296. Tapia was charged with investigating "alguna desorden e innovación" and was told that don Martín had caused much "desasosiego." Gerhard, *Síntesis e índice*, 290. Author's translation. In the second half of the sixteenth century, Indigenous nobles were often appointed to investigate such cases, since they could understand local circumstances and adjudicate sensibly. Lockhart, *The Nahuas After the Conquest*, 34–35.
61. Dehouve, "Les élites indiennes," 18; Gerhard, *Síntesis e índice*, 291. Complaints of this sort were frequent in New Spain. Borah, *Justice by Insurance*, 187–96.
62. Gerhard, *Síntesis e índice*, 308.
63. Zavala, *Libros de asientos*, 379–80.
64. Hernández Jaimes, "El cacicazgo de los Moctezuma"; and Lebeuf, "Origen y genealogía de los Moctezuma."
65. Haskett, "Not a Pastor," 302–3. Cabildo officials were also exempt. See Haskett, *Indigenous Rulers*, 66.
66. Haskett, "Not a Pastor," 299–304.

67. Haskett, "Not a Pastor," 300–301, 315–16.
68. Gerhard, *Síntesis e índice*, 299, 310.
69. Amith, *The Möbius Strip*, 145–51.
70. Paso y Troncoso, *Epistolario*, 8:120.
71. Borah, *Justice by Insurance*, 51, 71; Gibson, *The Aztecs Under Spanish Rule*, 78–81; Haskett, *Visions of Paradise*, 89.
72. Gerhard, *Síntesis e índice*, 573–74.
73. "Relación de Iguala," 352; Gerhard, *Síntesis e índice*, 287, 300, 302; Dehouve, *Quand les banquiers*, 118. In her study of the roles of Indigenous principales in the Sierra Norte of Oaxaca, Yannakakis, in *The Art of Being In-Between*, concludes that they both protected their privileges and tribute but also met at least some of their obligations to defend their community, which could be personally costly and dangerous.
74. Paso y Troncoso, *Epistolario*, 8:116–119, for the quote 116. Author's translation.
75. Borah, *Justice by Insurance*, 206.
76. Dehouve, *Quand les banquiers*, 90–91, 99–101, 168–69, 173, 177–88.
77. Gibson, *The Aztecs Under Spanish Rule*, 126, 185–86, 198–99, 213–17.
78. Haskett, *Indigenous Rulers*, 62–65. For cases concerning community funds in various parts of New Spain, Borah, *Justice by Insurance*, 132, 157–58, 158–60, 206, 211–12.
79. Terraciano, *The Mixtecs of Colonial Oaxaca*, 206, 286.
80. García Izcabalzeta and García Pimentel, *Descripción del Arzobispado*, 150–51, 170, 198.
81. Kartunnen and Lockhart, *Nahuatl in the Middle Years*, 56.
82. Lockhart, Schroeder, and Namala, eds., *Chimalpahin Quauhtlehuanitzin*, 201, 203, 213–17, 229, 237, 243–49.
83. Schwaller, "Constitution of the cofradía del Santissimo Sacramento."
84. Schroeder, "Jesuits, Nahuas, and the Good Death Society."
85. Velasco Murillo, *Urban Indians*, 53–55. For a survey of the cofradía in the late colonial period, see Taylor, *Magistrates of the Sacred*, 301–23, including examples from Guerrero of Ixcatepec in the Tierra Caliente (307), Mochitlán in the Center (313), and the complex case of Alahuiztlán in the Tierra Caliente (316–21).
86. García Izcabalzeta and García Pimentel, *Descripción del Arzobispado*, 150–51, 170, 198; Contreras, *Taxco en el siglo XVI*, 27–37; "Relación de los mandamientos . . . Tasco," 131.
87. Gruzinski, *The Conquest of Mexico*, 241–42; Haskett, "Not a Pastor," 302, 311, 313.

88. Lockhart, *The Nahuas After the Conquest*, 218–29.
89. Von Mentz, *Señoríos indígenas*, 364–68.
90. Amith, "The Möbius Strip," 1093–108.
91. Dehouve, *Quand les banquiers*, 156, cites one example of a woman, doña Gertrudis Maldonado, cacica of Alcozauca, functioning as the majordomo of the cofradía of the Virgin of the Rosary, but does not offer further information as to how frequently women held such positions, nor the nature of gender relations in Alcozauca. Participation of women was characteristic of Mixtec cofradías in Oaxaca. The cofradías of the Oaxacan Mixteca engaged in commerce like sodalities in the Montaña. Terraciano, *The Mixtecs of Colonial Oaxaca*, 206, 286.
92. Dehouve, *Quand les banquiers*, 152–57, 170–73, 200–205.
93. Labarthe R., "Provincia de Zacatula," 131–35.
94. Terraciano, *The Mixtecs of Colonial Oaxaca*, 286.
95. Haskett, *Visions of Paradise*, 106–7, 297.
96. Gibson, *The Aztecs Under Spanish Rule*, 127–32.
97. Velasco Murillo, *Urban Indians*, 53–54, 70–78.
98. Guardino, *Peasants, Politics*, 21–22, 31–33.
99. Von Mentz, *Señoríos indígenas*, 33–34, 92–98, 106.
100. Silverstein, "A Study of the Late Postclassic Aztec-Tarascan Frontier," 57–60, 72–74, 87–88, 314; Silverstein, "Aztec Imperialism."
101. García Castro, *Suma de visitas*, 428–45. This is not the modern Ayutla de los Libres, but another Ayutla in the region of Zacatula.
102. Labarthe R., "Provincia de Zacatula," 184.
103. García Castro, *Suma de visitas*, 480–81, 523; Rubí Alarcón, "El dominio español," 97–103.
104. Widmer, *Conquista y despertar*, 66–72.
105. Pavía Guzmán, "Tlappan," 412–16.
106. García Castro, *Suma de visitas*, 89–90, 150, 200–201, 261, 375–77, 517; Rubí Alarcón, "*República de indios*," 41–43; Rubí Alarcón, "*La encomienda de la Montaña*," 429–40; Dehouve, *Quand les banquiers*, 121–22.
107. García Izcabalzeta and García Pimentel, *Descripción del Arzobispado*, apéndice 2.
108. García Castro, *Suma de visitas*, 523; Rubí Alarcón, "*República de indios*," 39; Megged, "Salvaging Recurring Themes," 387–88. Díaz de Ordaz was a veteran of many campaigns and expediciones: Darien, Cuba, the Noche Triste in Tenochtitlan, and an expedition to explore the Orinoco. He owned land and livestock as well as horticultural land and

houses in Mexico City, and he intentionally avoided mining ventures as a declining and risky business. He died at sea in 1532. Chilapa reverted to the Crown for a time and was then inherited by his nephew Díaz de Ordaz Villagómez. Lope Blanch, *El habla de Diego de Ordaz*, 9–23, 195; Álvarez, *Diccionario de conquistadores*, 2:413–15.

109. García Castro, *Suma de visitas*, 205, 352, 393, 516; Rubí Alarcón, "*República de indios*," 52.
110. García Izcabalzeta and García Pimentel, *Descripción del Arzobispado*, 192. Author's translation.
111. García Izcabalzeta and García Pimentel, *Descripción del Arzobispado*, 192–99.
112. García Castro, *Suma de visitas*, 126, 166, 239, 461, 507, 508, 516.
113. Gerhard, *Síntesis e índice*, 584, 586–87.
114. Gerhard, *Síntesis e índice*, 302.
115. Gerhard, *Síntesis e índice*, 303–4.
116. Gerhard, *Síntesis e índice*, 305.
117. Gerhard, *Síntesis e índice*, 307–8.
118. Gerhard, *Síntesis e índice*, 571, 576.
119. Gerhard, *Síntesis e índice*, 575–76.
120. Terraciano, *The Mixtecs of Colonial Oaxaca*, 227–31.
121. Taylor, *Landlord and Peasant*, 197–201.
122. Barrett, *La Cuenca del Tepalcatepec*, 154–69.
123. Haskett, *Indigenous Rulers*, 73–75, 78–82, 98, 101; Borah, *Justice by Insurance*, 129–48, catalogued litigation concerning land in, for example, Oaxaca, Malinalco, Otumba, San Luis Potosí, and Zacatecas.
124. Wood, "Corporate Adjustments," 195–294; Amith, "Place Making," examines the case of Palula, a community in the North and originally a sujeto of Tepecoacuilco, settled by migrants from the Center on land in the Iguala Valley in the seventeenth century.
125. Dehouve, *Quand les banquiers*, 121–29; Dehouve, "Las separaciones de pueblos"; Dehouve, "Les élites indiennes"; Dehouve, "Historia del municipio," 102–6; Gutiérrez Mendoza, "La Organización político-territorial," 326–27.
126. *El libro de tasaciones*, 492.
127. *El libro de tasaciones*, 357–58.
128. Gerhard, *Síntesis e índice*, 310–11.
129. Martínez Baracs, "Documentos en náhuatl de Oztuma," 274–75. Note that even a sujeto had five rulers.
130. "Relación de Ichcateupan," 283, 292–93.

131. "Relación de Ichcateupan," 315–18.
132. "Relación de Ichcateupan," 321–22. Author's translation.
133. "Relación de Ichcateupan," 322.
134. Sousa and Terraciano, "The 'Original Conquest' of Oaxaca."
135. García Martínez, *Los pueblos de la Sierra*, 210–23, 278–305.
136. Gerhard, "Congregaciones de Indios"; Lockhart, *The Nahuas After the Conquest*, 44–46; Wood, "Corporate Adjustments," 24–49; Torre Villar, *Las congregaciones*, summarizes the sixteenth-century civil congregaciones and provides a detailed study of the seventeenth-century program.
137. Lockhart, *The Nahuas After the Conquest*, 44–46.
138. Wood, "Corporate Adjustments," 24–49.
139. Paredes Martínez, "Los pueblos originarios," 41–43.
140. García Martínez, *Los pueblos de la Sierra*, 152–79.
141. Rubí Alarcón, "El dominio español," 104–8. Porcallo was evidently given to violence. In 1525 he was imprisoned for killing Hernando Cabrera, although he declared himself innocent. In the early 1530s he became encomendero of Tlalcozautitlán in northern Guerrero. The encomienda was still held by his family in 1611. Himmerich y Valencia, *The Encomenderos*, 217–18; Álvarez, *Diccionario de conquistadores*, 2:457.
142. Labarthe R., "Provincia de Zacatula," 153–56; Gerhard, "Congregaciones," 380–82. For the cases of Yanhuitlán and Tecpan, see Torre Villar, *Las Congregaciones*, 136–37, 302–3.
143. Widmer, *Conquista y despertar*, 174–81. For the Cosoyoapan and Ometepec cases, Torre Villar, *Las Congregaciones*, 239, 305–6.
144. Dehouve, *Quand les banquiers*, 105–9.
145. Dehouve, *Quand les banquiers*, 109–12. For the case of Totomixtlahuaca, Torre Villar, *Las Congregaciones*, 305–6.
146. Torre Villar, *Las Congregaciones*, 239–40.
147. Torre Villar, *Las Congregaciones*, 169–71, 228–29, 243–44, 250–52, 255–56; Rubí Alarcón, "El dominio español," 52–57; Rubí Alarcón, "La encomienda de la Montaña," 308–13; García Castro, *Suma de visitas*, 157. A half tributary was an unmarried adult who paid half the amount of a head of household.
148. Torre Villar, *Las Congregaciones*, 181–82; Rubí Alarcón, "El dominio español," 64–70; Rubí Alarcón, "La encomienda de la Montaña," 319–24; García Castro, *Suma de visitas*, 157; *Historia de Chilpancingo*, 103–16. Reading between the lines of Megged's study, "Salvaging Recurring Themes," one suspects that preexisting community animosities also played a part.

149. Torre Villar, *Las Congregaciones*, 311–12; Rubí Alarcón, "El dominio español," 57–61; Rubí Alarcón, "La encomienda de la Montaña," 313–17.
150. Amith, *The Möbius Strip*, 120, 129–38, 145–46, 159–98; Amith, "Place Making," 163–164, 172.
151. Rubí Alarcón, "El dominio español," 116–20, 122–25.
152. Torre Villar, *Las Congregaciones*, 230.
153. Torre Villar, *Las Congregaciones*, 268.
154. Von Mentz, *Cuauhnáhuac*, 87, 337, 342–64; Von Mentz, *Señoríos indígenas*, 156–71; García Izcabalzeta and García Pimentel, *Descripción del Arzobispado*, 125–27. De la Peña arrived in New Spain in 1525 and purchased Tetipac in 1530. In 1527 he was factor of the treasury in Mexico City and later alcalde mayor of Taxco. In 1545 he purchased land, and in 1555 he was given a grant of further land, near Tacuba in the Valley of Mexico. His heirs lost Tetipac to Luis Velasco the younger in 1586. Himmerich y Valencia, *The Encomenderos*, 213; Ruiz Medrano, *Reshaping New Spain*, 163.
155. Von Mentz, "Aproximaciones," 50.
156. Amith, *The Möbius Strip*, 136.
157. Von Mentz, *Cuauhnáhuac*, 25–34, 87–93, 162–83, 337–42; Von Mentz, *Señoríos indígenas*, 49–50.
158. Torre Villar, *Las Congregaciones*, 81–83, 144–49; Rubí Alarcón, "El dominio español," 127–40; García Castro, *Suma de visitas*, 71, 127–28, 239, 257, 270; "Relación de Ajuchitlán." Concerning the rose bush of Ajuchitlán, see Torre Villar, *La Congregaciones*, 178–79.
159. Von Mentz, *Señoríos indígenas*, 310–18, 327.
160. Aguirre Beltrán, *Cuijla*, 177–84, for example, cites cultural traits of African origin such as the *sombra*, an intangible entity that accompanies the person to the grave and beyond.
161. Ochoa Campos's study of 1964, *Guerrero: Análisis de un estado problema*, identifies the Montaña as the Indigenous region par excellence of Guerrero and discusses its associated social problems. See 10, 128–38.

Chapter Six

1. Simpson, *The Encomienda*; Miranda, *El tributo indígena*; Ruiz Medrano, *Reshaping New Spain*, 31–95.
2. Rubí Alarcón, "El dominio español," 31–89; Dehouve, "Historia del municipio en la Montaña."

3. "Tributos de pueblos de indios."
4. *El libro de Tasaciones*, 449–52. Tribute also included daily delivery of a chicken, four quails, firewood, grass, and pitch pine, presumably for a royal official.
5. *El libro de Tasaciones*, 553–56. An assessment of 1562 notes that tribute had not been paid for the last two years.
6. Puga, ed., *Provisiones*, 7v, 9r, 15r–v, 64–67r; Sánchez-Arcilla Bernal, ed., *Las ordenanzas*, 103–12, 113–16.
7. Miranda, *El tributo indígena*, 92.
8. "*Tributo de los indios*." The document includes Tlapa in a list of pueblos whose tribute belonged to Cortés: "Relacion de los pueblos que estan en corregimiento de que el marques del valle ha de aver y le pertenece el residuo pagado a los corregidores." Other sources state that Cortés lost Tlapa in 1525; e.g., Himmerich y Valencia, *The Encomenderos*, 221.
9. Himmerich y Valencia, *The Encomenderos*, 144, 152, 157, 161, 169, 190, 219, 223, 229, 231, 237, 242, 252, 255; Gerhard; *Síntesis e índice*, 589.
10. Himmerich y Valencia, *The Encomenderos*, 190; Millares Carlo and Mantecón, eds., *Índice y extractos*, 1:237, 241, 256, 261–64, 272; Von Mentz, *Señoríos indígenas*, 222; Porras Muñoz, *El gobierno de la ciudad de México*, 391–96; Álvarez, *Diccionario de conquistadores*, 2:444–45. For Pérez de Bocanegra's political offices and social relations, Álvarez, *Diccionario de conquistadores*, 2:444–45; Porras Muñoz, *El gobierno de la ciudad de México*, 218–19, 267–71, 391–96.
11. Himmerich y Valencia, *The Encomenderos*, 125; Icaza, *Diccionario autobiográfico*, 1:40; Dorantes Carranza, *Sumaria relación*, 184–93, 202, 446; Álvarez, *Diccionario de conquistadores*, 1:64–65; *El libro de tasaciones*, 261–64. Orduña was the secretary and close friend of Cortés, although he later turned against him. In 1523 he was escribano of Mexico City, in 1528 a regidor of Mexico City, in 1529 visitador (government inspector) of Guatemala, in 1531 procurador mayor (senior attorney) of Mexico City, in 1537 veedor (supervisor) of the Casa de la Moneda, in 1542 regidor of Puebla, and in 1543 alcalde ordinario (magistrate) of Puebla. In 1524 and 1528, he was given house sites and horticultural land in Mexico City. He purchased half of Igualapa, Ometepec, and Xochistlahuaca about 1548. He invested in slaves and mining on the Michoacán coast. A daughter married Bernaldino del Castillo, owner of livestock ranches in central Mexico and Huatusco

(Veracruz), who received Igualapa, Ometepec, and Xochistlahuaca as a dowry. Himmerich y Valencia, *The Encomenderos*, 139, 174–75, 208–9; Millares Carlo and Mantecón, eds., *Índice y extractos*, 1:184; Porras Muñoz, *El gobierno de la ciudad de México*, 379–83; Álvarez, *Diccionario de conquistadores*, 1:122–24, 2:415–18.

12. Millares Carlo and Mantecón, eds. *Índice y extractos*, 1:79; Álvarez, *Diccionario de conquistadores*, 1:64–65.
13. Von Mentz, *Señoríos indígenas*, 203; Álvarez, *Diccionario de conquistadores*, 1:64–65.
14. Paso y Troncoso, *Epistolario de Nueva España*, 3:91.
15. El *libro de tasaciones*, 511–13.
16. Paso y Troncoso, *Epistolario de Nueva España*, 8:34–46.
17. Himmerich y Valencia, *The Encomenderos*, 145–48.
18. Himmerich y Valencia, *The Encomenderos*, 131, 154, 257; Dorantes Carranza, *Sumaria relación*, 278–79; Von Mentz, *Señoríos indígenas*, 204; Álvarez, *Diccionario de conquistadores*, 2:439–41, 444–45, 581–83; García Martínez, *El Marquesado del Valle*, 47, states that Cortés requested three other encomiendas in Guerrero: Ayacastla and Nexpa on the Costa Chica and Zacatula on the Costa Grande.
19. "Relación de méritos y servicios del conquistador Bernardino Vázquez de Tapia," 154. Writing between 1542 and 1546, Vázquez de Tapia complained that the reinstatement of Churubusco left him with only one quarter (not the original half) of Tlapa. He reported that his quarter of Tlapa yielded about 600 pesos, while Churubusco provided only 160 pesos. Millares Carlo and Mantecón, eds., *Índice y extractos*, 1:79; Porras Muñoz, *El gobierno de la ciudad de México*, 459.
20. Himmerich y Valencia, *The Encomenderos*, 221, 256–57; Dorantes Carranza, *Sumaria relación*, 439; Icaza, *Diccionario autobiográfico*, 1:2–4; Álvarez, *Diccionario de conquistadores*, 1:13–18, 87–89, 2:575–80; Porras Muñoz, *El gobierno de la ciudad de México*, 453–54, 457–61; "La vida en la colonia," 597–98.
21. Porras Muñoz, *El gobierno de la ciudad de México*, 459, notes that Bernardino was one of the richest men in New Spain. For Bernardino's funeral, "Vida en la colonia," 597–98; Álvarez, *Diccionario de conquistadores*, 1:13–18, 87–89, 2:575–80; "Relación de méritos y servicios del conquistador Bernardino Vázquez de Tapia," 153–54 for the quote. Author's translation.
22. Paso y Troncoso, *Epistolario de Nueva España*, 8:3–46.

23. See chapter 8.
24. Himmerich y Valencia, *The Encomenderos*, 161, 194; Megged, "Salvaging Recurring Themes," 387–88. Cortés gave Zumpango, with Tixtla, to Diego de Santa Cruz, majordomo of the treasurer of Mexico City, and then assigned Zumpango to Pedro Zamorano Cendejas.
25. *El libro de tasaciones*, 654–59.
26. *Historia de Chilpancingo*, 81–86.
27. Zavala, *Libros de asientos*, 226–27.
28. Himmerich y Valencia, *The Encomenderos*, 177–78; Dorantes Carranza, *Sumaria relación*, 215, 221; Icaza, *Diccionario autobiográfico*, 1:30–31; *El libro de tasaciones*, 489–90; Álvarez, *Diccionario de conquistadores*, 1:159–61; Amith, *The Möbius Strip*, 138–40.
29. *El libro de tasaciones*, 489–90. Author's translation.
30. Himmerich y Valencia, *The Encomenderos*, 200; Von Mentz, *Señoríos indígenas*, 59–60, 64, 114; Álvarez, *Diccionario de conquistadores*, 2:375–76.
31. *El libro de tasaciones*, 210.
32. Amith, *The Möbius Strip*, 145–50; Von Mentz, *Señoríos indígenas*, 114; Álvarez, *Diccionario de conquistadores*, 2:375–376. Tlaxmalac and Mayanalán were granted to Juan de Cisneros, who by the 1530s, owned houses in Mexico City. He fought in the battles of Tenochtitlan and died in fighting in Jalisco in 1542. His widow, María Medina/Cisneros, and son Mateo Vázquez de Cisneros inherited the encomienda, which remained in private hands as late as 1688. One of Juan's daughters married a son of the wealthy miner and encomendero of Coyuca in Tierra Caliente, Pedro de Meneses. Himmerich y Valencia, *The Encomenderos*, 142; Icaza, *Diccionario autobiográfico*, 1:117; Porras Muñoz, *El gobierno de la ciudad de México*, 361; Álvarez, *Diccionario de conquistadores*, 1:137.
33. Himmerich y Valencia, *The Encomenderos*, 133; Icaza, *Diccionario autobiográfico*, 1:85–86; "Relación de las minas de Tasco," 116–17; Álvarez, *Diccionario de conquistadores*, 1:92–93.
34. Millares Carlo and Mantecón, eds., *Índice y extractos*, 1:239; *El libro de tasaciones*, 272–73; Gerhard, *Síntesis e índice*, 308–9.
35. Von Mentz, *Señoríos indígenas*, 220–21, 297; Gerhard, *Síntesis e índice*, 305–6; Álvarez, *Diccionario de conquistadores*, 1:92–93; Otte and Albi, *Cartas privadas*, 193–95.
36. Litvak King, *Cihuatlán y Tepecoacuilco*.

37. Himmerich y Valencia, *The Encomenderos*, 251–252; Icaza, *Diccionario autobiográfico*, 2:5–6; Porras Muñoz, *El gobierno de la ciudad de México*, 441–44; Álvarez, *Diccionario de conquistadores*, 2:550–52. Juan's brother Luis held official positions and was given land in Mexico City and an encomienda. Álvarez, *Diccionario de conquistadores*, 2:552–54.
38. Himmerich y Valencia, *The Encomenderos*, 180, 251–52; Millares Carlo and Mantecón, eds., *Índice y extractos*, 1:117, 119, 202, 307, 312.
39. Himmerich y Valencia, *The Encomenderos*, 251–52; Icaza, *Diccionario autobiográfico*, 2:8; Von Mentz, *Señoríos indígenas*, 237; Gerhard, *Síntesis e índice*, 301, 305–6; Álvarez, *Diccionario de conquistadores*, 2:425; Ruiz Medrano, *Reshaping New Spain*, 109.
40. Gerhard, *Síntesis e índice*, 311.
41. Otte and Albi, *Cartas privadas*, 39–41.
42. Himmerich y Valencia, *The Encomenderos*, 181–82. For Loa's career, Álvarez, *Diccionario de conquistadores*, 2:296.
43. Himmerich y Valencia, *The Encomenderos*, 194; Dorantes Carranza, *Sumaria relación*, 222–23; Icaza, *Diccionario autobiográfico*, 1:41; Álvarez, *Diccionario de conquistadores*, 2:352–355; Porras Muñoz, *El gobierno de la ciudad de México*, 361; Ruiz Medrano, *Reshaping New Spain*, 42–52, 65–66, 70–72, 183–84; García Mendoza, "La formación de grupos de poder," 82. Sources differ as to exactly which encomiendas Meneses purchased from Ramírez. I have preferred the account in Icaza taken from the probanza de méritos that Meseses submitted to the royal government.
44. *El libro de tasaciones*, 146–49. I have not identified the current location of Acayo. Copper sent to Mexico City presumably came from mines in Coyuca, since the "Relación de Ajuchitlán," 43, notes, "There is a great quantity of copper, although it is not mined." Author's translation.
45. Fernández del Castillo, "Gil González de Benavides"; Porras Muñoz, *El gobierno de la ciudad de México*, 300–306.
46. *El libro de tasaciones*, 190–92; Scholes and Adams, *Documentos para la historia del México*, 29; Álvarez, *Diccionario de conquistadores*, 1:219–21.
47. Porras Muñoz, *El gobierno de la ciudad de México*, 300–306. Both sons were executed in 1566 for involvement in the conspiracy of Martín Cortés.
48. For Burgos' career, see Himmerich y Valencia, *The Encomenderos*, 131; Álvarez, *Diccionario de conquistadores*, 1:87–89; Porras Muñoz, *El gobierno de la ciudad de México*, 204–9; García Mendoza, "La formación de grupos

de poder," 139. Burgos was close to Cortés. His daughter doña Guiomar Vázquez de Escobar married Luis Cortés, an illegitimate son of Cortés made legitimate in 1529. Burgos owned land for housing and a horticultural plot in Mexico City. He was appointed procurador mayor (attorney general) and majordomo of Mexico City in 1539, alcalde of Mexico City in 1532, 1540, and 1545, and alcalde of the cattlemen's guild in 1541, 1542, and 1546. He was recommended to the king to be a permanent regidor of Mexico City, and in 1527 he was granted a coat of arms by the monarch.

49. Himmerich y Valencia, *The Encomenderos*, 257; Dorantes Carranza, *Sumaria relación*, 186–87, 278–79, 284–87; Álvarez, *Diccionario de conquistadores*, 2:444–45, 581–83; Porras Muñoz, *El gobierno de la ciudad de México*, 267–71, 391–96.
50. *El libro de tasaciones*, 158–61. The community's cotton was distributed to tributaries (7 pounds each) and widows (3.5 pounds), presumably to be woven to raise funds.
51. "Relación de Ichcateupan," 303–4, 319–21; Himmerich y Valencia, *The Encomenderos*, 224.
52. Von Mentz, *Señoríos indígenas*, 204, 236, 277; Álvarez, *Diccionario de conquistadores*, 1:89–90; Porras Muñoz, *El gobierno de la ciudad de México*, 283–86, 405–7. Gaspar was a regidor of Mexico City, alguacil real in the mining town of Tejupilco, and alcalde mayor of Temascaltepec from 1588 to 1594. His sister married encomendero Juan de Busto.

Chapter Seven

1. Gibson, *The Aztecs Under Spanish Rule*, 94–96, reports forced sales of agricultural goods and candles by corregidores.
2. Millares Carlo and Mantecón, eds., *Índice y extractos*, 1:28, 32, 237, 276, 322.
3. Labarthe R., "Provincia de Zacatula," 74–76, 100–101; García Izcabalzeta and García Pimentel, *Descripción del Arzobispado*, 147–52; Himmerich y Valencia, *The Encomenderos*, 229, 255.
4. Labarthe R., "Provincia de Zacatula," 102.
5. Álvarez, *Diccionario de conquistadores*, 1:122–24. Del Castillo had livestock ranches in Coyoacán, Toluca, and Huatusco (modern Veracruz).
6. Miranda, *El tributo indígena*, 194.
7. Gerhard, *Síntesis e índice*, 578.

8. Aguirre Beltrán, *Cuijla*, 41–51, 216–17.
9. "Relación de Xalapa, Cintla y Acatlan," 286. At Nexpa there was also a fishing lagoon and woodlands for timber and the large coastal plains were suitable for cattle. Some were already being grazed.
10. Widmer, *Conquista y despertar*, 125–26. Between 1542–1594, thirty-one grants of livestock estancias were given in the neighboring province of Huatulco, suggesting that fifteen on the Costa Chica may be an underestimate. Vázquez Mendoza, *Pueblo a orilla del mar*, 163–65. "Relación de Xalapa, Cintla y Acatlan," 286, notes that the coastal pueblo of Nexpa had large plains for cattle and that cattle was already grazing on some.
11. "Relación de Xalapa, Cintla y Acatlan," 292.
12. "Relación de la Villa de Zacatula," 460; Dehouve, *Entre el caimán*, 72; Labarthe R., "Provincia de Zacatula," 90–92, 131–35.
13. Labarthe R., "Provincia de Zacatula," 99; *El libro de tasaciones*, 261–64; Álvarez, *Diccionario de conquistadores*, 1:122–24. Except for Vargas, the Costa Grande plantation owners are not listed among the recipients of land grants. Exactly how they acquired the land is not clear.
14. *El libro de tasaciones*, 9–10, 395–96.
15. Hernández Jaimes, "El fruto prohibido," 52–53; Chávez Orozco, *Índice del Ramo de Indios*, 1:62; Labarthe R., "Provincia de Zacatula," 90–92.
16. "Relación de la Villa de Zacatula," 460; "Relación de Citlaltomahua y Anecuilco," 118–21.
17. "Tributos de pueblos de indios"; *El libro de tasaciones*, 120–22, 281–82, 288–89, 420, 649.
18. Chávez Orozco, *Índice del Ramo de Indios*, 1:55.
19. Hernández Jaimes, *Cacao de Guayaquil*, 54–63.
20. "Tributos de pueblos de indios."
21. The extent and complexity of precontact tribute of woven cotton goods, some very elaborate, is evident in the Codex Mendoza. Berdan and Anawalt, *The Essential Codex Mendoza*, 2:76–79, 80–85.
22. For the examples of Olinalá in the Montaña and Atenango and Zacango in the North, see *El libro de tasaciones*, 63–65, 275–76.
23. Dehouve, *Quand les banquiers*, 92–96; Dehouve, *Entre el caimán*, 76; Labarthe R., "Provincia de Zacatula," 138–39.
24. Oropeza Keresey, "La esclavitud asiática," 5–40.
25. Oropeza Keresey, "La esclavitud asiática," 37; Machuca, "La palma de

coco," 321–25, 327–37; Machuca, *El vino de cocos*; Machuca, "The Arrival of American Plants," 234–35.

26. "Relación de la Villa de Zacatula," 456–59; "Relación de Citlaltomahua y Anecuilco," 118–21; "Relación de Justlahuaca," 310.
27. *Cartas de Indias*, 267.
28. Puga, ed., *Provisiones*, 7v–9r.
29. Puga, ed., *Provisiones*, 33r–36r.
30. Gerhard, *Síntesis e índice*, 583–84.
31. Zavala, *El Servicio personal*, 1:151–52, 164, 193.
32. "Relación de la Villa de Zacatula," 451, 456.
33. Labarthe R., "Provincia de Zacatula," 150–56.
34. Labarthe R., "Provincia de Zacatula," 157–59.
35. Widmer, *Conquista y despertar*, 121–24, 135, 138–40.
36. Widmer, *Conquista y despertar*, 138, citing a document in the Archivo General de la Nación, Ramo de Inquisiciones, 48:294–300.
37. Lockhart, Schroeder, and Namala, *Chimalpahin Quauhtlehuanitzin*, 213–25.
38. Aguirre Beltrán, *Cuijla*, 52–64; Widmer, *Conquista y despertar*, 135, 138–40.
39. Widmer, *Conquista y despertar*, 84–92. For the specifics of the Coyuca case, 87–88.
40. Dehouve, *Quand les banquiers*, 30–41; Dehouve, *Entre el caimán*, 96–100; Chávez Orozco, *Índice del Ramo de Indios*, 2:273.
41. Dehouve, *Quand les banquiers*, 37–41; Dehouve, *Entre el caimán*, 96–100; Jacobs, *Ranchero Revolt*, 18.
42. Millares Carlo and Mantecón, eds., *Índice y extractos*, 2:169–70.
43. *El libro de tasaciones*, 490–91.
44. Amith, "The Möbius Strip," 1134–35; Gerhard, *Síntesis e índice*, 287, 289, 293; for Cerezo, see Álvarez, *Diccionario de conquistadores*, 1:126–28; for the marital connections of the Ircio-Mendoza-Velasco family, Amith, *The Möbius Strip*, 140–42. Haskett, *Visions of Paradise*, 114–15, describes an inn managed by the Indigenous municipality in Cuernavaca.
45. Álvarez, *Diccionario de conquistadores*, 1:159–61; Amith, *The Möbius Strip*, 138–45, 151–53, 209–16; Zavala, *Libros de asientos*, 68.
46. "Relación de Tistla y Muchitlan," 274; "Relación de Chilapan," 117–18; Gerhard, *Síntesis e índice*, 294; Dehouve, *Quand les banquiers*, 86–90, 97–101; Pavía Guzmán, "*Tlappan*," 416–17.
47. "Relación de Chilapan," 117–18; "Relación de Tistla y Muchitlan,"

275; Mota y Escobar, *Memoriales*, 106–7; Dehouve, *Quand les banquiers*, 86–89, 97–99, 152–57, 191–98.
48. *El libro de tasaciones*, 489–90; Dehouve, *Quand les banquiers*, 86.
49. Dehouve, *Quand les banquiers*, 97–99.
50. Dehouve, *Quand les banquiers*, 97–100. A parallel arrangement consisted of forced labor, for example, compelling Indians to spin and weave cotton. See 92–96. Indigenous nobles not infrequently collaborated with Spaniards in these practices.
51. Amith, "The Möbius Strip," 1109–12, 1115.
52. Amith, "The Möbius Strip," 1109–12, 1115; Amith, *The Möbius Strip*, 134–53 159–98; Gerhard, *Síntesis e índice*, 307.
53. Von Mentz, *Señoríos indígenas*, 357–68; Chávez Orozco, *Índice del Ramo de Indios*, 1:96, 202, 212–13, 281, 2:109, 273, 281.
54. Von Mentz, *Señoríos indígenas*, 368–72; Amith, *The Möbius Strip*, 54–56.
55. Amith, *The Möbius Strip*, 8–9, 129–34, 198–208.
56. Chávez Orozco, *Índice del Ramo de Indios*, 1:186; Puga, ed., *Provisiones*, f89, f105–106, f200r–202r; Gerhard, *Síntesis e índice*, 301.
57. "Relación de Iguala," 343. Author's translation.
58. Chávez Orozco, *Índice del Ramo de Indios*, 1:31, 38. Author's translation.
59. Von Mentz, *Señoríos indígenas*, 231, 247–49, 340–41.
60. Álvarez, *Diccionario de conquistadores*, 2:352–55.
61. García Izcabalzeta and García Pimentel, *Descripción del Arzobispado*, 242. On Maese de Roa, see Porras Muñoz, *El gobierno de la ciudad de México*, 186, 293–95; and Millares and Mantecón, eds. *Índice y extractos*, 1:92, 140–41, 145, 181–82, 319–20, 326–27, 329, 343.
62. Von Mentz, *Señoríos indígenas*, 313–14, 359, 362, 364–65.
63. García Izcabalzeta and García Pimentel, eds., *Descripción del Arzobispado*, 242.
64. For reports on these towns, "Relación de Ichcateupan," 262–68, 268–75, 275–81, 281–93, 293–98, 304–8, 314–21, 327–31.
65. "Relación de Ichcateupan," 263, 289, 303, 320, 330.
66. Von Mentz, *Señoríos indígenas*, 387–404, 413–33.
67. "Relación de Ichcateupan," 267, 274–75, 280–81, 289, 303, 307–8, 313, 320, 326, 330.
68. "Relación de Ichcateupan," 267, 275, 280, 289 304, 307–8, 326–27.

Chapter Eight

1. See 4.1.
2. Millares Carlo and Mantecón, eds., *Índice y extractos*, 1:45.
3. Millares Carlo and Mantecón, eds., *Índice y extractos*, 1:194–96, 222, 269, 279.
4. Millares Carlo and Mantecón, eds., *Índice y extractos*, 1:117, 119; Himmerich y Valencia, *The Encomenderos*, 180, 251–52.
5. Millares Carlo and Mantecón, eds., *Índice y extractos*, 1:239. These examples of the use of encomienda labor in gold mining constitute partial exceptions to the observation of Lockhart and Schwartz, *Early Latin America*, 100–101, that gold mining relied on Indian slave labor.
6. Millares Carlo and Mantecón, eds., *Índice y extractos*, 1:262; Himmerich y Valencia, *The Encomenderos*, 113–14. Alonso de Aguilar y Córdoba fought in military expeditions to Yopecingo, Pánuco, and Jalisco. He married Isabel de Lara, encomendera of Jalatlaco and eldest daughter of a powerful commander of the Order of Santiago, Leonel de Cervantes. He was a visitador (government inspector) of several provinces, in 1535 and 1551 alcalde ordinario (magistrate) of Mexico City, and in 1552 and 1558 alcalde (magistrate) of the *mesta* (cattlemen's guild). In 1557 and 1558 he had the contract to supply meat to Mexico City. Álvarez, *Diccionario de conquistadores*, 1:3–4; Porras Muñoz, *El gobierno de la ciudad de México*, 175–79; Icaza, *Diccionario autobiográfico*, 1:193–94.
7. Millares Carlo and Mantecón, eds., *Índice y extractos*, 1:175, 177, 185–86.
8. Millares Carlo and Mantecón, eds., *Índice y extractos*, 1:243, 303.
9. Millares Carlo and Mantecón, eds., *Índice y extractos*, 1:274.
10. Millares Carlo and Mantecón, eds., *Índice y extractos*, 2:114–15.
11. "Relación de la Villa de Zacatula," 441–42, 449–51, 456. Author's translation.
12. "Relación de las minas de Zumpango," 196–97; Zavala, *Tributos y servicios personales*, 97–98.
13. Icaza, *Diccionario autobiográfico*, 1:299–300. Author's translation.
14. Icaza, *Diccionario autobiográfico*, 2:92, 329–330.
15. Zavala, *Tributos y servicios personales*, 97–98.
16. Icaza, *Diccionario autobiográfico*, 2:111, 196, 337; Millares Carlo and Mantecón, eds., *Índice y extractos*, 2:34. For Talavera's claims, Icaza, 196. Author's translation.
17. *Historia de Chilpancingo*, 81–86.

18. "Relación de las minas de Zumpango," 196–97.
19. Millares Carlo and Mantecón, eds., *Índice y extractos*, 2:262; "Relación de Chilapan," 117; "Relación de Tistla y Muchitlan," 274.
20. "Relación de Ichcateupan," 273–74. Mansanilla was a conquistador and regidor of Mexico City from 1532 to 1538. He was given the encomienda of Tetela del Río by Cortés and by 1532 was also encomendero of Ixcapuzalco. He sold Tetela to Francisco Rodríguez del Guadalcanal in 1538. In 1542 he was granted a cattle estancia near Taxco. He died in 1545, but his family retained Ixcapuzalco until 1600. Himmerich y Valencia, *The Encomenderos*, 188–89, 223–24; Álvarez, *Diccionario de conquistadores*, 2:325.
21. "Relación de Ichcateupan," 303–4.
22. "Relación de Ichcateupan," 313.
23. Von Mentz, *Señoríos indígenas*, 209–14.
24. Von Mentz, "Aproximaciones."
25. Velasco Murillo, *Urban Indians*, 18–43.
26. See chapter 6.
27. See 4.4.
28. "Relación de las minas de Tasco," 110–11; Haskett, "Our Suffering with the Taxco Tribute," 449.
29. Porras Muñoz, *El Gobierno de la ciudad de México*, 234; Álvarez, *Diccionario de conquistadores*,1:120; González Leal, ed., *Relación secreta*, 53–57.
30. Dorantes Carranza, *Sumaria relación*, 302–3; Millares Carlo and Mantecón, eds., *Índice y extractos*, 2:71; Álvarez, *Diccionario de conquistadores*, 1:120–21; Porras Muñoz, *El gobierno de la ciudad de México*, 234–42; Scholes and Adams, *Cartas del licenciado Jerónimo Valderrama*, 48, 55, 210, 212, 224–25, 229–30. For Valderrama's dismissive comment about Juan Gutiérrez de Bocanegra, 210. Author's translation.
31. Icaza, *Diccionario autobiográfico*, 2:7.
32. Dorantes Carranza, *Sumaria relación*, 302–3. Author's translation.
33. Haskett, "Our Suffering," 449; Von Mentz, *Señoríos indígenas*, 221. Perhaps the 1530 strike was also the work of Indigenous seekers of mines. Velasco Murillo notes that local Indians directed Spaniards to the mines in Zacatecas. See *Urban Indians*, 18–19.
34. Von Mentz, *Cuauhnáhuac*, 342–56.
35. Gerhard, *Síntesis e índice*, 309.
36. Chávez Orozco, *Índice del Ramo de Indios*, 1:79.
37. Millares Carlo and Mantecón, eds., *Índice y extractos*, 2, 31, 43–44.

38. Ruiz Medrano, *Reshaping New Spain*, 198–201.
39. Millares Carlo and Mantecón, eds., *Índice y extractos*, 2:43–44, 47, 99–100, 118, 123.
40. Millares Carlo and Mantecón, eds., *Índice y extractos*, 2:131; Von Mentz, *Señoríos indígenas*, 176; Sarabia Viejo, *Don Luis de Velasco*, 464–67.
41. Millares Carlo and Mantecón, eds., *Índice y extractos*, 2:30; Von Mentz, *Señoríos indígenas*, 175–76; for more cases, 179–81. Quintero was also encomendero of Petatlán and Xalxucatitan on the Costa Grande. He was a veteran of Santo Domingo and Cuba, as well as of Tenochtitlan. He sold Tetipac to Juan de la Peña Vallejo in the late 1530s, and in 1537 he traded his coastal holding with Francisco Rodríguez for Taimeo and Yetecomac in Michoacán and 2,100 pesos. His encomiendas reverted to the Crown ca. 1548 when he left for Peru.
42. Millares Carlo and Mantecón, eds., *Índice y extractos*, 2:43, 71, 79–80, 97, 123.
43. Millares Carlo and Mantecón, eds., *Índice y extractos*, 2:23, 34, 39–40. For the quote concerning Carmona's sale of foodstuffs, 23. Author's translation.
44. Haskett, "Our Suffering," 451.
45. Millares Carlo and Mantecón, eds., *Índice y extractos*, 2:79–80.
46. Millares Carlo and Mantecón, eds., *Índice y extractos*, 2:108; Haskett, "Our Suffering," 451; Paso y Troncoso, *Epistolario de Nueva España*, 11:44–46. By 1568 Cortés had built houses for his mineworkers, a church, and three refining mills in Cantarranas. In 1568–1569 Cantarranas earned 3,690 pesos.
47. Zavala, *El servicio personal*, 3:521; Contreras, *Taxco en el siglo XVI*, 49–51.
48. Von Mentz, *Señoríos indígenas*, 277–80. Von Mentz does not state what was sold in de la Peña's shop.
49. Hawks, "A Relation of the Commodities," 289.
50. Zavala, *Servicio personal*, 3:320–24.
51. Gerhard, *Síntesis e índice*, 299–300.
52. *El libro de tasaciones*, 210, 357–58, 395–96.
53. Gerhard, *Síntesis e índice*, 299, 303.
54. García Izcabalzeta and García Pimentel, *Descripción del Arzobispado*, 124, 178, 181. For the quote concerning Acamixtlahuaca, 181. Author's translation.
55. Roskamp, *La historiografía indígena*, 235, 237, 255, 352.

56. Haskett, "Not a Pastor"; Von Mentz, *Señoríos indígenas*, 130–37, 148–49.
57. Contreras, *Taxco en el siglo XVI*, 39; García Zapoteco, "La población en Taxco," 149–51; King, *Juan Ruiz de Alarcón*, 23–30. For a description of Gonzalo Cerezo's lavish Mexico City household, Conway, *An Englishman and the Mexican Inquisition*, 14–15.
58. The following discussion is based on Contreras, *Taxco en el siglo XVI*, 43–89; and Zavala, *Trabajo indígena*, 28–29, except where otherwise noted.
59. Contreras, *Taxco en el siglo XVI*, 43–56; Ruiz Medrano, *Reshaping New Spain*, 198–201.
60. Contreras, *Taxco en el siglo XVI*, 56–57; Zavala, *Trabajo indígena*, 28–29. For pre- and postcontact mining technologies, West, "*Aboriginal Metallurgy*"; and Bargalló, *La minería*. For smelting in Zacatecas, Velasco Murillo, *Urban Indians*, 41–43, 45–46, 67–68. As late as 1788 and 1789, mining technology was still primitive, and ore was contaminated with sulphur, arsenic, and antimony. Tavera Alfaro, "De una mina de cobre."
61. Contreras, *Taxco en el siglo XVI*, 84–89; Studnicki-Gizbert and Schecter, "The Environmental Dynamics."
62. Contreras, *Taxco en el siglo XVI*, 66–73 Concerning the problem of undesirables, 57–58.
63. Contreras, *Taxco en el siglo XVI*, 56–66, 83
64. Contreras, *Taxco en el siglo XVI*, 90–94; "Relación de los mandamientos."
65. "Ordenanzas de las Minas de Tasco"; "Relación de los mandamientos"; Contreras, *Taxco en el siglo XVI*, 115–55. *Sonsaque* was practiced in Zacatecas. Velasco Murillo, *Urban Indians*, 42.
66. Gerhard, *Síntesis e índice*, 305–6.

Chapter Nine

1. Mota y Escobar, *Memoriales del Obispo de Tlaxcala*, 106–7, 110, 113–15.
2. Bernal, *México en Filipinas*, 23–24; Kamen, *Spain's Road to Empire*, 197–99.
3. "Expedition of García de Loaisa 1525–26," in Blair and Robertson, eds., *The Philippine Islands*, 2 (n.p.).

4. "Voyage of Alvaro de Saavedra," in Blair and Robertson, eds., *Philippine Islands*, 2 (n.p.).
5. "Expedition of Ruy Lopez de Villalobos 1541–46," in Blair and Robertson, eds., *Philippine Islands*, eds., 2 (n.p.).
6. Machuca, *Élites y gobierno en Colima*, 54, 57–61; Vázquez Mendoza, *Pueblo a orilla del mar*, 199–211; Pinzón Ríos, "Descubriendo el Mar del Sur."
7. Bernal, *México en Filipinas*, 47–54. The King to Viceroy Velasco, September 24, 1559; Memorial of Urdaneta to the King, Mexico 1561; "Relation of the expedition, from November 19, 1564, to the end of May 1565, when the 'San Pedro,' under command of Felipe de Salcedo, left Cebú for New Spain," in Blair and Robertson, eds., *Philippine Islands*, 2 (n.p.).
8. "Expedition of Miguel Lopez de Legazpi 1564–68," in Blair and Robertson, eds., *Philippine Islands*, 2 (n.p.); Bernal, *México en Filipinas*, 52–57.
9. "Copia de Vna Carta Venida de SeUilla a Miguel Saluador de Valencia. La Qual Narra El VentuRoso DesCubrimiento Que los Mexicanos Han Hecho, NaueGando con la Armada Quesu Magestad Mando Hazer en Mexico. Con Otras Cosas MarAuillosas, y de Gran Proecho [sic] Para Toda la ChrisTiandad: ConDignas De Ser Vistas y Leydas," Blair and Robertson, eds., *Philippine Islands*, 2 (n.p.). Author's translation.
10. For a map of Saavedra's failed attempts, León Portilla, "Lo que supo," 64. For a map of Urdaneta's route, Maquivar, "Derrotero histórico," 7. See also map by Weexsteen, "The Manila Galleons and Their Trade Network in 1610," showing the Acapulco-Manila, Manila-Acapulco routes and trade routes to Manila from Japan, China, Southeast Asia, and India, in Pierce and Otsuka, *Asia and Spanish America*.
11. Tempère, "Vida y muerte," 114–15; Machuca, "Fortuna de mar," is a case study of the death from disease of the scribe Gaspar Pagés de Moncada, a passenger on *Nuestra Señora de Antocha*.
12. Chávez Orozco, *Índice del Ramo de Indios*, 1:133–34, 187, 266.
13. Zavala, *El Servicio personal*, 3:277–78.
14. Widmer, *Conquista y despertar*, 103–10; Chávez Orozco, *Índice del Ramo de Indios*, 2:154, 244, 247; Zavala, *El Servicio personal*, 3:277–78.
15. Lockhart, Schroeder, and Namala, *Chimalpahin Quauhtlehuanitzin*, 171–73, 273–77, 297, 305–7.
16. Slack, "The Chinos," 36–42, 49–52, 55–56; Oropeza Keresey, "La Esclavitud asiática." Slack, 36–37, estimates total Asian immigration (free and slave) at 100,000. Oropeza Keresey states that 3,872 Asians arrived as slaves 1565–1673.

17. González Claverán, *Malaspina en Acapulco*, 67–69; Gonzales Claverán, *La expedición científica*, 96–97, 128–30, 134, 138.
18. Serrera, "El Camino de Asia," 218, 228; Yuste López, *El comercio de la Nueva España*, 23.
19. Serrera, "El Camino de Asia." For journey times and the length of the road, see 219, 229, 233. On the narrow stretches of the road, see Amith, *The Möbius Strip*, 320.
20. Amith, *The Möbius Strip*, 329.
21. Serrera, "El Camino de Asia," 214–15; Bonialian, *La América española*, 35–80; Bonialian, "El galeón de Manila"; Bonialian, "Panamá, Perú."
22. *Historia de Chilpancingo*, 84–90, 123; Serrera, "El Camino de Asia," 227, 229.
23. *Historia de Chilpancingo*, 23–38; Reyna Robles and González Quintero, *Rescate arqueológico*; Pye and Gutiérrez, "The Pacific Coast Trade Route"; Niederberger, "Nácar."
24. *Historia de Chilpancingo*, 81–116, 123, 130–31. For the quote, 100. Author's translation. Amith, *The Möbius Strip*, 316–18.
25. *Cartas de Indias*, 284–85. Author's translation.
26. Blair and Robertson, eds., *The Philippine Islands*, 3:187, 191–92. For the quote, 191–92. Author's translation.
27. "Relon délo q traen los dos nauios q Vinieron delas yslas del ponite y otros Cosas qe á esto tocã qe fe ponen pa qe mejor fe entienda la Calidad de aquellos proujas," Blair and Robertson, eds., *The Philippine Islands*, 3:220–22.
28. *Cartas de Indias*, 297–8. Author's translation.
29. Bonialian, *La América española*; Bonialian, "La seda china"; Blair and Robertson, eds., *Philippine Islands*, 6:157–234. For examples of Peruvian agents and merchants and Manila traders involved in the Acapulco trade, see appendix 3.
30. Alvarez de Abreu, *Extracto historial*.
31. Guido de Lavezaris [sic] to Felipe II, July 17, 1574, Blair and Robertson, eds., *Philippine Islands*, 3:246–56. For the quote, 250.
32. Don Gonzalo Ronquillo de Peñalosa to Felipe II, June 16, 1582, Blair and Robertson, eds., *Philippine Islands*, 4:16–27. For the quote, 22. Author's translation.
33. Miyata Rodríguez, "The Early Manila Galleon," 40, 42–43.
34. Miyata Rodríguez, "The Early Manila Galleon," 40, 42, 46–55.
35. Curiel, "De cajones," 196–204.
36. Curiel, "De cajones," 204–11.

37. Hoberman, *Mexico's Merchant Elite*, 39–41.
38. Bonialian, *La América española*, 84–85, 374–76; Ruiz Gutiérrez, "La figura del comerciante," 16–17; Del Valle Pavón, "Los mercaderes de México," 220.
39. Del Valle Pavón, "Los mercaderes de México," 228–30. Álvaro and Diego were consulado members.
40. Arenas Frutos and Pazos Pazos, "Una estirpe lepera," 3–4.
41. Ruiz Gutiérrez, "La figura del comerciante," 18–24.
42. Cohen, "Antonio Díaz de Cáceres," 171–74, 176–79; Cohen, *The Martyr*, 186–94; Uchmany, *La vida entre el judaísmo*, 57–58. For Díaz de Cáceres's investigation by the Inquisition, *Procesos de Luis de Carvajal*, 14, 42, 118–19, 458–59. According to Cohen, "Antonio Díaz de Cáceres," 177, the unregistered metal was gold, while Uchmany, 57–58, states that it was iron.
43. Sales Colín, *El movimiento portuario*, 171.
44. Sales Colín, *El movimiento portuario*, 170.
45. Yuste López, *El comercio de la Nueva España*, 89–91.
46. Blair and Robertson, eds., *The Philippine Islands*, 9:298–99.
47. Cervera, *Cartas de Parián*, 92.
48. Cervera, *Cartas de Parián*, 114.
49. Álvarez Delgado, "Los límites del Imperio hispánico," 121.
50. Cervera, *Cartas de Parián*, 144.
51. Álvarez Delgado, "Los límites del Imperio hispánico," 120.
52. "A Letter from the Royal Officials of the Filipinas Accompanied by a Memorandum of the Necessary Things to Be Sent to the Colony 28/05/1565," in Blair and Robertson, eds., *The Philippine Islands*, 2 (n.p.).
53. Blair and Robertson, eds., *The Philippine Islands*, 5:23–24. It would not be surprising if Peñalosa also had a commercial interest in this matter.
54. Blair and Robertson, eds., *The Philippine Islands*, 6:157–234.
55. Blair and Robertson, eds., *The Philippine Islands*, 6:242–47.
56. Blair and Robertson, eds., *The Philippine Islands*, 7:144–45.
57. Blair and Robertson, eds., *The Philippine Islands*, 7:250–53.
58. Blair and Robertson, eds., *The Philippine Islands*, 10:92–93.
59. Blair and Robertson, eds., *The Philippine Islands*, 10:162–67, 248–51, 255–56, 11:86–120.
60. Blair and Robertson, eds., *The Philippine Islands*, 7:279–90.
61. Blair and Robertson, eds., *The Philippine Islands*, 7:297–311.
62. Rodríguez, *AGI Filipinas*, no. 675.

63. Del Valle Pavón, "Los mercaderes de México," 219; Rodríguez, *AGI Filipinas*, nos. 318, 319, 320, 526.
64. Blair and Robertson, eds., *The Philippine Islands*, 8:298–300.
65. Del Valle Pavón, "Los mercaderes de México," 227–28, 230.
66. Bonialian, *La América española*, 35–57, 85–117; Bonialian, "El galeón de Manila"; Bonialian, "La seda china"; Bonialian, "La historia económica del Pacífico"; Hernández Jaimes, "El fruto prohibido," 76.
67. Bonialian, *La América española*, 144–48; Bonialian, "Acapulco. Puerta abierta del Pacífico," 135.
68. Bonialian, *La América española*, 110–11.
69. Vázquez Mendoza, *Pueblo a orilla de mar*, 207–8.
70. Machuca, *Élites y gobierno*, 54, 59.
71. Bonialian, *La América española*, 147.
72. Chaunu, *Las Filipinas*, 98–99, 233–45.
73. Bonialian, "La historia económica del Pacífico"; Bonialian, *La América española*.
74. Alvarez de Abreu, *Extracto historial*.
75. "Copia de Vna Carta Venida de SeUilla a Miguel Saluador de Valencia. La Qual Narra El Ventu|Roso DesCubrimiento Que los Mexicanos Han Hecho, NaueGando con la Armada Quesu Magestad Mando Hazer en Mexico. Con Otros Cosas MarAuillosas, y de Gran| ProneCho [sic] Para Toda la ChrisTiandad: ConDignas De Ser Vistas y Leydas," Blair and Robertson, eds., *The Philippine Islands*, 2 (n.p.). Author's translation.
76. Bjork, "The Link that Kept the Philippines Spanish."
77. Alvarez de Abreu, *Extracto historial*.
78. Chaunu, *Las Filipinas*, 220–27; Serrera, "El camino de Asia," 228.
79. Serrera, "El camino de Asia," 216. Emphasis in the original. Author's translation.
80. Vázquez de Espinosa, *Compendio y descripción*, 157–58, 248. Author's translation.
81. Serrera, "El camino de Asia," 216. Author's translation.
82. Dehouve, *Entre el caimán*, 107–9.
83. González Claverán, *Malaspina en Acapulco*, 93.
84. González Claverán, *Malaspina en Acapulco*, 97–99.
85. González Claverán, *Malaspina en Acapulco*, 93, 97, 101–5. Lockhart and Schwartz, *Early Latin America*, 86–90, notes that Spanish reluctance to reside in the port reflected a general attitude that proper cities should be inland and applied even to New Spain's largest port, Veracruz.

86. González Claverán, *Malaspina en Acapulco*, 110–11.
87. González Claverán, *Malaspina en Acapulco*, 113–14.
88. Bonialian, "México: De epicentro a la periferia"; Amith, *The Möbius Strip*, 325–31.

Concluding Observations

1. Hirth, The *Aztec Economic World*, 6–10.
2. Terraciano, *The Mixtecs*, 354–55, observes that Mixtec language sources contradict the traditional assessment that the Mexicas had surpassed the Mixtecs culturally and politically and that the Mixteca was a region of marginal chiefdoms. This point could be examined over a longer period than Terraciano's study by drawing on surveys such as Pérez Rodríguez and Heredia Espinoza, *La epopeya de la Mixteca*. Guerrero has, similarly, been considered a marginal region of Mesoamerica, a conclusion contradicted by the longue durée archaeological evidence.
3. Restall, *Seven Myths*, 100–130. The cultural vitality that afforded considerable agency to the Nahuas of central Mexico to play a role in molding New Spain was, of course, documented in 1964 in Charles Gibson's classic *The Aztecs Under Spanish Rule* and in James Lockhart's *The Nahuas After the Conquest* in 1992. Haskett's *Indigenous Rulers* documents substantial continuity in terms of both personnel and resilience in forming a synthesis of Indigenous and Iberian government and social organization. Terraciano, in his *The Mixtecs*, examines the distinctive Mixtec response to the Spanish invasion, for example, the tradition of dual rulership cemented by marriage, the *yuhuitayu*, which afforded a governing role as of right to female rulers, a tradition that colonial changes to governing arrangements did not eliminate. William Taylor's *Landlord and Peasant* shows that because of a relative lack of Spanish interest in land in the Valley of Oaxaca, the Indigenous peoples of the Valley conserved substantial holdings into the late colonial period. In a very different region of Oaxaca, the Sierra Norte, Yannakakis, *The Art of Being In-Between*, demonstrates that the region was seen as peripheral by Spaniards but not by the Indians who determinedly defended local communities. In the Sierra Norte of Puebla, García Martínez, in *Los pueblos de la Sierra*, finds that pueblos close to the altiplano underwent significant change in the colonial period but that in the more remote communities change was almost zero. While Wood's investigation of

the colonial trajectory of towns in the Valley of Toluca, *Transcending Conquest*, finds that Indigenous determination to defend the status and autonomy of their communities was a constant in colonial Mexico, their ability to do so varied with their ecological niche and distance from the centers of Spanish commerce.

4. Guardino, *Peasants, Politics*, 22–24.
5. Guardino, *Peasants, Politics*, 23.
6. Guardino, *Peasants, Politics*, 21–22.
7. More pictographic documents from the Montaña have survived than those from other regions of Guerrero. While it is possible that this could be an accident of preservation, the number of documents that relate to the lineage and history of Tlapa-Tlachinollan alone, along with other indicators of particularly vigorous cultural traditions in the Montaña, suggest that the region did, indeed, produce more such documents than other areas.
8. The process of separation begun in the 1570s and 1580s continued throughout the colonial period, and after independence Indigenous communities fiercely defended municipal autonomy. Guardino, *Peasants, Politics*, 95–103, 152, 173–74. By 2000 there were seventy-six municipalities in the Montaña. The population of the municipality of Acapulco was 722,499, while Atlamajalcingo del Monte had only 5,080 inhabitants and Cualác 6,575. These two municipalities were the smallest in the state in population terms. Eleven Montaña municipalities had fewer than 10,000 inhabitants, and twenty-two between 10,000 and 20,000. Only five exceeded 100,000. *XII Censo General de Población*. This disparity was emphasized at a meeting of municipal treasurers in Chilpancingo that I attended in 1975, when Governor Rubén Figueroa commented that some municipalities in the state had budgets so small they could barely afford pencils.
9. Amith, *The Möbius Strip*, 206–7.
10. Guardino, *Peasants, Politics*, 22; Montes Vega, *Héroes pioneros*, 90, 94–95, 97.
11. Von Mentz, *Señoríos indígenas*, 474.
12. Von Mentz, *Señoríos indígenas*, 83–85, plate 1.
13. Miranda Arrieta, *Economía y comunicaciones*, 89, describing Guerrero in the late nineteenth century. Author's translation.
14. Ochoa Campos, *Guerrero: Análisis de un estado problema*, 11. Author's translation.
15. Bartra, "Sur profundo," 13–14. Author's translation.

16. Good Eshelman, "Los estudios etnohistóricos," addresses this question in brief. She argues that for the Indigenous peoples of Guerrero the balance of the colonial period was not entirely negative. In particular, the communities of the Montaña were able to establish a moderately comfortable rural way of life. Things began to go wrong in the nineteenth century, especially during the Porfiriato, when Indigenous lands were lost to mestizos who also controlled credit. After the Revolution of 1910–1920, fought ostensibly to further the interests of rural communities, the activities of monopolist merchants and moneylenders combined with new governmental structures that undermined traditional community governance to marginalize the Indigenous peoples of the Montaña further still.

Bibliography

Published Primary Sources

XII censo general de población y vivienda 2000. Síntesis de los resultados. Guerrero, https://www.inegi.org.mx/programas/ccpv/2000/default.html#Datos_abiertos.

Acuña, René, ed. *Relaciones geográficas del Siglo XVI: Antequera*. México: UNAM, 1984.

———. *Relaciones geográficas del Siglo XVI: México*. México: UNAM, 1985.

———. *Relaciones geográficas del Siglo XVI: Michoacán*. México: UNAM, 1987.

———. *Relaciones geográficas del Siglo XVI: Tlaxcala*. México: UNAM, 1985.

Álvarez de Abreu, Antonio. *Extracto historial del comercio entre China, Filipinas y Nueva España, Introducción, notas y arreglo del texto por Carmen Yuste*. México: Instituto Mexicano de Comercio Exterior, vol. 1, 1977.

Berdan, Frances F., and Patricia Rieff Anawalt, eds. *The Essential Codex Mendoza*, 2 vols. Berkeley: University of California Press, 1997.

Blair, Emma Helen, and James Alexander Robertson, eds. *The Philippine Islands, 1492–1898*, 55 vols. Cleveland: A. H. Clark, 1903–1909. http://www.gutenberg.org/ebooks/54740.

"Cargos al Alcalde Mayor de Acapulco en su juicio de residencia." *Boletín del archivo General de la Nación* no. 2 (marzo–abril 1935): 263–66.

Carrillo Cázares, Alberto. *Partidos y padrones del obispado de Michoacán*. Zamora: Colegio de Michoacán, 1996.

Cartas de Indias. Publícalas por primera vez el Ministerio de Fomento. Madrid: Imprenta de Manuel G. Hernández, 1877.

Chávez Orozco, Luis, ed. *Índice del Ramo de Indios del Archivo General de la Nación*, 2 vols. México: Archivo General de la Nación, 1951–1953.

Colección de documentos para la historia de Oaxaca. Contribución del Museo Nacional de Arqueología, Historia y Etnografía, al Primer Congreso Mexicano de Historia que se celebra en la ciudad de Oaxaca. México: Secretaría de Educación Pública, 1933.

Dirección General de Estadística. *Quinto censo de población, 15 de mayo de 1930, Estado de Guerrero.* https://www.inegi.org.mx/programas/ccpv/1930/#Tabulados.

Dirección General de Geografía, Meteorología e Hidrología. *Atlas geográfico por estados: República Mexicana.* México: Secretaría de Agricultura, 1951.

Dorantes Carranza, Baltasar. *Sumaria relación de las cosas de la Nueva España con noticia individual de los conquistadores y primeros pobladores españoles.* México: Imprenta del Museo Nacional, 1902.

García Castro, René, ed. *Suma de visitas de pueblos de la Nueva España, 1548–1550.* Toluca: Universidad Autonóma del Estado de México, 2013.

García Izcabalzeta, Joaquín, and Luis García Pimentel, eds. *Descripción del Arzobispado de México hecha en 1570 y otros documentos.* Guadajalara: Edmundo Aviña Levy Editor, 1976.

Gemelli Carreri, Giovanni Francesco. *Viaje a la Nueva España, estudio preliminar, traducción y notas de Francisca Perujo.* México: UNAM, 1976.

Gerhard, Peter. *Síntesis e índice de los mandamientos vierreinales 1548–1553.* México: UNAM, 1992.

González Leal, Mariano, ed. *Relación secreta de conquistadores. Informes del archivo personal del Emperador Carlos I que se conserva en la Biblioteca del Escorial años1539–1542.* Guanajuato: Taller de Investigaciones Humanísticas de la Universidad de Guanajuato, 1979.

Grijalva, Juan de. *Crónica de la orden de N. P. S. Agustín en las Provincias de la Nueva España, en cuatro edades desde al año de 1533 hasta el de 1592.* México: Editorial Porrúa, S.A., 1985.

Hawks, Henry. "A Relation of the Commodities of Nova Hispania and the Manners of the Inhabitants, written by Henry Hawks merchant, which lived five yeeres in the sayd contrey, and drew the same at the request of M. Richard Hakluyt Esquire of Eiton in the county of Hereford, 1572." In Richard Hakluyt, *Voyages*, vol. 6, 279–96. London: J. M. Dent & Sons, 1962.

Icaza, Francisco A. de. *Diccionario autobiográfico de Conquistadores y Pobladores de la Nueva España sacado de los textos originales*, 2 vols. Guadalajara: Edmundo Aviña Editor, 1969.

"Instrucción y memoria de las relaciones que se han de hacer para la descripción de las Indias, que su majestad manda hacer, para el buen gobierno y ennoblemeciento dellas." In Acuña, ed., *Relaciones geográficas del Siglo XVI: Tlaxcala*, vol. 2, 17–23.

El libro de las tasaciones de pueblos de la Nueva España: siglo XVI, con prólogo de Francisco González de Cossío. México: Archivo General de la Nación, 1952.

Libro Primero de votos de la Inquisición de México. Introducción de Edmundo O'Gorman. México: Archivo General de la Nación, 1952.

Lockhart, James, Susan Schroeder, and Doris Namala, eds. and trans. *Chimalpahin Quauhtlehuanitzin, Don Domingo de San Antón Muñón. Annals of His Time*. Stanford: Stanford University Press, 2006.

Martínez Baracs, Rodrigo. "Documentos en náhuatl de Oztuma, Guerrero: 1574–1692." In Paredes Martínez and Martínez Ayala, *Alzaban banderas de papel*, 253–97.

Millares Carlo, A., and J. I. Mantecón, eds. *Índice y extractos de los Protocolos del Archivo de Notarías de México D.F.*, 2 vols. México: Colegio de México, 1945.

Mota y Escobar, Fray Alonso de la. *Memoriales del Obispo de Tlaxcala: un Recorrido por el Centro de México a Principios del Siglo XVII, Introducción y notas de Alba González Jácome*. México: SEP, 1987.

"Ordenanzas de las Minas de Tasco, 22 noviembre 1575." *Boletín del Archivo General de la Nación* 7, no. 3 (julio–agosto–septiembre 1936): 324–42.

Otte, Enrique, and Guadalupe Albi, eds. *Cartas privadas de emigrantes a Indias (1540–1616), Prólogo de Ramón Carande y Thovar*. Seville: Consejería de Cultura, Junta de Andalucía: Escuela de Estudios Hispano Americanos de Sevilla, 1988.

Paso y Troncoso, Francisco del, ed. *Epistolario de Nueva España 1505–1818*, 16 vols. México: Antigua Librería Robredo, de José Porrúa e Hijos, 1939.

Procesos de Luis de Carvajal (el Mozo), Publicaciones del Archivo General de la Nación, XXVIII. México: Talleres Gráficas de la Nación, 1935.

Puga, Vasco de, ed. *Provisiones, cédulas, instrucciones para el gobierno de la Nueva España*. Madrid: Ediciones Cultura Hispánica, 1945.

"Relación de Ajuchitlan y su partido." In Acuña, *Relaciones geográficas del Siglo XVI: Michoacán*, 27–45.

"Relación de Chilapan." In Acuña, *Relaciones geográficas del Siglo XVI: Tlaxcala*, vol. 2, 107–19.

"Relación de Citlaltomahua y Anecuilco." In Acuña, *Relaciones geográficas del Siglo XVI: México*, vol. 1, 109–22.

"Relación de Ichcateupan y su partido." In Acuña, *Relaciones geográficas del Siglo XVI: México*, vol. 1, 257–334.

"Relación de Iguala y su partido." In Acuña, *Relaciones geográficas del Siglo XVI: México*, vol. 1, 335–56.

"Relación de Justlahuaca." In Acuña, ed. *Relaciones geográficas del Siglo XVI: Antequera*, vol. 1, 278–324.

"Relación de la Villa de Zacatula." In Acuña, ed., *Relaciones geográficas del Siglo XVI: Michoacán*, 439–62.

"Relación de las minas de Tasco." In Acuña, ed., *Relaciones geográficas del Siglo XVI: México*, vol. 2, 107–32.

"Relación de las minas de Zumpango." In Acuña, ed., *Relaciones geográficas del Siglo XVI: México*, vol. 3, 191–202.

"Relación de los mandamientos que se han despachado los años pasados para las minas de Tasco, en el oficio del Secretario Juan de Cueva y refrendados de él." *Boletín del Archivo General de la Nación* 7, no. 4 (octubre–noviembre–diciembre 1936): 524–26.

"Relación de méritos y servicios del conquistador Bernardino Vázquez de Tapia, vecino y regidor de esta gran ciudad de Tenuxtitlan México." In *La conquista de Tenochtitlan*. Crónicas de América 40, edited by Germán Vázquez, 125–54. Madrid: Historia 16, 1988.

"Relación de Sirandaro y Guayameo." In Acuña, ed., *Relaciones geográficas del Siglo XVI: Michoacán*, 259–70.

"Relación de Tistla y Muchitlan." In Acuña, ed., *Relaciones geográficas del Siglo XVI: Tlaxcala*, vol. 2, 263–77.

"Relación de Xalapa, Cintla y Acatlan." In Acuña, ed., *Relaciones geográficas del Siglo XVI: Antequera*, vol. 2, 279–94.

Reynolds, Winston A., ed. *El Corregidor Diego Díaz del Castillo (hijo del conquistador) ante la Inquisición de México (1568–1571)*. Colección Chimalistac de libros y documentos acerca de la Nueva España. Madrid: Ediciones José Porrúa Turanzas, 1973.

Ruiz de Alarcón, Hernando. *Tratado de las idolatrías, supersticiones, dioses, ritos, hechicerías y otras costumbres gentilicias de las razas aborígenes de México, notas, comentarios y un estudio de Don Francisco del Paso y Troncoso*. México: Ediciones Fuente Cultural, 1892.

Sánchez-Arcilla Bernal, José, ed. *Las ordenanzas de las Audiencias de Indias (1511–1821)*. Madrid: Editorial Dykinson, 1992.

Scholes, France V., and E. B. Adams, eds. *Cartas del licenciado Jerónimo Valderrama y otros documentos sobre su visita al gobierno de Nueva España, 1563–1565*. México: José Porrúa e hijos, 1961.

———, eds. *Documentos para la Historia del México Colonial. Relación de las Encomiendas de indios hechas en Nueva España a los conquistadores y pobladores de ella. Año de 1564*. México: José Porrúa e Hijos, Sucs., 1955.

Schwaller, John Frederick, ed. "Constitution of the Cofradía del Santissimo Sacramento of Tula, Hidalgo, 1570," n.d. https://www.historicas.unam.mx/publicaciones/revistas/nahuatl/pdf/ecn19/310.pdf.

———. *Partidos y parrocos bajo la real corona en la Nueva España, Siglo XVI*. México: INAH, 1981.

"Tributo de los indios de la Nueva España." *Boletín del Archivo General de la Nación* 7, no. 2 (abril–mayo–junio 1936): 185–226.

"Tributos de pueblos de indios (Virreinato de Nueva España)." *Boletín del Archivo General de la Nación* 11, no. 2 (abril–mayo–junio 1940): 195–243.

Vázquez de Espinosa, Antonio. *Compendio y descripción de las Indias Occidentales, por Antonio Vázquez de Espinosa, transcrito del manuscrito original por Charles Upson Clarke*. Smithsonian Miscellaneous Collections, Vol. 108 (whole volume). Washington, DC: Smithsonian Institution, 1948.

"La vida en la colonia. Cuaderno de apuntes de un ministro del Santo Oficio 1606–1617." *Boletín del Archivo General de la Nación* 14, no. 4 (octubre–noviembre–diciembre, 1943): 590–615.

Wood, Stephanie, ed. "Nahuatl Dictionary," n.d. https://nahuatl.wired-humanities.org.

Zavala, Silvio. *Libros de asientos de la gobernación de la Nueva España (periodo del virrey don Luis de Velasco, 1550–1552)*. México: Archivo General de la Nación, 1982.

———, ed. *El servicio personal de los indios en la Nueva España*, 3 vols. México: Colegio de México/Colegio Nacional, 1984–1987.

———, ed. *El trabajo Indígena en los libros de gobierno del virrey Luis de Velasco 1550–1552*. México: Centro de Estudios Históricos del Movimento Obrero Mexicano, 1981.

———, ed. *Tributos y servicios personales de indios para Hernán Cortés y su familia (Extractos de documentos del siglo XVI)*. México: Archivo de la Nación, 1984.

Secondary Sources

Adler, Cyrus, ed. *Trial of Jorge de Almeida by the Inquisition in Mexico*. Publications of the American Jewish Historical Society, No. 4. Baltimore: Johns Hopkins University Press, 1896, https://www.jstor.org/stable/43057457.

Aguirre Beltrán, Gonzalo. *Cuijla: esbozo etnográfico de un pueblo negro*. México: Fondo de Cultura Económica, 1985.

Albiez-Wieck, Sarah. "Contactos exteriores del Estado tarasco: Influencias desde dentro y fuera de Mesoamérica," Revised typescript of PhD diss., University of Bonn, 2010. https://kompetenznetz-lateinamerika.academia.edu/SarahAlbiezWieck.

Altamirano, Ignacio. "Paisajes y Leyendas." In *Tradiciones y costumbres de México no. 275*. México: Ed. Porrúa, 1997.

Álvarez, Víctor M. *Diccionario de conquistadores*, 2 vols. México: INAH, 1975.

Alvarez de Abreu, Antonio. *Extracto historial del comercio entre China, Filipinas y Nueva España. Introducción, notas y arreglo del texto por Carmen Yuste*, vol. 1. México: Instituto Mexicano de Comercio Exterior, n.d.

Álvarez Delgado, Lorena. "Los límites del Imperio hispánico en la confluencia de fronteras del Mar del Sur." In *Las Fronteras en el mundo atlántico (siglos XVI–XIX)*, edited by Susana Truchuelo and Emir Reitano, 97–140. Buenos Aires: Universidad Nacional de la Plata, 2017. https://unican.academia.edu/LorenAlvarezDelgado.

Amith, Jonathan David. "The Möbius Strip: A Spatial History of a Colonial Society: Central Guerrero, Mexico, from the Sixteenth to the Nineteenth Centuries." PhD diss., Yale University, 2000.

———. *The Möbius Strip: A Spatial History of Colonial Society in Guerrero, Mexico*. Stanford: Stanford University Press, 2005.

———. "Place Making and Place Breaking: Migration and the Development Cycle of Community in Colonial Mexico." *American Ethnologist* 32, no. 1 (2005): 159–79.

Anderson, Edgar, and R. H. Barlow. "The Maize Tribute of Moctezuma's Empire." *Annals of the Missouri Botanical Garden* 30: 413–18, 420. http://www.jstor.org/stable/2394304.

Arana, Raúl Martín. *Proyecto Coatlan. Area Tonatico-Pilcaya*. México: INAH, 1990.

Arana, Raúl M., and Gerardo Cepeda C. "Localización de sitios arqueológicos en el Vaso de la Presa de Palos Altos, Guerrero." *Boletín del INAH* 26 (1966): 14–16.

Arenas Frutos, Isabel, and María Luisa Pazos Pazos. "Una estirpe lepera en México: Baltasar Rodríguez de los Ríos y sus primeros descendientes." *Nuevo Mundo/Mundos Nuevos*, Debates, 2009: 473–506. DOI: https://doi.org/10.4000/nuevomundo.56077.

Armillas, Pedro. "Expediciones en el occidente de Guerrero: II, el grupo de Armillas." *Tlalocan* (febrero–marzo 1944): 73–85.

Ball, Hugh G., and Donald L. Brockington. "Trade and Travel in Prehistoric Oaxaca." In *Mesoamerican Communication Routes and Cultural Contacts*. Papers of the New World Archaeological Foundation, edited by Hugh G. Ball and Donald L. Brockington, 107–14. Provo: Brigham Young University, 1978.

Bargalló, Modesto. *La minería y la metalurgia en la América española durante la época colonial*. México: Fondo de Cultura Económica, 1955.

Barlow, Robert H. "Conquistas de los antiguos mexicanos." *Journal de la Société des américanistes*, n.s., 36 (1947): 215–22. http://www.jstor.org/stable/24601905.

———. *The Extent of the Empire Culhua-mexica*. Ibero-Americana, 28. Berkeley: University of California Press, 1949.

———. "El palimsesto de veinte mazorcas." *Revista de Estudios Antropológicos* 17: 97–110.

Barrett, Elinore M. *La Cuenca del Tepalcatepec. I. Su colonización y tenencia de la tierra*. México, DF: SepSetentas, 1975.

Bartra, Armando. "Sur profundo." In *Crónicas del sur. Utopías campesinas en Guerrero*, edited by Armando Bartra, 13–74. México, DF: Ediciones Era, 2000.

Batalla Rosado, Juan José. "*El Códice de Ohuapan II* (Estado de Guerrero). Un nuevo documento pictográfico sobre tributos de mediados del siglo XVI firmado por el oidor Antonio Rodríguez de Quesada." In *Códices y cultura indígena en México. Homenaje a García-Gallo*, edited by Juan José Batalla Rosado, José Luis Rojas, and Lisardo Pérez Lugones, 141–202. Madrid: BRF Servicios Editoriales, 2018.

Beekman, Christopher S. "Recent Research in Western Mexican Archaeology." *Journal of Archaeological Research* 18, no. 1 (2010): 41–109.

Berdan, Frances F. "Aztec Merchants and Markets: Local-Level Economic Activity in a Non-Industrial Empire." *Mexicon*, 2, no. 3 (July 1980): 37–41. http://www.jstor.org/stable/23757459.

———. "Cotton in Aztec Mexico: Production, Distribution and Uses." *Mexican Studies/Estudios Mexicanos* 3, no. 2 (Summer 1987): 235–62. http://www.jstor.org/stable/1051808.

———. "Economic Dimensions of Precious Metals, Stones and Feathers: The Aztec State Society." *Estudios de cultura náhuatl* 22 (1992): 291–322.

———. "Ports of Trade in Mesoamerica: A Reappraisal." In *Mesoamerican Communication Routes, and Cultural Contacts*. Papers of the New World Archaeological Foundation, edited by Hugh G. Ball and Donald L. Brockington, 187–98. Provo: Brigham Young University, 1978.

Berdan, Frances F., Richard E Blanton, Elizabeth Hill Boone, Mary G. Hodge, Michael E. Smith, and Emily Umberger, eds. *Aztec Imperial Strategies*. Washington, DC: Dumbarton Oaks, 1996.

Bernal, Rafael. *México en Filipinas*. México, UNAM: 1965.

Bittmann Simons, Bente. "Further Notes on the Map of Tepecoacuilco, a Pictorial Manuscript from the State of Guerrero, Mexico." *Indiana* 2 (1974): 97–131. https://doi.org/10.18441/ind.v2i0.97-131.

Bjork, Katharine. "The Link that Kept the Philippines Spanish: Mexican Merchant Interests and the Manila Trade, 1571–1815." *Journal of World History* 9, no. 1 (Spring 1998): 25–50. http://www.jstor.org/stable/20078712.

Blomster, Jeffrey P., and David Cheetham. *The Early Olmec and Mesoamerica: The Material Record*. Cambridge: Cambridge University Press, 2017.

Blomster, Jeffrey P., Hector Neff, and Michael D. Glascock. "Olmec Pottery Production in Ancient Mexico Determined Through Elemental Analysis." *Science*, n.s., 307, no. 5712 (2005): 1068–72. http://www.jstor.org/stable/3840153.

Bonfil Batalla, Guillermo. *México Profundo: Reclaiming a Civilization*. Austin: University of Texas Press, 2007.

Bonialian, Mariano. "Acapulco. Puerta abierta del Pacífico, válvula secreta del Atlántico." In *Relaciones Intercoloniales: Nueva España y Filipinas*, edited by Jaime Olveda. 127–46. Zapopan: El Colegio de Jalisco, 2015. https://independent.academia.edu/MarianoBonialian.

———. *La América española: entre el Pacífico y el Atlántico: globalización mercantil y economía política, 1580–1840*. Ciudad de México: Colegio de México, 2012.

———. "El galeón de Manila y el comercio entre Filipinas, México y Perú en la época colonial." In *Tornaviaje: la Nao de China y el Barroco en México 1565–1815*, 38–43. Puebla: Museo Internacional del Barroco; Ciudad de México: Museo Franz Mayer, 2016. https://independent.academia.edu/MarianoBonialian.

———. "La historia económica del pacífico en su larga duración una revisión a *Las Filipinas y el Pacífico de los Ibéricos* de Pierre Chaunu." *Illes i imperis* no. 19 (2017): 77–99. http://dx.doi.org/10.2436/20.8050.02.21.

———. "México: de epicentro a periferia. La desintegración del modelo semiinformal del comercio hispanoamericano (1750–1840)." *Historia Mexicana* 67, no. 1 (junio 2017): 61–123. http://dx.doi.org/10.24201/hm.v67i1.3441.

———. "Panamá, Perú y el universo económico del Pacífico en la temprana globalización, 1580–1640." *Nuevo Mundo/Mundos Nuevos* (2019): 1–14. https://journals.openedition.org/nuevomundo/76620.

———. "La seda china en Nueva España a principios del siglo xvii. Una mirada imperial en el memorial de Horacio Levanto." *Revista de Historia Económica / Journal of Iberian and Latin American Economic History* (2016): 147–71. http//:doi.org/10.1017/S0212610915000385.

Borah, Woodrow Wilson. *Justice by Insurance: The General Indian Court of Colonial Mexico and the Legal Aides of the Half-Real*. Berkeley: University of California Press, 1983.

Borah, Woodrow, and Sherburne F. Cook. *The Aboriginal Population of Central Mexico on the Eve of the Spanish Conquest.* Ibero-Americana: 45. Berkeley: University of California Press, 1963.

———. *The Population of Central Mexico in 1548: An Analysis of the Suma de visitas de pueblos.* Ibero-Americana: 43. Berkeley: University of California Press, 1960.

Brush, Charles F. "Pox Pottery: Earliest Identified Mexican Ceramic." *Science*, n.s., 149, no. 3680 (1965): 194–95. http://www.jstor.org/stable/1716311.

———. "Pre-Columbian Alloy Objects from Guerrero, Mexico." *Science*, n.s., 138, no. 3547 (1962): 1336–38. https://www.jstor.org/stable/1709711.

Burkhart, Louise. "Flowery Heaven: The Aesthetic of Paradise in Nahuatl Devotional Literature." *RES: Anthropology and Aesthetics* no. 21 (Spring 1992): 88–109. www.jstor.org/stable/20166843.

———. *The Slippery Earth: Nahua-Christian Moral Dialogue in Sixteenth-Century Mexico.* Tucson: University of Arizona Press, 1989.

Cabrera Castro, Rubén. "Arquitectura y sistemas constructivos en sitios prehispánicos del valle de Cocula en el estado de Guerrero." In Niederberger and Robles, *El Pasado arqueológico de Guerrero*, 259–.81.

———. "El desarrollo cultural prehispánico en la región del Bajo Río Balsas." In *Primer coloquio de arqueología y etnohistoria del estado de Guerrero*, 119–151.

———. "El proyecto arqueológico 'Cocula', resultados generales." In *Primer coloquio de arqueología y etnohistoria del estado de Guerrero*, 173–200.

Cabrera Guerrero, Martha. "The Cave of the Bat, a primordial Cave of the Sun, Acapulco, Mexico." In *Rock Art in the Americas: Mythology, Cosmogony and Rituals, Proceedings of the 2nd REEA Conference Ritual Americas: Configurations and Recombining of the Ritual Devices and Behaviors in the New World*, in *Historical and Contemporary Societies, Louvain-la-Neuve (Belgium) April 2–5, 2008.* Edited by Françoise Fauconnier and Serge Lemaitre, 89–102. Oxford: BAR Publishing, 2012. https://independent.academia.edu/MarthaCabreraGuerrero.

———. *Las grutas de Juxtlahuaca. Santuario al dios olmeca del maíz.* México: Secretaría de Cultura, 2017. https://independent.academia.edu/MarthaCabreraGuerrero.

———. "Las pinturas rupestres de la Cueva de Pie de la Cuesta." In *II Mesa Redonda el conocimiento antropológico e histórico sobre Guerrero. Las regiones histórico-culturales: sus problemas e interacciones, 23–25 agosto 2006*. México: INAH, 2006, https://independent.academia.edu/MarthaCabreraGuerrero.

———. *Los pobladores prehispánicos de Acapulco: Proyecto Arqueológico Renacimiento*. México DF: INAH, 1990.

Cabrero G., María Teresa. "El modo de vida marítima en el occidente de México." *Revista de Arqueología Americana* no. 16 (1999): 183–92.

Campbell, Lyle. "Middle American Languages." In *The Languages of Native America: Historical and Comparative Assessment*, edited by Lyle Campbell and Marianne Mithun, 902–1000. Austin: University of Texas Press, 1979.

Canger, Una. "Los dialectos náhuatl de Guerrero." In *Primer coloquio de arqueología y etnohistoria del estado de Guerrero*, 281–92.

Carrera Stampa, Manuel. "El sistema Monetario Colonial." *Memoria de la Academia Mexicana de la Historia* 27, no. 1 (enero–marzo 1968): 15–62. https://www.academiamh.com.mx/memorias-de-la-amh/tomo-xxvii.

———. "El sistema de pesos y medidas coloniales." *Memoria de la Academia Mexicana de la Historia* 26, no. 1 (enero–marzo 1967): 1–37. https://www.academiamh.com.mx/memorias-de-la-amh/tomo-xxviii-2.

Castelló Iturbide, Teresa. "El Maque: Lacas de Michoacán, Guerrero y Chiapas." *Artes de México* no. 153 (1972): 92–101. http://www.jstor.org/stable/24317090.

Castrejón Díez, Jaime. "Una ciudad minera en sus orígenes." *Artes de México*, nueva época, no. 5 (1995): 26–33. http://www.jstor.org/stable/24326818.

Castro, Efraín, ed. *El arte de Mezcala*. Chilpancingo: Gobierno Constitucional del Estado de Guerrero, 1993.

———. "El estilo Mezcala." In *El arte de Mezcala*, edited by Castro, 72–95.

Cepeda Cárdenas, Gerardo. "Estela del Cerro de los Monos, Tlalchapa, Guerrero." *Boletín del INAH* no. 40 (1970): 15–20.

Cervera, José Antonio, ed. *Cartas de Parián. Los chinos de Manila a finales del siglo XVI a través de los ojos de Juan Cobo y Domingo de Salazar*. México, DF: Palabra de Clío, 2015. https://colmex.academia.edu/JoseCervera.

Chadwick, R. "Archaeological Synthesis of Michoacán and Adjacent Regions." In *Archaeology of Northern Mesoamerica*, vol. 11, Part 2: *Handbook of Middle American Indians*, edited by G. F Ekholm and I. Bernal, 657–93. Austin: University of Texas Press, 1971.

Chaunu, Pierre. *Las Filipinas en el Pacífico de los siglos ibéricos. Siglos XVI, XVII y XVIII.* México: Instituto Mexicano de Comercio Exterior, 1974.

Clark, John E., and Mary E. Pye. "The Pacific Coast and the Olmec Question." *Studies in the History of Art*, vol. 58: *Olmec Art and Archaeology in Mesoamerica*, 216–51. http://www.jstor.org/stable/42622275.

Coe, Michael D., and Rex Koontz. *Mexico: From the Olmecs to the Aztecs*, 7th ed. London: Thames & Hudson, 2013.

Coe, Michael, Dean Snow, and Elizabeth Benson. *Atlas of Ancient America*. New York: Facts on File, 1986.

Coe, Sophie D., and Michael D. Coe. *The True History of Chocolate*. Thames & Hudson: London, 2003.

Cohen, Martin A. "Antonio Díaz de Cáceres: Marrano Adventurer in Colonial Mexico." *American Jewish Historical Quarterly* 60, no. 2 (December 1970): 169–84.

———. *The Martyr: Luis de Carvajal, a Secret Jew in Sixteenth-Century Mexico*. Albuquerque: University of New Mexico Press, 2001.

Coloquio de Arqueología y Etnohistoria del Estado de Guerrero. *Primer Coloquio de Arquelogía y Etnohistoria del Estado de Guerrero*. 1st ed. México, DF: Instituto Nacional de Antropología e Historia; Chilpancingo, Mexico: Gobierno del Estado de Guerrero, 1986.

Contreras, José Enciso. *Taxco en el siglo XVI: sociedad y normatividad en un real de minas novohispano*. Zacatecas: Ayuntamiento de Zacatecas and Universidad Autónoma de Zacatecas, 1999.

Conway, G. R. G., ed. *An Englishman and the Mexican Inquisition, 1556–1560: being an account of the voyage of R. Tomson to New Spain, his trial for heresy in the City of Mexico, and other contemporary historical documents*. México: Privately printed, 1927.

Curiel, Gustavo. "De cajones, fardos y fardillos. Reflexiones en torno a las cargazones de mercaderías que arribaron desde el Oriente a la Nueva España." In *A 500 años del hallazgo del Pacífico. La presencia novohispana en el Mar del Sur*, edited by Yuste López, y Guadalupe Pinzón Ríos, 191–216. México: UNAM, 2016. http://www.historicas.unam.mx/publicaciones/publicadigital/libros/hallazgo_pacifico/novohispana.html.

Dakin Anderson, Karin. "El náhuatl del Norte y Sur de Guerrero: Relaciones lingüísticas con el náhuatl del occidente y la costa del Pacífico." In Miller, Johnson, and von Mentz, eds., *Por el norte de Guerrero*, 311–17.

Daneels, Annick, and Gerardo Gutiérrez Mendoza, eds. *El poder compartido: Ensayos sobre la arqueológica de organizaciones políticas segmentarias y oligárquicas*. México and Zamora: Publicaciones de la Casa Chata, 2012.

Davies, Claude Nigel. *The Aztec Empire: The Toltec Resurgence*. Norman: Oklahoma University Press, 1987.

Davies, Claude Nigel Byam. *Los señoríos independientes del imperio Azteca*. México: INAH, 1968.

Dehouve, Danièle. "Dos relatos sobre migraciones nahuas en el estado de Guerrero." *Estudios de Cultura Náhuatl* 12 (1976): 137–48.

———. "Les élites indiennes du Mexique central face à la conquête espagnole." *Caravelle (1988–)* no. 67 (1996): 9–21. http://www.jstor.org/stable/40852584.

———. *Entre el caimán y el jaguar: los pueblos indios de Guerrero*. México: CIESAS, 1994.

———. *Hacia una historia del espacio en la Montaña de Guerrero*. México: CESMECA, 1995.

———. "Historia del municipio en la Montaña." In *Multipardismo y poder en municipios indígenas de Guerrero*, edited by Danièle Dehouve, Víctor Franco Pellotier, and Aline Hémond, 97–197.

———. "Les Lienzos de Malinaltepec (.tat de Guerrero). Reproduction et analyse." *Cahiers des Amériques Latines* 25 (1982): 95–121.

———. "La migración, una tradición prehispánica: la Montaña de Guerrero." *Rutas de campo* no. 9 (enero-ferbero 2015), 20–28. https://u-paris10.academia.edu/dehouvedani%C3%A8le.

———. *Quand les banquiers étaient des saints: 450 ans de l'histoire économique et sociale d'une province indienne du Méxique*. Paris: Éditions du Centre National de la Recherche Scientifique, 1990.

———. "Las separaciones de pueblos en la región de Tlapa (siglo XVIII)." *Historia Mexicana* 33, no.4 (abril–junio 1984), 379–404. www.jstor.org/stable/25732118.

Del Valle Pavón, Guillermina. "Los mercaderes de México y la transgresión de los límites al comercio pacífico en Nueva España, 1550–1620." *La Economía en tiempos del Quijote*, número extraordinario (2005): 213–40. https://mora.academia.edu/GuillerminadelValle/Historia-del-comercio-Pac%C3%ADfico.

Dewan, Leslie, and Dorothy Hosler. "Ancient Maritime Trade on Balsa Rafts: An Engineering Analysis." *Journal of Anthropological Research* 64, no. 1 (2008): 19–40. https://www.jstor.org/stable/20371179.

Díaz Oyarzábal, Clara Luz. "La presencia teotihuacana en las estelas de Tepecuacuilco." In *Primer coloquio de arqueología y etnohistoria del estado de Guerrero*, 203–8.

Dibble, Charles E., and Arthur J. O. Anderson, eds. and trans. *Florentine Codex. General History of the Things of New Spain, Fray Bernardino de Sahagún*, Book 10, *The People*. Santa Fe, NM: The School of American Research and the University of Utah, 1961.

Diehl, Richard A. "Olmec Archaeology After 'Regional Perspectives': An Assessment of Recent Research." In *Studies in the History of Art*, Vol. 58: *Olmec Art and Archaeology in Mesoamerica*, 18–29. Washington, DC: National Gallery of Art, 2006. http://www.jstor.org/stable/42622265.

Drennan, Robert D. "Long-Distance Movement of Goods in the Mesoamerican Formative and Classic. *American Antiquity* 49, no. 1 (1984): 27–43. http://www.jstor.org/stable/280510.

———. "Long-Distance Transport Costs in Pre-Hispanic Mesoamerica." *American Anthropologist*, n.s., 86, no. 1 (1984): 105–12. http://www.jstor.org/stable/679394.

Ebert, C. E., M. Dennison, K. G. Hirth, S. B. McClure, and D. J. Kennett. "Formative Period Obsidian Exchange Along the Pacific Coast of Mesoamerica." *Archaeometry* (2014): 1–20. https://psu-us.academia.edu/DouglasKennett.

Espejel, Claudia. "Reflexiones acerca del estado Tarasco a partir de las nuevas investigaciones etnohistóricas y arqueológicas." In *Nuevas contribuciones al estudio del antiguo Michoacán*, edited by Sarah Albiez-Weick and Hans Roskamp, 73–94. Zamora: Colegio de Michoacán, 2016.

Evans, Susan Toby. *Ancient Mexico and Central America: Archaeology and Culture History*, 3rd ed. London: Thames & Hudson, 2013.

Fernández del Castillo, Francisco. "Gil González de Benavides." *Memorias de la Academia Mexicana de la Historia* 28, no. 3 (1969): 313–20. https://www.academiamh.com.mx/memorias-de-la-amh/tomo-xxviii.

Gadow, Hans. *Through Southern Mexico, Being an Account of the Travels of a Naturalist*. London: Witherby & Co., 1908.

Galarza, Joaquín. *Lienzos de Chiepetlan: Manuscrits pictographiques et manuscrits en caractères latins de San Miguel Chiepetlan, Guerrero, Mexique.* Mexico: Mission Archéologique et Ethnologique Française au Mexique, 1972.

Galeana Cruz, Elizabeth J. "Resultados preliminares del salvamento arqueológico realizado en El Embarcadero I, estado de Guerrero." Unpublished manuscript, n.d. http://remarq.ning.com/page/resultados-preliminares-del-salvamento-arqueologico-realizado-en-. Accessed June 11, 2017.

García Abasolo, Antonio. "Problemas para gobernar un imperio. Aspectos del modelo colonial en Filipinas, siglos XVI–XVIII." In *España, el Atlántico y el Pacífico. V Centenario del descubrimiento de la Mar del Sur (1513–2013) y otros estudios sobre Extremadura, XIV Jornadas de Historia en Llerena.* Edited by Félix Iñesta Mena, 9–29. Llerena: Sociedad Extremeña de Historia, 2015.

García Cook, Ángel. "Las cerámicas más tempranas en México." *Revista de Arqueología Americana* no. 14 (1998): 7–64.

García Martínez, Bernardo. *El Marquesado del Valle. Tres siglos de régimen señorial en Nueva España.* México: Colegio de México, 1969.

———. *Los pueblos de la Sierra: El poder y el espacio entre los indios del norte de Puebla hasta 1700.* México: Colegio de México, 2005.

García Mendoza, Jaime. "La formacion de grupos de poder en la provincia de la plata en el siglo XVI." PhD diss., UNAM, 2002. https://repositorio.unam.mx/contenidos/8402.

García Payón, José. "Estudio Preliminar de la Zona Arqueológica de Texmelincan, Estado de Guerrero." *El México Antiguo* 5, no. 11/12 (1941): 361–64.

García Zapoteco, Mercedes. "La población en Taxco: siglos XVI al XIX." In *Por el norte de Guerrero*, edited by María Teresa Pavía Miller, Anne Warren Johnson and Brígida von Mentz, 149–177.

Gay, Carlo T. E. *Mezcala: Architecture in Miniature.* Brussels: Académie Royale de Belgique, Mémoires de la Classe des Beaux-Arts, Collection in-8, 2ᵉ série, T. XV, Fascicule 3, 1987.

———. "Mezcala: Herencia cultural de Guerrero." In *El arte de Mezcala*, edited by Castro 186–225.

———. *Xochipala: The Beginnings of Olmec Art.* Princeton, NJ: Princeton University Museum, 1972.

Gerhard, Peter, "Congregaciones de Indios en la Nueva España antes de 1570." *Historia Mexicana* 26 no. 3 (1977): 347–95.

———. *A Guide to the Historical Geography of New Spain*. Cambridge: Cambridge University Press, 1972.

Gibson, Charles. *The Aztecs Under Spanish Rule. A History of the Indians of the Valley of Mexico, 1519–1810*. Stanford, CA: Stanford University Press, 1964.

González, Carlos Javier, and Bertina Olmedo Vera. *Esculturas mezcala en el Templo Mayor*. México, DF: INAH, G. V. Editores, Asociación de Amigos del Templo Mayor, 1990.

González Claverán, Virginia. *La expedición científica de Malaspina en Nueva España, 1789–1794*. México: Colegio de México, 1988.

———. *Malaspina en Acapulco*. Madrid: Turner, 1989.

González Crespo, Norberto. *Patrón de asentamiento prehispánico en la parte central del bajo Balsas: un ensayo metodológico*, vol. 1. México: SEP INAH, 1979.

González Quintero, Lauro, and Jesús Ignacio Mora Echeverría. "Estudio arqueológico-ecológico de un caso de explotación de recursos litorales en la Costa Grande de Guerrero (1300–600 a.C.)." In *El Pasado arqueológico de Guerrero*, edited by Niederberger and Robles, 321–37.

Good, Catherine. "Salt Production and Commerce in Guerrero, Mexico: An Ethnographic Contribution to Historical Reconstruction." *Ancient Mesoamerica* 6, no. 1 (1995): 1–14.

Good Eshelman, Catherine. "Los estudios etnohistóricos." In *Guerrero: una mirada antropológica e histórica*, edited by Gloria Artis, Miguel Ángel Rubio, and Mette Marie Wacher, 251–79. México, INAH, 2007.

Griffin, Gillett G. "Xochipala, the Earliest Great Art Style in Mexico." *Proceedings of the American Philosophical Society* 116, no. 4 (1972): 301–9. http://www.jstor.org/stable/985900.

Grove, David C. *Chalcatzingo: Excavations on the Olmec Frontier*. London: Thames & Hudson, 1984.

———. "Olmec Archaeology: A Half Century of Research and its Accomplishments." *Journal of World Prehistory* 11, no. 1 (1997): 51–101. http://www.jstor.org/stable/25801106.

———. "Olmec Horizons in Formative Period Mesoamerica: Diffusion or Social Evolution?" In *Latin American Horizons*, edited by D. S. Rice, 83–111. Washington, DC: Dumbarton Oaks, 1993.

———. "The Olmec Paintings of Oxtotitlan Cave, Guerrero, Mexico." *Studies in Pre-Columbian Art and Archaeology* no. 6 (1970): 2–36. http://www.jstor.org/stable/41263411.

Grove, David C., and Louise I. Paradis. "An Olmec Stela from San Miguel Amuco, Guerrero." *American Antiquity* 36, no. 1 (1971): 95–102. http://www.jstor.org/stable/278026.

Gruzinski, Serge. *The Conquest of Mexico: The Incorporation of Indian Societies into the Western World, 16th–18th Centuries.* Cambridge: Polity Press, 1988.

Guardino, Peter F. *Peasants, Politics and the Formation of Mexico's National State: Guerrero, 1800–1857.* Stanford, CA: Stanford University Press, 1996.

Gutiérrez, Gerardo. *The Aztec Conquest of the Kingdom of Tlapa, Guerrero. La conquista mexica de Tlapa, Guerrero.* Mexico City: Leonel Rivera Editor, 2017. https://colorado.academia.edu/GerardoGutierrez.

———. "The Cohimbre Stela: Death, Sacrifice and Political Ideology on the Guerrero Coast." *Mexicon* 37, no. 1 (2015): 19–26. https://colorado.academia.edu/GerardoGutierrez.

———. "The Expanding Polity: Patterns of the Territorial Expansion of the Post-Classic Señorío of Tlapa-Tlachinollan in the Mixteca-Nahuatl-Tlapaneca Region of Guerrero." PhD diss., Pennsylvania State University, 2002. http://etda.libraries.psu.edu/theses/approved/WorldWideIndex/ETD-166/index.html.

———. "Negotiating Aztec Tributary Demands in the Tribute Record of Tlapa." In *Merchants, Markets, and Exchange in the Pre-Columbian World*, edited by Kenneth G. Hirth and Joanne Pillsbury, 141–64. Washington, DC: Dumbarton Oaks, 2013. https://colorado.academia.edu/GerardoGutierrez.

Gutiérrez, Gerardo, and Baltazar Brito, eds. *El Códice Azoyú 2: política y territorio en el señorío de Tlapa-Tlachinollan, Siglos XIV–XVI.* México: SEP; Conaculta: INAH, Raíz del Sol, 2014. https://colorado.academia.edu/GerardoGutierrez.

Gutiérrez, Gerardo, Viola König, and Baltazar Brito, eds. *Códice Humboldt Fragmento 1 Ms. amer. 2 y Códice Azoyú 2 reverso. Nómina de tributos de Tlapa y su provincia al Imperio Mexicano.* México: CIESAS; Berlin: Stiftung Preussischer Kulturbesitz, 2009. https://colorado.academia.edu/GerardoGutierrez.

Gutiérrez, Gerardo, and Mary E. Pye. "Los gobernadores de Techan, Guerrero: anatomía de una cueva del Preclásico medio en Guerrero." *Arqueología Mexicana* no.142 (2016): 77–83.

Gutiérrez, Gerardo, Alfredo Vera, Mary E. Pye, and Juana Mitzi Serrano. *Contlalco y La Coquera: Arqueología de Dos Sitios Tempranos del*

Municipio de Tlapa, Guerrero, Con Otros Ensayos Sobre el Período Formativo y los Desarrollos Culturales del Oriente de Guerrero Hasta el Período Postclásico. Tlapa: Municipio de Tlapa de Comonfort, 2011. https://colorado.academia.edu/GerardoGutierrez.

Gutiérrez Mendoza, G. *Catálogo de sitios arqueológicos de las regiones Mixteca-Tlapaneca-Nahua y Costa Chica de Guerrero*, vol. 1. México: CIESAS, 2007.https://colorado.academia.edu/GerardoGutierrez.

———. "La organización político-territorial del "Reino" de Tlapa, siglos xv y xvi: Elementos empíricos para entender la estructura espacial de la unidad política mesoamericana." In *Bases de la complejidad social en Oaxaca: memoria de la Cuarta Mesa Redonda de Monte Albán*, edited by Nelly M. Robles García, 309–78. México: INAH, 2009. https://colorado.academia.edu/GerardoGutierrez.

———. "Territorial Structure and Urbanism in Mesoamérica: Huaxtec and Mixtec-Tlapanec-Nahua Cases." In *El urbanismo mesoamericano. Urbanism in Mesoamerica*, edited by William T. Saunders, Alba Guadalupe Mastache, and Robert H. Cobean, 85–118. México, DF: INAH; University Park: Pennsylvania State University, 2003.

Haskett, Robert. *Indigenous Rulers: An Ethnohistory of Town Government in Colonial Cuernavaca*. Albuquerque: University of New Mexico Press, 1991.

———. "Living in Two Worlds: Cultural Continuity and Change among Cuernavaca's Indigenous Ruling Elite." *Ethnohistory* 35, no. 1 (Winter 1988): 34–59. https://www.jstor.org/stable/482432.

———. "'Not a Pastor, but a Wolf": Indigenous-Clergy Relations in Early Cuernavaca and Taxco." *Americas* 50, no. 3 (1994): 293–336. http://www.jstor.org/stable/1007163.

———. "'Our Suffering with the Taxco Tribute': Involuntary Mine Labor and Indigenous Society in Central New Spain." *Hispanic American Historical Review* 71, no. 3 (1991): 447–75. http://www.jstor.org/stable/2515879.

———. *Visions of Paradise. Primordial Titles and Mesoamerican History in Cuernavaca*. Norman: University of Oklahoma Press, 2005.

Hassig, Ross. *Aztec Warfare, Imperial Expansion and Political Control*. Norman: University of Oklahoma Press, 1988.

Henderson, John S. *Atopula, Guerrero and Olmec Horizons in Mesoamerica*. Yale University Publications in Anthropology,

No.77. New Haven, CT: Department of Anthropology, Yale University, 1979.

Hendrichs Pérez, Pedro R. *Por tierras ignotas: viajes y observaciones en la región del río de las Balsas*, 2 vols. México: Editorial Cultura, 1945–1946.

Hepp, Guy David. "La Consentida: Initial Early Formative Period Settlement, Subsistence, and Social Organization on the Pacific Coast of Oaxaca, Mexico." PhD diss., University of Colorado, 2015. https://csusb.academia.edu/GuyDavidHepp.

Hernández Jamies, "El cacicazgo de los Moctezuma y la comunidad indígena en la alcaldía mayor de Chilapa druante la colonia." Revised manuscript of licenciatura thesis, UNAM, 1998. https://unam.academia.edu/Jes%C3%BAsHern%C3%A1ndezJaimes.

———. "El fruto prohibido. El cacao de Guayaquil y el mercado novohispano, siglos XVI–XVIII." *Estudios de historia novohispana* no. 39 (julio–diciembre 2008): 43–79. https://unam.academia.edu/Jes%C3%BAsHern%C3%A1ndezJaimes.

Herrera Muñoz, Alberto, and Elizabeth Mejía Pérez Campos. "Minería prehispánica de Querétaro." In *Tributo a Jaime Litvak King*, edited by Paul Schmidt Schoenberg, Edith Ortiz Díaz, and Joel Santos Ramírez, 219–31. México: UNAM, 2008.

Hill Boone, Elizabeth. "Manuscript Painting in Service of Imperial Ideology." In Berdan, Blanton, Hill Boone, Hodge, Smith, and Umberger, eds., *Aztec Imperial Strategies*, 181–206.

Himmerich y Valencia, Robert. *The Encomenderos of New Spain 1521–1555*. Austin: University of Texas Press, 1996.

Hirth, Kenneth. *The Aztec Economic World: Merchants and Markets in Ancient Mesoamerica*. Cambridge: Cambridge University Press, 2016.

Historia de Chilpancingo. Chilpancingo: Asociación de Historiadores de Guerrero, A. C., H. Ayuntamiento de Chilpancingo, Gobierno del Estado de Guerrero, Universidad Autónoma de Guerrero, 1999.

Hoberman, Louisa Schell. *Mexico's Merchant Elite. 1590–1660, Silver, State and Society*. Durham: Duke University Press, 1991.

Hosler, Dorothy. "Ancient West Mexican Metallurgy: South and Central American Origins and West Mexican Transformations." *American Anthropologist*, n.s., 90, no. 4 (1988): 832–855. http://www.jstor.org/stable/680760.

———. "Excavations at the Copper Smelting Site of El Manchon, Guerrero, México, 2004." http://www.famsi.org/reports/01058/.

———. "Nuevos hallazgos sobre la metalurgia antigua de Guerrero." In Niederberger and Reyna Robles, eds., *El Pasado arqueológico de Guerrero*, 225–41.

———. "Sound, Color and Meaning in the Metallurgy of Ancient West Mexico." *World Archaeology* 27, no. 1 (1995): 110–15. http://www.jstor.org/stable/124780.

———. "West Mexican Metallurgy Revisited and Revised." *Journal of World Prehistory* 22, no. 3 (2009): 185–212. http://www.jstor.org/stable/25801271.

Hosler, Dorothy, Heather Lechtman, and Olaf Holm. "Axe-monies and Their Relatives." *Studies in Pre-Columbian Art and Archaeology* no. 30 (1990): 1–97, 99–103.

Huerta Carrillo, Alejandro and Eugenia Berthier Villaseñor. "Análisis y técnica de manufactura del Códice Azoyú 2." *Antropología. Boletín Oficial del INAH* no. 69 (2003): 50–60. https://revistas.inah.gob.mx/index.php/antropologia/article/view/4956/4982.

Iwaniszewski, Stanislaw. "De Nahualac al Cerro Ehécatl: una tradición prehispánica más en Petlacala." In *Primer coloquio de arqueología y etnohistoria del estado de Guerrero*, 497–518.

Jacobs, Ian. *Ranchero Revolt: The Mexican Revolution in Guerrero*. Austin: University of Texas Press, 1982.

Jacobs Muller, E. Florencia. *El Códice de Cualác*. México: INAH, 1958.

Jiménez García, Elizabeth. "Apuntes sobre la arqueología de Tlapa, Guerrero." In Niederberger and Reyna Robles, eds., *El Pasado arqueológico de Guerrero*, 387–407.

———. "Materiales arqueológicos de orígen orgánico procedentes de la región norte del estado de Guerrero." In Niederberger and Reyna Robles, eds., *El Pasado arqueológico de Guerrero*, 487–504.

Jiménez García, Esperanza Elizabeth. "La nobleza indígena de la Montaña de Guerrero: Tlapa-Tlachinolla 1499–1800." PhD diss., UNAM, 2016. http://132.248.9.195/ptd2016/octubre/0751193/Index.html.

Jiménez García, Elizabeth, Guadalupe Martínez Donjuán, and Aarón Arboleyda Castro. "Época prehispánica." In Jiménez García, Martínez Donjuán, Castro, Calvo eds., *Historia General de Guerrero*, , vol. 1, 1–139.

Jiménez García, Elizabeth, Guadalupe Martínez Donjuán, Aarón Arboleyda Castro, and Raúl Vélez Calvo, eds. *Historia General de Guerrero*, 3 vols. México, DF: INAH, Gobierno del Estado de Guerrero, JGH Editores, 1998.

Jiménez P., Blanca M., and Samuel L. Villela F. *Historia y cultura trás el glifo: los códices de Guerrero*. México: INAH, 1998.

Jiménez Padilla, Blanca, and Samuel Villela Flores. "Rituales y protocolos de posesión territorial en documentos pictográficos y títulos del actual estado de Guerrero." *Relaciones* 24 (verano 2003): 94–112.

Just, Bryan. "Xochipala: Salvaging a Looted Culture and Its Art." Online lecture, June 25, 2020. https://artmuseum.princeton.edu/false/video/xochipala-salvaging-looted-culture-and-its-art.

Kamen, Henry. *Spain's Road to Empire. The Making of a World Power 1492–1763*. London: Penguin Books, 2002.

Kartunnen, Frances, and James Lockhart. *Nahuatl in the Middle Years: Language Contact in Texts of the Colonial Period*. Berkeley: University of California Press, 1976.

Kennett, Douglas J., Dolores R. Piperno, John G. Jones, Hector Neff, Barbara Voorhies, Megan K. Walsh, and Brendan J. Culleton. "Pre-pottery Farmers on the Pacific Coast of Southern Mexico." *Journal of Archaeological Science* 37 (2010): 3401–11. https://psu-us.academia.edu/BrendanCulleton.

Kennett, Douglas J., Barbara Voorhies, Thomas A. Wake, and Natalia Martínez. "Long-Term Effects of Human Predation on Marine Ecosystems in Guerrero, Mexico." In *Human Impacts on Ancient Marine Ecosystems: A Global Perspective*, edited by Torben C. Rick and Jon M. Erlandson, 103–24. Berkeley: University of California Press, 2008.

King, Willard F. *Juan Ruiz de Alarcón, letrado y dramaturgo: Su mundo mexicano y español*. México: Colegio de México, 1989.

Kurtz, Donald V. "Peripheral and Transitional Markets: The Aztec Case." *American Ethnologist* no. 4 (1974): 685–705. http://www.jstor.org/stable/643375.

Kyle, Chris. "From Burros to Buses: Transport Efficiency and Economic Development in Guerrero, Mexico." *Journal of Anthropological Research* 52, no. 4 (1996): 411–32. http://www.jstor.org/stable/3630295.

Labarthe R., María de la Cruz. "Provincia de Zacatula: historia social y económica." Master's thesis, Escuela Nacional de Antropología e Historia, 1969.

Lebeuf, Arnold. "Origen y genealogía de los Moctezuma, caciques de Chilapa." *Estudios Latinoamericanos* no. 29 (2009): 253–66. https://jagiellonian.academia.edu/ArnoldLebeuf.

Leibsohn, Dana. "Colony and Cartography: Shifting Signs on Indigenous Maps of New Spain." In *Reframing the Renaissance: Visual Culture in Europe and Latin America 1450–1650*, edited by Claire Farago, 265–340. New Haven, CT: Yale University Press, 1995.

León Portilla, Miguel. "Lo que supo y lo que no supo Hernán Cortés acerca del Océano Pacífico." In *A 500 años del hallazgo del Pacífico. La presencia novohispana en el Mar del Sur*, edited by Carmen Yuste López and Guadalupe Pinzón Ríos, 53–82. México: UNAM, 2016. http://www.historicas.unam.mx/publicaciones/publicadigital/libros/hallazgo_pacifico/novohispana.html.

Lister, Robert H. "Archaeology of the Middle Rio Balsas Basin, Mexico." *American Antiquity* 13, no. 1 (1947): 67–78. http://www.jstor.org/stable/275756.

Litvak King, Jaime. *Cihuatlán y Tepecoacuilco: Provincias tributarias de México en el siglo XVI*. Instituto de Investigaciones Históricas, Sección de Antropología, Serie Antropológica, 12. Mexico: UNAM, 1971.

Lobato, Rodolfo. "El sistema de comunicación religiosa de Xihuacan, un ejemplo de la iconografía de la Costa Grande de Guerrero." In *Geometrías de la imaginación: Diseño e iconografía de Guerrero*, edited by Fernando Ygnacio Cuauhtémoc Reyes Álvarez and Gerardo Guerrero Gómez, 181–82. México, DF: CONACULTA, 2014.

Lockhart, James. *The Nahuas After the Conquest: A Social and Cultural History of the Indians of Central Mexico Sixteenth Through Eighteenth Centuries*. Stanford, CA: Stanford University Press, 1992.

———. *Nahuas and Spaniards: Postconquest Central Mexican History and Philology*. Stanford, CA: Stanford University Press, 1991.

Lockhart, James, Frances Berdan, and Arthur J. O. Anderson, eds. *The Tlaxcalan Actas: A Compendium of the Records of the Cabildo of Tlaxcala (1545–1627)*. Salt Lake City: University of Utah Press, 1986.

Lockhart, James, and Stuart B. Schwartz. *Early Latin America. A History of Colonial Spanish America and Brazil*. Cambridge Latin American Studies, 46. Cambridge: Cambridge University Press, 1983.

Lope Blanch, Juan M. *El habla de Diego de Ordaz: contribución a la historia del español americano*. México: UNAM, 1985.

López, Julieta. "Teotihuacan y el estado de Guerrero, interacción tecnológica y cultural." *Boletin del Centro INAH de Guerrero*, año 2, no. 7 (enero–marzo 2006): 16–19. https://www.academia.edu/5843887/Tecnolog%C3%ADa_de_cuentas_en_piedra_caliza_del_%C3%A1rea_Mezcala_Guerrero.

López, Rick. *Crafting Mexico: Intellectuals, Artisans, the State after the Revolution*. Durham, NC: Duke University Press, 2010.

Love, Michael. "Recent Research in the Southern Highlands and Pacific Coast of Mesoamerica." *Journal of Archaeological Research* 15, no. 4 (2007): 275–328. http://www.jstor.org/stable/41053242.

Machuca, Paulina. "El arribo de plantas a las Indias Occidentales: el caso del Balsas-Jalisco a través de las Relaciones geográficas del siglo xvi." *Relaciones* 34, no. 136 (2013): 73–114. https://colmich.academia.edu/PaulinaMachuca.

———. "The Arrival of American Plants in the Philippines: Ecological Colonialism in the Sixteenth-to-Eighteenth Centuries." *Anais de história de além-mar* 15 (2014): 231–60. https://colmich.academia.edu/PaulinaMachuca.

———. *Élites y gobierno en Colima de la Nueva España siglo XVII*. Colima: Secretaría de Cultura, Archivo Histórico del Municipio de Colima, 2017. https://colmich.academia.edu/PaulinaMachuca.

———. "Fortuna de mar. Enfermedad y muerte en la carrera de Filipinas, siglo XVII." In *El mar: percepciones, lecturas y contextos. Una mirada cultural a los entornos marítimos*, edited by Guadalupe Pinzón Ríos and Flor Trejo Rivera, 321–40. México: UNAM, 2015.

———. "La palma de coco: regalo de Filipinas a México (siglos XVI–XVII)." In *México y Filipinas: culturas y memorias sobre el Pacífico*, edited by Thomas Calvo and Paulina Machuca, 321–40. Zamora: Colegio de Michoacán; Manila: Ateneo de Manila University, 2016. https://colmich.academia.edu/PaulinaMachuca.

———. *El vino de cocos en la Nueva España. Historia de una transculturación en el siglo XVII*. Zamora: Colegio de Michoacán, 2018. https://colmich.academia.edu/PaulinaMachuca.

Maldonado, R. *Ofrendas asociadas a entierros del Infiernillo en el Balsas*. México: SEP-INAH Colección Científica, 1980.

Maldonado Cárdenas, Rubén. "Las paletas del Infiernillo, Michoacán, Guerrero y las Hohokam del Suroeste de los Estados Unidos." In Niederberger and Reyna Robles, eds., *El Pasado arqueológico de Guerrero*, 151–73.

Manzanilla López, Rubén. "La investigación arqueológica de la Costa Grande." In *Guerrero: una mirada antropológica e histórica*, edited by Gloria Artis, Miguel Ángel Rubio, and Mette Marie Wacher, 107–31. México: INAH, 2007.

———. *La región arqueológica de la Costa Grande de Guerrero: su definición a través de la organización social y territorialidad prehispánicas*. México: INAH, 2008.

———. "La zona arqueológica de Cuetlajuchitlán: Nuevos hallazgos en el estado de Guerrero." *Boletín "Cemanáhuac"* no. 16 (julio 1992): 11–17. https://independent.academia.edu/Jagonzalezg.

Manzanilla López, Rubén, and Alberto Mena Cruz. "Arqueología de la Punta Diamante, Puerto Marqués, estado de Guerrero." *Arqueología* 51 (diciembre 2016): 153–66. https://revistas.inah.gob.mx/index.php/arqueologia/article/view/10865/11633.

Manzanilla López, Rubén, and Jorge Arturo Talavera González. "Cuetlajuchitlan, sitio preurbano en la región Mezcala." *Arqueología Mexicana* 14, no. 82 (noviembre–diciembre 2006): 47–51.

Manzanilla López, Rubén, Jorge Arturo Talavera González, and Juan Martín Rojas Chávez. "Interpretaciones de la dinámica cultural en el Noreste de Guerrero durante el Preclásico Tardío y Terminal: el caso de Cuetlajuchitlán." In Niederberger and Reyna Robles, eds., *El Pasado arqueológico de Guerrero*, 283–300.

Maquivar, Consuelo. "Derrotero histórico del galeón de Acapulco." *Artes de México* no.190 (1976–1977): 5–20. http://www.jstor.org/stable/24324400.

Marino Flores, Anselmo. "Panorama étnica del estado de Guerrero en la época prehispánica." In *Primer coloquio de arqueología y etnohistoria del estado de Guerrero*, 521–35.

Martínez Donjuán, G. "Los olmecas en el Estado de Guerrero." In *Los Olmecas en Mesoamérica*, edited by John E. Clark, 143–63. México: El Equilibrista; Madrid: Turner Libros, 1994.

Martínez Donjuán, Guadalupe. "Sculpture from Teopantecuanitlan, Guerrero." In *The Place of Stone Monuments: Context, Use and Meaning in Mesoamerica's Preclassic Transition*, edited by Julia Guernsey, John E Clark, and Barbara Arroyo, 55–76. Washington, DC: Dumbarton Oaks, 2010.

———. "Teopantecuanitlán." *Arqueología Mexicana* 2, no. 12 (1995): 58–62.

———. "Teopantecuanitlán." In *Primer coloquio de arqueología y etnohistoria del estado de Guerrero*, 55–80.

———. "Teopantecuanitlan, Guerrero: Un sitio olmeca." *Revista Mexicana de Estudios Antropológicos* 28, no. 3 (enero–abril 1982): 123–32.

Martínez Donjuán, Guadalupe, and Reyna Beatriz Solís Ciriaco. "Producción especializada de bienes de prestigio en concha de Teopantecuanitlán," 2011. https://www.academia.edu/9717062/Producci%C3%B3n_especializada_de_bienes_de_prestigio_en_concha_de_Teopantecuanitl%C3%A1n_Guerrero.

Matos Moctezuma, Eduardo. "Los mexicas y el rumbo sur del universo." In Castro, *El arte de Mezcala*, 120–39.

———. "Presencia del Sur en el Templo Mayor de Tenochtitlan." In Niederberger and Reyna Robles, eds., *El Pasado arqueológico de Guerrero*, 127–49.

Meanwell, Jennifer. "Technical Requirements and Technical Choices in Pottery Production: A View from the Middle Balsas Region of Guerrero, Mexico." *American Antiquity* 80. no. 2 (2015): 312–31.

Megged, Amos. "Salvaging Recurring Themes of Historical Memory in the Cohuixca Province of Tepecoacuilco (Cohuixcatlacapan), Guerrero, Mexico, 1460 to 1580." *Ancient Mesoamerica* 28 (2017): 383–401. https://www.cambridge.org/core.

Melgar Tísoc, Emiliano, and Reyna Solís Ciriaco. "El estilo Mezcala en el Templo Mayor: Manufacturas." *Boletín del Centro INAH de Guerrero* 2, no. 7 (enero–marzo 2006): 11–15. https://inah.academia.edu/REYNABEATRIZSOL%C3%8DSCIRIACO.

Meza Herrera, Malinali. "Yopes y tlapanecas en el siglo XVI: intento de una diferenciación." In *Primer coloquio de arqueología y etnohistoria del estado de Guerrero*, 391–403.

Michelet, Dominque. "Apuntes para el análisis de las migraciones en el México prehispánico." In *Movimientos de población en el occidente de México*, edited by T. Calvo and G. López, 13–24. México: CEMCA and Colegio de Michoacán, 1988.

Miller, Mary Ellen. *The Art of Mesoamerica: From Olmec to Aztec*, 3rd ed. London: Thames & Hudson, 2001.

———. "The Ballgame." *Record of the Art Museum, Princeton University* 48, no. 2 (1989): 22–31. http://www.jstor.org/stable/3774731.

Miranda Arrieta, Eduardo. *Economía y comunicaciones en el estado de Guerrero 1877–1910*. Morelia: Universidad Michoacana de San Nicolás Hidalgo, 1994.

Miranda, José. *El tributo indígena en la Nueva España durante el siglo XVI*. México: Colegio de México, 1952.

Miyata Rodríguez, Etsuko. "The Early Manila Galleon Trade: Merchants' Networks and Markets in Sixteenth- and Seventeenth-Century Mexico." In *Asia and Spanish America: Trans-Pacific Artistic and Cultural Exchange 1500–1850; Papers from the 2006 Mayer Center Symposium at the Denver Art Museum*, edited by Donna Pierce and Ronald Otsuka, 37–58. Denver, CO: Denver Art Museum, 2009.

Moedano Navarro, Gabriel. "Notas etnohistóricas sobre la población negra de la Costa Chica" In *Primer coloquio de arqueología y etnohistoria del estado de Guerrero*, 551–62.

Moguel, María Antonieta. "Exploraciones arqueológicas en el Valle del río Cutzamala." In Niederberger and Reyna Robles, eds., *El Pasado arqueológico de Guerrero*, 321–37.

Monterrosa Desruelles, Hervé. "Proyecto Arqueológico Pezuapan (INDECO): Temporada 2007, Chilpancingo, Guerrero." In *3a. Mesa Redonda, El conocimiento antropológico e histórico sobre Guerrero, "Reflexiones sobre la investigación multidisciplinaria e integral y su impacto social,"* 1–12. https://enah.academia.edu/Herv%C3%A9MonterrosaDesruelles.

Monterrosa Desruelles, Hervé Víctor, and Emiliano Melgar Tísoc. "Tecnología de cuentas de piedra caliza del área Mezcala, Guerrero." *Boletín del Centro INAH de Guerrero* 2, no. 7 (enero–marzo 2006): 4–6. https://independent.academia.edu/Herv%C3%A9MonterrosaDesruelles.

Montes Vega, Octavio Augusto. *Héroes pioneros, padres y patrones. Construcción de la cultura política en los pueblos del Medio Balsas (Tierra Caliente de Michoacán y Guerrero)*. Zamora: Colegio de Michoacán; México: INAH and CONACULTA, 2011.

Moreno Hernández, Juana. "Excavación y restauración integral del juego de pelota de Tehuacalco, Gro." Master's thesis, Escuela Nacional de Antropología e Historia, 2012. http://200.188.19.20/islandora_74/islandora/object/tesis%3A854.

Niederberger, Christine. "Antiguos paisajes de Guerrero y el papel de su fauna en las creencias míticas." In Niederberger and Reyna Robles, eds., *El Pasado arqueológico de Guerrero*, 17–75.

——. "Excavación de un área de habitación doméstica en la capital "olmeca" de Tlacozotitlán. Reporte Preliminar." In *Primer coloquio de arqueología y etnohistoria del estado de Guerrero*, 83–103.

——. "Nácar, 'jade' y cinabrio: Guerrero y las redes de intercambio en la Mesoamérica antigua (1000–600 a.C.)." In Niederberger and Reyna Robles, eds., *El Pasado arqueológico de Guerrero*, 175–223.

Niederberger, Christine, and Rosa Ma. Reyna Robles, eds. *El Pasado arqueológico de Guerrero*. México, DF: CEMCA, Gobierno del Estado de Guerrero, INAH, 2002.

Nielsen, Jasper, Elizabeth Jiménez García, and Iván Rivera. "Across the Hills, Toward the Ocean: Teotihuacan-Style Monuments in Guerrero, Mexico." In *Interregional Interaction in Ancient Mesoamerica*, edited by Joshua D. Englehardt and Michael D Carrasco, 176–208. Louisville: University Press of Colorado, 2019.

Noguez, Xavier. "Tres documentos pictográficos sobre tributación indígena del estado de Guerrero, siglo XVI." *Historia Mexicana* 36, no. 1 (July–September 1986): 5–48. http://www.jstor.org/stable/25138091.

Nuttall, Zelia. "Chalchihuitl in Ancient Mexico." *American Anthropologist*, n.s., 3, no. 2 (April–June 1901): 227–38. http://www.jstor.org/stable/658979.

Ochoa Campos, Moisés. *Guerrero: Análisis de un Estado problema*. México: Editorial F. Trillas, S.A., 1964.

Oettinger, Marion Jr., and Fernando Horcasitas. "Lienzo of Petlacala: A Pictorial Document from Guerrero, Mexico." *Transactions of the American Philosophical Society* 72, no. 7 (1982): 1–71. http://www.jstor.org/stable/1006358.

Oropeza Keresey, Déborah. "La esclavitud asiática en el virreinato de la Nueva España, 1565–1673." *Historia Mexicana* 61, no. 1 (julio-septiembre 2011): 5–57. http://www.jstor.org/stable/23032051.

Ortega Ortiz Montero, Pedro. "Tetela del Río: iglesia colonial en la cuenca de Río Balsas." In *Primer coloquio de arqueología y etnohistoria del estado de Guerrero*, 353–70.

Oudijk, Michel R. "El Señorío de Tlapa-Tlachinollan: Los documentos pictográficos de la región de la Montaña, Guerrero." In *Códice Azoyú 2: El señorío de Tlapa-Tlachinollan*, edited by Constanza Vega Sosa and Michel R. Oudijk, 73–229. México: INAH and El Fondo de Cultura Económica, 2011. https://unam1.academia.edu/micheloudijk.

Oudijk, Michel R., and Matthew Restall. *Conquistas de buenas palabras y de guerra: una vision indígena de la Conquista*. México: UNAM, 2013. https://unam1.academia.edu/micheloudijk.

Padilla Gutiérrez, Eliseo Francisco. "La cerámica blanco granular de Guerrero: implicaciones de su distribución temporal y espacial." Master's thesis, México, UNAM, 2009.

Papers of the New World Archaeological Foundation, Number 68. Provo, UT: Brigham Young University, 2007, https://colorado.academia.edu/GerardoGutierrez.

Paradis, Louise I. "Ahuináhuac, una aglomeración urbana al final del Preclásico y principio del Clásico en la región de Mezcala-Balsas, Guerrero." In Niederberger and Reyna Robles, eds., *El Pasado arqueológico de Guerrero*, 77–97.

———. "El estilo Mezcala en contexto. Hallazgos en Ahuináhuac, Guerrero." *Arqueología* no.5 (enero–junio 1991): 59–68. http://mediateca.inah.gob.mx/islandora_74/islandora/object/issue%3A1350.

———. "The Tierra Caliente of Guerrero, Mexico: An Archaeological and Ecological Study." PhD diss., Yale University, 1974.

Paradis, Louise I., C. Bélanger, D. Raby, and B. Ross. "Le style Mezcala découvert en contexte au Guerrero (Méxique)." *Journal de la Société des américanistes* 76 (1990): 199–212. http://www.jstor.org/stable/24605622.

Paredes M., Carlos. "Sistemas de intercambio en el Estado Tarasco." In *Origen y desarrollo de la civilización en el occidente de México: homenaje a Pedro Armillas y Angel Palerm*, edited by Brigitte Boehm de Lameiras, Phil C. Weigand, Pedro Armillas García, and Ángel Palerm, 295–305. Zamora: Colegio de Michoacán, 1992.

Paredes Martínez, Carlos. "Los pueblos originarios del oriente y la Tierra Caliente de Michoacán. Ensayo historiográfico (época prehispánica y colonial)." In Paredes Martínez and Martínez Ayala, *Alzaban banderas de papel*, 18–67.

Paredes Martínez, Carlos, and Jorge Amós Martínez Ayala, eds. *Alzaban banderas de papel: los pueblos originarios del oriente y la Tierra Caliente de Michoacán*. México: Comisión Nacional para el Desarrollo de los Pueblos Indígenas, 2012.

Pavía Guzmán, Edgar. "Tlappan, una provincia guerrerense: datos y hechos históricos (siglos XVI al XVIII)." In *Primer coloquio de arqueología y etnohistoria del estado de Guerrero*, 407–22.

Pavía Miller, María Teresa. "Mulatos, moriscos y negros en Taxco." In Pavía Miller, Johnson, and von Mentz, eds., *Por el norte de Guerrero*, 111–48.

Pavía Miller, María Teresa, Anne Warren Johnson, and Brígida von Mentz, eds. *Por el norte de Guerrero: Nuevas miradas desde la antropología y la historia*. México: INAH, 2016.

Pérez Negrete, Miguel. "Arqueología de Guerrero." *Boletín del Centro INAH Guerrero* 1, no. 2 (2004): 16–17.

Pérez Negrete, Miguel, and Raúl M. Arana Álvarez. "Proyecto arqueológico Tehuacalco (Proyecto de investigación y conservación del sitio arqueológico de Tehuacalco, Guerrero)." Unpublished manuscript, n.d.

Pérez Negrete, Miguel, Hans Martz de la Vega, Guadalupe Paoky Rueda Robledo, and José Aguilera Almanza, eds. *De árboles cósmicos y jaguares: los petrograbados de La Gloria, Arqueología de Atoyac de Álvarez, Guerrero, Número 1*. México: CONACYT, 2013.

Pérez Negrete, Miguel, and Erica Arias Vázquez. "Proyecto de investigación y conservación de la zona arqueológica de Indeco (Pezuapan)." *Boletín Consejo de Arqueología*, n.d. https://www.yumpu.com/es/document/view/15887999/zona-arqueologica-pezuapan-boletin-consejo-de-arqueologia-1-.

Pérez Rodríguez, Verónica. "Recent Advances in Mixtec Archaeology." *Journal of Archaeological Research* 21, no. 1 (2013): 75–121.

Pérez Rodríguez, Verónica, and Verenice Y. Heredia Espinoza. *La epopeya de la Mixteca. Cómo se hicieron y rehicieron las sociedades complejas en la Mixteca Alta*. Zamora: Colegio de Michoacán, 2020.

Pierce, Donna, and Ronald Otsuka, eds. *Asia and Spanish America: Trans-Pacific Artistic and Cultural Exchange 1500–1850; Papers from the 2006 Mayer Center Symposium at the Denver Art Museum*. Denver, CO: Denver Art Museum, 2009.

Piña Chan, Román. "Algunos sitios arqueológicos de Oaxaca y Guerrero." *Revista Mexicana de Estudios Antropológicos* 16 (1960): 65–76.

Pineda Santa Cruz, Edgar. "Análisis de huellas de manufactura de objetos de estilo Mezcala en Guerrero." *Boletín del Centro INAH de Guerrero* 2, no. 7 (enero–marzo 2006): 7–10. https://independent.academia.edu/Herv%C3%A9MonterrosaDesruelles.

Pinzón Ríos, Guadalupe. "Descubriendo el Mar del Sur de los puertos novohispanos en las exploraciones del Pacífico (1522–1565)." In *El mundo de los conquistadores*, edited by Martín F. Ríos Saloma,

749–74. México: UNAM and Silex Ediciones, 2017. http://www.historicas.unam.mx/publicaciones/publicadigital/libros/mundo/conquistadores.html.

Polaco Ramos, Oscar J. "Restos biológicos de la costa del Pacífico." In *Primer coloquio de arqueología y etnohistoria del estado de Guerrero*, 255–63.

Pollard, Helen Perlstein. "Recent Research in West Mexican Archaeology." *Journal of Archaeological Research* 5, no. 4 (December 1997): 345–84. http://www.jstor.org/stable/41053149.

———. *Taríacuri's Legacy: The Pre-Hispanic Tarascan State*. Norman: University of Oklahoma Press, 1993.

Porras Muñoz, Guillermo. *El gobierno de la ciudad de México en el siglo XVI*. México: UNAM, 1982.

Primer coloquio de arqueología y etnohistoria del estado de Guerrero. México: INAH/Gobierno del Estado de Guerrero, 1986.

Pulido Méndez, Salvador. "Datos para la historia arqueológica de la desaparecida Zacatula." In Niederberger and Reyna Robles, eds., *El Pasado arqueológico de Guerrero*, 301–20.

Punzo Díaz, José Luis. "Presencia tarasca en el centro sur de Michoacán. Nuevas investigaciones, Morelia." Unpublished manuscript, 2018.

Punzo Díaz, José Luis, Diego Rangel, Erika Ibarra, Jesús Zarco, and Mijaely Castañón. "Revisiting the Archaeology of the Huetamo Area, South-Eastern Michoacán, Mexico." In *Ancient West Mexicos: Time, Space, and Diversity*, edited by Joshua Englehardt, Verenice Heredia, and Christopher Beekman, 103–30. Gainesville: University Press of Florida, 2020.

Pye, Mary E., and Gerardo Gutiérrez. "The Pacific Coast Trade Route of Mesoamerica: Iconographic Connections Between Guatemala and Guerrero." In *Archaeology, Art and Ethnogenesis in Mesoamerican Prehistory: Papers in Honor of Gareth W. Lowe*, edited by Lynneth S. Lowe and Mary E. Pye, 229–46. Provo, UT: New World Archaeological Foundation, Brigham Young University, 2007.

Ramírez C., Alfredo. *El Códice de Teloloapan*. México: CONACULTA, INAH, Miguel Ángel Porrúa, 2006.

Ramírez Celestino, Alfredo. "El mapa de Tepecuacuilco. Relaciones temáticas." In *Primer coloquio de arqueología y etnohistoria del estado de Guerrero*, 321–30.

Ranere, Anthony J., Dolores R. Piperno, Irene Holst, Ruth Dickau, José Iriarte, and Jeremy A. Sabloff. "The Cultural and Chronological Context of Early Holocene Maize and Squash Domestication in the Central Balsas River Valley, Mexico." *Proceedings of the National Academy of Sciences of the United States of America* 106, no. 13 (2009): 5014–18. http://www.jstor.org/stable/40455140.

Renfrew, Colin, and Paul Bahn. *Archaeology: Theories, Methods and Practice*, 7th ed. London: Thames & Hudson, 2016.

Restall, Matthew. "Black Conquistadors: Armed Africans in Early Spanish America." *Americas* 57, no. 2 (October 2000): 171–205. http://www.jstor.org/stable/1008202.

———. *Seven Myths of the Spanish Conquest*. Oxford: Oxford University Press, 2003.

Reyes Álvarez, Cuauhtémoc. "Piedra Labrada: escultura de un sitio del Clásico en Guerrero." In *3a Mesa Redonda: El conocimiento antropológico e histórico sobre Guerrero. Reflexiones sobre la investigación multidisciplinaria e integral y su impacto social*, edited by Rosa María Reyna Robles, 62–89. México: INAH, 2017.

Reyes Álvarez, Fernando Ygnacio Cuauhtémoc, and Gerardo Guerrero Gómez. *Geometrías de la imaginación: Diseño e iconografía de Guerrero*. México, DF: CONACULTA, 2014.

Reyes García, Luis. *Documentos manuscritos y pictóricos de Ichcateopan, Guerrero*. México: UNAM, 1979.

Reyna Robles, Rosa María. "De la antigüedad de la bóveda corbelada en Guerrero." In Niederberger and Reyna Robles, *El Pasado arqueológico de Guerrero*, 243–58.

———. "La cultura arqueológica Mezcala en Guerrero: datos e interpretación" In Niederberger and Reyna Robles, eds., *El Pasado arqueológico de Guerrero*, 99–126.

———. "La época Clásica en el Estado de Guerrero." In *La época Clásica: nuevos hallazgos, nuevas ideas*, edited by Amalia Cardos de Méndez, 221–36. México: INAH, 1980.

———. "Esculturas, estelas y lápidas de la región del Balsas: acercamiento a su cronología e interpretación." In Niederberger and Reyna Robles, eds., *El Pasado arqueológico de Guerrero*, 321–37.

———. "Inspección arqueológica en la Alta Sierra Madre del Sur de Guerrero." *Arqueología* no. 46 (julio 2013): 137–52. https://revistas.inah.gob.mx/index.php/arqueologia/article/view/3512.

———. "Movimientos de población y rutas de intercambio en el Guerrero prehispánico." *Rutas de Campo* (enero–febrero 2015): 10–19.

———. *La Organera-Xochipala: un sitio del epiclásico en la región Mezcala de Guerrero*. México, DF: INAH, 2003.

———. "La Organera-Xochipala, Guerrero." *Arqueología Mexicana*, 14, no. 82 (noviembre–diciembre 2006): 42–46.

———. "Las pinturas de la cueva del Cerro Tláloc en Xochipala, Guerrero." *Arqueología* no. 40 (enero–abril 2009), 8–19. https://revistas.inah.gob.mx/index.php/arqueologia/article/view/3558/3442.

Reyna Robles, Rosa Ma., and Lauro González Quintero. *Rescate arqueológico de un espacio funerario de época olmeca en Chilpancingo, Guerrero*. México, DF: INAH, 1998.

Rodríguez, Lorena. *AGI Filipinas*. Publicación de la Subdirección General de los Archivos Estatales, n.d. https://independent.academia.edu/LorenaRodriguez140.

Rodríguez Betancourt, Felipe. "Desarrollo cultural en la región de Mezcala-Tetela del Río." In *Primer coloquio de arqueología y etnohistoria del estado de Guerrero*, 155–70.

Román Ramos, Israel. "Primeras aproximaciones sobre estudios de patrón de asentamiento en Tehuacalco, Guerrero, México." Unpublished manuscript, n.d.

Roskamp, Hans. *Los códices de Cutzio y Huetamo: encomienda y tributo en la Tierra Caliente de Michoacán, siglo XVI*. Zamora: El Colegio de Michoacán; Zinacantepec: El Colegio Mexiquense, 2003.

———. "Historia, mito y legitimación: el Lienzo de Jicalán." In *Tierra Caliente de Michoacán*, edited by José Eduardo Zárate Hernández, 119–51. Zamora: El Colegio de Michoacán; Morelia: Gobierno del Estado de Michoacán, 2001.

———. *La historiografía indígena de Michoacán: el Lienzo de Jucutácato y los Títulos de Carapan*. Leiden: Research School CNWS, Leiden University, 1998. http://colmich.repositorioinstitucional.mx/jspui/handle/1016/242

Rubí Alarcón, Rafael. "Comunidades indígenas, siglos XVI y XVII del centro y la Montaña de Guerrero." *Estudios de Cultura Náhuatl* 23 (1993): 297–343.

———. "El dominio español. Era de los Habsburgos: 1521–1700." In Jiménez García, Martínez Donjuán, Castro, and Calvo, *Historia General de Guerrero*, vol. 2, 11–232.

———. "La encomienda de la Montaña." In *Primer coloquio de arqueología y etnohistoria del estado de Guerrero*, 425–40.

———. "República de indios, siglo XVI y XVII (en territorio guerrerense)." In *Códices y Documentos sobre México, Segundo Simposio*, edited by Salvador Rueda Smithers, Constanza Vega Sosa, and Rodrigo Martínez Baracs, vol. 2., 37–61. México: INAH, 1997.

Ruiz Gutiérrez, Ana. "La figura del comerciante y benefactor lepero, Baltasar Rodríguez de los Ríos: 1543–1620." In *Andalucía en América: Arte y Patrimonio*, edited by Rafael López Guzmán, 13–28. Granada: Editorial Atrio, Universidad de Granada, 2012. https://ugr.academia.edu/AnaRuizGuti%C3%A9rrez.

Ruiz Medrano, Ethelia. *Mexico's Indigenous Communities: Their Lands and Histories 1500–2010*, translated by Russ Davidson. Boulder: University Press of Colorado, 2011.

———. *Reshaping New Spain: Government and Private Interests in the Colonial Bureaucracy, 1531–1550*, translated by Julia Constantino and Pauline Marmasse. Boulder: University Press of Colorado, 2006.

Russ, Jon, Mary D. Pohl, Christopher L. von Nagy, Karen L. Steelman, Heather Hurst, Leonard Ashby, Paul Schmidt, Eliseo F. Padilla Gutiérrez, and Marvin W. Rowe. "Strategies for 14C Dating the Oxtotitlán Cave Paintings, Guerrero, Mexico." *Advances in Archaeological Practice* 5, no. 2 (May 2017), 170–83.

Sales Colín, Otswald. *El movimiento portuario de Acapulco: El protagonismo de Nueva España en la relación con Filipinas, 1587–1648*. México: Plaza y Valdés, 2000.

Sandstrom, Alan R., and Pamela Effrein Sandstrom. *Traditional Papermaking and Paper Cult Figures of Mexico*. Norman: University of Oklahoma Press, 1986.

Sarabia Viejo, M Justina. *Don Luís de Velasco: virrey de Nueva España 1550–1564*. Seville: Consejo Superior de Investigaciones Científicas, Escuela de Estudios Hispano-Americanos, 1978.

Schávelzon, Daniel. *Treinta siglos de imágenes: maquetas y representaciones de arquitectura en México y América Central prehispánica*. Buenos Aires: Ediciones Fundación CEPPA, 2004. http://www.danielschavelzon.com.ar/?page_id=3.

Schmidt, Paul. "Arqueología de Superficie en el área de Chilapa-Zitlala, Guerrero, México. Temporadas 2 y 3 (2004–2005)." FAMSI, 2005. http://www.famsi.org/reports/03015es/.

Schmidt Schoenberg, Paul. *Arqueología de Xochipala*. México: UNAM, Instituto de Investigaciones Arqueológicas, 1990.

———. "La época prehispánica en Guerrero." *Arqueología Mexicana* 14, no. 82 (noviembre–diciembre 2006): 28–37.

———. "Secuencia arqueológica de Xochipala." In *Primer coloquio de arqueología y etnohistoria del estado de Guerrero*, 107–16.

Schmidt Schoenberg, Paul, and Eliseo Padilla Gutiérrez. "William Niven y la Estela de Quechomictlipan, Guerrero." Online Lecture, December 2, 2021. https://www.youtube.com/watch?v=uNcKXMh9zrM.

Schmidt Schoenberg, Paul, and Jaime Litvak King. "Problemas y perspectivas de la arqueología de Guerrero: 1984–2002." In *Guerrero. Una Mirada Antropológica e Histórica*, edited by Gloria Artis, Miguel Angel Rubio, and Mette Marie Wacher, 23–44, Serie Regiones de México. México: INAH, 2007.

Schroeder, Susan. "Jesuits, Nahuas, and the Good Death Society in Mexico City, 1710–1767." *Hispanic American Historical Review* 80 no. 1 (February 2000): 43–76.

Serrera, Ramón María. "El camino de Asia: la ruta de México a Acapulco." In *Rutas de la Nueva España*, edited by Chantal Cramaussel, 211–34. Zamora: El Colegio de Michoacán, 2006.

Servín Carlos, Blanca Esthela. "La frontera multilingüe de la Tierra Caliente en la época prehispánica." In Paredes Martínez and Martínez Ayala, eds., *Alzaban banderas de papel*, 152–61. México: Comisión Nacional para el Desarrollo de los Pueblos Indígenas, 2012.

Sharer, Robert J., Andrew K. Balkansky, James H. Burton, Gary M. Feinman, Kent V. Flannery, David C. Grove, Joyce Marcus, Robert G. Moyle, T. Douglas Price, Elsa M. Redmond, Robert G. Reynolds, Prudence M. Rice, Charles S. Spencer, James B. Stoltman, and Jason Yaeger. "On the Logic of Archaeological Inference: Early Formative Pottery and the Evolution of Mesoamerican Societies." *Latin American Antiquity* 17, no. 1 (2006): 90–103. http://www.jstor.org/stable/25063038.

Silverstein, Jay E. "Aztec Imperialism at Oztuma, Guerrero: Aztec-Chontal Relations During the Late Postclassic and Early Colonial Periods." *Ancient Mesoamerica* 12, no. 1 (2001): 31–48. https://www.researchgate.net/publication/231982499_Aztec_imperialism_

at_Oztuma_Guerrero_Aztec-Chontal_relations_during_the_late_postclassic_and_early_colonial_periods.

———. "Un Estudio de la Frontera Azteca-Tarasca del Posclásico Tardío en el Norte de Guerrero, México: El Proyecto Oztuma-Cutzamala, 1998." FAMSI, 2004. www.famsi.org/reports/97014es/97014esSilverstein01.pdf.

———. "La frontera mexica-tarasca en el norte de Guerrero." In Niederberger and Reyna Robles, *El Pasado arqueológico de Guerrero*, 409–28.

———. "A Study of the Late Postclassic Aztec-Tarascan Frontier in Northern Guerrero, México: The Oztuma-Cutzamala Project." PhD diss., Pennsylvania State University, 2000. https://etda.libraries.psu.edu/catalog/5860.

Simpson, Lesley Byrd. *The Encomienda in New Spain: The Beginnings of Spanish Mexico*. Berkeley: University of California Press, 1950.

Slack, Edward R., Jr. "The Chinos in New Spain: A Corrective Lens for a Distorted Image." *Journal of World History* 20, vo. 1 (March 2009): 35–67.

Smith, C. B., C. E. Ebert, and D. J. Kennett. "Human Ecology of Shellfish Exploitation at a Prehistoric Fishing-Farming Village on the Pacific Coast of Mexico." *Journal of Island and Coastal Archaeology* 9 (2014): 183–202. https://pitt.academia.edu/ClaireEbert.

Smith, Michael E. "The Expansion of the Aztec Empire: A Case Study in the Correlation of Diachronic Archaeological and Ethnohistorical Data." *American Antiquity* 52, no. 1 (1987): 37–54. http://www.jstor.org/stable/281059.

Smith, Michael E., Adrian L. Burke, Timothy S. Hare, and Michael D. Glascock. "Sources of Imported Obsidian at Postclassic Sites in the Yautepec Valley, Morelos: A Characterization Study Using XRF and INAA." *Latin American Antiquity* 18, no. 4 (2007): 429–50. http://www.jstor.org/stable/25478196.

Solar Valverde, Laura, Ben A. Nelson, and Michael A. Ohnersorgen. "Aztatlán: Una red de interacción en el Occidente de México." In *Aztatlán: Interacción y cambio social en el Occidente de México ca, 850–1350 d.C.*, edited by Laura Solar Valverde and Ben A. Nelson, 1–38. Zamora: El Colegio de Michoacán; Tempe: Arizona State University, 2019.

Solís Ciriaco, Reyna Beatriz, and Guadalupe Martínez Donjuán. "Specialized Shell Object Production at Teopantecuanitlan Site, Guerrero, Mexico." *Munibe Suplemento–Gehigarria*, no. 20, 20–20 (2010): 34–41. https://www.academia.edu/7378440/Specialized_Shell_Object_Production_at_Teopantecuanitlan_Site_Guerrero_Mexico?auto=download.

Solís Ciriaco, Reyna Beatriz, and Hervé Victor Monterrosa Desruelles. "Malacological Material from Pezuapan's Archaeological Site, Chilpancingo, Guerrero, Mexico." *Munibe Suplemento Gehigarria* n°. 20, 20–20 (2010): 34–40. https://www.academia.edu/7378403/Malacological_Material_from_Pezuapans_Archaeological_site_Chilpancingo_Guerrero_Mexico.

Sousa, Lisa, and Kevin Terraciano. "The 'Original Conquest' of Oaxaca: Nahua and Mixtec Accounts of the Spanish Conquest." *Ethnohistory* 50, no. 2 (Spring 2003): 349–400.

Spinden, H. J. "An Ancient Sepulchre at Placeres Del Oro, State of Guerrero, Mexico." *American Anthropologist*, n.s., 13 (1911): 29–55. http://www.jstor.org/stable/659807.

Studnicki-Gizbert, Daviken, and David Schecter. "The Environmental Dynamics of a Colonial Fuel-Rush: Silver Mining and Deforestation in New Spain, 1522 to 1810." *Environmental History* 15, no. 1 (January 2010): 94–119.

Tarkanian, Michael J., and Dorothy Hosler. "America's First Polymer Scientists: Rubber Processing, Use and Transport in Mesoamerica." *Latin American Antiquity* 22, no. 4 (2011): 469–86. http://www.jstor.org/stable/23072570.

Tavera Alfaro, Xavier. "De una mina de cobre en la Tierra Caliente." In *La Tierra Caliente de Michoacán*, edited by José Eduardo Zárate Hernández, 181–200. Zamora: El Colegio de Michoacán; Morelia: Gobierno del Estado de Michoacán, 2001.

Taylor, William B. *Drinking, Homicide, and Rebellion in Colonial Mexican Villages*. Stanford, CA: Stanford University Press, 1979.

———. *Landlord and Peasant in Colonial Oaxaca*. Stanford, CA: Stanford University Press, 1972.

———. *Magistrates of the Sacred: Priests and Parishioners in Eighteenth-Century Mexico*. Stanford, CA: Stanford University Press, 1996.

Tempère, Delphine. "Vida y muerte en alta mar. Pajes, grumetes y marineros en la navegación española del siglo XVII." *Iberoamericana*, n.é., 2, no. 5 (marzo 2002): 103–20. https://www.jstor.org/stable/41672821.

Terraciano, Kevin. *The Mixtecs of Colonial Oaxaca: Ñudzahui History, Sixteenth Century Through Eighteenth Centuries.* Stanford, CA: Stanford University Press, 2001.

Torre Villar, Ernesto de la. *Las congregaciones de los pueblos de indios: Fase terminal: aprobaciones y rectificaciones.* México: UNAM, 1995.

Torres Aguilar, Javier. "Aculturación religiosa en la Mar del Sur de la Nueva España (1533–1810). Un acercamiento al desempeño de los evangelizadores novohispanos en la región Centro y la Costa Grande del Actual Estado de Guerrero." Master's thesis, Universidad Autónoma de Guerrero, 2014. https://uagro-mx.academia.edu/JavierTorresAguilar.

Townsend, Richard Fraser. "State and Cosmos in the Art of Tenochtitlan." *Studies in Pre-Columbian Art and Archaeology* no. 20 (1979), State and Cosmos in the Art of Tenochtitlan: 1–78. http://www.jstor.org/stable/41263442.

Uchmany, Eva Alexandra. *La vida entre el judaísmo y el cristianismo en la Nueva España 1580–1606.* México: Archivo General de la Nación, Fondo de Cultura Económica, 1992.

Umberger, Emily. "Antiques, Revivals, and References to the Past in Aztec Art." *RES: Anthropology and Aesthetics* no. 13 (1987): 62–105. http://www.jstor.org/stable/20166764.

———. "Aztec Presence and Material Remains in the Outer Provinces." In Berdan, Blanton, Hill Boone, Hodge, Smith, and Umberger, eds. *Aztec Imperial Strategies*, 151–79.

Urcid, Javier. "The Pacific Coast of Oaxaca and Guerrero: The Westernmost Extent of the Zapotec Script." *Ancient Mesoamerica* 4 no. 1 (1993): 141–66.

Vázquez Mendoza, Nahui Ollin. *Pueblo a orilla del mar. Huatulco en el siglo XVI (1522–1616).* Santa Lucía del Camino, Oaxaca: Secretaría de las Culturas y Artes de Oaxaca, 2012. https://unam1.academia.edu/NahuiOllinV%C3%A1zquezMendoza.

Vega Sosa, Constanza. "The Annals of the Tlapanecs." In *Handbook of Middle American Indians: Epigraphy Supplement 5*, edited by Victoria Bricker, 34–52. Austin: University of Texas Press, 1992.

———. "El Códice Azoyú 1 y el Lienzo de Tlapa. Relaciones temáticas." In *Primer coloquio de arqueología y etnohistoria del estado de Guerrero*, 79–109.

———. "Códice Azoyú 2 y Humboldt Fragmento 1: Historia y tributación del Reino de Tlapa-Tlachinollan, 1425–1564." In *Códice Azoyú 2: El señorío de Tlapa-Tlachinollan*, edited by Constanza

Vega Sosa and Michel R. Oudijk, 1–72. México: INAH and El Fondo de Cultura Económica, 2011. https://unam1.academia.edu/micheloudijk.

———. "La Ruta de Ahuitzotl a la Provincia Tributaria de Tlapan. Códice Azoyú 2." In *Códices y Documentos sobre México, Segundo Simposio*, edited by Salvador Rueda Smithers, Constanza Vega Sosa, and Rodrigo Martínez Baracs, vol. 1, 505–20. México: INAH,1997.

Velasco Murillo, Dana. *Urban Indians in a Silver City: Zacatecas, Mexico, 1546–1810*. Stanford, CA: Stanford University Press, 2020.

Velázquez-Castro, Adrián. "The Study of Shell Object Manufacturing Techniques from the Perspective of Experimental Archaeology and Work Traces." In *Archaeology, New Approaches in Theory and Techniques*, edited by Imma Ollich-Castanyer, 229–50. London: IntechOpen, 2012. https://www.intechopen.com/chapters/36574.

Vélez Calvo, Raúl. "Etnohistoria (¿–1521)." In Jiménez García, Martínez Donjuán, Arboleyda Castro, and Vélez Calvo, eds. *Historia General de Guerrero*, vol. 1, 140–478.

Vié-Wohrer, Anne-Marie. "Huellas del culto de Xipe Totec en la toponimia del estado de Guerrero. In Niederberger and Reyna Robles, eds. *El Pasado arqueológico de Guerrero*, 533–66.

Villela F., Samuel. "El Códice Panel de Chiepetlán y las migraciones nahuas a la Montaña de Guerrero." *Estudios de Cultura Náhuatl* 26 (1996): 133–46.

Von Mentz, Brígida. "Aproximaciones a una historia social del norte del actual estado de Guerrero." In Miller, Johnson, and von Mentz, eds., *Por el norte de Guerrero*, 29–63.

———. *Cuauhnáhuac 1450–1675: Su historia indígena y documentos en "mexicano." Cambio y continuidad de una cultura nahua*. México: Miguel Ángel Porrúa, 2008.

———. *Señoríos indígenas y reales de minas en el norte de Guerrero y comarcas vecinas: etnicidad, minería y comercio. Temas de historia económica y social del periodo Clásico al siglo XVIII*. México: Ciesas and Juan Pablos Editor, 2017.

Voorhies, Barbara, and Douglas J. Kennett. "Reanalizando el 'Pox Pottery' de la costa de Guerrero." In *El conocimiento antropológico e histórico sobre Guerrero: Reflexiones sobre la investigación multidisciplinaria e intergal y su impacto social*, edited by Rosa María Robles, vol. 3, 20–25. México: INAH, 2017.

Voorhies, Barbara, Douglas J. Kennett, John G. Jones, and Thomas A. Wake. "A Middle Archaic Archaeological Site on the West Coast of Mexico." *Latin American Antiquity* 13, no. 2 (2002): 179–200. http://www.jstor.org/stable/971913.

Weitlaner, Robert J., and R. H. Barlow. "Breve Nota Sobre las Peregrinaciones." *Boletín de INAH* no. 27 (1967): 29–30.

Weitlaner Johnson, Irmgard, and Alba Guadalupe Mastache. "Tejidos prehispánicos de Guerrero." In Niederberger and Reyna Robles, eds., *El Pasado arqueológico de Guerrero*, 443–70.

West, Robert C. "Aboriginal Metallurgy and Metalworking in Spanish America: A Brief Overview." In *Mines of Silver and Gold in the Americas*, edited by Peter Bakewell, 41–56. Aldershot: Variorum, 1997.

Widmer, Rolf. *Conquista y despertar de las costas de la Mar del Sur (1521–1684)*. México: CONACULTA, 1990.

Williams, Eduardo. "The Ethnoarchaeology of Salt Production at Lake Cuitzeo, Michoacán, Mexico." *Latin American Antiquity* 10, no. 4 (1999): 400–414. http://www.jstor.org/stable/971964.

Wood, Stephanie Gail. "Corporate Adjustments in Colonial Mexican Towns: Toluca Region, 1550–1810." PhD diss., University of California, Los Angeles, 1984.

Wood, Stephanie. *Transcending Conquest. Nahua Views of Spanish Colonial Mexico*. Norman: University of Oklahoma Press, 2003

Yannakakis, Yanna. *The Art of Being In-Between: Native Intermediaries, Indian Identity, and Local Rule in Colonial Oaxaca*. Durham, NC: Duke University Press, 2008.

Yuste López, Carmen. *El comercio de la Nueva España con Filipinas 1590–1785*. México: INAH, 1984.

Index

Page numbers in italic text indicate illustrations and tables.

Señor Abeja, ruler of Tlapa-Tlachinollan, 79, 93–94, *95*
Acamixtlahuaca, 231
Acapetlahuaya, 103, 165, 171, 180, 219
Acapulco, 165, *239*, *245*, 261; Asian influence in, 209, 240–41; Asian trade in, 133; discovery of return route from Philippines to, 236–38; future of, 252–55; Manila and, 238–39, 248–50; parishes of, 141; Philippines trade centered in, 242–49; population of, 141; Puerto Marqués in, 19, 89, 290n91; rock art in, 295; Spanish officials in, 253–54; trade fair, consumption during, 254; trade in, 242–43, 247–50; Western Isles and, 237
Acapulco–Mexico City road, 176–77, 183–84, 213, 241–42, 260
Acatlán, 168
administrative centers, of Tarascan empire, 106
Afromestizo, 180, 211, 275, 317n160
aguafuerte, 239–40, 275
Señor Agua, ruler of Tlapa-Tlachinollan, 298n78
Aguilar y Córdoba, Alonso de, 122–24, 144, 157–58, 201, 208, 222, 326n6
Aguilera, Juan, Mexica *calpixqui* in Tepecoacuilco, 99
Aguirre Beltrán, Gonzalo, 211
Ahuatepec Pueblo (church), *131*
Ahuináhuac, 33–34, 58, 61, *72*, 74, 288n73, 289n81
Ahuítzotl, Mexica *tlatoani*, 101, 102, 144
Aixpotetle, Indigenous ruler of Tixtla, 144

ají, 118, 275
Ajuchitlán, 106, 139–40, *142*, 160, 168, 179–80, 186–87, 219
Alahuiztlán, 45, 101–3, 161, 218–19, 310n27
Albornoz, Bernardino de, 190
Albornoz, García de, 204, 206, 247
alcalde, 147, 148, 155, 158, 171, 197, 275
alcalde de mesta, 197, 275
alcalde mayor, 117–19, 210, 275; of Acapulco, 240, 253; of Taxco, 227, 229, 230, 234–35; of Tlapa, 150
alcaldía mayor, 117, 165–66, 275
Alcozauca, 126, 133, 314n91
alguacil, alguacil mayor, 128, 146, 152, 155, 167, 189, 224, 229, 246, 275
Almaráz, Diego García de, 127, 130
Almeida, Jorge de, 135, 246–47
Almoguer, Antonio de, 195–96, *215*, 216
almojarifazgo, *245*, 246, 275
Alpoyeca-Las Minas, 27
Alta California, 238
Altamirano, Ignacio, commenting on nineteenth-century Tixtla, 24
altepetl, 12, 48, 93, 99, 105, 275, 276: of Chontal Oztuma, 151–52; conflicts between, *107*, 168; in Mexica empire, 99–100, 102, 103, 144, 150, 171; model of, 26–27; nucleation of in central Mexico, 173; Spanish understanding of, 284n47
Alvarado, Leonor de, 199
Alvarado, Pedro de, 112, 199
Amalpilli, Postclassic Indigenous ruler of Oztuma, 138, 151

377

amate, 74–75, *80*, *95*, 146, 149, 275, 276
amatlacuilo, 145, 275
Amith, Jonathan David, 6
Amuco Abelino, 35, 63, *64*, 289n81. *See also* San Miguel Amuco
Amuzgo language, 82–83
Amuzgo people, 25, 86
anahuatl, 39, 275
Anawalt, Patricia Rieff, *104*
Ángeles, Don Domingo de los, Indigenous cacique of San Luis Acatlán, 133
animals, food for, 228–29
Apango, 133
Apaxtla, 161, 168, 171–72
Apelo, Baltasar and Salvador, 247
archaeological sites in precontact Guerrero, *14–15*
Archaic period, *18*, 56–57, 89–90; Cerro de las Conchas (Chiapas) during, 17–18; La Consentida (Oaxaca) during, 18; Formative period and, 89–90; Puerto Marqués during, 19–20
architectural innovation, 33, 288n72
architectural models (sculpture), 58, *60*
Armillas, Pedro, 35
arriero, 118, 125, 275
artifacts, 4, 19, 36, 39, 47, 51, 69, 88, 90, 275
Asia, 209, 236–37, 240–41
Asian trade, Guerrero: in Acapulco, 133; corruption and, 246, 250–51, 254; royal decrees not controlling, 251; short- and long-term consequences of, 239–41
Atenango, 166, 168
Atlamajac, 170, 176, 301n20
Atlixtac, 126, 170, 176
Atoyac, *141*, 206, 285n22
Atoyac River. *See* Balsas River
Audiencia, 99, 129–30, 144, 154, 189–90, 197

Augustinians, 126, 133–34, 175–76, 237, 259
Ávila, Alonso de, 198
Ávila, Jorge de, 126
Ávila, Rodrigo de, 229
Axayácatl, Mexica *tlatoani*, 39, 101, 144, 156
Ayacastla kingdom, 98
Ayllón, Joan de, 129
Ayutla, 133, 165
Azoyú, 141, 165
Azoyú-Tenconahualle, 286n26
Aztecs. *See* Mexicas

baby-face figurines, in Olmec style, 53, 74, 297n59
bachiller, 275
Badajoz, Gutierre de, 188–89, 206
Baez, Juan, 116
Bahn, Paul, 84
ballcourt, 26, 27, *30*, *32*, 33, 275; at La Organera, 20; at La Soledad de Maciel, *21*; at Tehuacalco, *97*
ballgame, 45
Balsas region, 34; Amuco Abelino in, 63, *64*; in Classic period, 49; copper in, 40; El Infiernillo in, 36, *38*, *41*; during Formative period, 35; middle, 49, 61, 63, 83; population of, 35; Tarascan empire expanding into, 101
Balsas River (Mezcala River or Atoyac River), 16–17; Balsas delta during Postclassic period, 23; hydrological system of, 2; settlement pattern of lower Balsas, 289n85; settlement patterns influenced by, 34–35
barrio, 161, 275
Bazán, Gonzalo, 188, 224
beeswax, mines lit using, 230
bells, types of West Mexican bronze, *41*
Benavides, Gil de, 198–99
Benavides family, 199

Berdan, Frances F., 37, 102, 103, *104*
biombo, 245, 275
Bird Man (sculpture), at Villa Rotaria, 285n22
Blanco Granular, 49, 293n146
Bocanegra, Bernardino de, 190
Bocanegra, Bernardino Pacheco de, 199, 200
Bocanegra, Hernán Pérez de, 123, 188, 199, 200
Bocanegra family, 199, 226
Bonfil Batalla, Guillermo, 2
Borah, Woodrow Wilson, 86–87, *184*
botijo, 125, 275
Brito, Baltazar, 298n78
bronze, 36, *41*, 106, 244
Brush, Charles, 19
Burgos, Juan de, 123, 188, 190, 199–200, 229, 321n48
Burkhart, Louise, 134

caballería (44 hectares), 265, 275
cabecera, 12, 127, 156–57, *164*, 168, 172–73, 275, 277; in the Center, 166, 170–71; on the Costa Chica, 166; in the Montaña, 169–70; in the North, 166–67; Spaniards' designation of, 284n47; in Taxco, 128; in Tepecoacuilco, 149; in Tierra Caliente, 143, 167, 171–72; in Tlapa, 142, 166, 169, *170*
cabecera de doctrina, 126, 127, 129, 175, 276
cabildo, 151, 152, 180–81, 276, 311n50
Cabra, Juan de, 109, 112, 194
Cabrera, Hernando, 316n141
cacahuatl, 276
Cacalotenango, 144
cacao, 206, 251; coastal economy impacted by, 208; as currency, 45, 118; Mexica empire acquiring, 42; in Postclassic period, 43; slaves processing, 210–11
cacao plantation (*cacahuatl*), 276

cacique, 133–34, 276; administrative-political functions of, 152–53; change and continuity of, 311n48; *Códices de Azoyú 1* and *2* named in, 298n78; lineages disrupted and disputed, 154–55; of the Montaña, 152; as officials under Spanish rule, 144, 155, 159; polities governed by, 164; by right of descent, 280; royal government protecting, 155–56; sacred function of, 100, 152–53, 261; Spaniards, reaction to, 257–58; of Tlapa-Tlachinollan, 298n78, 312n57
Caesalpinia cacalaco. *See cascalote*
caja de comunidad, 8, 158–59, 163, 260, 276; in the Montaña, 159; tribute paid to, *160*, 310n39
Señor Calandria Flecha, ruler of Tlapa, 93–94
Calens, Guillermo, 135
calli, 149, 276
calpixqui, 99–100, 171, 276
calpolli, 276
cantor (Indigenous singer in church), 276
Cardero, José, *239*
Carletti, Francesco, 253
Carmona, Antón de, 118
Carrasco, Cristóbal, 125
Carreño, Hernando de, 132–33, 136
Cartagena, Juan de, *122*, 221
Carvajal, Antonio de, 190
Carvajal el Mozo, Luis, 135
casa de comunidad, 276
cascalote (Caesalpinia cacalaco), 157, 194, 216, 276
castas, 138–39, 276
Castilla, Luisa de, 190
Castilla, Luis de, 117, 178, 190, 196, 226–27, 235
Castillo, Bernaldino del, 206, 318n11
Castrejón, Antonio, 117, *205*, 206
Castrillo, Álvaro de, 117, 268–71

Castro, García, 309n21

Cauadzidziqui Cave, 56–57

Cave of the Governors (*Cueva de los Gobernadores*), in Techan, 56, 57

caves, ceremonial importance of, 99, 295n16

cazonci, 101, 106, 181, 276

Cebú, Philippines, 238, 248–49

the Center region, 17, 176–77, 212–14; *cabeceras* and *sujetos* in, 166–67; *congregaciones* in, 176–77; *encomienda* in, 191; geography and settlement pattern in, 28–30; landowners in, *213*; Mezcala sculpture in, 61, 260–61; Oxtotitlán Cave in, 2, 6, *52*, 53–54, 70, 89–90, 294n13; separation of pueblos in, 170; Spanish enterprises in, 212–14; Xochipala in, 29, *30*, 61–62, 162; Xochipala, sculpture in, 61–62, 260–61. *See also* Chilapa; Chilpancingo; Tixtla; Zumpango

Cerezo, Gonzalo, 117, 213, 231, 329n57

Cerro de las Conchas, Chiapas, 17–18

Cerro de los Brujos, *21*

Cerro de Los Monos, 67–68

Cerro Quemado-La Coquera, 25–27

Cervantes de Salazar, Francisco, 289n80

Chalcatzingo, Morelos, 39, 53, 56, 57, 63

chalchihuite or *chalchihuitl*, 28, 103, 276

Chalmeca Cihuatl "the white god," 45

Chamorro, Nicolás, 194

charape, 241, 276

charcoal, use in mining of, 220, 230, 231, 233

Charles V (Emperor), 75, 79, 209–10

Chaunu, Pierre, 252

chía, 45, 47, 103, 147, 191, 200, 276

Chiapas, Cerro de las Conchas in, 17–18

chicovite, 184, 276

Chiepetlán, 75–76, *131*

Chilacachapa, 201

Chilapa, 50, 126, 156, 176, 214, 223–25

Chilapa huipil, 43, *44*

Chilpancingo, 28–29, 70, 74, 99, 162, 177, 241–42, 261

Chimalpahin Quauhtlehuanitzin, Don Domingo de San Antón Muñón, 211, 240

Chinese goods, cheapness of, 249

Chinese person (*chino*), 141, 240, 253, 276

Cintla, 174

Chontal language, 87, 127, 263; Nahuatl replacing, 82–83

Chontal people, 61, 87, 109, 145–46, 151–52, 180; altepetl of, 151–52; Cuetzala in conflict with, 171; kingdoms of, 100, 102, 138; lineage of, 100, 103; *sujetos* of, 172. *See also* Oztuma

churches, 125–26, 131, *132*, 151–52, 176, 181, 225, 240; in Ahuatepec Pueblo, *131*; behavior of, 146; in Petlacala, *132*; regular orders, 113, 116, 126–27, 164. *See also* evangelization; friars; priests; *cofradía*

church officials, Indigenous, 126–29, 134, 137, 146, 152–53, 156

Cihuatlán, 40, 42–43, 47, *104*

Cisneros, Cristóbal de, 228–29

Cisneros, Juan de, 320n32

Cisneros, María de, 157, *215*, 216

Citlaltomahua, 165, 166, 191, 209

civil or parochial jurisdiction (*partido*), 279

Classic period, *18*, *67*, *68*, *69*; Balsas region in, 49; Costa Grande during, 21; Indigenous rulers during, 256; monumental stone sculpture during, 64–69; site design during, 34; Teotihuacan and Guerrero during, 23, 33, 64–68, 74, 90–91, 296n43

clavos (architectural feature), 71, *72*, *73*, 260, 276

Cobo, Fray Juan, 248

Coacoyula, 70

cochineal, 133, 214

Cochoapa-Yuu Kivi, 27
coconuts, 174, 209, 240
Cocula, 128, 152, 162, 216
Cocula River Valley, 34
codex (*códice*), 276
Codex Mendoza, 104
códice. *See* codex
Códice Azoyú 2, 301n20
Códice de Cualác, 98–99, 198n77
Códice de Totomixtlahuaca, 175
Códices de Azoyú 1 and *2*, 5, 12, *94–95*, 102–3, 299n81; Indigenous rulers named in, 298n78; lineage recorded in, 79–81, *80*; Tlapa-Tlachinollan documented by, 10, 93–96
cofrade, 159, 276
cofradía, 8, 159–63, 169, 179, 262–63, 276, 314n91; livestock owned by, 161–62, 169, 216; member of, 276; of Mixtecs, 314n91; in the Montaña, 162–63, 260
Cohimbre stela, Costa Chica, 68
comal, 276
commoners, burdened under Mexica empire, 104
communications, 35, 51, 83, 177, 214, 241–42, 263, 289n78
community finances, pictographic documents for managing, 146–48
composición de tierras, 109, 276
Señor Conejo, ruler of Tlapa, *80*, 81, 298n78
conflade. *See cofrade*
congregaciones, 82–83, 173, 276; Ajuchitlán, sujetos reduced by, 179–80; in the Center, 176–77; on the Costa Chica, 175; on the Costa Grande, 174; evangelization facilitated by, 173; friars carrying out, 175; in the Montaña, 175–76; in the North, 177–78; population, impact on, 178–80, 210, 260; Spaniards acquiring land after, 177–78

La Consentida, Oaxaca, 18–19, 20
Consulado de México, 246
Contlalco, 25–27
converso, 276
Cook, Sherburne F., 86–87
copal, 45, 75, 186
copper, 36, 43, 112; in Balsas region, 40; Mexico City delivered to, 321n44; Tarascan empire seeking, 101
corbelled arch (architectural feature), 29, 33, 70–71, *72*, 256, 260, 288n70
corregidor, 117–18, 119, 145, 151, 159, 164, 167, 276; of Ajuchitlán, 168; on the Costa Chica, 165–66; of Iguala, 157, 167, 216, 239; of Teloloapan, 239
corregimiento, 117, 119, 165, 277; Castilla family and, 226–27
corruption, 246, 250, 254
Cortés, Hernán, 109, 112, 118, 165, 182, 183, 195, 197, 321n48, 328n46; *encomienda* in Tlapa, 189–90; gold sought by, 40; tribute to, 318n8
Cortés, Luis, 321n48
Cortés, Martín, 117, 321n47
Costa Chica region, 16–17, 23, 64–67, 112, 183; Cohimbre stela, 68, *69*; *congregaciones* in, 175; *encomienda* in, 115, 188; epidemics impacting, 133, 139, 141; evangelization of, 133–34; landowners in, *207*
Costa Grande region, 16–17, 21–23, 159, 210–11, 285n22; during Classic period, 21; *congregaciones* in, 174–75; *encomienda* in, 183–86, 187–88; epidemics impacting, 139, 140; landowners on, 203–6, *204*, *205*; land used for grazing in, 207; Manzanilla López, R., 5; population of, 140, *141*, 142, 165–66; settlement patterns in, 5, 21

Cototolapan kingdom, 98–99, 257
cotton, 43–45, 277, 322n50; Costa Grande producing, 208–9; cost of water compared with cost of, 292n125; Tierra Caliente producing, 208–9, 219; tribute of, *104*, 208–9, 323n21
Covarrubias, Miguel, 11–12
Señor Coyote-Abuelo, ruler of Tlapa-Tlachinollan, 298n78
Coyuca (Costa Grande), 161, 211, 240
Coyuca (Tierra Caliente), 106, 168, 179, 197–99, 206, 217
credit, 114–16, 123–24, 196, 221, 228, 336n16
crops, Spaniards introducing, 209, 213–14, 215–16, 219
the Crown: Asian trade regulated by, 250–51; revenues of, 143–44, 182–86, *184*, *185*, 250–51
Cuajinicuilapa, 211
Cualác, 69, 91, 98–99, 170
Cuetlajuchitlán, 33, 39, *71*, 168
Cuetzala, *107*, 168, 171–72, 200, *201*, 219, 230
Cueva de los Gobernadores. *See* Cave of the Governors
Cuevas de Atzcala, 43–44
Cuitlatec language, 82, 263, 299n86
Cuitlatec people, 83, *85*, 86, *87*, 98, 106, 299n86
customs duty (*almojarifazgo*), 245, 246, 275
Cutzamala, 106, *142*, 167, 168, 179, 199–200, *201*, 245
Cutzamala valley, 289n83
Cuytlacinchitlan, 155

Davies, Claude Nigel Byam, 96
Dávila, Alonso de, *122*, 124
Dávila, Gregorio, 188

Dávila, Pedrarias, 198
debt, 123–25, 189, 196; mining and, 221–22, 227–28; power of attorney and, 114–15
Dehouve, Danièle, 5, 9, 140, 141, 142, 309n21
Castillo, Bernaldino del, 206, 208, 209, 318n11
Díaz de Cáceres, Antonio, 135, 136, 246–47, 332n42
Díaz del Castillo, Diego, 129–31
Díaz de Vargas, Gonzalo, 157, 158–59
diezmo, *185*, 186, 277
diputado de minas, 234, 277
Dorantes Carranza, Baltasar, 191, 227
Drennan, Robert, 46

eastern Guerrero, polities in, 92
ecological niches, of Guerrero, 37, 46, 255–56, 334n3
elites, of Guerrero: figurines representing, 89; Mexicas influencing, 102–3; of mining towns, 229; of Olinalá, 155; privileges and powers of, 150–58; Spanish systems adapted to by, 145–46; Tarascan empire, influence of, 105–6; of Taxco mining, 226–29, 231
El Embarcadero, 285n19
encomendero, 8–9, 99, 187–201, 277; abuse of power by, 157–58
encomienda, 8–9, 165, 182, 201–2, 277, 326n5; in the Center, 166, 191–92; on the Costa Chica, 188–89; on the Costa Grande, 183–86, 187–88; Crown *encomiendas*, *184*, 185–88; distribution of, 182–86; individuals holding, *183*; labor and supplies for mining supplied by, 115–16, 192–93, 222, 305n15, 326n5; in the Montaña, 166; regional distribution of, 182, *183*, *184*, *185*; in Tierra Caliente, 185–86

engasamiento, 232, 277
Enríquez, Martín, Viceroy, 151–52, 243
entrada, 117, 277
epcololli, 39, 277, 290n97
epidemics: Costa Chica impacted by, 139; Costa Grande impacted by, 139; Indigenous communities damaged by, 8; lineages disrupted by, 154; the North impacted by, 139, 177–78; population reduced by, 180, 210; Tierra Caliente impacted by, 139, 179–80
escribano, 117, 277
escribano de registro, 117, 250, 277
Espinoza, Alonso, 118
Espinoza y Tello, José, 254
estancia (cattle ranch), 277
estancia. See *sujeto*
Esteban, Fray Jerónimo de S., 126
Estrada, Alonso de, governor and treasurer of New Spain, 187, 190–91, 195, 199
Estrada, Beatriz de, 154, 189, 190
ethnicity, 84, 88, 140
evangelization, 4, 125–27, 134; *congregaciones* and, 173–75
exchange, 20; costs associated with, 47–48; for cotton, 104; ecological niches influencing, 37, 46; in the Montaña, 27–28; networks of, 3, 89; obsidian indicating, 19, 48; Oztuma controlling, 35–36; pigments and, 73–74; resources and, 37–39, 50; routes of, 4, 7, 27–28, 51, 256–57, 259; settlement patterns and, 92–93; shells confirming, 26; Tarascan empire relying on, 101; transport and, 46–50
expression, media of, 73–74

familiar (constable of the Inquisition), 277
Fernández, Juan (*arriero*), 239
figurines, 23, 45, 74

firewood, heating ore with, 230
fiscal, 146, 152, 277
fishing, 19
Señor Flecha, ruler of Tlapa-Tlachinollan, *80*, 81
Fonseca Castellanos, Tomás de, 118, 135
Formative period, *18*, *52*, *55*; Ahuináhuac during, 74; Balsas region during, 35; Mezcala sculpture during, 74; monumental stone sculpture during, 63–64; in the North, 30–34; Olmec during, 51–53; relative chronology of sites from, *72*; rock art from, 53–57; Techan in, *56*; Teopantecuanitlán in, 63–64; Xochipala in, 61–62
friars, 133, 137; *congregaciones* carried out by, 175; involved in trade, 133; Viceroy Gaspar de Zúñiga opposed by, 175–76

Gajo, Martínez del, 196
Gallego, Gonzalo, 210
Gallego, Hernando, *122*, 124, 222
ganado mayor, 162, 277
ganado menor, 219, 277
García, Alonso, *122*, 124, 221
García, Don Juan, Indigenous governor of Iguala, 151
García de Almaráz, Diego, 127, 130, 218, 219
García Martínez, Bernardo, 172, 334n3
García Moreno, Pedro, *122*, 221
Garrido, Juan, 112, 222, 304n8
Garrovillas, Fray Pedro de, 126
Don Gaspar, Indigenous governor of Oapan, income of, 147–48
Gay, Carlo T. E., 61
Gaspar de Zúñiga, Viceroy, Augustinian friars opposing, 175–76
gente de razón, 135, 277
geography and settlement patterns, 16–17
Gerhard, Peter, 84, 98
Gibson, Charles, 159, 334n3

glyphs, Postclassic, in pictographic documents, 146
gobernador (governor of an Indigenous municipality), 79, 138, 147, 157, 167, 277; income of, 147, 151; in the Montaña, 152; of Oztuma, 151; powers of challenged, 154–55; of Tixtla, 144; of Tlapa, 154
Godoy, Luis de, 196, 226
gold: Cortés, H., seeking, 40; mining of, 113–15, 222–23, 305n15, 326n5; Spanish invasion financed with, 112; in Zacatula, 113
González, Francisco, 206, 223
González, Francisco, Indigenous governor of Iguala, 153
governor of an Indigenous municipality. *See gobernador*
Gre, Juan, 135
greenstone, 4, 28, 39, 93, 276
Grijalva, Juan de, 126
Grove, David, 6, 51, 53–54
Gruzinski, Serge, 79–80
Guayameo, *198*, 199. *See also* Zirándaro
Gutiérrez, Francisco, 207
Gutiérrez, Gerardo, 5, 17, 23, 25–26, 57, 85, 92, 298n78
Guzmán, Gerónimo de, Indigenous governor of Tlapa, 154–55
Guzmán, Nuño de, 197

hacienda volante, 259, 261, 277
Haskett, Robert, 129, 152, 159, 334n3
Hassig, Ross, 92, 93, 102
Hawks, Henry, 230
hermandad, 161–62, 277
Hernández, Gaspar, 231
Herrera, María de, 144, 194
hierarchy: Indigenous church officials altering, 156–57; among settlements, 34, 169–71; 256–57; in *Suma de Visitas*, 165–67; in Tlapa-Tlachinollan, 166
hierarchy in Indigenous settlements, social, 18, 20–21, 40–41, 89–90, 156–57
Hirth, Kenneth, 17, 46, 47–48, 49, 50
honey, 186, 189, 191, 192, 193, 199, 214, 216
hortelano, 277
Hosler, Dorothy, 40
Hoyos, Francisco de, 223
Huamuxtitlán, 25, 27, 132, 152, 155, 166; *encomienda* of, 190–91
Huatulco, Oaxaca, 237, 251, 252, 323n10
huauhtli, 45, 277
huerta, 277
Hueyistac, 178
huipil, 43, *44*, 277
Huitzapula, 40
Huitzilopochtli (Mexica deity), 37, 45
Huitzuco, 73, 162, 192, 216, 230; *congregaciones* in, 177–78; disputes in, 157, 168; *encomienda* of, 192–94
Humboldt Fragment 1, 79
hunter gatherers, social hierarchy not present among, 20–21

ichcatl (Nahuatl cotton), 277
icpalli, 75, 277
Iguala, 161, 178, 216, 227, 230, 241; church in, 126, 128, 129, 152; *congregaciones* in, 178; Indigenous rulers of, 151, 153; land and livestock, 177–78, 186–87, 216–17; population of, 139, 166
Igualapa, 119, 126, 154, 165–66, 206, 207, 208
Iguala Valley, 25, 31, 177, 255, 262
illegally acquired land, 214–16
INAH. *See* Instituto Nacional de Antropología e Historia

Indians. *See* Indigenous people
Indigenous church officials, 134, 137
Indigenous communities, 149, *160*, 163, 212, 219; adaptation of tools for government of, 145; colonial legal processes used to advantage by, 157; during Colonial period and in independent Mexico, 336n16; conflict between, *107*, 308n1; epidemics damaging, 8; government of in sixteenth century, 151–58, 310n28; Indigenous and Spanish concepts of land ownership, 311n42; land use during Late Postclassic, 179; mining and, 231; in the Montaña, 259–60, 336n16; municipal autonomy defended by, 335n8; resources available to, 255–56; rights defended by, 145; salt produced by, 219; Spanish colonization, impact of, 180–81; during Spanish invasion, 109; *See also cabacera; caja de comunidad; sujeto; encomienda*
Indigenous people, 137–39, 278; Acapulco trade impacting, 240; the Crown, response of Indigenous nobles to, 143–44; decline in, 140; enslavement of, 119, 222, 305n15; forced resettlement of in sixteenth century, 173–74; friars relying on, 134; Iberian practice modified by, 180–81; labor, obligations of in Acapulco trade, 239–40; mines discovered by, 327n33; religious practices investigated by Hernando Ruiz de Alarcón, 134–35; Spaniards resisted by, 136; Spanish governmental structures adapted to by, 150–51. *See also encomienda*
indio mandón, 277
indio naborío, 233, 277
indio de servicio, 229, 277
El Infiernillo, 21, 36, *38*, *41*, 49, 289n85; possible Toltec contact, 91

Inquisition, 130, 135–36, 197, 232, 246, 247, 277
Instituto Nacional de Antropología e Historia (INAH), 2
Ircio, Agustín de, Indigenous ruler of Oapan, 153
Ircio, Martín de, 144, 153, 154–55, 191–92, *193*
isolation and marginality, of Guerrero, 263
Isquinantzin, Antonio, ruler of Tlapa, 156
Ixcapuzalco, 167, 219, 327n20
Ixcateopan, 126, 157, 219

Jacinta, María Nicolasa, Indigenous founder of Petlacala, 79
Jaramillo, Diego, 144, 187, 191, 223, 224
Jerez, Martín de, 117, *122*, 123–24, 187–88
Jerónimo, Francisco, Indigenous landowner on the Costa Grande, 208
Jews, punished by the Inquisition, 135, 136, 246–47
jícara or *jícara pintada*, 41–43, *42*, 199, 278
Jiménez, Martín, 222
José, Miguel, Indigenous miner, 227
judicial processes, administration of, 146
juez de comisión, 151
Juxtlahuaca cave, 54, *55*, 56, 89–90, 294n13

Labarthe R., María, 5
labor: in Acapulco, 240; access to, 222; competition for scarce, 234; forced Indigenous, 203, 209–10, 222, 325n50; mass death causing shortages of, 210–11; slaves, 9; in Taxco mines, 115–16. *See also repartimiento de indios*; slaves
ladino, 133, 278
Laguna de Coyuca, El Embarcadero on, 285n19

landowners: in the Center, *213*; on the Costa Chica, *207*; on the Costa Grande, 203–6, *204*, *205*; in the Montaña, *212*; in the North, *215*, 216–17; in Teloloapan, 218–19; in Tierra Caliente, 218

language: Amuzgo, 82, 83, *85*, 87, 263; Chontal, 87, 127–28, 263, 299n86; Cuitlatec, 106, 263, 299n86; ethnicity conflated with, 84; Mixtec, 82–83, 263; Nahuatl, 12, 25, 82–83, 263; Tarascan, 106; Tlapanec, 25, 82–83, 93, 263, 302n22; Yope, 83

language groups, regional distribution of, 87

Lavezares, Guido de, 209, 244

legal processes, 157

Legazpi, Miguel, 228, 229, 238

León, Diego de, 212–13

León, Jerónimo de, 228–29

El libro de tasaciones, 5

lienzo, 297n64, 278. *See also* pictographic documents

Lienzo de Aztatépec y Citlaltépec, 79

Lienzo de Chiepetlán I, 76

Lienzo de Chiepetlán II, 75, 76, *76*, 78

Lienzo de Chiepetlán III, *77*, 78, 298n71

Lienzo de Petlacala, *78*, 79

Lienzo de Tlapa, 79

Lienzo de Totomixtlahuaca, 311n43

Lienzos de Malinaltepec, 149–50

lineage: of Chilapa, 156; of Chontal polities, 100; *Códices de Azoyú 1* and *2* recording, 79–81, *80*; epidemics disrupting, 153–54; of Oztuma, 103, 151–52; after Spanish invasion, 138; of Tlapa-Tlachinollan, 10, 95, 259

Lister, Robert, 35, 289n80

Litvak King, Jaime, 42, 44–47, 86, 103, 303n46

livestock, 212–13, 216, 219, 220, 277, 323n10; *cofradías* owning, 161–62; *congregaciones* and, 174–75; grazing of, 116, 212, 262–63; mining linked to in Tierra Caliente, 217–18; Spaniards introducing, 119; Zacatula, introduced to, 203–6

Llerena, Gonzalo de, *122*, 124

Señor Lluvia, ruler of Tlapa-Tlachinollan, 79, 93–94, *95*, 298n78, 301n20

Loa, Guillén de, 197

Loaysa, Juana de, 195–96

Lockhart, James, 84, 152, 173, 284n47, 298n71, 305n15, 310n39, 311n48, 312n56, 312n60, 333n85, 334n3

Logroño, Diego de, 228–29

López, Bartolomé, 116

López, Pedro, *122*, 125, 306n44

Luján, Isabel de, 190, 199, 245

Lutheranism, 135

macegual or *macehual*, 278

maestre, 278

Magariño family, 200–201

Magellan, Ferdinand, 236

maize, 47; consumption of, 119; cultivation of, 20, 155; domestication of, 2, 31; tribute of, 188–90, 191–92, 193, 199–200, *201*, 208

Malaspina, Alessandro, 240, 254

Maldonado, Alonso de, 128, 129

Maldonado, Gertrudis, 314n91

Malinaltepec, 149–50, 176

Manila, in the Philippines, 209, 244, 248–49, *250*, 252–53, 331n29

Manila Galleon, 238, 241, 248–49, 250, 252, 253, 254, 259

Manrique de Zúñiga, Álvaro, Marqués de Villamanrique, Viceroy, 251

Mansanilla, Juan de, 224, 327n20

manta, 278

manta de Ilocos, 245, 278

Mantecón, J. I., 113
Manzanilla López, Rubén, 5, 20, 89, 285n22
Mapa de Tepecoacuilco (1576), 149
mapas, 278, 311nn42–43
marco, 278
Marino Flores, Anselmo, 82
maritime navigation in Late Archaic and Formative, 19
Martín, Don, Indigenous governor of Cuytlacinchitlan, 155, 312n60
Martínez, Francisco, *122*, 124, 125, 208
Martínez, Joan, 127, 167
Martínez del Gajo, Juan, 196
maxtlatl, 278
Mayacat, Indigenous governor of Tixtla, 144, 192
Mayanalán, 100, 157, 162, 194
Mayeque, Martín, Indigenous *cacique* of Tixtla, 154–55
media, of expression, 73–74
Medinilla, Pedro de, 117
Melgosa, Pablo de, 228
Mendoza, Antonio de, Viceroy, 191, 198, 199, 210, 232
Mendoza, Don Miguel de, Indigenous noble of Oapan, 153
Mendoza, María de, 213
Meneses, Pedro de, 197–98, 217, 320n32, 321n43
merced, 203–7, 212–13, 214–16, 217–19, 278, 305n22
mercury, 116, 224, 230, 234, 251–52
mestizaje, 278
metallurgy, 4, 40–41, 116, 214, 232–33, 256, 291n109, 329n60
metals, 4, 40–41, 256, 277; salt used in processing, 219; Spaniards searching for, 235; Taxco refining, 214–16, 232–33, 262, 328n46. *See also* copper; gold; silver

Mexcaltépec, 98, 207
Mexica empire, 45, 93–94, 108, 165, 257; cacao acquired by, 42; commoners, tribute burden under, 104; conflict under rule of, *107*; expansion in Guerrero of, 101; Indigenous allies of Spaniards opposing, 112; Indigenous settlements reconquered by, *102*; the North expanded into by, 100–101; the South, importance of in Mexica cosmology, 37–39, 290n90; Tenochtitlan, 37–39, *76*, 95; tribute paid to, 44, 103–5; Yopes successfully resisting, 97–98, 102
Mexicas (Aztecs), 12, 93, 97, 171, 278; Guerrero elites influenced by, 103; Mexica officials in Guerrero, 99; Mixtecs compared to, 334n2; significance of the South to, 37–38
Mexico City, 190, 197, 280; copper sent to, 321n44; merchants of, 244, 247, 250; tribute delivered to, 186, 188
Mexico City–Acapulco road, 126, 176–77, 184, 191, 213, 220, 237, 241–42
Mexiquito, 68
Mezcala River. *See* Balsas River
Mezcala sculpture, 39, 58–61, *59*, *60*, 67–68, 290n90; at Ahuináhuac, 74; in the Center, 260–61; relative chronology of, *72*
migration: linguistic diversity reflecting, 82; to the Montaña, 78–79, 83; of Nahuas, 75–76; to Teotihuacan, 91
Millares Carlo, A., 113
minero, 278
mines: Indigenous people discovering, 327n33; inputs, 230–31; of Silver Province, 117, 184, 225; slaves working in, 115, 118, 188, 191; Spaniards prospecting for, 224; in Taxco region, 225; in Zumpango, 115

mining, 9, *114*, 186, 195, *226*; debt and, 221–22, 227–28; deforestation caused by, 233; *encomienda* linked to, 192–93, 222; of gold, 113–15, 223, 305n15, 326n5; Indigenous communities and, 231; livestock linked to, 217–18; Magariño family enriched by, 200; in the Montaña, 189; in the North, 6, 214–16, 261; priest Garci Rodríguez investing in, 130; in Sierra Gorda, Querétaro, 291n109; of silver, 115–16; Spanish activities driven by, 221; in Taxco, 177–79, 227–30, 261–62; technologies for, 329n60; in Tierra Caliente, 261; tribute funding, 188, 196–97, 199–200; Zacatula an early center of, 114–15, 223

Miranda, Dr. Lope de, *oidor* of the *Audiencia*, 234

Mixtec language, 25

Mixtecs, 172; governmental system of Montaña influenced by, 93; Mexicas compared to, 334n2; response of to Spanish invasion, 334n3; women participating in *cofradías* of, 314n91

Mochitlán, 109, 132–33, 154–55, 162, 170, 213–14, 261

Moctezuma, Indigenous noble family of Chilapa, 156

Moctezuma Ilhuicamina, Mexica *tlatoani*, 39, 93, *95*, 99, 101, 102

Moctezuma Xocoyotzin, Mexica *tlatoani*, 101

monolithic sculpture, Teopantecuanitlán, *65*

the Montaña region, 3, 24, 214; archaeology of, 5; *cajas de comunidad* wealthy, 159; Cauadzidziqui Cave in, 56–57; *cofradías* in, 162–63, 260; *congregaciones* in, 175–76; Costa Chica contrasted with, 115; Cototolapan in, 98–99, 257; exchange in, 27–28; Indigenous communities in, 259–60, 336n16; Indigenous rulers of, 152; landowners in, *212*; migration to, 78–79, 83; mining in, 189; municipalities of, 335n8; Olinalá in, 132–33, 155, 157; pictographic documents from, 335n7; population, 141–42; Postclassic period in, 4; San Pedro Petlacala in, *132*; separation of pueblos in, 169–70; settlement patterns in, 25–28, *170*, 175; Teotihuacan influencing, 90–91; Texmelincan in, 69, 74. *See also* Huamuxtitlán; Tlapa; Tlapa-Tlachinollan

Monte Albán, Oaxaca, 23, 64, 65, 68, 69, 74, 90, 256

El Monte Don Venus, 23, 49

Monterroso, Blas de, 165

Montúfar, Archbishop Fray Alonso de, 127, 159–60

monumental stone sculpture, 22–23, 285n22; during Classic period, 64–69, *66*, *68*, *69*; during Formative period, *56*, 57, 63–64, 65

Moreno, Francisco, 224

Moreno, Isidro, 157, 192–93

Moreno de Casasola, Bernardino, 157, 177, 194, *215*, 216

Morón, Alonso, 123, 124

Mota y Escobar, Bishop Fray Alonso de la, 130–31, 236

Moya y Contreras, Archbishop Don Pedro de, 127, 129, 130, 131

Muela, Diego de la, *122*, 124, 222

mules, used for transport, 118, 125, 217

Muñoz, Benito, 116

Mural C-1 in Oxtotitlán cave, *52*

Mural Group 2, Scene 1, in Juxtlahuaca cave, *55*

Nahua iconography, 81, 147

nahualli, 134, 278

Nahua people, 147; migration of, 75–76; Nahua migrants in the Montaña, 93–94; nobility of, 312n56; priests venerated by, 129
Nahuatl language, 12, 25, 83, 100
Negrete, Francisco Hernández, 116–17
Nexpa, 188, 206–7, 323n9, 323n10
the North region, 3; clergy in, 116–17; *congregaciones* in, 177–78; epidemics impacting, 140, 177–78; Formative period in, 34; Iguala in, 128, 129, 151, 153, 161–62, 216; landowners in, *215*, 217; Mexica empire expanding into, 100–101; mining in, 6, 214–16, 261; Palula in, 315n124; priests in, 128; silver mined in, 6, 226; *sujetos* in, 166–67; Taxco, importance of, 220; Teotihuacan and, 67; Tepecoacuilco in, *68*, 103, 127, 167, 177, 195. *See also* Huitzuco; Mayanalán; Tlaxmalac
Noxtepec, 83, 109, 125–26, 130, 144, 165, 178, 194, 222
Núñez, Andrés, 222
Núñez, Juan, 123, 124
ñuu, 27, 93, 278

Oapan, 99–100, 146, *147*, *148*, 149, 153, 155, 162
Oaxaca: Monte Albán in, 23; San José Mogote in, 31; Sierra Norte of, 313n73; Tututepec in, 112, 126. *See also* La Consentida
obsidian, 5, 20, 285n19; exchange indicated by, 19, 48; in Puerto Marqués, 290n91; shells possibly exchanged for, 39
Ocampo, Diego de, 229
ocote, 278
Ocotequila, settled by migrants from Xochimilco, 75–76
Oettinger, Marion, 74
oidor, 278

ojos sin pupila (Olmec figurine), 74, 278
Olid, Cristóbal de, 112, 198
Olinalá, 25, *42*, 74, 126, 131–32, 155, 157, 166, 214
Oliveros, Francisco de, *122*, 124
Olmec culture, 11–12, 278; achievements of, 2; as mother culture, 6–7, 51–52; Olmec style contrasted with, 51
Olmec style, 31, 52; at Amuco Abelino, 63, *64*; baby-face figurines in, 53, 74, 297n59; at Cauadzidziqui Cave, 56–57; at the Cave of the Governors, Techan, 56, 57; definition of, 51; during Formative period, 90; at Juxtlahuaca, *55*, 56; at Oxtotitlán, *52*, 53–54
ololiuhqui (Turbina corymbosa), 134, 278
Ometepec, 126, 141, 165, 175, 318n11
Ordaz, Díaz de, 166, 187, 314n108
Ordaz Villagómez, Diego de, 156, 206–7
Orduña, Francisco de, 188, 318n11
La Organera-Xochipala, 29, *30*, 70–71, *73*, 74, 288n62, 295n24
oro común, 278
Ortiz, Rodrigo, 146
Osorio, Don Diego, Chontal governor of San Simón Oztuma, 138, 151–52
Osorio, Pedro de, 196, 235
Otomí people, 96, 100, 261
Oxtotitlán Cave, 6, *52*, 53–54, 89–90, 294n13
Oztuma, 45, 74, 161, 167, 180, 219, 293n149; Acapetlahuaya in conflict with, 171; exchange, 35–36, 49; lineage of, 151–52; and the Mexicas, 83, 101–2, 103, 105

Pacheco, Pedro, 154
Pacheco de Bocanegra, Bernardino, 199–200
painted gourds, 41–43, *42*
Señor Pájaro-Lagarto, ruler of Tlapa-Tlachinollan, *95*

INDEX 389

Palacios, Baltasar de, 223
Palula, 315n124
Pantla, 23, 285n19
pantli (glyph), 146, 279
Papalutla, 158–59, 222
Paradis, Louise I., 33, 35, 58, 288n73, 289n81
pardo, 141, 279
Pardo, Diego de, 112, 224, 304n6
partido (definition), 279
partidos (parishes), 127; of Acapulco, 141; of the Costa Grande, 140; priests and, 117–18, 131–32; royal treasury funding secular priests, 126; in Tierra Caliente, 128
patache, 238, 279
Peñalosa, Don Gonzalo Ronquillo de, governor of the Philippines, 244, 249, 332n53
Peña, Joan de la, 178
Peña Vallejo, Joan de la, 178, 317n154
Pérez, Tomás, 207
Pérez de Bocanegra, Hernán, 123, 188, 199, 228
Pérez Desmariñas, Gómez, governor of the Philippines, 248
Pérez Desmariñas, Luis, interim governor of the Philippines, 248
Pérez Payán, Francisco, 247
Pérez de Soto, Juan and Melchor, 247
Peru, Asian trade and, 251–52, 331n29
petate, 147, 240, 241, 279
Petatlán, 23, *141*, 165, 208, 285n19
Petlacala, *24*, 78–79, 93. *See also* San Pedro Petlacala
Pezuapan, 28–29
the Philippines, 238–39, 278; Cebú in, 248–49; Manila in, 209, *250*, 252–53, 331n29; population of, *248*
Philippines trade, 244–45, 250–51; Acapulco as center of, 242–43, 247–50; Díaz de Cáceres investing in, 246–47; Rodríguez de los Ríos investing in, 246; royal decrees and, 252–53

pictographic documents (*pinturas* or *lienzos*), 74–75, 145, 149, 227, 260, 279; community finances managed with, 146–47; hybrid character of, 75; from the Montaña, 335n7; from Postclassic period, 3; from Tierra Caliente, 10. *See also* codex; *mapas*
Piedra Labrada, 23, 64–65, *66*, 67, 286n25m 296n42
pigments, exchange and, 73–74
Pilcaya, 144, 165, 178, 194, 231
Piña Chan, Román, 64–65
piñol, 279
Pinto, Captain Lucas, 171
pintura. *See* pictographic documents
Placeres de Oro, 67, *69*
poblador, 279
polished stone, *59, 60*, 290n90. *See also* greenstone
Pollard, Helen, 101
population, 138–39; of Acapulco, 141; of Alahuiztlán, 310n27; of Balsas region, 35; Cervantes de Salazar on, 289n80; *congregaciones* and, 174–75, 180; of the Costa Chica, 165–66; of the Costa Grande, *141*, 165; decline of, 140, 141, 174–75; density of, 84–86, 165–67; epidemics reducing, 139, 141, 180, 210; estimated ca. 1520, 86–87; of Huitzuco, 178; labor shortages caused by mass Indigenous deaths, 210–11; by language, *85*; in the Montaña relatively dense, 257; in Silver Province, *226*; and slavery, 210; Spanish population of the Philippines, *248*; of Taxco, 225; of Tierra Caliente, 140, *142, 143*; of Tlapa-Tlachinollan, 85–86
Porcallo, Vasco, 173, 224, 316n141
porcelain, 245

Portobello fair, on Isthmus of Panama, 251–52
Postclassic period, *18*, 87, 98–100, 108, 171; administrative and judicial processes in, 146; Cocula River valley, settlement pattern during, 34; importance of cacao in, 43; Indigenous polities, structure of during, 164–65; Indigenous rulers, challenges to during, 153–54, 164–65; land of Indigenous communities during, 179; in the Montaña, 4–6; pictographic documents from, 3; settling of disputes in, 144; Tlapa-Tlachinollan polity developed, 90–96; Yopecingo during, 90–96
potrero, 279
power of attorney, 114–15, 125
priests, 116–17, 307n64; abuse of position by, 129–30; in the Center, Costa Chica, and the Montaña, 130–32; in the North, 127–29; parishes and, 131–32, 156–57; precontact Nahuas venerating, 129; secular, 126–27, 132–33, 164, 175–76; in Tierra Caliente, 127, 128–29; wealthy, 130
Princeton University Art Museum, 61–62
principal, 279
probanza de méritos, 223, 227, 279
procurador a la corte, 279
Provincia de la Plata. *See* Silver Province
Puerto Marqués, Acapulco, 19, 89, 290n91
pulque, 279, 307n62, 309n6
Pungarabato, 106, 139, *142*, 143, 167, 168
Purhépecha people, 12, 279. *See also* Tarascan empire

Quechultenango, 176–77
quesos (architectural feature), *71*, *72*, 260–61, 279
quezquémetl, 279
Quintero de Zamora, Francisco, 228

quinto, 279
Quiroga, Bishop Vasco de, 173

Ramírez, Francisco, 197
Ramírez Bravo, Francisco, 194–95
Real Hacienda, 113, 126, 279
real de minas, 279
regidor, 279
regional contexts, settlement patterns and, 37
regular orders, 113, 116, 126–27, 164
reino, 279
"Relación de Ajuchitlán y su partido," 179
"Relación de Ichcateupan," 171, 200–201, 224
"Relación de Iguala y su partido," 139, 153, 217
"Relación de las minas de Zumpango," 223, 224
"Relación de la Villa de Zacatula," 139, 223
"Relación de Sirandaro y Guayameo," 112
"Relación de Tistla y Muchitlán," 213–14
"Relación de Xalapa, Cintla y Acatlán," 139, 207, 309n21
Relaciones Geográficas, 10–11, 82, 106, 283n38
religious practices, Indigenous, 22, 37, 45, 57, 63, 65, 68, 76, 81, 88, 97, 99, 134–35, 156; caves and, 295n16; *clavos* depicting, 71; metallurgy and, 40–41; rulers, sacred functions of, 88, 100, 108, 152–53, 261; at Teopantecuanitlán, 63
Renfrew, Colin, 84
renters of land, in Tierra Caliente, *218*
repartimento de efectos, 203, 214, 279
repartimiento de indios, 203, 209–10, 222, 279, 324n50
república de indios, 157, 279
El Rey de la Chole (statue), 22
Reyna Robles, Rosa María, 29, 91

Ribadeo, Francisco de, 189–90
rock art, 54–56, 295n18; elites represented in, 89; from Formative period, 89; Olmec style of, 53, 57, 73, 256; polychrome, 88, 91
Rodas, Juan de, *122*, 221
Rodríguez, Garci, 130
Rodríguez, Martín, 116, 128, 129
Rodríguez de Guadalupe, Miguel, 124
Rodríguez de los Ríos, Baltasar, 246
Rodríguez de Magariño, Francisco, 200
Rodríguez de Villafuerte, Juan, 112, *122*, 187, 206, 224
Rodríguez de Zacatula, Francisco, *122*
Ronquillo de Peñalosa, Don Gonzalo, governor of the Philippines, 249
royal decrees, 251–53
royal government, Indigenous rulers protected by, 155–56
Ruiz de Alarcón, Hernando, 134
Ruiz de Alarcón, Juan, 231
Ruiz de Baeza, Jerónimo, 224

Saavedra, Álvaro de, 237–38
salaries, sample of, in Guerrero, 119, *121*
Salazar, Fray Domingo de, 248
Salcedo, Domingo de, 216
Salcedo, Juan de, 112, 228
salt, 116, 118, 200, 234; Chalmeca Cihuatl associated with, 45, 100; Indigenous communities in Tierra Caliente producing, 219; transport of, 50
Sánchez, Antón, *122*, 124, 208, 221
sangley, 280
San José Mogote, in Oaxaca, 31
San Luis Acatlán, 112, 126, 133
San Martín, Diego de, 227–28
San Miguel Amuco (sculpture), 63, *64*. *See also* Amuco Abelino

San Pedro Petlacala (church), *132*. *See also* Petlacala
Santa Cruz y Aguilar, Diego, 229
Santa María de la Asunción (church). *See* Tetela del Río
Santa Prisca (church), Taxco, 225
Santiago, Alonso de, Indigenous noble of Iguala, 153
Schmidt Schoenberg, Paul, 29, 285n22
separation of pueblos (*separación de pueblos*), 162, 168–72, 260, 335n8; in the Center, 170–71; in the Montaña, 169–70; *sujetos* and, 169
Señor Serpiente-Espina de Maguey, ruler of Tlapa, 298n78
settlement patterns, *14–15*, *110–11*, 178, 256–57; Balsas River influencing, 35; on the Costa Grande, 5, 21; dispersed, 70, 173, 175; exchange and, 92–93; geography and, 16–17; in the Montaña, 26–27, 175; regional contexts and, 37. *See also congregaciones*
settlements, in precontact Guerrero, *14–15*
shellfish, 19, 20
shell mounds, 17–18, 20, 236
shell pendant, from El Infiernillo, *38*
shells, 4, 29, 290n96; exchange confirmed through, 28; obsidian possibly exchanged for, 39; transport of, 39, 103; value of, 39
shippers from Acapulco and Manila, 245, *250*
Sierra Gorda, Querétaro, mining in, 291n109
Sierra Madre del Sur, 16, 28
Sierra Norte, of Oaxaca, 313n73
silver, 226–27; in Chilapa, 224; mining of, 115–16; in the North, 6; Spaniards seeking, 261–62; in Taxco, 115–16, 225; in Zumpango, 223–24
Silver Province (*Provincia de la Plata*), 9, 225, 279; Crown *encomienda* in, 183–84;

mineowners as royal officials in, 117; population of, *226*; Spanish population of, 229
Silverstein, Jay E., 10
slaves, 227; African, 210–11, 220; Asian, 220, 240; cacao cultivated by, 210–11; the coast, demography impacted by, 211; demography changed by importation of, 133–34; food for, 228–29; Indigenous people as, 119, 222, 305n15; labor of, 9; mines worked in by, 115–16, 118, 188, 191, 225, *226*, *227*; of Moreno, I., 192–93; Yopes as, 173–74
Smith, Michael, 11
Sochitonala, 134,
social hierarchy, not present among hunter gatherers, 20–21
La Soledad de Maciel, *21*, *22*, 23, 285n22
sonsaque, 234, 280, 329n65
soplillos, 232–33, 280
Soria, Diego de, 135
Soria, Gaspar de, 227
Sosa, Juan Alonso de, Royal Treasurer, 199, *215*, 226, 229
the South, importance in Mexica cosmology of, 37–38
Souza, Bartolomé de, 149
Spaniards, *114*, 138–39, 277; cabeceras designated by, 284n47; and Chilapa, prospecting for mines in, 224; *congregaciones* benefiting, 177–78; crops introduced by, 119; Guerrero invaded by, 8; Indigenous communities impacted by, 180–81; Indigenous people not opposing, 136; Indigenous rulers reacting to, 257–58; livestock introduced by, 119, 124; metals searched for by, 235; mines sought by, 224–25; population of in Philippines, *248*; population of in Silver Province, *226*; silver and gold sought by, 118, 261–62; in Silver Province, 229; Taxco resided in by, 118; in Tierra Caliente, 262; in Zacatula, 114
Spanish governmental structures, Indigenous people adapting, 150–51
Spanish governmental systems, Indigenous elites adapting to, 145–46
Spanish invasion, 12, 107–13, 258; the Crown not funding, 182; cultures disrupted by, 1–2; gold and silver financing, 112; Indigenous response to, 138–39; Mixtecs responding to, 334n3
stelae, 63–65, 67–69, 90, 296n43. *See also* monumental stone sculpture
Stelae 1 and 2, of Tepecoacuilco, *68*
Stela Monument 3, from Piedra Labrada, *66*
Structure 11, at La Organera-Xochipala, *73*
sugar, 159, 216–19, 241, 254
sujeto, 12, 127–28, 154–55, *164*, 171, 172, 277, 280; in the Center, 166; in the North, 166–67; reduction in number of, 176; and separation of pueblos, 169; in Tierra Caliente, 167; in Tlapa, *170*
Sultepec, *226*; land for cattle near, 197, 217; shortage of flour in, 232; Spanish mineowners in, 229
Suma de Visitas, population data in, 309n21

Tacatecla, Indigenous noble of Tixtla, 144, 192
taleguilla, 280
talud-tablero (architectural feature), 70, *73*, 90, 280
tameme, 47–48, 103, 118, 280; restrictions on use of, 209
Tapia, Andrés de, 109
Tapia, Tomás de, Indigenous governor of Tepeaca, 312n60

Tarascan empire, 12, 100, 108, 280, 284n46, 293n149; administrative centers of, 106; Balsas region, incentives to expand into, 101; character of, contrasted with Mexica empire, 105–6; copper sought by, 101; cotton tribute paid to, 44–45; Cuitlatecs of the Costa Grande encroached on by, 82; nucleus of state, no longer economically viable, 101

Taxco, 136; flour shortages in, 232; health endangered by technologies used in, 232–33; importance of, 231; Inquisition active in, 136; metals refined in, 214–16; mines neighboring, 225; mining elites of, 226–29, 231; mining in, 177–79, 227–30, 261–62; mining regulations in, 232–35; the North shaped by, 220; population of, 225, *226*; silver in, 115–16, 225; Spaniards residing in, 118; Spanish officials in, 227, 229; Tetelzinco, *barrio* of, 161–62

Taxco el Viejo, 166–67, 171, 186

Techan, *56*, 57

tecoçahuitl, 103, 280

tecomate, 104–5, 208, 280

tecpan, 25, 26, 34, 70, 280

Tecpan, 141, 174, 206

Tecuiciapan, payments to municipal officials of, *148*

Tehuacalco, *97*, 98, 302n26

Tejada, Lorenzo de, 130, 228, 232–33

Tejada, Gaspar de, 129–30

Teloloapan, 61, 83, 101–3, 127, 145–46, 167, 218–19

Templo Mayor in Tenochtitlan: offerings from Guerrero in, 37–39

tenedor de bienes de difuntos, 280

teniente de corregidor, 280

10 Knot (*10 Nudo*), Indigenous ruler of Piedra Labrada, 66

Teopantecuanitlán, 6, 7, 12; architecture and site design, 31–33; baby face figurines, 74; Cerro Quemado-La Coquera compared to, 26; Chalcatzingo, ceremonial center compared to, 63; *clavos* in, 71; corbelled arches in, 70; Cuicuilco and San José Mogote compared to, 31; in Formative period, 63–65; La Organera-Xochipala compared to, 29; manufacture, transport and exchange of prestige goods, control of, 47–48, 49, 61, 89–90; pigments, 73–74; plan of ceremonial precinct, *32*; sculpture in, 52, 63–64, *65*; shell processing in, 39, 48; site plan, *32*; urbanism, earliest example in Guerrero, 31–32; workshop zones, 48

Teotihuacan: ceramics influenced by, 286n24; migration from Guerrero to, 91; the Montaña influenced by, 90–91; monumental sculpture influenced by, 64–67; the North impacted by, *68*; possible direct control of Guerrero by, 296n43

Tepecoacuilco, 44, 47, 67, *68*, 85–86, 103–4, 127, 167, 177, 195–96, 262

tepixqui, 128, 280

tepotzoicpalli or *tolicpalli*, 77, 147, 280, 201

Tequicuilco, 67

tequio, 234, 280

tequitato, 127, 167, 280

terrrazguero, 280

territorial extent, of Guerrero, 300n103

Tetela de Río, 83, 126, 167, 219, 224, 327n20

Tetelzinco *barrio* of Taxco, 161–62

Tetipac, 83, 130, 144, 155, 178, 216, 227, 317n154

Tetitlán, 20

teuctli, 99, 280

Teulistaca, 186

Texmelincan, 40, 69, 74, 91

textiles, 43–45, 214, 241, 244–45, 249. *See also* cotton

tianguis, 280

Tierra Caliente region, 34–36, 196–201, 217–19, 224, 293n149; Alahuiztlán, population of, in, 310n27; *cabeceras* in, 167; *congregaciones* in, 179–80; cotton produced in, 219; Cutzamala in, 199, 200, *201*, 245; epidemics impacting, 139–40, *142*, 143, 179–80; land grants in, 305n22; landowners in, *218*; metals processed in, 219; pictographic documents from, 10; population of, 140, *142*; renters of land in, *218*; salt in, 261; Spaniards in, 262; Teloloapan in, 127, 218–19; Utatlan in, 192, 219. *See also* Ajuchitlán; Cuetzala; Guayameo; Oztuma; Pungarabato; Zirándaro

tierras baldías, 280

tilma, 281

Tixtla, 99, 161–62, 177; commerce in, 133, 161, 162, 166, 177, 213–14, 241, 254, 261; described by Ignacio Altamirano, 24; *encomienda* of, 191–92, 193; landowners, 154, 213; Mayacat, governor of, 144, 192; mining in, 224; precontact government of, 99; Tacatecla, Indigenous noble of, 144, 192; tribute from, 192, *193*

tlacatecuhtli, 103, 281

Tlacotepec, 83, 219, 224

Tlalcozautitlán, 102, 103, 191, 141n36

tlacuilo, 103, 281

Tlamacazapa, 170–71

Tlapa, 154, 159, 169, *170*, 189–90, 318n8; *cabeceras* and *sujetos* in, 169, *170*; evangelization of, 126, 131–33; nobility of in sixteenth century, 152; population of, 141–42; precontact tribute from, 104–5; ruling lineage disrupted by epidemics, 154; separation of pueblos in, 170; sixteenth-century tribute from, 189; Spanish officials of, 150, 166

Tlapanec language, 25, 83, 302n22

Tlapanec people, 78, 86, 87, 93, 95, 302n22

Tlapa-Tlachinollan, 10, *79*, 92–96, *94*, 138, 259, 263; *Códices de Azoyú 1* and *2* documenting, 10, 93, 95–96; creation of, 95–96; expansion of, 93; Indigenous rulers of, 298n78; lineage ruling, 10, 312n57; Mexicas capturing, 95; Nahuas migrating to, 93–94; population of, 85–86; Yoallan incorporated into, 299n81

tlatoani, 10, 39, 93, *95*, 99, 101, 102, 144, 156, 171; during Classic period, 256–57; during Postclassic period, 153–54, 164–65

Tlaxcala, Indigenous rulers of, 311n50

Tlaxmalac, 134, 157, 178, 194

tolicpalli. *See tepotzoicpalli*

Toltecs, 69, 91, 96

tonelada, 281

topile, 152, 156, 281

De la Torre, Juan, 195

Torres, Bernardina de, 196

Torres, Hernando de, *122*, 195, 196, 222

Totomixtlahuaca, 126, 133, 175–76

Tototepec, conquered by Tlapa-Tlachinollan, 95

Tovar, Isabel de, 195

towns and settlements, in sixteenth-century Guerrero, *110*, 111

trade: in Acapulco, 242–43, 247; Indigenous peoples impacted by Acapulco trade, 240; Manila, trade with impacting coast, 209; Manila and, 248–50; Mexico City merchants and, 243, 246; with Peru, 251–52. *See also* Asian trade; Philippines trade

transport, 125; costs associated with, 47–48, 241; exchange and, 46–50; mules used for, 118, 217; of salt, 49–50; of shells, 39, 103; of tribute, 47, 103

tributary provinces, of Postclassic Guerrero, *104*
tribute, 143–44, 147; *caja de comunidad*, tribute paid into, *160*, 310n39; to Cortés, H., 318n8; of cotton, *104*, 208–9, 323n21; to Crown, 184–87; to Don Gaspar of Oapan, 147–48; *encomienda* and, 181, 184–87; of Guayameo and Zirándaro, *198*, 199; of Huitzuco, 193; of maize, 199–200, 228; to Mexica empire, 44, 103–5; Mexico City, delivered to, 188, 199, 321n44; mining funded by, 188, 196–97, 199–200; to Tarascan empire, 44–45, 105–6; of Tixtla, *193*; of Tlapa-Tlachinollan, 104–5; transport of, 49, 103; from tributary provinces in Postclassic, *104*; value of Crown, *185*
Turbina Corymbosa. See *ololiuhqui*
Tututepec, in Oaxaca, 112, 126
Tuzantla, 186

Umbría, Gonzalo de, 112
urban city, archaeological model of not applicable to Mesoamerican urban centers, 287n60
Urdaneta, Andrés de, 237–38
Urizar, Joseph de, 224
Utatlan, Tierra Caliente, 192–93, 219

Valderrama, Jerónimo de, 226
Valdivieso, Juan de, 190
Valley of Mexico, 2, 29, 51, 90, 103; *caja de comunidad* in, 159; *cofradía* in, 163; Cuicuilco in, 31; migrations from, 78, 171; Teohihuacan in, 23
Valley of Toluca, 36, 49, 225, 261
Valverde, Tomás de, 223
Vargas, Francisco, 205–6
Vargas, Juan de, *122*, 125

Vargas, Juan Alonso de, 206
Vázquez de Cisneros, Mateo, 194, 320n32
Vázquez de Coronado, Francisco, 117, 190, 199, 200
Vázquez de Escobar, Guiomar, 321n48
Vázquez de Espinosa, Antonio, 119, 253
Vázquez de Tapia, Bernaldino (father), 154, 166, 188–91, 212, 319n19
Vázquez de Tapia, Bernardino (son), 189, 319n21
vecino, 281
Velasco, the elder, Luis de, Viceroy, 155, 173, 209, 226, 237–38
Velasco, the younger, Luis de, Viceroy, 175, 189, 191–92, 213, 234, 239
Vélez Calvo, Raúl, 82, 84, *85*
Señor Venado, ruler of Tlapa-Tlachinollan, 95
Vera, Santiago, Bishop of the Philippines, 249
Veracruz, 63, 74, 89, 241, 244, 247, 253, 333n85
Villafuerte, Juan Rodríguez de, 112, 187, 206, 224
village government, change and continuity in, 150
Villa Rotaria, Bird Man (sculpture) at, 285n22
Virgin of the Rosary (*cofradía*), female majordomo of, 314n91
Vitoria, Francisco de, Indigenous landowner, 219
Von Mentz, Brígida, 6, 82

Western Isles, Acapulco and, 237
wine, 309n6

Xicayán, 139, 165, 168, 208, 209
xicolli, 44, 281
Xipe Tótec, cult of, 22, 41, 76, 97
Xiquipilco, hospital of, 219

Xochimilco, 75–76
Xochipala, 29, *30*, 61–62, 70, 71, *72*, *73*, 74, 162, 287n60, 288n62, 295n18
Xochipala sculpture, 45, 61, *62*, *72*, 260–61, 296n35
Xochistlahuaca, 165, 318n11
Xocutla, 141, 165, 176
X-ray fluorescence, 20, 281

Yáñez de Burgos, Gregorio, 227–28
Yannakakis, Yanna, 7, 313n73, 334n3
Ynfante, Pedro, 129
Yoallan, incorporated into Tlapa-Tlachinollan polity, 299n81
Yopecingo (polity), 92, 96–98, 102, 105, 112, 113, 257
Yope language, 83
Yope people, 96, 165, 173–74, 304n6
yuhuitayu, 27, 79, 93, 98, 281, 334n3

Zacatula, 86–87, 112, 114–15, 125, 165, 208–9; epidemics, population devastated by, 139, 141; figurines in, 74; forced labor in, 210; independent of Mexicas and Tarascans, 106; individuals cited in legal documents concerning, *122*; land and livestock, 203–6; mining in, 136, 221–23; population of, 86–87, 139, *141*; in the Postclassic, 23; prices and salaries in, 119–21; slavery in, 210; Spaniards in, *114*, *121*, 122–25; Spanish officials in, 117; Toltec-style ceramics at, 91; tradespeople attracted to, 124–25; Zacatula civil province, 165
Zambrano, Álvaro, 196
Zambrano, Juan Rodríguez, 196
La Zanja, 20
Zapotitlán, 132
Zavala, Martín de, 228
Zazacatla, Morelos, 56, 63
Zihuatanejo, 23, 237, 251–52
Zirándaro, *142*, 143. *See also* Guayameo
Zitlala, 131, 176–77
Zumárraga, Bishop Fray Juan de, 192
Zumpango, 99–100, 144, 177, 191; livestock in, 212–13; mining in, 112, 115, 183–84, 223–25, 242, 261; silver in, 223–24
Zúñiga, Juana de, 139

www.ingramcontent.com/pod-product-compliance
Lightning Source LLC
Chambersburg PA
CBHW030104010526
44116CB00005B/89